Liturgical Reform After Vatican II

Liturgical Reform After Vatican II

The Impact on Eastern Orthodoxy

Nicholas E. Denysenko

Fortress Press
Minneapolis

BX
350
.D46
2015

LITURGICAL REFORM AFTER VATICAN II

The Impact on Eastern Orthodoxy

Copyright © 2015 Fortress Press. All rights reserved. Except for brief quotations in critical articles or reviews, no part of this book may be reproduced in any manner without prior written permission from the publisher. Visit http://www.augsburgfortress.org/copyrights/ or write to Permissions, Augsburg Fortress, Box 1209, Minneapolis, MN 55440.

Cover image: a-poselenov, ThinkstockPhotos-470923502

Cover design: Joe Reinke

Library of Congress Cataloging-in-Publication Data

Print ISBN: 978-1-4514-8615-5

eBook ISBN: 978-1-5064-0144-7

The paper used in this publication meets the minimum requirements of American National Standard for Information Sciences — Permanence of Paper for Printed Library Materials, ANSI Z329.48-1984.

Manufactured in the U.S.A.

This book was produced using Pressbooks.com, and PDF rendering was done by PrinceXML.

To Kevin Irwin, Dominic Serra, and Mark Morozowich
Friends and Teachers
for steadfast encouragement

Contents

Acknowledgments

Many people helped me think about and write this book. First, I thank my teachers at The Catholic University of America, Msgr. Kevin Irwin, Father Dominic Serra, and Father Mark Morozowich, whose passion and love for the liturgy inspired me to study it critically, and receive it as a gift of the Holy Spirit. I am also thankful to Paul Meyendorff, who not only continues Alexander Schmemann's work at St. Vladimir's Seminary, but enriches it by exposing students to the riches of the method of comparative liturgy.

Numerous friends and colleagues directed me to precious sources, read chapters, assisted with translations, and commented on excerpts and ideas, especially Father Michael Plekon, Father Stefanos Alexopoulos, Deacon Andrei Psarev, Sister Vassa Larin, Father Alkiviadis Calivas, Father Peter Galadza, Father Cyril Hovorun, Father Thomas Pott, Deacon Paul Gavrilyuk, Petros Vassiliadis, Daniel Galadza, Elizabeth Ledkovsky, David Drillock, Alexander Lingas, Vitaly Permiakov, and Roberto Dell'Oro. I would like to single out Brother Stavros Winner, the ecclesiarch at New Skete Monastery, who read several chapters and provided me with precious background on New Skete's process of studying the liturgy and developing its own Typikon: thank you! Thank you to Eleana Silk and Matthew Garklavs who granted me access to the

Schmemann archives at the Georges Florovsky library at St. Vladimir's Seminary. Thanks to Amy Van Mechelen, my research assistant at LMU, who developed helpful bibliographies. Thanks to Tresja and Sophia, my wife and daughter, who offer ongoing support through my maze of intersecting research projects.

Last, but not least, I offer thanks to the ever-memorable Father Alexander Schmemann, whose writings inaugurated my journey and inspired my development of this book. May his memory be eternal.

A note to readers about terms: this book is a study of liturgical reform. Throughout the book, I use reform, renewal, and rebirth interchangeably. My reading of the stories foregrounding this study demonstrates a fluidity of vocabulary which permits the employment of multiple terms referring to the same basic idea. Unless otherwise noted, all translations of foreign language texts are mine. I have employed the terms native to the Byzantine tradition for most liturgical offices and books. Hence, the office for morning prayer is Orthros, not Matins; the title for Sunday Eucharist is the Divine Liturgy, not Mass; the term for the service book is Euchologion or hieratikon, not sacramentary.

Publication Credits

The following publishers are acknowledged for permission to reprint material in this book:

Excerpts from Alexander Schmemann, *For the Life of the World: Sacraments and Orthodoxy* (Crestwood, NY: St. Vladimir's Seminary Press: 1963). Used by permission.

Excerpts from Thomas Fisch, ed., *Liturgy and Tradition: Theological Reflections of Alexander Schmemann* (Crestwood, NY: St. Vladimir's Seminary Press, 1990). Used by permission.

Excerpts from Alexander Schmemann, *The Journals of Father Alexander Schmemann, 1973-1984* (Crestwood, NY: St. Vladimir's Seminary Press, 2000). Used by permission.

Excerpts from Alexander Schmemann, *The Eucharist: Sacrament of the Kingdom*, trans. Paul Kachur (Crestwood, NY: St. Vladimir's Seminary Press, 1987). Used by permission.

Excerpts from Alexander Schmemann, Syllabus. "Liturgical Theology 22/31A," Spring 1982-83. Fr. Alexander Schmemann Papers at the Father Georges Florovsky Library, St. Vladimir's Theological Seminary, Box 18, Document 8. Used by permission.

Excerpts from David Drillock, "My Life in Liturgical Music," lecture delivered at the Institute of Liturgical Music and Pastoral Practice at St. Vladimir's Seminary, Crestwood, NY, June 2004. Used by permission.

Excerpts from Alexander Schmemann, Syllabus. "Liturgical Theology 57," Winter 1978. Fr. Alexander Schmemann Papers at the Father Georges Florovsky Library, St. Vladimir's Theological Seminary, Box 18, Document 9. Used by permission.

Excerpts from Alexander Schmemann, "Transformation of the Parish." Lecture at St. Andrew's parish, 1971. Fr. Alexander Schmemann Papers at the Father Georges Florovsky Library, St. Vladimir's Theological Seminary, Box 17, Document 12. Used by permission.

Excerpts from Monks of New Skete, *The Divine Liturgy* (Cambridge, New York: New Skete Monastery, 1987). Used by permission.

Excerpts from Monks of New Skete, *Passion and Resurrection* (Cambridge, NY: New Skete Monastery, 1995). Used by permission.

List of Tables

Preface

I never thought I would write a book about liturgical reform and Orthodoxy. Numerous life events contributed to the genesis of this book. I spent countless hours of my youth in the company of my grandfather, a priest of the Ukrainian Orthodox Church. I served as an altar boy, sang in the parish choir, and began to conduct choir when I turned 18. These activities included the familiar tasks of preparing and evaluating music, learning the appointed ritual movements of the liturgy, and debating the "right" way to liturgize. When I was in college, a friend from the local chapter of the Orthodox Christian Fellowship at the University of Minnesota introduced me to the writings of Alexander Schmemann. Schmemann answered my questions about the ultimate purpose of the liturgy. I found his explanation of the liturgy as the Church's ascent into the kingdom of God more persuasive than anything I had ever read. I continued my inquiry into Orthodox theology by reading Schmemann; his explanations were not only informative, but also inspiring and edifying. In my first quarter at "The U," I requested information on theological education from every Orthodox seminary in North America.

The next step occurred much later in my career, when I began to teach liturgy to undergraduates at The Catholic University of

America (CUA). The question of liturgical renewal captured my full attention with my attempt to understand the so-called liturgy wars in the Catholic Church, especially since students did not withhold their opinions about more noteworthy dimensions of the wars. The only way I could attempt to address the controversial liturgical issues in the classroom was to seriously read the pertinent documents of Vatican II, especially *Sacrosanctum Concilium* and *Lumen Gentium*. In reading these documents and the history of the liturgical movement, I began to recognize common theological patterns shared between the Orthodox and Catholic churches. The fiftieth anniversary of the proclamation of *Sacrosanctum Concilium*, and its commemoration at a special symposium in September 2013 at CUA, afforded me the opportunity to begin the process of working out my reflections on the question of liturgical reform. I was particularly struck by Schmemann's dismissal of the possibility of a significant liturgical reform for the Orthodox Church. His conservative approach to reform seemed dissonant with his liturgical theology, which shared much in common with *Sacrosanctum Concilium*. At the time, I was putting the finishing touches on my book on Chrismation (The Liturgical Press, 2014), and the memory of the similarity between Schmemann's and Yves Congar's notion of the priesthood of the laity only enhanced my awareness of the dissonance between a conservative approach to liturgical reform and the common enterprise of *ressourcement* in sacramental theology.

After the symposium at CUA, I wrote a formal proposal for the book project and was rewarded with a contract by the generosity of Michael Gibson and Fortress Press. The pages awaiting your attention are the result of this work. In these pages, I explore the phenomenon of liturgical reform in the Orthodox Church in dialogue with the impact of Vatican II on Christendom. My study attempts to show that *Sacrosanctum Concilium* is the product of the liturgical movement, and that contemporaneous Orthodox models of liturgical reform are grounded by the same theological rationale supporting the Roman Catholic reform. After analyzing *Sacrosanctum Concilium*, I examine and assess four Orthodox models of liturgical reform: Schmemann's Eucharistic revival, liturgical renewal in the Russian Orthodox Church Outside of Russia, liturgical rebirth in the Church of Greece, and the creation of a new liturgical order at New Skete Monastery. I conclude with extensive reflections on what we can learn from these recent reform models and how we might update the agenda for liturgical reform to achieve the ecumenical liturgical objectives.

Introduction

Academic discourse on liturgical reform tends to employ a rigorous methodology and use complex terms to narrate history, establish patterns, and provide platforms for the agenda of liturgical reform. Ultimately, however, the source of discourse on liturgical reform comes from the Church itself. This reference to "the Church" should not evoke an image of a dozen or so men sitting around a table at a meeting and deliberating on the pros and cons of excising material from the liturgy or adding new components. Internal Church discourse involves ordinary people and their experiences of the liturgy.

Christian faithful attend liturgy for many reasons. For what one might refer to as the "core group," attending liturgy is an obligation required by divine law. God commands Christians to keep the Sabbath, to remember and honor God one day a week, and in obedience to this command, Christians attend liturgy. Others attend liturgy according to an irregular schedule. Many adults work on Sundays, so it is not possible for them to attend Sunday liturgy.

Others attend alternative events: soccer games for their children, birthday parties, and other social gatherings. For some, Sunday is a day entirely devoted to rest, relaxation, and recreation. Of course, there are families who desire to attend liturgy, but after spending a week hurrying through the morning routine of packing lunches, waiting for the shower, shuffling children off to school, sitting in traffic jams, and trying to finish nine hours of work in seven hours, only to return home to prepare a dinner, help children with homework, and collapse on the couch—with no maid service to clean the house—a family's most earnest intention to arrive at liturgy on time might fall short.

Pastors who devote the entirety of their lives to ministry express their frustration with people who arrive late to church. Church bulletins contain messages with rules stipulating the degree to which people participate depending on their arrival time. Samples of rules I have seen in parish bulletins include "faithful who wish to receive Holy Communion must arrive no later than the Gospel reading, and should really strive to arrive for the beginning of liturgy." Pastors and their assistants have dreamt up dozens of strategies and tactics to garner the people's attention. They attempt to enliven liturgy by adding music that appeals to the people, delivering special sermons and related programs for children, integrating catechesis into the liturgy, opening up ritual actions to laity to enhance participation, and removing material that appears to make the liturgy burdensome. Recognizing the liturgy as the sole opportunity to speak to the people, pastors tend to communicate dozens of messages to the people in the course of one liturgy. A homily may be lengthened to expose the people to the life of a saint or material from historical theology that is essential for their salvation. Catechesis or impromptu sermons may be added to the end of the liturgy to continue the theme started at the homily, or to introduce a new one. Pastors may remind people of the rules they are to observe during solemn seasons: they must make an annual confession or follow the Church's fasting guidelines.

One can understand why pastors attempt to seize crucial moments within the liturgy to address the assembly. These moments, usually near the dismissal or before Holy Communion, are the times during the liturgy where attendance is the highest. Pastors are often occupied with urgent business after the liturgy: meetings with parish officials, visits to the sick, and unscheduled prayers for the dead, among other items. This pastoral business cannot be ignored, but it precludes the possibility of transitioning from the liturgy to the next community gathering, where the pastor can mix with the people. Hence, pastors maximize the limited time they have to talk to the people.

What do the people experience in this convergence of disparate messages? Did the exhausted parents who arrived during the Gospel reading absorb each bullet point of the pastor's thirty-minute sermon? Did they remember to populate their grocery list with foods that adhere to their Church's fasting rules? Were they attuned to the music specially chosen and rehearsed for this assembly after spending an evening listening to their children play and sing the Frozen playlist eight consecutive times? Will they remember the significance of the life of the saint celebrated, along with the meaning of living in God's communion through Christ and in the Spirit?

Obviously, the answers to these hypothetical questions will vary, but it is my conviction that these are the kinds of questions pastors should ask when they think about the liturgy, after considering two fundamental questions: did God attend the liturgy? Did the order of liturgy permit the people to meet and relate to God, to have an audience with God in the context of a meal? I ask these two fundamental questions as a serious consideration of the interplay between the order of liturgy and the people's engagement with it. Readers already know that most folks view their encounters and dialogues with God through the multidimensional lens of daily life and participation in liturgy. Church attendance is formative, and the time one spends in the midst of a praying assembly matters because

3

an encounter with God has the capacity to inscribe meaning on one's life. The reality of what happens at liturgy can matter even for Christians on the far ends of the Church's periphery, who often attend Church only once or twice each year. The finest contributions of liturgical theology from theologians of the apostolic age, late antiquity, monastic communities, scholasticism, the Reformation, the modern *ressourcement* movement, and postmodernity can assure the reader of one absolute truth: God is present at liturgy, eternally reaching out to seek covenantal communion with those who have gathered in response to the divine invitation to convene. Furthermore, God invites those who are gathered to receive a divine blessing, so they can change by gradually becoming citizens of the royal nation and kingdom of priests God invites them to join. Most experts agree that minor variations in order, style, and content do not change the truth of God's presence and the capacity of the people to receive a divine blessing to become God's people. Historically, the fissure between the core foundation of the liturgy and the people's perception of it has occurred in the dynamic interplay of space, place, rite, word, music, and art. Pastors have failed, albeit involuntarily, to celebrate liturgy in such a way that the people can fully sense God reaching out to them.

Meticulous study of liturgical history facilitated by the *ressourcement* movement enabled liturgical historians to narrate the development of liturgy through Christian history, and has illuminated how the people gradually became disconnected from the liturgy and attempted to find new ways to seek union with God through individualized spiritual and devotional practices, sometimes employed during the liturgical celebration. This project of academic liturgical scholarship, better known to academics as *Liturgiewissenschaft*, has shed light squarely on the liturgy as the primary theological event, the source of encounter with and reflection on God that provides the spiritual energy informing Christian life. In the nineteenth and twentieth centuries, the ecumenical movement included the collaboration of academics and pastors who identified the liturgy as the primary event where the Church encountered God.[1] Given that liturgy was the people's primary experience of Church and had a vast capacity to transform them into a kingdom of priests, numerous Christian bodies studied, deliberated, and implemented programs of reform that would reconstruct liturgical celebrations that communicated the royal and priestly vocation to participants and invited them to actively engage the liturgy, ultimately equipping them to be God's servants in, to, and for the life of the world.

This long introduction constitutes my attempt to explain the significance of this book studying the history of liturgical reform in modern Orthodoxy in dialogue with the legacy of Vatican II: liturgical reform is relevant for the past, present, and future of a vibrant Christianity and its ministry to the world. The reforms imagined and implemented in the Roman communion and in some Orthodox Churches were inspired by the pastoral recognition of a renewed liturgy as the source of a renewed Church. Numerous studies and ongoing colloquia treat liturgical reform by debating the details on spatial configuration, euchology, aesthetics, and *ars celebrandi* because these are the primary experiential elements perceived by the senses in liturgy, and consequently spark the most heated debate, better known to readers as "liturgy wars." However, examinations which focus exclusively on specific liturgical components or a selection of controversial issues run the risk of ignoring the theological foundations that support each liturgical ordo.

---

1. For an overview of the liturgical movement, see John Fenwick and Bryan Spinks, *Worship in Transition: The Liturgical Movement in the Twentieth Century* (New York: Continuum, 1995).

In this study, I examine the theological foundations of contemporary liturgical reform in the Roman Catholic and Eastern Orthodox Churches to show how the reconfiguration of the layered orders of priesthood restored the order of the laity, revealing the priestly, prophetic, and royal dignity of each Christian man, woman, and child. Liturgical structures that clearly communicate the priestly vocation to each participant invite the faithful to actively engage the liturgy, and it is through this engagement where they receive divine blessings from God and are equipped to be God's priests in service to the world.

Vatican II and Orthodox Liturgical Reform

The title of this monograph pairs Vatican II and Orthodox liturgical reform in the same descriptive sentence, suggesting that they are related. A common perception among Orthodox people is that Vatican II invented liturgical reform, especially instances that appear to be radical. This perception tends to appear in response to changes in liturgical aesthetics, especially in sacred architecture and music. Orthodox people familiar with the celebration of Mass according to the Missal of Pius V, or the Tridentine Mass, identify qualities of liturgical celebration that evoke the Byzantine liturgy. Besides the obvious differences between the two traditions, especially the Roman practice of celebrating private Mass, the pre–Vatican II liturgy was performed entirely in Latin, the prayers were recited quietly, the altar table was on the back wall of the Church and the priest celebrated *ad orientem*, with his back to the people. Churches were decorated with stained glass windows and had many shrines, and it was common for the priest and singers to employ Gregorian chant or polyphonic choral music in liturgical performance.

Orthodox laity found shared practices in the Roman tradition of making an annual Lenten confession and receiving Holy Communion once a year. Like the Orthodox, Catholics observed Lent with fasting, baptized babies in water in the name of the Trinity, and delineated the roles of the clergy and laity in Church clearly. To be sure, Orthodox were likewise aware of the significant differences in liturgical practices between the two churches (such as Confirmation and Chrismation), but there were enough similarities in aesthetics and lay participation to identify common ground.

When Vatican II proclaimed its first official teaching on the sacred liturgy, *Sacrosanctum Concilium* (henceforth, "*SC*"), the council initiated a process of reforming the liturgy that resulted in an enormous experiential change for the people.[2] Besides the introduction of a new order of Mass, which required a considerable adjustment by the clergy and laity, the environmental context of the Roman liturgy changed drastically in accordance with regional applications. The presider celebrated the liturgy *versus populum* (facing the people rather than away), ministers introduced new music and art, and encouraged the people to participate in acclamations and psalm refrains. Frequent participation in Holy Communion became the norm, and in many places, the vernacular was used instead of Latin. The list of changes mentioned here barely scratches the surface of the impact of liturgical reforms on the people: we can summarize this impact as dramatic, requiring a generation of faithful accustomed to one style of liturgical celebration to adjust to an entirely new one.

The global nature of Roman liturgy exposed these changes to all Christian communities, which resulted in a prevalent perception: Vatican II inaugurated radical liturgical reform for the sake of encouraging the active and conscious participation of the faithful in the liturgy, but the actual outcome was chaos. Certainly, this

---

2. For a helpful overview, see Massimo Faggioli, *True Reform: Liturgy and Ecclesiology in Sacrosanctum Concilium* (Collegeville, MN: Liturgical Press, 2012), 132-45.

perception was not held universally, but Orthodox who paid attention to the structural and aesthetical changes of the liturgy took note and began to view Vatican II's liturgical reform as a cautionary tale and an anti-model for Orthodox liturgical renewal.

The perception of Vatican II as the harbinger of radical liturgical reform resulting in chaos is unfortunate not only for Roman Catholics, but also for Orthodox who attend only to perceptions. In reality, *SC* was the result of a long process of liturgical scholarship drawing from tradition and presenting possibilities for liturgical reform that would update and energize the life of the Church.[3] In other words, Vatican II and *SC* did not inaugurate liturgical reform, but were instead the results of a lengthy process of study, reflection, and deliberation on the liturgy. Vatican II received the reputation of causing liturgical reform because of its stature, its enormous impact, and the authority vested in the teaching of an ecumenical council. *SC*'s teaching on the active and conscious participation of the laity in liturgy were not invented by Vatican II, but achieved fame and stature because *SC*'s statements enshrined them permanently into the global theological vocabulary where they became fixtures of Roman Catholic doctrine.

In this study, I will analyze the impact of Vatican II on Orthodox liturgical reform by attending to the reality of *SC* as the result of the liturgical movement and the perception of Vatican II as inaugurating liturgical reform. The first part of my study will explore aspects of the liturgical movement as a common ecumenical enterprise, emphasizing themes of common interest between Catholic and Orthodox theologians. The rediscovery of the laity as an ancient and legitimate order of the Church, established by the laying on of hands and anointing with Chrism, catapulted the laity into the

---

3. On Vatican II's true place in liturgical reform, see Arthur Sippo, "Liturgical Reform Did Not Start with Vatican II," *New Oxford Review* no. 3 (2011): 40–43.

shared focus of Catholic and Orthodox theologians of the twentieth century, such as Yves Congar, Virgil Michel, Nicholas Afanasiev, and Alexander Schmemann.[4] These theologians arrived at similar theological notions of the royal priesthood of the laity through the process of studying the sources, even though they represented different ecclesial traditions. The work of theologians such as Congar, Schmemann, Afanasiev, and many others shows that Orthodox and Catholic theologians did not study liturgical history without reference to other ecclesial traditions, but engaged in frequent and often fruitful exchanges that facilitated the cross-pollination of one another's methodologies and proposals for liturgical reform. The frequency with which Schmemann draws from Catholic theologians attests to this process of cross-pollination.

Vatican II was the result of the liturgical movement and also the primary beneficiary of the cross-pollinating exchanges between the Orthodox and Catholic churches. One could argue that Eastern Orthodoxy had more of an impact on Vatican II in the liturgical reform because of the number of new prayers, structures, and formulae inspired by the Eastern Christian tradition that Vatican II added to the liturgy.[5] Massimo Faggioli argues persuasively that the addition of Easternisms to Roman liturgy were to honor the Church's adoption of a more Catholic view.[6] Robert Taft traces the origins of Roman interest in Eastern liturgy and notes the development of a pattern of Romans turning to the East to reform the Roman liturgy.[7]

---

4. See my treatment of this matter in *Chrismation: A Primer for Catholics* (Collegeville, MN: Liturgical Press, 2014), 118-32.
5. See Robert F. Taft, "Between Progress and Nostalgia: Liturgical Reform and the Western Romance with the Christian East; Strategies and Realities," in *A Living Tradition: On the Intersection of Liturgical History and Pastoral Practice*, ed. David Pitt, Stefanos Alexopoulos, and Christian McConnell (Collegeville, MN: Liturgical Press, 2012), 29-39; Anne McGowan, "Eastern Christian Insights and Western Liturgical Reforms: Travelers, Texts, and Liturgical Luggage," in *Liturgy in Migration: From the Upper Room to Cyberspace*, ed. Teresa Berger (Collegeville, MN: Liturgical Press, 2012), 179-208.
6. Faggioli, 34-42.

The composition and addition of three new Eucharistic prayers, including split epicleses and the wholesale adoption of the Byzantine formula for anointing with Chrism for Confirmation, are the ritual reforms that best represent the influence of Eastern liturgy on Roman reforms.[8]

In this study, I assert that the most important aspect of cross-pollination between East and West has been underdeveloped and functions as the apparatus for the liturgical reform: the common development of a definition of Christian priesthood grounded by Christ as the High Priest who eternally offers the liturgy to the Father, and the communication of this religious identity to lay men and women who actively participate in the liturgy to minister as God's priests to the world. The multi-layered priesthood rooted in Christ the High Priest and the active participation of the laity in the liturgy are the two central pillars of liturgical reform that illuminate its ultimate aim. The relationship between priesthood and active participation in the liturgy is not linear, but circular and reciprocal. Liturgical structures, contents, and rituals communicate priestly identity to the people, who are then enabled to embrace their priestly vocation and actively participate in the liturgy. The people's active and conscious participation in the liturgy facilitates more frequent and clear communication of their priestly identity. Ideally, as the people gradually grow into this priestly identity, they become capable of translating the principles of offering, gift-giving, and service rehearsed in the world to all aspects of their daily lives.[9]

Liturgical reform does not stop at the transformation of the

---

7. Taft, "Between Progress and Nostalgia: Liturgical Reform and the Western Romance with the Christian East," 29-36.

8. See Paul Bradshaw and Maxwell Johnson, *The Eucharistic Liturgies: Their Evolution and Interpretation* (Collegeville, MN: Liturgical Press, 2012), 313-17, and Denysenko, *Chrismation*, 144-46.

9. See Mark Searle, *Called to Participate: Theological, Ritual, and Social Perspectives*, ed. Barbara Searle and Anne Y. Koester (Collegeville, MN: Liturgical Press, 2006), and Stephen Wilbricht,

Church: through the service by the people of God to the world in their daily lives, liturgical reform seeks the transformation and transfiguration of the world as well. The aims of liturgical reform are thus quite bold: ideally, people would notice the effects of liturgical reform in daily life through the behaviors, habits, relationships, and service of Christian people who are transformed into *christs* (anointed ones) and present God to society on a regular, daily basis. This explains why the council fathers elevated liturgy to the highest stature in the life of the people; liturgy provides the spiritual energy required to achieve the noble and bold objectives of Vatican II: to build up a church of priests who transform and transfigure the world. In the fifty-plus years that have elapsed since the council's promulgation of *SC*, much of the discussion of liturgical reform has focused on the legitimacy of specific reforms. This study is an attempt to redirect the focus of liturgical theology towards the theological rationale underpinning the reforms of Vatican II and the Orthodox churches that deliberated and implemented variants of liturgical reform.

The Limits of This Study

The reader will note that I have selected four models of Orthodox liturgical reform as the primary narrative stories that unveil the impact of the liturgical movement. The four models of liturgical reform examined here are attributed to Alexander Schmemann, the Russian Orthodox Church Outside of Russia (ROCOR), the Church of Greece, and New Skete Monastery. Having established that Vatican II was a result of the liturgical movement, and not its cause, I will briefly explain why I have chosen these four models of liturgical reform in Orthodoxy, and will also direct readers to sources that narrate the other stories of Orthodox liturgical reform.

Rehearsing God's Just Kingdom: The Eucharistic Vision of Mark Searle, foreword Kevin W. Irwin (Collegeville, MN: Liturgical Press, 2013).

11

Liturgical Archaeology in Pre-Revolutionary Russia

Above, I alluded to the fact that the liturgical reform of Vatican II is a result of the contributions of the liturgical movement. I also noted that Vatican II embraced Eastern Christian traditions, principles, and practices in its liturgical reform. The Orthodox Church was active in engaging liturgical study and constructing its history, and one of the most critical periods and contexts for Orthodox liturgiology was in pre-revolutionary Russia. Many pioneers of the study of the liturgical sources established a path for scholars by creating editions of liturgical sources representing numerous centers of Eastern Christianity. Perhaps the most renowned pioneer of Eastern liturgical sources was Jacques Goar, whose Euchologion presenting the contents of numerous medieval Euchologia is still consulted by contemporary liturgiologists.[10] The publication of such editions made the study of Byzantine liturgical history possible, and numerous scholars in the pre-revolutionary Russian academies engaged the enterprise, adding to the repository of liturgical sources. These scholars include Alexei Dmitrievsky (also known as the "Russian Goar") Mikhail Skaballanovich, Ivan Mansvetov, Alexander Golubtsov, Nikolai Krasnoseltsev, Athanasy Papadopoulos-Kerameus, and many others.[11] Among their many contributions are publications that remain useful for the contemporary liturgiologist, including Dmitrievsky's three-

---

10. Jacques Goar, *Euchologion sive rituale graecorum*, 2d ed. (Venice: Typographia Bartholomaei Javarina, 1730; Graz: Akademische Druck und Verlagsanstalt, 1960).

11. For a list of pre-revolutionary Russian liturgiologists, see the web site of Michael Zheltov, *Logike Latreia*, http://www.mhzh.ru/en/authors1/ (accessed November 21, 2014). Zheltov's site provides some biographical information and links to literature published by each scholar. Also see Peter Galadza, "Liturgy and Life: The Appropriation of the 'Personalization of Cult' in East-Slavic Orthodox Liturgiology, 1869-1996," *Studia Liturgica* 28 (1988): 210-31; Paul Meyendorff, "The Liturgical Path of Orthodoxy in America," *St. Vladimir's Theological Quarterly* 40, nos. 1-2 (1996): 44-49, and Taft, "The Liturgical Enterprise Twenty-five Years after Alexander Schmemann," *St. Vladimir's Theological Quarterly* 53, nos. 2-3 (2009): 143-44.

volume series of Typika and Euchologia and Skaballanovich's seminal study of the Typikon.[12]

Liturgical scholars did not merely compile editions for the purpose of narrating liturgical history: they also posed questions directed towards understanding the historical development of the liturgy from antiquity to the received tradition of the synodal-era Russian church. In the late-nineteenth century, the bishops of the Orthodox Church in Russia inaugurated a process of church-wide discussion on potential reforms that would equip the Church to meet the pastoral challenges confronting modern Russia.[13] Russia's contact with the West permitted the permeation of ideas of Enlightenment, and the rise of nationalism and collapse of empires in Western Europe challenged the longstanding hegemony of the Romanov dynasty and the unchallenged authority of the Russian Church. For the bishops, the most pressing issue was the Church's subservience to the state. Tsar Peter I had abolished the patriarchate and established a ruling synod with a lay presider, based on a Reformed model. A movement to re-establish the patriarchate gained momentum among the bishops who anticipated that an emancipated Russian Church would have the necessary freedom to respond to the challenges afflicting their flock.

The challenges confronting the bishops were formidable. It is outside the scope of this study to even summarize the problems of this

12. Aleksei Dmitrievsky, *Описаніе Литургическихъ Рукописей*, 3 vols. (Kiev: Typographia G. T. Korchak-Novitskago, 1895. Reprint, Hildesheim: Georg Olms Verlagbuchhandlung, 1965). For a biography of Skaballanovich, see Peter Galadza, "Baumstark's Kievan contemporary, Mikhail N. Skaballanovich (1871-1931 [?]): A Sketch of his Life and Heortology," *Orientalia christiana analecta* 265 (2001): 761-75.
13. On the preconciliar discussions, see Günther Schulz, "Das Landeskonzil der Orthodoxen Kirche in Russland 1917/1918 und seine Folgen für die russische Geschichte und Kirchengeschichte," *Kirche im Osten* 42-43 (1999-2000), 11-28; James Cunningham, *A Vanquished Hope: The Movement for Church Renewal in Russia, 1905-1906* (Crestwood, NY: St. Vladimir's Seminary Press, 1981); and Hyacinthe Destivelle, *The Moscow Council (1917-1918): The Creation of the Conciliar Institutions of the Russian Orthodox Church*, ed. Michael Plekon and Vitaly Permiakov, trans. Jerry Ryan, foreword by Metropolitan Hilarion (Alfeyev) (Notre Dame, IN: University of Notre Dame Press, 2015).

period, but it is relevant because the bishops recognized the role of liturgy in engaging the people and reinvigorating their faith in God. Vera Shevzov's study on the pre-revolutionary Russian Orthodox Church provides crucial insights on the impact societal upheaval had on the lived faith of parish communities in Russia.[14] Shevzov pairs the "social and political climate" of pre-revolutionary Russia with Orthodoxy's attempt to respond the modernity's challenges. A recent example of the impact of political movements on the life of real communities appears in Gregory's Freeze's English translation of the "Report on the Commission on Raising the Religious and Moral Condition of the Population of Vladimir Diocese (1913)":[15]

> The waves of the 'liberation movement' of 1905-1906 also reached the rural population, and life in the countryside then reflected a lot of the senseless willfulness and unbridled passion. . . . Among the rural and factory population, periodically there still appear false teachers; they continue to incite people by disseminating illegal literature, by distributing free brochures and leaflets with anti-religious, socialist, sectarian, and even immoral content. All this plainly aims to undermine the foundations of faith and morality in popular life, to sunder the ties between parishioners and pastors and the trust in them.

The same commission made several recommendations for restoring faith and morality among the people, and their seventh point referred to the liturgy as a primary way of evangelizing the people:[16]

> The Commission finds it highly useful to conduct church services on patron saint festivals in as grand and celebratory manner as possible. . . . The first concern of each pastor should be the majesty of church services and sacred rites, which have great importance for the Christian education of believers and for combating rationalist sectarianism.

14. Vera Shevzov, *Russian Orthodox on the Eve of the Revolution* (Oxford: Oxford University Press, 2004), 5-6.
15. Gregory Freeze, "Dechristianization in Holy Rus?," in *Orthodox Christianity in Imperial Russia: A Source Book on Lived Religion,* ed. Heather Coleman (Bloomington, IN: Indiana University Press, 2014), 218.
16. Ibid., 222.

This excerpt from the commission of the Vladimir diocese in 1913 is one example of how pastors attended to the liturgy as a primary way of rejuvenating faith and morals among the people and strengthening intra-community fraternal bonds. The Vladimir Commission hardly exhausts the pre-revolutionary Russian perspective on the role of liturgy in addressing the needs of modernity. In preparation for the convening of a council of the Russian Orthodox Church that would seek to restore the patriarchate, among the many pre-conciliar commissions established was one devoted to liturgical renewal. Nikolai Balashov has documented the deliberations, contributions, and fate of the proposals of this commission in his magisterial study.[17] I will refer to select aspects of Balashov's study in two of the four Orthodox models because the scope of the reforms considered and proposed by the preconciliar commission was broad and would have introduced significant changes to the liturgy. However, the Russian council convened in 1917 in the midst of the revolution's turbulence, and its work was interrupted on several occasions by the Russian civil war. Because many bishops were murdered and the Bolsheviks launched a fierce campaign of persecution against the Russian Church, the council's capacity to implement a broad platform of reforms was severely compromised. The council restored the patriarchate, but most of its efforts were reactionary, devoted to addressing the Russian populace, attempting to find a new place in a society governed by a regime hostile to the Church, and mourning the mounting death toll of clergy and laity.

The pre-conciliar deliberations on the liturgy did not cease, however. Thousands of Russians fled to the West, and the debates on the place of liturgy and modernity accompanied them to their new homes. As Russian émigrés acclimated to their new homes—a slow

17. Nikolai Balashov, *На пути к литургическому возрождению* (*On the Path of Liturgical Renewal*) (Moscow: Round Table on Religious Education and Service, 2001).

15

process hampered by the hopes that the Bolsheviks would be ousted and they could return home—they established theological schools in cities such as Paris, Belgrade, and eventually New York.[18] While the sciences of liturgical archaeology continued, and were cultivated by scholars associated with the Pontifical Oriental Institute in Rome, the Orthodox émigrés transitioned from liturgical archaeology to liturgical theology.[19] Orthodox liturgical theology centered on the relationship between the Church and the Eucharist, and the primary figures who developed this Eucharistic ecclesiology were Kyrpian Kern, Nicholas Afanasiev, Alexander Schmemann, and Boris Bobrinskoy.[20] Schmemann cultivated the Eucharistic ecclesiology at St. Vladimir's Seminary in New York which resulted in its implementation by the school's graduates, hence the first model of Orthodox liturgical reform which originated with the pre-revolutionary Russian deliberations on the liturgy.

Orthodox Model No. 1: Alexander Schmemann

Schmemann's model of Orthodox liturgical reform is the most renowned and analyzed instance of renewal in contemporary Orthodoxy. Schmemann's stature among scholars and pastors of East and West is such that several commemorative events were held on the twenty-fifth anniversary of his death in 2008, with numerous

18. The realities faced by the Russian immigrants are depicted soberly by Paul Gavrilyuk, *Georges Florovsky and the Russian Religious Renaissance* (Oxford: Oxford University Press, 2014), 53-59.

19. See Job Getcha "Les études liturgiques russes aux XIXe-XXe siècles et leur impact sur la pratique," in *Les mouvements liturgiques: corrélations entre pratiques et recherché, conferences Saint-Serge, Le Semaine d'études liturgiques*, Bibliotheca Ephermerides Liturgicae, Subsidia (Rome: Edizione liturgizhe, 2004), 279-91.

20. Nicholas Afanasiev, *The Church of the Holy Spirit*, ed. Michael Plekon, trans. Vitaly Permiakov (Notre Dame, IN: University of Notre Dame Press, 2007). Idem, *Трапеза Господня* (The Lord's Supper) (Kyiv: Temple of the Venerable Agapit of the Caves, 2003); Kyprian Kern, *Eucharistia* (Paris: YMCA, 1947); Boris Bobrinskoy, *The Mystery of the Trinity: Trinitarian Experience and Vision in the Biblical and Patristic Tradition*, trans. Anthony P. Gythiel (Crestwood, NY: St. Vladimir's Seminary Press, 1999); Alexander Schmemann, *The Eucharist: Sacrament of the Kingdom*, trans. Paul Kachur (Crestwood, NY: St. Vladimir's Seminary Press, 1987).

liturgical scholars reflecting on various aspects of his legacy. Schmemann's model sets the stage for this study for several reasons. First, Schmemann's liturgical theology has been received more enthusiastically in the West than the East. Currently, Schmemann is referred to as a founding figure of the so-called Schmemann-Kavanagh-Fagerberg-Lathrop school of liturgical theology, which cultivates the notion of liturgy as *theologia prima*, the revelatory event that makes the activity of theologizing possible.[21] The reader should note that Schmemann is the only Orthodox theologian in this group, which is ironically consistent with his own career, as Schmemann engaged in exchanges on the place of liturgy in theology with Western interlocutors primarily.

Despite Schmemann's voluntary engagement with the West, a close reading of his program of liturgical renewal demonstrates his attempt to retrieve and implement prominent aspects of the liturgical reforms proposed by the pre-revolutionary Russian Church. In fact, Schmemann refuted the appeals for liturgical reform in Orthodoxy coming from some of his Western interlocutors and viewed Vatican II with caution. Schmemann's stated reluctance for liturgical reform did not prohibit him from implementing a certain degree of renewal through his position as professor of liturgy and dean at St. Vladimir's Seminary. The chapter on Schmemann assesses his legacy of liturgical renewal by identifying his articulation of a theological rationale for reform and establishing a center for study and reform at St. Vladimir's Seminary. My assessment reflects on the limits of Schmemann's reform by focusing on the central role exercised by parish clergy as the primary catalysts of renewal in the local community.

21. Michael Aune, "Liturgy and Theology: Rethinking the Relationship, Part 1, Setting the Stage" *Worship* 81, no. 1 (2007): 48; David Fagerberg, *On Liturgical Asceticism* (Washington, DC: The Catholic University of America Press, 2013), ix.

Orthodox Model No. 2:
Russian Orthodox Church Outside of Russia (ROCOR)

Schmemann was not the only inheritor of the pre-revolutionary
Russian liturgical legacy. The turbulence caused by the Bolshevik
Revolution and Russian Civil War resulted in confusion and a
desperate desire for survival on the part of various bishops of the
Russian church. One of the most influential bishops who favored
the restoration of the patriarchate was Metropolitan Antony
(Khrapovitsky). In the election for the office of patriarch,
Metropolitan Antony had the most votes, but the name chosen from
the chalice belonged to Metropolitan Tikhon (Bellavin) of Moscow,
who became the new patriarch.[22] Metropolitan Antony was assigned
to the cathedral in Kyiv, but spent very little time in the capital as
Ukrainian nationalists and Bolsheviks fought for control. Antony was
briefly imprisoned, and was eventually forced to take refuge outside
of Russia, first in Istanbul, and then in Belgrade.

Antony attained fame in the history of Russian Orthodoxy because
he was the chief figure who sustained the traditions of the Synodal-
era Church in exile. Antony led a synod of bishops who rejected the
pledge of allegiance decreed by Moscow's Metropolitan Sergius in
1927 ("Sergianism"), thus temporarily severing communion between
the patriarchate and a large body of Orthodox Russians outside of
Russia. While the separation of these communities is largely
attributable to politics and ROCOR's devotion to the Russian
monarchy, ROCOR also bore other characteristics distinguishing it
from progressive Orthodox Russians who settled in Paris. Antony
was a leader and active participant in the dialogues preparing for the

22. For the story of the patriarchal election, see James Cunningham, "Reform Projects of the
Russian Orthodox Church at the Beginning of the Twentieth Century," in *The Legacy of
St. Vladimir: Byzantium, Russia, America*, ed. John Breck, John Meyendorff, and Eleana Silk
(Crestwood, NY: St. Vladimir's Seminary Press, 1990), 116-23.

Russian Council of 1917, and he exuded a consistently conservative approach to the liturgy. Antony represented a group of bishops and theologians that did not support a surgical approach to liturgical reform because they viewed the pastoral problems of liturgical engagement as attributable to impoverished pastoral leadership and the permeation of alien Western elements and ideas into Orthodox liturgy.

In the chapter on ROCOR, I discuss how Antony's conservative views on the liturgy have been consistently cultivated throughout its history. My analysis includes a detailed exploration of Antony's proposed solutions to the problem, which placed the burden of responsibility on the clergy and focused on liturgical aesthetics, especially music. I then show how ROCOR continued one of the renewal programs inaugurated prior to the revolution as the primary catalyst for liturgical renewal: the promotion of chant-based liturgical music that promotes the people's engagement of the liturgy, as opposed to constructing a liturgy that entertains the people. I also identify areas of convergence and separation between the Schmemann and ROCOR models as both emphasized the clergy as the chief proprietors of renewal, but diverged in their interpretations of the development of liturgical history. The models of Schmemann and ROCOR share one aspect in common that warrants further reflection: their renewal efforts occurred in immigration, which resulted in a paradoxical phenomenon particular to Orthodox liturgical reform, namely the implementation of renewal programs which were originally designed for Russia, but ultimately occurred outside of their native liturgical habitat.

Orthodox Model No. 3: The Church of Greece

The third Orthodox model of liturgical reform in this study is the ongoing program of liturgical renewal occurring in the Church of Greece. The Church of Greece is an autocephalous Orthodox Church that is a direct inheritor of the legacy of the Ecumenical Patriarchate of Constantinople, but independent in its governance and attention to matters of faith and morals since 1833. The Church of Greece observed the traditional Byzantine liturgy that remained largely unchanged through the periods of Turkocratia, nationalist aspirations, and eventual state independence. In the late-nineteenth century, the Ecumenical Patriarchate initiated modest liturgical reforms which were also adopted by the Church of Greece. In the late-twentieth century, as Greece confronted postmodernity, the prospect of association with the European Union, secularism, and ecclesial attrition, the Synod of Bishops of the Church of Greece established several special committees to address pastoral areas of need, including liturgical renewal. The synodal committee on liturgical renewal hosted several symposia consisting of scholars and pastors who deliberated on the liturgy and made recommendations for reform to the bishops of the Church of Greece.[23] The bishops then implemented some of the suggested reforms through churchwide and diocesan encyclicals.

The reform platform in the Church of Greece offers several unique aspects that do not appear in our other models. First, the spirit and mechanism for reform follows a pattern of scholars and pastors gathering together to discuss and flesh out potential areas of liturgical reform. The symposia then make specific recommendations to the bishops for implementing reform. The pattern is unique within the Orthodoxy as it occurs under the aegis of an autocephalous Church, which means that the process is Churchwide and represents diverse

23. Stefanos Alexopoulos, "The State of Modern Greek Liturgical Studies and Research: A Preliminary Survey," in *Inquiries into Eastern Christian Worship*, Selected Papers of the Second International Congress of the Society of Oriental Liturgy, Rome, 17-21 September 2008, ed. Bert Groen, Steven Hawkes-Teeples, and Stefanos Alexopoulos, Eastern Christian Studies 12 (Leuven: Peeters, 2012), 375-92.

views from all of Greece; the pattern honors liturgical scholarship, both native to Greece and also within the larger Orthodox communion. Furthermore, the liturgical renewal enterprise adopts the pattern of gathering and presenting information from liturgical history to show what is possible and handing it over to the authority and competence of bishops, who are ultimately responsible for pastoral implementation.

In addition to presenting the most prominent aspects of the reform platform, my chapter on the Church of Greece attends to three additional issues. First, I show how the Church of Greece follows a conservative and careful approach to reform by recommending changes that do not alter the structure of the received liturgical tradition but instead emphasize catechesis. Second, I shed light on the problems encountered during the implementation of liturgical reforms and the frustrations expressed by a minority of proponents who view the received tradition as having decayed to such a degree that a more radical and surgical approach to reform is required. Third, I remark on the striking similarities between the Greek and Roman Catholic programs of liturgical renewal in emphasizing the place of the liturgy in the life of the people, the appeal for their active and conscious participation in the liturgy, and the role of priesthood in implementing renewal. The similarity between the Greek Orthodox and Roman Catholic approaches suggests that Vatican II exercised some influence on the Greek program for liturgical renewal, a hypothesis contradicted by statements from leading Greek liturgists who perceive Vatican II as a model of reform ill-suited for the Church in Greece.

Orthodox Model No. 4: New Skete Monastery

The final Orthodox model examines liturgical reform at New Skete Monastery in Cambridge, New York. New Skete is unique because

21

the monastery was established by Franciscan friars who had experienced Vatican II and desired to draw from tradition to pray a monastic office that cohered with the demands of their daily work.[24] The friars embarked on the challenging process of creating a new ordo that they could observe in concert with the other requirements of religious life. New Skete followed the received Byzantine office and turned to liturgical scholarship in their efforts to create an office suitable for their circumstances.

The result of New Skete's drawing from academic scholarship was the construction of a new liturgical order that privileged aspects from the ancient cathedral traditions of Jerusalem and Constantinople and entailed a more surgical and radical approach to liturgical reform and renewal. In this chapter, I present and analyze several elements from New Skete's liturgical reforms with emphasis on the following: their freedom in consulting tradition to renew contemporary monastic life; their diagnosis of the deep decay of the received Byzantine liturgy; their articulation of a rationale that views surgery as the only viable route to unveil the theological foundations of the liturgy that permit the people to actively engage it; their construction of the liturgy that facilitated the communication of a common priesthood (especially in their reform of the rite of Holy Communion); and their creativity in composing new prayers, translating texts for improved comprehension and theological soundness, and cultivating an *ars celebrandi* that permits symbols to communicate the liturgy without confusion or obstruction. My analysis in this chapter includes reflections on a monastic attempt to rejuvenate cathedral liturgy, the limits of New Skete's influence as a small monastic community in a remote location of New York state, and the convergences of their principles for liturgical reform that are common with and divergent

24. The Monks of New Skete, *In the Spirit of Happiness* (Boston: Little, Brown, and Company, 1999), 8-23.

from Vatican II and the three Orthodox models discussed in this paper.

Alternative Models for Orthodox Liturgical Reform

I have selected the four Orthodox models of liturgical reform belonging to Schmemann, ROCOR, the Church of Greece, and New Skete for the following reasons. First, all four models are contemporary, and the primary elements of reform remain relevant, since many of the strategies and tactics designed to implement reform remain in-progress. These elements of reform have evolved since their inceptions, and the perceptions of reform permit the reader to perform an initial evaluation of their impact. Second, all four of these models occurred in the environments of the ecumenical and liturgical movements and Vatican II's implementation of liturgical reform. The Orthodox models are premium resources for studying the cross-pollination of traditions in ecumenical dialogue and rejection of external influences in Orthodox theology. Furthermore, three of the four models occurred in predominantly Western contexts. Because the models of Schmemann and ROCOR involve implementation of reform outside of its native habitat (Russia), these reforms invite us to reflect on the legitimacy of implementing liturgical reforms in Western environments when they were designed for church communities of specific historical epochs and places. This reflection includes consideration of an alternative approach: an attempt to restore tradition in dialogue with the cultural, social, political, and economic challenges of contemporary society as they impact people in today's times and places. I address these issues as an extended reflection in the penultimate chapter of this book, which I refer to as "lessons from history." I include a veritable ecumenical dimension: because of the vast cross-pollination of Catholic and Orthodox ideas in the liturgy, even when they are interpreted as alien or hostile, I also reflect on what continued efforts in Roman liturgical reform might glean from these lessons in history.

The reader should note that there are other models of Orthodox liturgical reform in addition to those I treat here. To understand the fullness of the genesis of liturgical reform, readers should consult the history of the liturgy in the Byzantine tradition. Robert Taft's short book on the Byzantine liturgy consolidates and synthesizes the primary periods of development in Byzantine liturgical history.[25] Central to understanding these developments is some familiarity with epic historical events and the Church's adjustment to them. For example, the Persian and Arabic invasions of Jerusalem in the seventh and eighth centuries necessitated the rebuilding of monastic life in the Palestinian monastery of St. Sabas; an important component in this rebuilding process was the composition of new hymns, and this creative flourish gradually permeated liturgy and populated its components. After the triumph of Orthodoxy over iconoclasm in the eighth and ninth centuries, the Studite monks in and around Constantinople grew in prestige and imported monks from the Palestinian Sabaitic monastery, which resulted in the diffusion and continued addition of hymnography to the liturgy. Furthermore, the monks' new prestige inaugurated the process of monasticizing urban liturgy; churches became increasingly adorned by icons, and the monastic communities adjusted the cathedral liturgy to fit their needs.[26] Constantinople was so devastated by the Latin Crusade of 1204 that the cathedral liturgy, which was already in decline, gave way to an increasingly monasticized liturgy. This process continued

---

25. Robert F. Taft, *The Byzantine Rite* (Collegeville, MN: Liturgical Press, 1996).

26. Hans-Joachim Schulz, *The Byzantine Liturgy: Symbolic Structure and Faith Expression,* trans. Matthew J. O'Connell (New York: Pueblo, 1986), 50–59; Vasileios Marinis, *Architecture and Ritual in the Churches of Constantinople: Ninth to Fifteenth Centuries* (Cambridge: Cambridge University Press, 2014), 30–41; Cyril Mango, *Byzantine Architecture* (New York: Harry N. Abrams, Inc., 1976), 196–97.

in the prestigious hesychastic community of Mount Athos and the monastic hegemony of the liturgy was essentially complete by the fall of Constantinople in 1453.[27] At this point in the history of Byzantine liturgy, liturgical creativity began to decline for two reasons. With the fall of Constantinople, the most vibrant metropolis in Orthodox was silenced. The invention of the printing press facilitated a broader dissemination of liturgical books, and a common book became a reference point for liturgical uniformity.

As the Greek populations of the fallen Byzantine Empire adjusted to their new conditions as religious minorities ruled by a bishop-ethnarch, the Slavic peoples who had embraced Orthodoxy took the mantle of leadership in liturgical creativity. Select episodes from the liturgical history of the Eastern Slavs, Russians and Ukrainians in particular, inform us on different aspects of liturgical reform. The Union of Brest-Litovsk in 1596 not only resulted in the temporary absence of a hierarchy for the Orthodox people in the Kyivan Metropolia, but was also influenced, in part, by liturgy.[28] After the restoration of an Orthodox episcopate in Kyiv at the initiative of Jerusalem Patriarch Theophanes in 1620, the lay brotherhoods who had sustained Orthodoxy by adopting Western educational models employed the new system in an effort to cultivate clergy who could dialogue with their Polish rulers while remaining Orthodox. The Kyivan Metropolitan Peter Mohyla not only created an academy that adopted Western scholasticism, but he also reformed the liturgy by providing lengthy pastoral introductions to liturgical and sacramental offices intended to aid clergy in catechizing the people. The

27. Robert F. Taft, "Mount Athos: A Late Chapter in the History of the Byzantine Rite," *Dumbarton Oaks Papers* 42 (1988): 179-93.
28. See Peter Galadza, "Seventeenth-century Liturgicons of the Kyivan Metropolia and Several Lessons for Today," *St. Vladimir's Theological Quarterly* 56, no. 1 (2012): 73-91; and Paul Meyendorff, "The Liturgical Reforms of Peter Moghila: A New Look," *St. Vladimir's Theological Quarterly* 29, no. 2 (1985): 101-14.

importation of Western methods included the integration of some prayers and formulas from Roman Catholic sacramentaries. Equally significant was the steady permeation of polyphonic music into Ukraine via contact with musical maestros of Poland and Italy.[29] The regional chants that had held hegemony gradually gave way to the entertaining and decorated concert polyphonies. Ukraine became a conduit for the migration of new liturgical styles into Russia, as Ukrainian educators and musicians began to settle in Moscow.

Mohyla and his Kyivan contemporaries developed educational, aesthetical, and liturgical programs in dialogue with the realities of their environment. Like their Palestinian and Constantinopolitan predecessors, they attended to the impact of political and ecclesial events on their churches and responded pastorally by adopting programs and systems of their immediate milieu. The process of adopting elements of Western Jesuit, Roman Catholic provenance was dialogical: the intent was to remain fully Orthodox through the cultural media of the environment, not to become Jesuit Roman Catholics. In the twentieth century, Orthodox theologians, under the influence of Georges Florovsky, referred to this period in Orthodox history as a Western captivity, as Western scholasticism superseded the Orthodox approach to theology inspired by the patristic era.[30] Most contemporary Orthodox theologians accept the *ressourcement* theological method, which seeks a neo-patristic revival. In the desire to adopt a more traditional theological method, the creativity generated by Mohyla and the lay brotherhoods in adapting to their immediate politico-ecclesial environment is easily obscured. Rather than dismiss the adoption of such systems as Western captivity or pseudomorphosis, perhaps a more accurate perspective is to describe

---

29. For an overview, see Vera Shevzov, "The Russian Tradition," in *The Orthodox Christian World*, ed. Augustine Casiday (London and New York: Routledge, 2012), 20-23.
30. Gavrilyuk, 53-59.

them as legitimate liturgical adaptations that honor the reality of cultural cross-pollination in the local population. The reader is free to choose his or her position; both sides can agree that the liturgical creativity of seventeenth-century Ukraine and Russia resulted in adoptions of Western forms and systems that changed the landscape of Orthodox liturgy and became sources of inspiration for subsequent liturgical reform.

Mohyla's reforms were not the only ones to occur in Russia prior to the late-nineteenth century. In the seventeenth century, Patriarch Nikon inaugurated a process of liturgical reform that resulted in schism.[31] Nikon concluded that the liturgical books of the Russian Church had fallen into decay and differed significantly from the books of Greek-speaking patriarchates, so he initiated a liturgical reform that sought to bring the Russian books into conformity with those of the Orthodox patriarchates. The response of the Russian people to these reforms was fierce and resulted in a tragic schism enduring to this day. Three aspects of the Nikonian reforms are pertinent to this assessment of modern liturgical reform. First, the reform was inspired by a perception that Orthodox liturgy should be uniform, and that the liturgical order used in Russia should conform to that of other patriarchates, which idealizes Orthodox liturgical uniformity. The Nikonian reform embellishes a myth on the liturgy that does not cohere with the entirety of Byzantine liturgical history, and this perception on liturgical uniformity holds hegemony among Orthodox people today. Second, the Nikonian reforms view the publication of books as the primary vehicle for implementing reform, a tactic which emphasizes the role of text in the larger scheme of liturgical ritual. Third, the reform resulted in a schism that remains unresolved, an instance of attempting to impose a reform that was

---

31. Paul Meyendorff, *Russia, Ritual, and Reform: The Liturgical Reforms of Nikon in the 17th Century* (Crestwood, NY: St. Vladimir's Seminary Press, 1991).

not received by the entirety of the Orthodox populace in a given patriarchate. These three elements of the Nikonian reforms reverberate in discourse on contemporary Orthodox liturgy and the reader will note their occasional appearance in the analysis of the four Orthodox models.

There are many other examples of attempts to implement Orthodox liturgical reform and figures who proposed programs for reform throughout modern history that I do not treat extensively in this study. Two recent monographs narrate the other stories of liturgical reform in Orthodoxy. Marcel Mojzeš published a revision of a doctoral dissertation that treats four modern models of Byzantine liturgical reform, namely the Russian council of 1917-1918, different currents of liturgical renewal in Greece, and proposals for liturgical reform in the Ukrainian Greco-Catholic Church and Melkite Greek Catholic Church.[32] My study presents aspects of the proposed Russian liturgical reforms and the precursors to contemporary reform in the Church of Greece that Mojzeš treats more extensively.

Thomas Pott published a groundbreaking monograph studying the nature of liturgical reform, first in French, and then in English.[33] Pott's study encompasses two parts. In the first part, he reviews the most prominent figures and documents of liturgical reform, including profiles of well-known figures and entities such as Cipriano Vaggagini, Alexander Schmemann, SC, and Robert Taft, but also less-known people whose contributions deserve a wider audience such as Emilianos Timiadis and Ene Branişte. In reviewing the contributions of these liturgical pioneers, Pott arrives at a definition

32. Marcel Mojzeš, *Il movimento liturgico nelle chiese bizantine. Analisi di alcune tendenze do riforma nel XX secolo,* Bibliotheca Ephemerides Liturgicae, Subsidia 132 (Rome: Edizione Liturgiche, 2005).

33. Thomas Pott, *Byzantine Liturgical Reform: A Study of Liturgical Change in the Byzantine Tradition,* trans. Paul Meyendorff, Orthodox Liturgy Series, book two (Crestwood, NY: St. Vladimir's Seminary Press, 2010).

of liturgical reform quite useful for the present study. First, Pott states that reform itself is "an action that implies . . . a determination about the state of things," a notion I frequently summarize in this study as "diagnosis."[34] Pott also notes the thematic equivalence of "reform" with several other expressions, including restoration, repair, renew, correct, and modification, among others.[35] Pott's arrival at how one experiences and apprehends reform is worthy of citation:[36]

> What is essential is that the action is aimed at the anterior form of something, which it transforms into something to a greater or lesser extent new. It seems to us that the term does not necessarily imply a total transformation of the form, although this is not excluded. . . . By the same token, one should not exclude minor modifications from the concept of reform. Indeed, because a form has multiple aspects, a small-scale reform can lead to a major reform, in which many small reforms can constitute a significant reform.

Pott asserts that earlier historical models often serve as the inspiration for reforms, but that the reconstruction and implementation result in new liturgical forms. Pott also notes that liturgical history manifests two separate moments of reform: spontaneous evolution and "the active and deliberate intervention of man," moments that will appear in this study as well.[37]

Pott's most significant contribution occurs in his creation of a taxonomy of liturgical reform. Pott discusses three categories: initiation, the restoration of the liturgy to its proper place in the life of the Church, and adaptation and restoration. One of his most significant observations is the distinction between two approaches to reform: appealing to participants so that they convert to the liturgy, and modifying the liturgy to conform to conditions in the

34. Ibid., 78.
35. Ibid.
36. Ibid.
37. Ibid., 80.

community.[38] The tension between these two approaches to reform occurs within and among the models of reform I present in this study, and I will refer to Pott's taxonomy at various points. Pott's study concludes with an examination of case studies that support his definitions in part two of his book, namely the Studite liturgical reform, the formation of the Byzantine Paschal Triduum, the Prothesis rite, and reform on the Slavic periphery. Readers will certainly learn some history here, but will also see how Byzantine liturgical history itself consistently manifests the central points of Pott's thesis.

In addition to these two seminal studies, there are new opportunities to explore liturgical reform in the Orthodox Church that are beginning to emerge. Nina Glibetic provides a comprehensive introduction to the background to liturgical reform in the Church of Serbia and initial efforts by leaders to implement it.[39] Readers should also investigate studies on the implementation of liturgical reform in the Orthodox Churches of Finland and Romania.[40]

North America has functioned as a workshop for liturgical reform

---

38. Ibid., 95-96.
39. Nina Glibetic, "Liturgical Renewal Movement in Contemporary Serbia," in *Inquiries into Eastern Christian Worship*, ed. Bert Groen, Steven Hawkes-Teeples, Stefanos Alexopoulos, Selected Papers of the Second International Congress of the Society of Oriental Liturgy, Rome, 17-21 September 2008, Eastern Christian Studies 12 (Leuven-Paris-Walpole, MA: Peeters, 2012), 393-414.
40. For the Romanian perspective, see Ene Branişte, "Le culte orthodoxe devant le monde contemporain: Opinion d'un théologien orthodoxe roumain," *Societas Liturgica: Documents for Liturgical Research and Renewal* 18 (1970). For background on Romanian participation in liturgical studies, see the chapter titled "Studies in Liturgical Theology in the Romanian Church in the 20th Century" in Viorel Ioniţă, ed., *Orthodox Theology in the 20th Century and Early 21st Century: A Romanian Orthodox Perspective*, trans. Adrian Agachi et al. (Bucharest: Basilica, 2013), 547-648. On the liturgical ethos of the Orthodox Church in Finland, see Archbishop Paul, *Feast of Faith* (Crestwood, NY: St. Vladimir's Seminary Press, 1988), and Brother Stavros Winner's analysis of this work, with reference to reforms adopted by the Church of Finland, in "Liturgy: Theory and Practice—An Example from Finland," *St. Vladimir's Theological Quarterly* 33, no. 2 (1989): 180-89.

in Orthodoxy on account of the freedom to implement aspects of reform afforded proponents there without interference from external entities. Three of our four models of reform represent the phenomenon of implementing reform in new places when the vision for reform originated in the contexts of regional centers in so-called "mother" churches. This creates the paradoxical situation of analyzing liturgical reform among "daughter" churches, which are much smaller and find themselves to be minorities in their new environments. I will address this paradox in this book and will reflect upon the potential of a small church in a Western context to function as a model for implementing reform in the mother church. Readers should note that deliberation on and implementation of these liturgical reforms occurred in dialogical continuity, as each model for reform involves disciples of particular schools of thought on the liturgy. Thus, one additional model for reform deserves the reader's attention, and this is the one that has occurred in the Greek Orthodox communities of North America, particularly through the contributions of Alkiviadis Calivas, professor emeritus of liturgy at Holy Cross Greek Orthodox School of Theology in Brookline, Massachusetts.[41]

In addition to monographs treating the history of liturgical reform in Orthodoxy, some theologians have also offered recommendations for specific revisions of the liturgy to restore it to its fullness. In general, these revisions are guided by the overarching purpose of studying liturgical history expressed by premier historians such as Robert Taft and Maxwell Johnson, that the duty of liturgical scholars is to inform, and not reform, which belongs to the competence of ecclesial authorities.[42] Peter Galadza, a scholar and priest of the

---

41. See Alkiviadis Calivas, *Essays in Theology and Liturgy*, vol. 3: *Aspects of Orthodox Worship* (Brookline, MA: Holy Cross Orthodox Press, 2003).
42. Robert F. Taft, "Response to the Berakah Award: Anamnesis," *Worship* 59 (1985), 311. Also see David Pitt, Stefanos Alexopoulos, and Christian McConnell, "Introduction," in *A Living*

Ukrainian Greco-Catholic Church, has established an initial agenda for Byzantine liturgical reform which applies to the Orthodox Church.[43] Galadza's article revisits the paradigm of liturgical theology that presumably follows the school attributed to Schmemann-Kavanagh-Lathrop-Fagerberg and points out that Schmemann failed to implement liturgical reforms he had identified in his scholarship, a puzzling gap between the lessons from history and contemporary pastoral practice. I responded to Galadza's fine article in an attempt to explain the rationale for Schmemann's reluctance to implement reform, and added several items to Galadza's virtual agenda.[44]

My study complements the fine contributions of the scholars mentioned above by returning to the sources of liturgical reform: a comprehensive examination of its theological rationale in the context of significant political, social, economic, and ecclesial paradigm shifts of the twentieth and twenty-first centuries. I attempt to show that Catholic and Orthodox theologians unearthed and refined the theological foundations for liturgy that had been obscured though centuries of neglect and decay, and that these foundations, particular the multilayered priesthood of the assembly grounded in Christ the High Priest and their active and conscious participation in the liturgy inspired several concurrent models for liturgical reform. While assessments of these reforms vary, the key for the Churches to move forward is to continue the process of studying liturgical history to recover and update the foundations for liturgical reform. I argue that this is possible only if we are willing to learn from the lessons of history, a topic I address at length in the penultimate chapter of this

---

Tradition: On the Intersection of Liturgical History and Pastoral Practice, ed. David Pitt, Stefanos Alexopoulos, and Christian McConnell (Collegeville, MN: Liturgical Press, 2012), vii-viii.

43. Peter Galadza, "Schmemann Between Fagerberg and Reality: Towards an Agenda for Byzantine Christian Pastoral Liturgy," *Bollettino della Badia Greca di Grottaferrata* 3, no. 4 (2007): 7-32.

44. Nicholas Denysenko, "Towards an Agenda for Byzantine Pastoral Liturgy: A Response to Peter Galadza," *Bolletino della Badia Greca di Grottaferrata* 7 (2010): 45-68.

book. One of the lessons from history is that Catholics and Orthodox have mutually benefitted from engaging in theological exchange while deliberating liturgical reform. In the spirit of being edified by gifts from the other in ecumenical dialogue, I make suggestions for liturgical reform to be considered by both Orthodox and Roman Catholics in the conclusion of this study. The primary lesson yielded for ongoing reform is that no one model of reform can be monopolized by the highest order of priesthood in the Church (the episcopacy), and that no single model can attain the perception of being so sacred that it cannot be updated in lieu of new paradigm shifts in culture, politics, and social structures. I argue that reform of the liturgy should not only continue, but should be reconfigured to maximize the people's exposure to God by illuminating the naturally close alignments between liturgy and daily life in its domestic and public aspects.

Ultimately, the liturgy is a gift from God to the Church, a sacred encounter that capacitates the Church's transformation into *christs* who are God's servants in, to, and for the life of the world. Reception of liturgical reform has varied and opposing camps have converged around perceptions of the liturgy in the respective churches. One of the aims of this book is to show that all who love God and the liturgy refer to a common theological core underpinning the liturgy, and that a return to studying this core and discovering its siblings is an opportunity to find common ground without being consumed by the passions of the liturgy wars. If representatives of all camps can agree that the liturgy is an opportunity to rehearse love for God and humanity and enflesh it by serving the world, then this is something for which all Christians can be grateful.

1

Sacrosanctum Concilium and Ecumenical *Ressourcement*

2013 marked the fiftieth anniversary of the Second Vatican Council's renowned Constitution on the Sacred Liturgy, *Sacrosanctum Concilium* (*SC*). In recent years, Catholic scholars throughout the world have debated the interpretation, impact, and implementation of *SC*. Frequently, sharp disagreement on particular aspects of *SC*'s implementation erupts into "liturgy wars."[1] The "Liturgy wars" cover several topics such as preferred musical styles, liturgical gestures, the position of the liturgical presider, the translation of the liturgy, and many others. Catholics from both sides often turn to the Byzantine

---

1. See the study by Massimo Faggioli, *True Reform: Liturgy and Ecclesiology in Sacrosanctum Concilium* (Collegeville, MN: Liturgical Press, 2012). Also see Rita Ferrone, *Liturgy: Sacrosanctum Concilium* (New York: Paulist Press, 2007); John O'Malley, *What Happened at Vatican II* (Cambridge: Belknap Press of Harvard University Press, 2008); John Baldovin, *Reforming the Liturgy: A Response to the Critics* (Collegeville, MN: Liturgical Press, 2008); and Kevin Irwin, *What We have Done, What We Have Failed to Do: Assessing the Liturgical Reforms of Vatican II* (New York: Paulist Press, 2014).

liturgy as a model of authentic tradition, expressing the devotion of Byzantine Rite while remaining faithful to their unchanging liturgy.[2] This devotion is perhaps stereotypically attributed to Russian Orthodox Christians, who supposedly observe an unadulterated ordo inherited from the Constantinopolitan patrons who initiated them into Christianity.

Fortunately, many liturgical scholars have labored hard to create a more accurate narrative of Byzantine liturgical history. The best of these works come from Jesuit scholars such as Juan Mateos, Miguel Arranz, and Robert Taft. Taft's detailed historical study of the liturgy of St. John Chrysostom and attention to the complex process of the formation of the Byzantine Rite demonstrates that the Orthodox liturgy underwent change and reform.[3] Taft, Paul Meyendorff, Thomas Pott, and others contribute further to the narrative by identifying particular episodes of reform in Byzantine liturgical history. In short, Byzantine liturgical reform followed the common thread of adjustment to new environmental circumstances.[4]

2. See Robert F. Taft, "Between Progress and Nostalgia: Liturgical Reform and the Western Romance with the Christian East; Strategies and Realities," in *A Living Tradition: On the Intersection of Liturgical History and Pastoral Practice: Essays in Honor of Maxwell E. Johnson,* ed. David Pitt, Stefanos Alexopoulos, and Christian McConnell (Collegeville, MN: Liturgical Press, 2012), 30-36, and Anne McGowan, "Eastern Christian Insights and Western Liturgical Reforms: Travelers, Texts, and Liturgical Luggage," in *Liturgy in Migration: From the Upper Room to Cyberspace,* ed. Teresa Berger, foreword by Martin Jean (Collegeville, MN: The Liturgical Press, 2012), 179-208.

3. In addition to Taft's five-volume *History of the Liturgy of St. John Chrysostom* published in the *Orientalia christiana analecta* series, also see idem, *The Byzantine Rite: A Short History* (Collegeville, MN: Liturgical Press, 1992), and "Mount Athos: A Late Chapter in the History of the Byzantine Rite." *Dumbarton Oaks Papers* 42 (1988): 179-94.

4. See Thomas Pott, *Byzantine Liturgical Reform: A Study of Liturgical Change in the Byzantine Tradition,* trans. Paul Meyendorff, Orthodox Liturgy Series, 2 (Crestwood, NY: St. Vladimir's Seminary Press, 2010); Paul Meyendorff, *Russia, Ritual, and Reform: The Liturgical Reforms of Nikon in the 17th Century* (Crestwood, NY: St. Vladimir's Seminary Press, 1991); Marcel Mojzeš, *Il movimento liturgico nelle chiese bizantine: analisi di alcune tendenze di riforma nel XX secolo,* Bibliotheca Ephemerides Liturgicae subsidia 132 (Rome: Edizione Liturgiche, 2005); Peter Galadza, "Schmemann Between Fagerberg and Reality: Towards an Agenda for Byzantine Christian Pastoral Liturgy," *Bolletino della Badia Greca di Grottaferrata* 4 (2007): 7-32;

The last one-hundred plus years witnessed a series of global events and developments necessitating ecclesial adjustments. In the twentieth century, Christianity adjusted to modernization, urbanization, nationalism, revolutions, totalitarianism, two horrifying world wars, the Cold War and the collapse of the Berlin wall, and the emergence of a professionalized workplace. The twenty-first century generates new challenges such as the information age and the technological revolution, globalization, egalitarianism, the emergence of new forms of slavery and human trafficking, and (according to some) the post-Christian era. Perhaps the most elaborate and instrumental ecclesial response to the challenges of modernity is the Second Vatican Council. Energized by *aggiornamento* and *ressourcement*, Vatican II promulgated a vision of the Church actively engaging and participating in the world as citizens of God's kingdom. The Council encouraged the conscious and active participation of the people in the Church's liturgy, a participation not limited to joining in the performance of gestures and singing of hymns, but also seeking to enter into the divine life of the Triune God. The Council envisioned a significant body of Christians participating in Christ's eternal liturgy offered to God; having partaken of God by hearing the proclamation of the word and receiving Holy Communion, Christians return to the world to bear Christ and contribute to society's transformation and transfiguration into an icon of God's kingdom.[5] Reform was to be implemented with structures and catechesis demanded by the nature of liturgy itself, with the hope that the reformed liturgy would shape and form

Nicholas Denysenko, "Towards an Agenda for Byzantine Pastoral Liturgy: A Response to Peter Galadza," *Bolletino della Badia Greca di Grottaferrata* 7 (2010): 45-68.
5. See Mark Searle, *Called to Participate: Theological, Ritual, and Social Perspectives*, ed. Barbara Searle and Anne Koester (Collegeville, MN: Liturgical Press, 2006), 2-16; Ferrone, *Liturgy*, 25-6.

multiple generations into a holy priesthood that served God in the world.

SC emerged within the context of the liturgical and ecumenical movements.[6] A core tenet of these movements was *ressourcement*, the return to the sources of antique Christianity, particularly the patristic epoch. *Ressourcement* aimed to illuminate a more holistic ecclesial history so that the contemporary Church would reform herself in light of her whole story. Vatican II did not inaugurate *ressourcement*, but the Council employed and encouraged it. At the same time, *ressourcement* was and remains an ecumenical endeavor. The Catholic dimension of the liturgical movement has a parallel in the Oxford movement of the Anglican tradition. Similarly, the Orthodox Church experienced periods of *ressourcement* from the eighteenth through the twentieth centuries.[7] The Russian Orthodox Church studied the history of the Byzantine liturgy and proposed and assessed numerous reforms that would bring the Church up to date, essentially an Orthodox version of *ressourcement*. For the Orthodox, the context of *ressourcement* shifted after the Bolshevik revolution, with the center moving from the academies of the Russian Empire to a variety of centers established by immigrants in the West. Among the most

6. See Faggioli, 30-37. Also see John Fenwick and Bryan D. Spinks, *Worship in Transition: the Liturgical Movement in the Twentieth Century* (New York: Continuum, 1995); Keith F. Pecklers, *The Unread Vision: the Liturgical Movement in the United States of America, 1926-1955* (Collegeville, MN: Liturgical Press, 1998). Michael Kinnamon and Brian E. Cope, eds., *The Ecumenical Movement: an Anthology of Key Texts and Voices* (Grand Rapids, MI: Eerdmans, 1996).

7. The most recent study is by Hyacinthe Destivelle, *The Moscow Council (1917–1918): The Creation of the Conciliar Institutions of the Russian Orthodox Church*, foreword by Metropolitan Hilarion [Alfeyev], preface by Hevré Legrand, trans. Jerry Ryan, ed. Michael Plekon and Vitaly Permiakov (Notre Dame, IN: University of Notre Dame Press, forthcoming in 2015). Also see Paul Valliere, *Conciliarism: A History of Decision-Making in the Church* (Cambridge, UK, and New York: Cambridge University Press, 2012). For additional background, see James Cunningham, *A Vanquished Hope: The Movement for Church Renewal in Russia, 1905-1906* (Crestwood, NY: St. Vladimir's Seminary Press, 1981); Nicholas Zernov, *The Russian Religious Renaissance of the Twentieth Century* (Salisbury, MA: Regina Orthodox Press, 1999).

important of these centers was St. Sergius Institute in Paris, which produced numerous theologians constituting the so-called "Paris School."[8] Some of the theologians formed at St. Sergius immigrated to the North America, establishing St. Vladimir's Orthodox Theological Seminary, an institution led by Alexander Schmemann and John Meyendorff. Schmemann and Meyendorff advocated the theological craft of *ressourcement* which occurred in pre-revolutionary Russia and continued in Paris. Orthodox *ressourcement* theology was not limited to these important centers: it was also cultivated by theologians such as John Zizioulas, Anthony Bloom, Olivier Clément, Christos Yannaras, and Kallistos Ware, *inter alia*.

Liturgy was one of the chief topics addressed by the Orthodox *ressourcement* theologians. In Paris, Kyprian Kern and Nicholas Afanasiev presented a renewed Eucharistic theology grounded by patristic sources.[9] Alexander Schmemann further advanced this Eucharistic theology in his writings and teaching. The theological contributions of the Orthodox theologians occurred largely in the West, among smaller Orthodox populations in North America and Western Europe. The Orthodox Church did not convene any councils at the global level during this period so no large-scale liturgical reform was promulgated by an ecumenical authority. The scale of liturgical reform distinguishes *SC* and its implementation from Orthodox liturgical reforms. *SC*, however, was one of the

8. Antoine Arjakovsky, *The Way: Religious Thinkers of the Russian Emigration in Paris and Their Journal, 1925-1940*, trans. Jerry Ryan, ed. John Jillions and Michael Plekon, foreword by Rowan Williams (Notre Dame, IN: University of Notre Dame Press, 2013); Aidan Nichols, *Theology in the Russian Diaspora: Church, Fathers, Eucharist in Nikolai Afanasiev, 1893-1966* (New York: Cambridge University Press, 1989); Antoine Kartachoff, "Orthodox Theology and the Ecumenical Movement," *The Ecumenical Review* 8, no. 1 (1955): 30-35; John A. Jillions, "Ecumenism and the Paris School of Orthodox Theology." *Theoforum* 39, no. 2 (2008): 141-74; Alexis Kniazeff, *L'Institut Saint-Serge: de l'académie d'autrefois au rayonnement d'aujourd'hui* (Paris: Beauchesne, 1974).

9. Cyprian Kern, *Eucharistija* (Paris: YMCA Press, 1947); Nicholas Afanasiev, *Трапеза Господня (The Lord's Supper)* (Kyiv: Temple of the Venerable Agapit of the Caves, 2003).

most influential ecclesial events of modernity and carried serious ecumenical reverberations. The implementation of *SC* influenced subsequent reforms in Reformed Churches, including the rites of initiation, the formation of a three-year lectionary, the composition of new Eucharistic prayers, and a revival of Eucharistic participation.[10] One could assert that *SC*'s teaching on active participation in the liturgy was the most influential of these reforms.

This background raises the question of the potential impact of *SC* on Orthodox liturgical reform. Because many Orthodox Churches participated in the ecumenical and liturgical movements and employed the methods of *ressourcement* theology alongside Catholics and Anglicans, one can plausibly query the impact of *SC* on Orthodox liturgical reform. This chapter surveys the development of a theology of priesthood developed and articulated by Orthodox and Catholic theologians which became a chief cornerstone of the theology of *SC*. I begin by examining the retrieval of a theology of the priesthood of the laity among select Orthodox theologians of the twentieth century. Then, I will survey the contributions of two Catholic theologians from this theological tradition, namely Yves Congar and Virgil Michel. Third, I will demonstrate how the theology of priesthood shared by Orthodox and Catholic *ressourcement* theologians became a staple of magisterial teaching, particularly in *Lumen Gentium* (*LG*), *Apostolicam Actuasitatem* (*AA*), and *SC*. Fourth, I will closely read sections of *SC* that articulate the place of priesthood in the liturgy and will discuss how the retrieved theology of priesthood and the active participation in the liturgy serve as the theological foundations for liturgical reform.

---

10. Paul Bradshaw and Maxwell Johnson, *The Eucharistic Liturgies: Their Evolution and Interpretation* (Collegeville, MN: Liturgical Press, 2012), 300. Also see James F. White, "Where the Reformation Was Wrong on Worship," *Christian Century* 99, no. 33 (1982): 1074-77.

Orthodox Liturgical *Ressourcement* and
the Priesthood of the Laity

The twentieth century witnessed the retrieval and restoration of the royal priesthood magisterially defined by Catholics as a priesthood bearing the Christic offices of king, priest, and prophet. Each Christian receives a divine blessing to exercise these offices in, to, and for the world at Baptism and Confirmation. Prominent Catholic and Orthodox theologians developed sophisticated theologies of the royal priesthood grounded by the exercise of king, priest, and prophet. These Christic offices are not mentioned by *SC*, but appear in *LG* and *AA*. I propose that the retrieval and articulation of this theology of the laity was an ecumenical endeavor, and that its restoration provided a common foundation for the Eucharistic theology expounded by Roman and Orthodox theologians.

In the twentieth century, four Orthodox theologians developed a theology of priesthood drawing from liturgical and patristic sources: Nicholas Afanasiev, Paul Evdokimov, Alexander Schmemann, and Dumitru Staniloae.[11] Afanasiev, Evodokimov, and Schmemann were products of the so-called Paris School, and Schmemann's Eucharistic ecclesiology is an elaboration and continuation of Afanasiev's pioneering work in this area. I will streamline this section by limiting the discussion to show how Afanasiev, Evdokimov, and Schmemann employed liturgical *ressourcement* to articulate this theology of the lay priesthood.

In his *Church of the Holy Spirit*, Afanasiev includes a chapter devoted to the "ordination of laics."[12] Afanasiev develops a theology

---

11. In this section, I will present perspectives on the three offices as presented by the first three theologians. For a brief overview of Staniloae's interpretation of the three offices, see Radu Bordeianu, "(In)Voluntary Ecumenism: Dumitru Staniloae's Interaction with the West as Open Sobornicity," in *Orthodox Constructions of the West*, ed. George Demacopoulos and Aristotle Papanikolaou (New York: Fordham University Press, 2013), 247-48.

12. Nicholas Afanasiev, *The Church of the Holy Spirit*, trans. Vitaly Permiakov, ed. Michael Plekon

of the priesthood of laics by interpreting select passages from liturgical sources of antiquity, especially the Apostolic Tradition attributed to Hippolytus of Rome, and the contemporary Orthodox rites. Afanasiev asserts that the handlaying gesture in the Apostolic Tradition performed by the bishop after the neophyte was baptized denoted the neophyte's ordination to the order of laics. Afanasiev views the handlaying gesture described by the Apostolic Tradition as symbolizing appointment to priestly ministry, both ordained and lay:

> In the ecclesial consciousness of the third century, the laying on of hands at the ordination for ministry signified the ordination for a priestly ministry. In the prayer formula, at the laying of hands on the newly-baptized we find the same verb *servire* (*leitourgein*) used in the prayer formula at the ordination of a bishop. The use of one and the same verb at the laying on of hands in both incidences is not coincidental. Rather this points to one and the same ministry: for one it is a high priestly ministry, for another it is a priestly ministry.[13]

Afanasiev continues to use the Apostolic Tradition as his primary liturgical source for developing a theology of the ordination of laics by referring to the anointing with Chrism performed by the bishop.[14] Afanasiev interprets the anointing as conferring both a royal and priestly ministry because "in the Old Testament only priests and kings were anointed."[15] It is important to note that the formula for the anointing in the Apostolic Tradition does not mention priests and kings.[16]

(Notre Dame, IN: University of Notre Dame Press, 2007). Afanasiev carefully defines "laic": "It is inaccurate to regard laymen as a separate group of the members of the Church. According to modern scholastic teaching, lay people are 'non-consecrated,' as opposed to the 'consecrated' which include all those who belong to the priesthood. As 'non-consecrated,' lay people do not receive any ordination and therefore the term 'lay ordination' contains in itself a contradiction. This would be accurate if the term 'lay people' is understood as 'laics,' i.e., the members of God's people. Therefore, we should speak not of a 'lay' but of a 'laic' ordination" (25).

13. Ibid., 25–26.
14. Ibid., 26.
15. Ibid.

Afanasiev turns to the contemporary Orthodox initiatory rites as he develops the theology of the ordination of laics. He infers that the Byzantine Rite once contained a handlaying gesture and points to the prayer recited at the rite of Ablution on the eighth day as evidence of the ancient episcopal handlaying since it "speaks of the laying on not of the bishop's but of God's mighty hand."[17] Afanasiev turns to the blessing of baptismal waters and cites one of the blessings requested of God for the neophytes, that they would "receive the prize of his high calling and be numbered with the firstborn."[18] Afanasiev says that the high calling to which the prayer refers is about the neophyte's priestly ministry.[19] The same is true of the anointing with holy oil in the contemporary Orthodox rite of Chrismation; this seal likewise signifies belonging to the people of God, or "holy priesthood," as does the donning of the white garment.[20]

Afanasiev describes the ordination of laics as initiating neophytes into "a nation of kings and priests" who exercise their ministry alongside those ordained to preside.[21] The ministry laics exercise is legitimate, and Afanasiev insists that "a laic cannot be viewed in opposition to the consecrated," because everyone who belongs to the Church has received the pledge of the age to come.

Paul Evdokimov was an important lay Orthodox theologian of the mid-twentieth century. Evdokimov wrote at length on a variety of topics in an ecumenical context. His most important works are his theology of marriage *The Sacrament of Love*, and his exposition

16. Afanasiev cites the formulary from the Apostolic Tradition: "I anoint you with holy oil in God the Father Almighty and Christ Jesus and the Holy Spirit" (ibid.).
17. Ibid. Afanasiev cites the text of the prayer in its entirety.
18. "His" refers to the Holy Spirit; for the text of the blessing of baptismal waters and its context, see the translation by Archimandrite Ephrem Lash, "Baptism," http://www.anastasis.org.uk/baptism.htm (accessed March 25, 2013).
19. Afanasiev, 27-28.
20. Ibid.
21. Ibid., 30-31. Afanasiev mentions "kings and priests" twice in his summary, manifesting the first foundation of his narrative.

of modern spirituality, *Ages of the Spiritual Life*.[22] One theological idea threads these two different works: an appeal to everyone—men, women and children—to respond to the universal call to priesthood. Evdokimov articulates a particularly Orthodox notion of lay priesthood by proposing a lifestyle embodying traditional monastic values in the contemporary environment, encapsulated by the now-famous notion of interiorized monasticism. Interiorized monasticism allows the Orthodox layperson an opportunity to employ the core values of the Orthodox ascetical tradition and witness to the world. It was important for Evdokimov to provide the laity with access to the venerable Orthodox way while fully engaging the world as men and women "on the street."

An important tenet of Evdokimov's universal priesthood of the laity is the theological contribution of the sacrament of Chrismation.[23] Like Afanasiev, Evdokimov views Chrismation as the ordination of the layperson to the priesthood.[24] The layperson's ministry is related to the bishop's: it is an exercise of the priesthood of Christ.[25] The anointing with Chrism equips the layperson with the spiritual gifts needed to exercise these ministries. Evdokimov interrogates several select liturgical sources to illuminate these gifts. For example, he refers to the occasional consecration of Chrism celebrated by the Orthodox Church and quotes the prayer recited by the bishop, which asks that God would seal the recipients so that

---

22. Paul Evdokimov, *The Sacrament of Love: The Nuptial Mystery in the Light of the Orthodox Tradition*, trans. Anthony P. Gythiel and Victoria Steadman, foreword by Olivier Clément (Crestwood, NY: St. Vladimir's Seminary Press, 1995).

23. Evdokimov expounds his theology of Chrismation in an essay titled "L'Esprit saint et l'Église d'après la tradition liturgique," in *L'Esprit Saint et l'Église. Catholiques, orthodoxes et protestants de divers pays confrontent leur science, leur foi et leur tradition: l'Avenir de l'Église et de l'oecuménisme*, ed. Académie internationale des sciences religieuses (Paris: Fanyard, 1969), 85-123, and also *Ages of the Spiritual Life*, trans. Michael Plekon and Alexis Vinogradov (Crestwood, NY: St. Vladimir's Seminary, 1998), 231-39.

24. Evdokimov, *Ages of the Spiritual Life*, 231.

25. Ibid., 232.

they would bear Christ in their hearts.[26] Evdokimov parenthetically elaborates the meaning of "seal" by defining it as making or anointing the participants into "christs."[27] He also views the tonsure that occurs at the rite of ablution as having a parallel to monastic tonsure: "In undergoing the rite of tonsure, every lay person is a monk of interiorized monasticism, subject to all the requirements of the Gospel."[28]

Evdokimov carefully distinguishes the priesthood of the laity from the other orders of the Church by elaborating their relevance in mission to the world. He cites, *inter alia*, St. Macarius of Egypt and Origen to state that the anointing with Chrism makes the laity into kings, priests, and prophets.[29]

Schmemann develops a theology of lay priesthood by describing the human being's ministry as following Christ's pattern. In Chrismation, the neophyte becomes priest, prophet, and king. He defines the content of each ministry in order, king, priest, and prophet, and the purpose of his exposition becomes clear: it is an exercise in theological anthropology. The gift of the Spirit makes one anointed in Christ's image, and Christ's priestly ministry is imparted to the restored human being, whose mission it is to carry out this threefold ministry in the world.

Schmemann's exposition consists of an essay on the theological anthropology of the rites of initiation and an underlying critique of secular culture. His discussion of the new human being who emerges from the font privileges what he calls "anthropological maximalism."[30] This new human being was once the king of creation who is now fallen; the human vocation has been restored and humans

---

26. Ibid., 235. Also see "L'Esprit saint et l'Église d'après la tradition liturgique," 101-2.
27. Evdokimov, *Ages of the Spiritual Life*, 235.
28. Ibid., 234-35.
29. Ibid., 238-39.
30. Schmemann, *Of Water and the Spirit*, 82.

are now kings again.[31] Later, Schmemann explains that humans exercise this restored vocation through the mystery of the cross.[32] Schmemann attributes the restoration of this gift to humanity to Baptism and the postbaptismal anointing with chrism: "In the eucharistic blessing of water . . . the entire cosmos is revealed again as God's gift to man, as man's kingdom. In the anointment with the 'oil of gladness,' the new life of the neophyte is announced as power and dominion. He is vested in royal garments, and it is Christ's own kingship that he receives in the 'seal' of the Holy Chrism."[33] Schmemann refers to a sequence of ritual components in initiation, namely the blessing of baptismal waters, the prebaptismal anointing of catechumens, and the postbaptismal Chrismation.

Schmemann's image of the restored human is positive (a word he frequently italicizes for emphasis), and seems to be suitable for Christian mission. But Schmemann also appears to have affixed a particular theological anthropology onto the ritual components by ascribing this definition of a Christian to the rite without more direct references to their content. One should also note that Schmemann completes his discussion on the content of kingship imparted to the neophyte by ascribing it solely to the anointing with chrism.[34] Schmemann's exposition on the second and third aspects of the human vocation is likewise attributed to the Holy Spirit. He briefly

---

31. Schmemann's distinctions are intriguing, and reveal his task of defining Christianity's theological anthropology in the context of secular culture. For example, he addresses the oft-repeated refrain on the universality of human failure by distinguishing between errors and the innate goodness of vocation when he says, "man misuses his vocation, and in this horrible misuse he mutilates himself and the world; but his vocation is good," ibid., 84.
32. Ibid., 85, 87.
33. Ibid., 83.
34. "Now, and only now, can we answer the question raised at the beginning of this chapter: about the meaning of our kingship bestowed upon us in the sacrament of Chrismation. We can answer it because in the Cross of Christ the content of this kingship is revealed and its power is granted. The royal anointment truly makes us kings, but it is the crucified kingship of Christ himself—it is the cross as kingship and kingship as cross—that the Holy Spirit bestows on us," ibid., 90.

states that Christ's priesthood is given to the neophyte at Chrismation,[35] along with the gift of prophecy.[36] His explanation of the features of these holy gifts follows the pattern he established with kingship: the gifts profoundly change the neophyte, but Schmemann does not establish how the initiatory rites communicate the imparting of these gifts.

In summary, Afanasiev, Evdokimov, and Schmemann developed a theology of the priesthood of the laity by examining the liturgical sources. Afanasiev views the laity as the first order of the Church appointed by God through the laying on of hands at Baptism. Evdokimov follows a similar pattern by defining the lay priesthood through the Christic offices of priest, prophet, and king imparted through the anointing with Chrism. Schmemann's theology is similar, and like Afanasiev and Evdokimov, he describes the imparting of these priestly gifts as designed for the lay person who exercises his or her ministry in the world. Thus, lay ministry originates with the mysteries of initiation, and the laity receives the spiritual energy required for priestly ministry through the Eucharist. The Orthodox theological teaching on the laity carried the weight of the prominence of its teachers' statures, so the dissemination of the teaching is directly connected with the influence wielded by Afanasiev, Evdokimov, and Schmemann. In other words, while many Orthodox theologians of the world would affirm and sustain this retrieval of the teaching on the priesthood of the laity, some Orthodox Churches and theologians could ignore it since it did not carry the authority of the canons or an Orthodox council. As we shall see later, the weight of authority distinguishes the impact of the Orthodox theological teaching from its Roman Catholic parallel,

---

35. Ibid., 94, 97.
36. Ibid., 101, 103.

which was inscribed upon the magisterial teaching of Vatican II and thus bore more authoritative weight in the Roman communion.

Catholic Theologians and the priesthood: Congar and Michel

In the West, the threefold division of Christ's ministry into the kingly, priestly, and prophetic offices has a long and rich history closely associated with the development of a priesthood of all believers.[37] Reformation theologians further refined this theology, especially John Calvin.[38] The triadic office continued to develop in the Catholic Reformation and was taken up by John Henry Newman.[39] One of the most substantial treatments of the Christic offices in modern Catholic theology occurs in Yves Congar's study of the laity in the Church.[40]

Congar's comprehensive study begins with a definition of the layperson and addresses the question of how laity exercise Christ's threefold ministry. Congar offers numerous contributions to lay ministry in the spirit of *ressourcement*, a careful and complete

37. Several seminal essays break open the historical development of the laity as kings, prophets, and priests in Roman Catholic theology. For the classical overview of the historical development of these offices and their interpretation, see Yves Congar, "Sur la trilogie: prophìte-roi-prêtre," *Revues des sciences philosophiques et théologiques* 67 (1983), 97-115. Also see David Power, "Priesthood Revisited: Mission and Ministries in the Royal Priesthood," in *Ordering the Baptismal Priesthood; Theologies of Lay and Ordained Priesthood,* ed. Susan Wood (Collegeville, MN: Liturgical Press, 2003), 97-120; Zeni Fox, "Laity, Ministry, and Secular Character," in *Ordering the Baptismal Priesthood,* ed. Susan Wood, 121-51; and Donald J. Goergen, "Priest, Prophet, King: The Ministry of Jesus Christ," in *The Theology of Priesthood,* ed. Donald Goergen and Ann Garrido (Collegeville, MN: Liturgical Press, 2000), 187-210. Also see the analysis by Susan Wood, *Sacramental Orders* (Collegeville, MN: Liturgical Press, 2000), 11-19.
38. Power, "Priesthood Revisited," in. Wood, ed., *Ordering the Baptismal Priesthood,* 107. For a complete treatment, see Rose Beal, "Priest, Prophet and King: Jesus Christ, the Church and the Christian Person," in *John Calvin's Ecclesiology: Ecumenical Perspectives,* ed. Gerard Mannion and Eddy van der Borght (London, New York: T & T Clark, 2011), 90-106.
39. See Goergen, "Priest, Prophet, King," in *The Theology of Priesthood,* ed. Goergen and Garrido, 191-92. See John Henry Newman, *Sermons Bearing on Subjects of the Day* (London, New York, Bombay: Longmans, Green, and Co., 1902), 52-62.
40. Yves Congar, *Lay People in the Church: A Study for the Theology of the Laity,* trans. Donald Attwater (Westminster, MD: Newman Press, 1957, 1963 reprint).

definition of a lay priesthood retrieved from the Church's patristic and liturgical heritage. Congar concludes that the three offices are not mutually exclusive, but reciprocally shape one another for the building up of the people of God, Christ's body.[41] He defines them as producing a plurality of ministries within the Church and is wary of attempting to apply them to the exercise of sacerdotal powers of order and jurisdiction.[42] For Congar, the notion of a plurality of ministries is perhaps best understood when noting that the ordained exercise ministries within the community, and not as external authorities imposing themselves upon the community.[43]

Central to Congar's ecclesiology, and consequently, to his definition of lay ministry, is his cosmology encompassing kingdom, Church, and world. After stating that God's purpose is to "bring mankind into fellowship with his divine life,"[44] Congar explains the intersections of kingdom, Church, and world through the image of the temple:

> God wills to make the world the temple of his power and glory; he wills to make mankind his temple built of living stones, his body made of free persons, in a word, the temple of his fellowship. This is whither it all tends: that God wills to dwell and to be praised in mankind as in a single temple, but the indwelling and the praise are spiritual, living.[45]

Congar continues by reviewing salvation history and the inauguration of God's kingdom in the Incarnation of Christ. He describes the present as a space between the fulfillment of the kingdom and its inauguration, and portrays the Church's role in fulfilling God's kingdom accordingly:

41. Congar, "Sur la trilogie: prophìte-roi-prêtre," 112.
42. Ibid.
43. Fox, "Laity, Ministry, and Secular Character," in 140–41.
44. Congar, *Lay People in the Church*, 53.
45. Ibid., 53–54.

The Church's constitution is in this, that she already has within herself, and as the very things that make her Church, the self-same and decisive causes of that renewal of which the Kingdom will be the consummation: the kingly, priestly, and prophetical power of Christ, and the Holy Spirit. Therefore, the Church co-operates directly in the constitution of the Kingdom, through the exercise of energies that are her won and constitute her reality as Church.[46]

Congar turns to the liturgy to connect the laity and Christ's threefold offices of king, priest, and prophet.[47] He identifies Confirmation as imparting the gift to exercise Christ's ministries to neophytes.[48] His teaching is quite similar to that of the Benedictine pioneer of the liturgical movement, Virgil Michel, who also understood the rites of initiation as imparting the divine vocation of king, priest, and prophet to neophytes, whose responsibility it is to manifest Christ to the world in which they live.[49] Michel's source for this vision of lay ministry is the doctrine of *theosis*, inaugurated by God at baptism. The gift of the indwelling of the Triune God is one Christians are to share with the world, with the priestly goal of transforming it in Christ. Rose Calabretta's description of Michel's last days echoes Congar's theological description of the present as the space between:

The object of this apostolic lifestyle was to obey the mandate of Christ given to his Church in its double commission: a) to announce to all human beings the highest truth about themselves: they were both children of God and members of Christ; and b) to capacitate them

---

46. Ibid., 88.
47. Congar, "Sur la trilogie: prophète-roi-prêtre," 99–100. Also see idem, *I Believe in the Holy Spirit*, vol. 3, trans. David Smith, 219–20.
48. Congar, *I Believe in the Holy Spirit*, vol. 3, trans. David Smith, 219–20. Congar also connects the imparting of these gifts to the anointing in his essay "The Structure of Christian Priesthood," in idem, *At the Heart of Christian Worship: Liturgical Essays of Yves Congar*, ed. and trans. Paul Philibert (Collegeville, MN: Liturgical Press, 2010), 90, esp. n. 39.
49. Rose B. Calabretta, *Baptism and Confirmation: The Vocation and Mission of the Laity in the Writings of Virgil Michel*, Tesi gregoriana, Serie Teologia 47 (Rome: Gregorian University Press, 1998), 166–67. For a survey of Michel's background, see Michael Woods, *Cultivating Soil and Soul: Twentieth-Century Catholic Agrarians Embrace the Liturgical Movement* (Collegeville, MN: The Liturgical Press, 2009), 66–100.

for living out their days, soaring even higher towards their sublimest dignity, thus experiencing new frontiers of authentic freedom. They were destined by their Father to enjoy even in time-bound existence the heavenly life that he wished to give them: to share in the eternal love in the inner communion of the Triune God.[50]

A crucial component of Michel's notion of a baptismal priesthood is its accessibility to the laity. Calabretta notes that Michel translates traditional monastic vocabulary by reintroducing terms such as "ascetic" and "mystical" to make it accessible to the layperson, who truly becomes a fellower of Christ and joins the communion of saints.[51] The transfiguration of social structures is a task belonging to the whole people of God, ordained and lay, each exercising the gifts of the Spirit they receive in the sacraments.

Priesthood in the Documents of Vatican II

The sacramental theology of priesthood developed by *ressourcement* theologians like Afanasiev, Evdokimov, Schmemann, Congar and Michel became official in two documents of Vatican II. In chapter four of *Lumen Gentium*, the constitution on the Church, Vatican II defines the laity accordingly:[52]

> The term laity is here understood to mean all the faithful except those in holy orders and those in the state of religious life specially approved by the Church. These faithful are by Baptism made one body with Christ and are constituted among the People of God; they are in their own way made sharers in the priestly, prophetical, and kingly functions of Christ; and they carry out for their own part the mission of the whole Christian people in the Church and in the world.

50. Calabretta, 213.
51. Ibid., 146-47, 160.
52. Second Vatican Council, *Lumen Gentium* no. 31, Vatican Web Site, http://www.vatican.va/archive/hist_councils/ii_vatican_council/documents/vat-ii_const_19641121_lumen-gentium_en.html (accessed April 8, 2013).

Lumen Gentium distinguishes the vocation of the laity from that of the ordained priesthood by emphasizing lay ministry to the world:

> But the laity, by their very vocation, seek the kingdom of God by engaging in temporal affairs and by ordering them according to the plan of God. They live in the world, that is, in each and in all of the secular professions and occupations. They live in the ordinary circumstances of family and social life, from which the very web of their existence is woven. They are called there by God that by exercising their proper function and led by the spirit of the Gospel they may work for the sanctification of the world from within as a leaven. In this way they may make Christ known to others, especially by the testimony of a life resplendent in faith, hope and charity. Therefore, since they are tightly bound up in all types of temporal affairs it is their special task to order and to throw light upon these affairs in such a way that they may come into being and then continually increase according to Christ to the praise of the Creator and the Redeemer.[53]

Vatican II echoes the teaching of theologians like Congar and Michel by placing the ministry of the laity in explicitly worldly terms. The Council connects lay ministry to the apostolate in *AA*. A strong sacramental theology grounded by the rites of initiation and the ministries of king, priest, and prophet again guides the mission of the laity in the world:[54]

> The laity derive the right and duty to the apostolate from their union with Christ the head; incorporated into Christ's Mystical Body through Baptism and strengthened by the power of the Holy Spirit through Confirmation, they are assigned to the apostolate by the Lord Himself. They are consecrated for the royal priesthood and the holy people (cf. 1 Pet. 2:4-10) not only that they may offer spiritual sacrifices in everything they do but also that they may witness to Christ throughout the world. The sacraments, however, especially the most holy Eucharist,

---

53. Ibid.
54. Second Vatican Council, *Apostolicam Actuasitatem*, Vatican website, http://www.vatican.va/archive/hist_councils/ii_vatican_council/documents/vat-ii_decree_19651118_apostolicam-actuositatem_en.html (accessed April 8, 2013).

communicate and nourish that charity which is the soul of the entire apostolate.

An emphasis on the legitimacy and power of the universal priesthood of the laity appears in the decree's description of the work of the lay apostolate. *AA* describes the laity as "sharers in the role of Christ as priest, prophet, and king," whose work is absolutely essential to the life of the Church.[55] The laity's ministry of creating encounters between the world and God's kingdom is essential to the divine will because the laity as the body of Christ is the tangible connection of kingdom, Church, and world.

The teachings of Vatican II here thus resonate significantly with the ecumenical *ressourcement* theology flourishing prior to the Council. This theology is a creative synthesis of liturgy, theological anthropology, and the sacramental theology gleaned from the historical development of the rites of initiation. Catholic theology defines the laity as becoming sharers of Christ and his threefold office, conferred through Baptism and Confirmation.[56] As well, the Council retrieves a sacramental theology subtending a salient, missional cosmology—the laity's purpose is to transform and transfigure the world by making Christ present in their daily secular activity. Theologians have assessed the status of this sacramental theology since Vatican II, but the theological anthropology of the laity as exercising Christ's ministries of king, priest, and prophet continues to hold sway in Catholic systematic theology.

The Direction of Theological Influence

The preceding section suggests that *LG* and *AA* espouse a theology of the laity that draws upon the contributions of Orthodox and

---

55. Second Vatican Council, *Apostolicam Actuasitatem* no. 10.
56. The documents of the Council underscore the former, whereas Congar focuses on the imparting of the Christic offices through the sacraments.

Catholic theologians. The evidence from the early-twentieth century suggests that the primary proponents of this theology in the respective Orthodox and Catholic traditions benefitted from the theological cross-pollination that occurs in dialogical exchange during ecumenical gatherings. Anastacia Wooden traces this process of mutual listening, commencing in the early-twentieth century, when Pope Pius XI instructed the Benedictines to work with the Russian Orthodox Church, resulting in a dual rite community now located at Chevetogne in Belgium.[57] Catholic-Orthodox dialogue flourished as well at the Liturgical Weeks symposia inaugurated by Afanasiev and Kyprian Kern in 1952 at St. Sergius Institute in Paris.[58] Wooden claims that Afanasiev's Eucharistic ecclesiology began to influence Catholic theologians during these encounters, evidenced by his appearance in the preparatory documents of Vatican II and his participation in the final session of the council, which contributed to the mutual lifting of anathemas between the Roman and Orthodox Churches.[59]

Another such example of mutual listening occurred during the Second Vatican Council itself. Orthodox theologians participated in Vatican II as observers, including representatives from the Moscow Patriarchate and Russian Church in Exile.[60] Yves Congar refers to

57. Anastacia Wooden, "Eucharistic Ecclesiology of Nicholas Afanasiev and Catholic Ecclesiology: History of Interaction and Future Perspectives," A Paper presented at the 50th International Eucharistic Congress in 2012, http://www.iec2012.ie/media/1AnastaciaWooden1.pdf (accessed October 11, 2013). "Wooden" hereafter.

58. Michael Plekon, "Nicholas Afanasiev," *Key Theological Thinkers: From Modern to Postmodern*, ed. Staale Kristiansen and Svian Reis (Farnham, Burlington: Ashgate, 2013), 374.

59. Wooden, 1. See Wooden's more substantial treatment of Afanasiev's contribution to ecumenical dialogue in her essay, "Eucharistic Ecclesiology of Nicolas Afanasiev and its Ecumenical Significance: A New Perspective," *Journal of Ecumenical Studies* 45, no. 4 (2010), 543-60. Also see Paul McPartlan, "*Ressourcement*, Vatican II, and Eucharistic Ecclesiology," in Ressourcement: *A Movement for Renewal in Twentieth-Century Catholic Theology*, ed. Gabriel Flynn and Paul D. Murray (New York: Oxford University Press, 2012), 403.

60. O'Malley, 96. Nikos Nissiotis, a Greek Orthodox layperson, represented the World Council of Churches.

several encounters with Orthodox observers at Vatican II, including contributions from Father Vitaly Borovoj from the Moscow Patriarchate and the active participation of Alexander Schmemann.[61] Besides exchanging ideas with Nikos Nissiotis and Schmemann during ecclesiological deliberations, Congar describes a meaningful conversation with both Orthodox representatives over lunch:

> We had an interesting chat: about ecclesiology. I told them my way of seeing the ecclesiology of the Fathers and of the liturgy, as including anthropology, and we agreed that the best ecclesiology would be . . . a development on the Christian human being. We also spoke of the *De Beata*. In their view, a *De Beata* is a fairly doubtful step. In the East, Mary is a DIMENSION of everything: of Christology, of the history of salvation (continuity with Israel), ecclesiology, of prayer. That is why the Orthodox mix her up with everything without ever producing a treatise *De Beata*.[62]

Congar's account provides a snapshot of the kind of theologically dense conversation that occurred between Catholics and Orthodox at Vatican II.

Robert Taft also attends to Catholic exchange with Orthodox.[63] Taft demonstrates that Catholic engagement with *ressourcement* theology oriented Catholic theologians towards Eastern sources. Taft states that the West discovered forms and ideas in the East that illuminated Western deficiencies: "the West has tended to define Eastern liturgy in terms of what it perceives itself as lacking."[64] Taft then identifies four areas of theological wealth (more or less) preserved in the East that enchanted the West: a balance of high

61. Yves Congar, *My Journal of the Council*, trans. Mary John Ronayne and Mary Cecily Boulding, ed. Dennis Minns (Collegeville, MN: Liturgical Press, 2012), 89, 329-31, 352. Congar also notes that the Ecumenical Patriarchate was opposed to sending observers to Vatican II, in contrast to the open ecumenical participation of the Moscow Patriarchate (82).
62. Ibid., 382-83.
63. Taft, "Between Progress and Nostalgia," in *A Living Tradition*, ed. Pitt, Alexopoulos, and McConnell, 19-42.
64. Ibid., 31.

Christology and the human, kenotic Christ; radical Trinitarianism; a sense of the holiness, transcendence, and unknowability of God (apophatic theology in the liturgy); and holistic liturgy.[65] Taft cautions the Orthodox that it is easy to misunderstand Western interest in Eastern liturgy, as Catholics were not seeking a return to Eastern Orthodoxy.[66] Catholic theologians are enchanted by the idea of the Orient, in an "attempt to recreate for itself a better present out of an imagined ideal past."[67] Taft also offers his own assessment of the cross-pollination between East and West in the Catholic liturgical reforms resulting in the promulgation and implementation of SC: "the process was . . . a fruitful influence in which both East and West influenced and enriched each other mutually."[68]

Anne McGowan presents several instances of Western Churches adopting Eastern liturgical practices and offices, including Catholic dependence on the Byzantine formula for anointing with Chrism and the identification of the anointing as the primary form (as opposed to the laying-on-of-hands) in Confirmation.[69] Together, Taft and Wooden suggest that Orthodox liturgy has contributed to the reform of Catholic liturgy in SC. Catholic recognition of authentically Eastern liturgical forms and content reached its apogee when the Holy See recognized the validity of the Assyrian form of the anaphora of Addai and Mari, a Eucharistic prayer which does not include the

---

65. "Eastern liturgy has created and retained a synthesis of ritual, art, church design, and symbolic structure that may at times seem inflexible but that permits it to do what liturgy is supposed to do without the self-consciousness of present-day liturgy in the West. For liturgy serves no purpose outside of itself," in ibid., 34-36.

66. Ibid., 32.

67. Ibid., 33.

68. Ibid., 37. On this topic, also see Mark Morozowich, "East Meets West in Liturgy: Mutual Influence Throughout the Centuries," in *Liturgies in East and West: Ecumenical Relevance of Early Liturgical Development. Acts of the International Symposium Vindobonense I, Vienna, November 17-20, 2007* (Vienne: International Specialized Book Services, 2013), 295-305.

69. McGowan, "Eastern Christian Insights and Western Liturgical Reforms," in *Liturgy in Migration*, ed. Berger, 200-203. Also see Nicholas Denysenko, *Chrismation: A Primer for Catholics* (Collegeville, MN: Liturgical, 2014), 144-50.

Words of Institution. Taft refers to this recognition as "the most remarkable magisterial document since Vatican II."[70]

The evidence examined to this point suggests that Roman Catholics consulted Orthodox sources in updating magisterial teaching on the Church and her liturgy and implementing liturgical reform. However, there is also evidence suggesting that the Orthodox also borrowed liberally from Roman Catholic voices. Mutual listening was not one-sided, as in only Catholics studying the Orthodox. Faggioli notes that some Orthodox listened to *SC*, including the prominent theologians Olivier Clément, who believed that *SC* could be modular for Orthodox liturgical reform.[71] Schmemann also indicates active listening to Catholics. For example, one of Schmemann's earliest and most important works, *Introduction to Liturgical Theology*, engages extensively Catholic theologians such as Louis Bouyer, Anton Baumstark, Yves Congar, and Olivier Rousseau.[72] Schmemann closely follows the Catholic tradition of explaining sacramental theology in his study of Baptism, *Of Water and the Spirit*.[73] In this work, Schmemann treats Baptism, Chrismation,

70. Robert F. Taft, "Mass Without the Consecration? The Historic Agreement on the Eucharist Between the Catholic Church and the Assyrian Church of the East Promulgated 26 October 2001," *Worship* 77, no. 6 (2003): 483. Also see Nicholas V. Russo, "The Validity of the Anaphora of Addai and Mari: Critique of the Critiques," in *Issues in Eucharistic Praying in East and West: Essays in Liturgical and Theological Analysis*, ed. Maxwell Johnson (Collegeville, MN: Liturgical Press, 2012), 21-62.

71. Olivier Clément, "Vers un dialogue avec le catholicisme," *Contacts* 14 (1965): 16-37, quoted in Faggioli, 111n58.

72. Alexander Schmemann, *Introduction to Liturgical Theology*, trans. Asheleigh E. Moorhouse (Crestwood, NY: St. Vladimir's Seminary Press, 1986), 9-32. Also see Plekon, *Living Icons*, 179-80; William Mills, *Church, World, and Kingdom: The Eucharistic Foundation of Alexander Schmemann's Pastoral Theology* (Chicago: Archdiocese of Chicago: Liturgy Training Publications, 2012), 37-39; and Robert Taft, "The Liturgical Enterprise Twenty-Five Years after Alexander Schmemann (1921-1983): The Man and His Heritage," *St. Vladimir's Theological Quarterly* 53, nos. 2-3 (2009): 163-64. See chapter 3 of this study for more evidence of Schmemann's "listening" to the West.

73. Alexander Schmemann, *Of Water and the Spirit: A Liturgical Study of Baptism* (Crestwood, NY: St. Vladimir's Seminary Press, 1974).

and Eucharist as three sacraments in order, and identifies Chrismation as the sacrament of the Holy Spirit. Schmemann also offers a rich presentation of Chrismation as the sacrament imparting the Christic offices of king, priest, and prophet, and his discussion of these offices is detached from his presentation on the liturgical components of the anointing with Chrism.

Besides Schmemann, other Orthodox seemed to have been influenced by Catholic *ressourcement* theology. For example, Alkiviadis Calivas, one of the most important teachers of Orthodox liturgy at Holy Cross Greek Orthodox School of Theology in Brookline, Massachusetts, refers to the Eucharist as the "source and summit of the Church's life" in his treatment of the Divine Liturgy, an obvious instance of adopting the vocabulary of *SC*.[74] The Church of Greece appears to adopt several aspects of the principles of Vatican II in the symposia its Holy Synod convoked in preparation for liturgical renewal.[75] Vatican II exercised considerable influence on Orthodoxy in America through sacred architecture. Kostis Kourelis and Vasileios Marinis argue that Vatican II "liberated Catholic churches from historical prototypes and precipitated an explosion of wild designs among the Irish, Italian, and Hispanic populations with whom Greeks socialized and intermarried," resulting in a new phase of Greek Orthodox architecture that abandoned traditional Greek prototypes.[76]

The preceding review of instances of mutual influence of Catholic and Orthodox theology and liturgy suggests that the contributions went in both directions. The ecumenical movement provided an environment for Catholics and Orthodox to engage in theological

---

74. Alkiviadis Calivas, *Essays in Theology and Liturgy,* vol. 3: *Aspects of Orthodox Worship* (Brookline, MA: Holy Cross Orthodox Press, 2003), 176-77.

75. I will treat the Church of Greece as a case study of liturgical renewal in chapter 5.

76. Kostis Kourelis and Vasileios Marinis, "An Immigrant Liturgy: Greek Orthodox Worship and Architecture in America," in *Liturgy in Migration,* ed. Berger, 166.

dialogue which impacted the participants from both traditions. One important difference emerges in the next section: Vatican II. The structure and environment of the council facilitates the inscription of this ecumenical theology onto Catholic magisterial theology. Because the Orthodox Church has not held a council of this magnitude, there is no parallel in Orthodoxy for assessing the permanent impact of Catholic contributions to Orthodox theology. Furthermore, one can only speak of the contribution of Catholic and Orthodox theologians to particular schools of thought within the Orthodox Church and her academy, since no Orthodox council, synod, or corpus of canons has made the reception of the *ressourcement* theology compulsory. Vatican II became a repository of theological contributions from the entire Church, both West and East.

The Impact of Ecumenical Cooperation on Vatican II

Multiple liturgical reforms, employing *ressourcement*, occurred in the twentieth century across ecclesial boundaries. *SC* is the most prominent of these reforms on account of the weight of its impact on the Christian world. On the surface, it appears sensible to assume that the promulgation and implementation of *SC* inaugurated a series of liturgical reforms in sister Churches. The ecumenical priority of Vatican II and the contribution of Eastern voices to its deliberations manifests the evidence of mutual listening discussed in the preceding section. Massimo Faggioli notes that *ressourcement* and its references to plurality in liturgical tradition illuminated the council fathers on the ecumenical nature of the Church.[77] Faggioli also highlights the bishops' experience of this plurality through the celebration of different Catholic rites during Vatican II, which "made the approach

---

77. Faggioli, 34.

to dialogue with Christians from other traditions, especially with the Eastern Orthodox Churches, much more possible."[78] Faggioli argues that the liturgical constitution was deliberately ecumenical, designed for rapprochement with estranged Churches, especially the notion of liturgy as the source and summit of the Church as appealing to the Orthodox and a renewed primacy of the Word in liturgy directed to Reformed Churches.[79] Contributions from Eastern Christians to the deliberations of Vatican II also illustrate the ecumenical character of Vatican II. In addition to the contributions of Orthodox observers, Eastern Catholics shaped the ecumenical lens of the Council. Patriarch Maximos IV of Antioch reminded the council fathers of the inherent plurality in liturgical tradition when he addressed them in French and presented the Eastern practice of worshiping in living languages as exemplary for the council fathers, who were then deliberating on the matter of retaining Latin and adopting the vernacular.[80]

The decree *Orientalium Ecclesiarum* (*OE*, promulgated by Pope Paul VI in 1964) implemented the ecumenical agenda established by *SC* and furthered by *Unitatis Redintegratio*.[81] *OE* encouraged the Catholic Churches of the Eastern rites to follow their own native liturgical traditions and to reform the liturgy only in accordance with its own inner organic development, as demonstrated by *OE*, no. 6:[82]

> All members of the Eastern Rite should know and be convinced that they can and should always preserve their legitimate liturgical rite and their established way of life, and that these may not be altered except to obtain for themselves an organic improvement. All these, then, must

78. Ibid.

79. Ibid., 107-11.

80. See O'Malley, *What Happened at Vatican II*, 136.

81. See the Vatican's English translation of this decree at http://www.vatican.va/archive/hist_councils/ii_vatican_council/documents/vat-ii_decree_19641121_orientalium-ecclesiarum_en.html (accessed October 11, 2013).

82. Ibid.

be observed by the members of the Eastern rites themselves. Besides, they should attain to an ever greater knowledge and a more exact use of them, and, if in their regard they have fallen short owing to contingencies of times and persons, they should take steps to return to their ancestral traditions.

Ironically, Thomas Pott identifies a dissonance in the rationale for reform between *SC* and *OE*. He states that *SC* encourages reform to meet the pastoral needs of the community whereas *OE* promotes restoration by returning to one's native tradition.[83] Pott's insightful distinction between the two types of reform seems to indicate an attitude on the part of the council fathers that the Eastern Churches did not need a liturgical reform, whereas conditions in the Roman liturgy necessitated one.[84] Pott's brief presentation on the reform of the Divine Liturgy in the Melkite Greek-Catholic Church is noteworthy, since this Church's patriarchal synod adopted and approved a new edition of the Divine Liturgy in 1998.[85] Pott states that the reform's aim was pastoral, and ultimately directed towards the reappropriation of the Church's Antiochian-Byzantine tradition.[86] In assessing this reform, Pott notes that the principles draw largely from *SC*.[87]

---

83. Pott, 43–46.
84. It is also possible that the council fathers hoped to demonstrate their fidelity to the autonomy of the Eastern Churches in ascertaining the need for a reform. *OE*'s respect for the Eastern Churches right for self-rule supports this hypothesis (*OE*, no. 5): "The Sacred Council, therefore, not only accords to this ecclesiastical and spiritual heritage the high regard which is its due and rightful praise, but also unhesitatingly looks on it as the heritage of the universal Church. For this reason it solemnly declares that the Churches of the East, as much as those of the West, have a full right and are in duty bound to rule themselves, each in accordance with its own established disciplines, since all these are praiseworthy by reason of their venerable antiquity, more harmonious with the character of their faithful and more suited to the promotion of the good of souls," http://www.vatican.va/archive/hist_councils/ii_vatican_council/documents/vat-ii_decree_19641121_orientalium-ecclesiarum_en.html (accessed October 11, 2013).
85. Pott, 59.
86. Ibid., 60–62.
87. Ibid., 61.

Conclusion on Catholic-Orthodox Theological Exchange

A long history of mutual exchange between Catholic and Orthodox *ressourcement* theologians occurred in the twentieth century, culminating, for Catholics, with *SC* and its implementation. One cannot connect the priesthood of the laity belonging to *LG* and *AA* directly to *SC*, but given the number of theologians who contributed to this theological thread, one can surmise that this understanding of the lay priesthood was gaining momentum in the consciousness of the Church. We have established instances of exchange and mutual influencing between Catholics and Orthodox in this section. Before we explore and assess instances of liturgical reform in modern Orthodoxy, we will establish one final foundation that serves as the key to understanding the rationale for both Orthodox and Catholic liturgical reform. This theological foundation is the result of the fruitful theological exchange that occurred between Catholic and Orthodox theologians during the course of the twentieth century. One of the chief cornerstones of modern liturgical reform in the Catholic and Orthodox Churches is that Christ's eternal priesthood grounds the priesthood of the laity, actualized in the Eucharistic liturgy and empowering the laity for service in, to, and for the life of the world. Because Vatican II functioned as a repository of the ecumenical theology of priesthood, its document on the liturgy (*SC*) serves as a crucial point of reference for analyzing the place of priesthood in the teaching on the liturgy and implementation of liturgical reform.

The Teaching of Vatican II:
Sacrosanctum Concilium and Priesthood

SC's Eucharistic priority is expressed through its definition of priesthood. An initial scan of the document seems to indicate that priesthood is not an important theme, as the word appears only two times. *SC* no. 14, its first statement on the active participation of the laity in the liturgy, links the laity with the royal priesthood of Christ.[88] The laity exercises a royal priesthood given to them in Baptism. The second reference to priesthood appears in *SC* no. 57, in encouraging liturgical concelebration. I will discuss the question of the laity as the liturgy's concelebrant, but *SC* clearly does not have the laity in mind with this reference.

Despite the rare appearance of "priesthood" in the document, I would argue that the notion of a lay priesthood is still prevalent. *SC* makes 29 references to "priest" (excluding the word "priesthood.") *SC* connects priest with Christ, the bishop, and ordained priests. The references to Christ as priest and the ordained priest illuminate the role of the laity as the royal priesthood of Christ. *SC* 7 defines the liturgy as an act of Christ and his body, the Church:[89]

> Rightly, then, the liturgy is considered as an exercise of the priestly office of Jesus Christ. In the liturgy the sanctification of the man is signified by signs perceptible to the senses, and is effected in a way which corresponds with each of these signs; in the liturgy the whole public worship is performed by the Mystical Body of Jesus Christ, that is, by the Head and His members. From this it follows that every liturgical celebration, because it is an action of Christ the priest and of His Body which is the Church, is a sacred action surpassing all others; no other action of the Church can equal its efficacy by the same title and to the same degree.

This passage articulates the ecclesiology of *SC*. The text identifies

---

88. "Mother Church earnestly desires that all the faithful should be led to that fully conscious, and active participation in liturgical celebrations which is demanded by the very nature of the liturgy. Such participation by the Christian people as 'a chosen race, a royal priesthood, a holy nation, a redeemed people' (1 Pet. 2:9; cf. 2:4-5), is their right and duty by reason of their baptism," *SC*, no. 14, http://www.vatican.va/archive/hist_councils/ii_vatican_council/documents/vat-ii_const_19631204_sacrosanctum-concilium_en.html (accessed July 18, 2013).
89. *SC* no. 7, http://www.vatican.va/archive/hist_councils/ii_vatican_council/documents/vat-ii_const_19631204_sacrosanctum-concilium_en.html (accessed July 18, 2013).

Christ as the true presider of every liturgy, with the Church as his body acting with him. One can interpret this passage as evidence for the entire body of Christ, ordained and lay, as concelebrants with Christ (the presider) at each liturgy. This notion of the laity as the liturgy's concelebrant is expressed with greater emphasis in *SC*'s treatment of the Eucharist, in no. 48:[90]

> The Church, therefore, earnestly desires that Christ's faithful, when present at this mystery of faith, should not be there as strangers or silent spectators; on the contrary, through a good understanding of the rites and prayers they should take part in the sacred action conscious of what they are doing, with devotion and full collaboration. They should be instructed by God's word and be nourished at the table of the Lord's body; they should give thanks to God; by offering the Immaculate Victim, not only through the hands of the priest, but also with him, they should learn also to offer themselves; through Christ the Mediator, they should be drawn day by day into ever more perfect union with God and with each other, so that finally God may be all in all.

The textual excerpt is again ecclesiological, consistent with the previous examples where Christ the presider is linked to his body, the Church. This passage from *SC* explicates how some of the orders of the Church participate in the liturgy. *SC* breaks open the theological significance of active participation in the liturgy. Christ's mediation grants the Church community access to the Triune God. The Eucharistic offering is an act of the entire Church, as the laity offers the Immaculate victim with the ordained priest, and offer themselves. The prerequisite for everyone who participates in the act of offering is good understanding and a conscious knowledge of what is being done. It is clear that *SC* does not merely call upon the laity to engage liturgical components (from the reference to silent spectators), but demands that the laity exercise the priesthood given to them. The

90. *SC* no. 48, http://www.vatican.va/archive/hist_councils/ii_vatican_council/documents/vat-ii_const_19631204_sacrosanctum-concilium_en.html (accessed July 18, 2013).

laity's exercise of this priesthood through the liturgy is not limited to the Eucharist, but also applies to the divine office. *SC* reformed the divine office, frequently referring to it as the public prayer of the Church, and calls upon the laity to pray the divine office on their own.[91] Thus both the Eucharistic theology and reform of the divine office in *SC* manifest the laity as the concelebrant of the liturgy. This does not mean that *SC* abrogates the orders of the Church. Rather, *SC* restores the dignity of the laity's priesthood and calls upon them to concelebrate the liturgy with the ordained priests. The distinction between the orders is that priests are granted the authority to preside, lead, and instruct, whereas the laity was called upon to join in the offering.

Most of the references to priests in *SC* are directed towards the ordained leaders of parishes or religious who live in community. The instructions directed to priests cohere with the theological emphasis on the priesthood of the laity, as illustrated by several examples. *SC* no. 18 calls upon priests to enrich their understanding of the sacred liturgy. *SC* offers this exhortation as a partial fulfillment of the restoration of the liturgy as the Church's source and summit, but it is also the chief means to reveal the power of the liturgy to the lay faithful who will experience and learn about the liturgy from their priest.[92] The priests do not learn about the liturgy merely for their

---

91. "Pastors of souls should see to it that the chief hours, especially Vespers, are celebrated in common in church on Sundays and the more solemn feasts. And the laity, too, are encouraged to recite the divine office, either with the priests, or among themselves, or even individually," *SC* no. 100, http://www.vatican.va/archive/hist_councils/ii_vatican_council/documents/vat-ii_const_19631204_sacrosanctum-concilium_en.html (accessed July 18, 2013).

92. "Priests, both secular and religious, who are already working in the Lord's vineyard are to be helped by every suitable means to understand ever more fully what it is that they are doing when they perform sacred rites; they are to be aided to live the liturgical life and to share it with the faithful entrusted to their care," http://www.vatican.va/archive/hist_councils/ii_vatican_council/documents/vat-ii_const_19631204_sacrosanctum-concilium_en.html (accessed July 18, 2013). Also see *SC* no. 19, which requires pastors to instruct the faithful on the liturgy with zeal and patience.

own edification, but to shape them into leaders whose liturgizing shapes and forms the people. *SC* underscores the concelebration of the laity in the liturgy in reforming the way that ordained priests offer prayers. *SC* no. 33 again connects the presidency of Christ exercised by the ordained priest with the concelebration of the people:[93]

> Although the sacred liturgy is above all things the worship of the divine Majesty, it likewise contains much instruction for the faithful. For in the liturgy God speaks to His people and Christ is still proclaiming His gospel. And the people reply to God both by song and prayer. Moreover, the prayers addressed to God by the priest who presides over the assembly in the person of Christ are said in the name of the entire holy people and of all present. And the visible signs used by the liturgy to signify invisible divine things have been chosen by Christ or the Church. Thus not only when things are read "which were written for our instruction" (Rom. 15:4), but also when the Church prays or sings or acts, the faith of those taking part is nourished and their minds are raised to God, so that they may offer Him their rational service and more abundantly receive His grace.

This passage indicates that the liturgical prayers and gestures performed by the priest are offered by the whole Church, even if the priest is the only one speaking. *SC* safeguards the priest's right and obligation to offer private Mass, but the instruction now favors a Eucharistic liturgy offered with the active participation of the whole church. The Church's liturgy is hierarchically ordered, so each ordained ministry has its specific role in liturgical celebration.

The notion that priesthood is one of the primary theological kernels of *SC*'s ecclesiology finds support in the writings of Congar. The feature of Congar's teaching that is distinct from the section I presented above is his connection between the exercise of Christian priesthood and the Eucharist. In an essay that outlines his sacramental

---

93. *SC* no. 33, http://www.vatican.va/archive/hist_councils/ii_vatican_council/documents/vat-ii_const_19631204_sacrosanctum-concilium_en.html (accessed July 18, 2013).

ecclesiology, Congar establishes Christ as the head priest with the ordained ministers and laity belonging to the priesthood of Christ's body.[94] Congar identifies the Eucharist as the mystery which connects Christ with his body, permitting the body—meaning the clergy and laity—to receive nourishment from Christ himself.[95] Christ extends the sacrifice he offers to God to the rest of his communal body, which makes the entire body of clergy and laity partakers or fellows of this sacrifice.[96]

Congar explicates this participation in Christ's priestly sacrifice as the laity's concelebration of the liturgy in an essay reflecting on magisterial documents, including SC.[97] In this essay, Congar emphasizes the ecclesiological substance of SC, which consistently refers to Christ's priestly activity performed as the high priest together with the rest of the body, including the laity. Congar also reviews aspects of liturgical celebration which indicate the priestly role performed by the people in affirming prayers.[98] When the people perform their part of the liturgy, the fullness of the liturgy's meaning is manifested and given to the people.[99] Congar preserves the distinctions between the types of priesthood and upholds the necessity of the ordained ministry, but he clarifies the meaning of ordination within these layers as a ministry of service performed within the church, and not above it.[100] Congar reflects on the

---

94. Yves Congar, "The Structure of Christian Priesthood," in *At the Heart of Christian Worship*, trans. Philibert, 69-107.
95. "The Eucharist shares with the personal body of Christ and will his communion-body or mystical body the same name of body. The Eucharist is precisely the dynamic link which unites one to the other, drawing from the first to nourish the second, just as the stem nourishes the fruit by drawing from its living roots," in ibid., 85.
96. Ibid., 88.
97. Yves Congar, "The Ecclesia or Christian Community as a Whole Celebrates the Liturgy," in *At the Heart of Christian Worship*, trans. Philibert, 15-67.
98. Ibid., 59-62.
99. Congar refers to this as "mutual consent that marks the entire life of the Church," ibid., 62.
100. "This theology situates the hierarchical priesthood within the church, not above it. . . . When we define church as Spouse of Christ or as the Great Sacrament, we understand by 'church' the

potential blessings the laity receives by actively participating in Christ's liturgy as his body: it is possible for them to become holy and cultivate sanctity in every aspect of their lives, including service to the world.[101] The excerpts from these two essays exhibit Congar's contribution to the ecclesiology of *SC*, and confirm the notion of a theology of layered priesthood rooted in Christ the high priest as a central theological foundation of *SC*.

I will now summarize the main points gleaned from this re-reading of *SC*:

1. In restoring the liturgy as the source and summit of Church life, *SC* expounded a potent theology of priesthood which is one of the foundations of the instruction, a notion which finds strong support in essays of Yves Congar both before and after Vatican II;

2. The theology of priesthood begins with Christ, who serves as the mediator between the Church and God in *SC*. By broadening the number of ways Christ is present in the liturgy, *SC* establishes Christ as the eternal priest of each liturgy, including the Eucharist and the Divine Office;

3. *SC*'s second theological foundation of priesthood is the body of Christ, which is inseparable from Christ himself. The body of Christ is ordered with the bishop exercising the office of high priest, and the ordained priests presiding in local parishes;

4. *SC*'s most significant contribution is its extension of priesthood to the laity, which is their right and obligation. The laity's priesthood is grounded sacramentally by Baptism and Eucharist.

---

totality of the People of God, ordered and structured in unity. *In order that it may become what it is called to be,* the church has been constituted by its Lord with a hierarchical priesthood within it," ibid., 64.

101. See Congar, "The Structure of Christian Priesthood," in *At the Heart of Christian Worship,* trans. Philibert, 74, 87.

This royal priesthood naturally invites the laity to actively participate in the liturgy;

5. This interpretation of the laity's active participation occurs through the ecclesiological lens that identifies Christ as the presider. *SC* presents multiple references to the necessity of the laity participating in the Eucharistic offering with understanding and conscious participation. By participating in the offering and actively participating in the liturgy through Christ, the laity is one of the liturgy's concelebrants, along with the bishop and ordained priest(s), a notion that finds support, again, with Congar;

6. *SC* contains numerous references to priests, and these instructions are designed to prepare the ordained priests to order their ministries towards the shaping of the laity into the royal priesthood of Christ envisioned by Vatican II. The instructions that call on priests to study the liturgy, instruct the faithful about the liturgy, and celebrate the liturgy in a style that invites the laity to participate are clearly aimed to draw the people into the liturgy's mystery for their transformation and preparation for priestly service to the world.

One final point rounds out this summary reading of *SC*. The sacramental grounding of the priesthood of the laity is a key point in comparing the liturgical reform authorized by *SC* and Orthodox liturgical reforms. The priesthood of the laity is the common denominator. For *SC* and the Orthodox theologians I have surveyed above, the priesthood of the laity is the key foundation of the entire enterprise. *SC* no. 71 calls for the revision of the sacrament of Confirmation and that "the intimate connection which this sacrament has with the whole of Christian initiation is to be more clearly set forth."[102] This point of the instruction occurs in a series of stipulated revisions for sacraments and appears to address only the addition of renewing baptismal promises to Confirmation. However, the actual revision of Confirmation was much more innovative, as the Roman Church adopted the Byzantine formula for anointing with Chrism and identified this ritual gesture as the chief one of the sacrament. Confirmation's renewed link to Baptism led to the expression of a theology of priesthood that came to underpin all the sacraments of initiation.

SC and Active Participation

The Council's inclusion of the laity in the eternal priesthood of Christ at the liturgy coalesces with the topic of the laity's active liturgical participation. Another area of cross-pollination between the Catholic and Orthodox Churches is the teaching on the active participation of the laity in the liturgy. I will explore this question by comparing SC's teaching to Orthodox liturgical reforms in these areas: the meaning of the active participation of the people in the liturgy and the goal of reforming liturgical offices.[103]

SC offers two seminal texts concerning the active participation of the laity in the liturgy:[104]

> Mother Church earnestly desires that all the faithful should be led to that fully conscious, and active participation in liturgical celebrations which is demanded by the very nature of the liturgy. Such participation by the Christian people as "a chosen race, a royal priesthood, a holy nation, a redeemed people (1 Pet. 2:9; cf. 2:4-5), is their right and duty by reason of their baptism. In the restoration and promotion of the sacred liturgy, this full and active participation by all the people is the aim to be considered before all else; for it is the primary and indispensable

---

102. SC No. 71, http://www.vatican.va/archive/hist_councils/ii_vatican_council/documents/vat-ii_const_19631204_sacrosanctum-concilium_en.html (accessed July 19, 2013).

103. On active participation, see Searle, *Called to Participate*.

104. Vatican II, SC nos. 30 and 14, http://www.vatican.va/archive/hist_councils/ii_vatican_council/documents/vat-ii_const_19631204_sacrosanctum-concilium_en.html (accessed June 26, 2013).

source from which the faithful are to derive the true Christian spirit; and therefore pastors of souls must zealously strive to achieve it, by means of the necessary instruction, in all their pastoral work (*SC* no. 30).

To promote active participation, the people should be encouraged to take part by means of acclamations, responses, psalmody, antiphons, and songs, as well as by actions, gestures, and bodily attitudes. And at the proper times all should observe a reverent silence (*SC* no. 14).

The active participation in the liturgy by the laity was the most important teaching of *SC*. An initial reading of the text from *SC* tempts one to adopt a superficial view of active participation. Number 14 in particular aligns the meaning of active participation with specific components and gestures of the liturgy. But the laity's active participation was not designed to be merely performative; rather, active participation refers to the engagement in a sequence of events that leads the participants, as a body, into the presence of the living God. The studies of Searle, Kimberly Belcher, and Gabriel Pivarnik connect ritual participation with life in the Triune God. Searle delineated three steps of ritual participation culminating in partaking of the divine nature, or theosis, as the original aim of *SC*.[105] More recently, Belcher has shown how infants participate in the life of the Trinity, and Pivarnik has assessed the Trinitarian dimensions of active participation.[106]

Whether or not Catholics are aware of the deeper implication of actively participating in the liturgy, which is theosis, is unclear. What is clear is that Catholic pastoral liturgy has encouraged and facilitated the people's active participation in the liturgy since the promulgation of *SC*. The laity's active participation in the liturgy

---

105. Searle, *Called to Participate*.
106. Kimberly Belcher, *Efficacious Engagement: Sacramental Participation in the Trinitarian Mystery* (Collegeville, MN: Liturgical Press, 2011), and Gabriel Pivarnik, *Towards a Trinitarian Theology of Liturgical Participation* (Collegeville, MN: Liturgical Press, 2012).

is a *sine qua non* for exercising their priesthood in the life of the world. Active participation makes the laity a participant in God's divine life, and this contact with God capacitates the laity to return to the world and minister to it. Thus, active liturgical participation is connected directly with the exercise of the royal priesthood of the laity in the world. Furthermore, the emphasis on active participation in the liturgy illuminates a thematic coherence in *SC*'s teaching.

Sacrosanctum Concilium and Eucharistic Reform

One of most frequently repeated phrases from *SC* is "the liturgy is the summit toward which the activity of the Church is directed; at the same time it is the font from which all her power flows."[107] *SC*'s acknowledgement of the liturgy as the source of the Church's theological and pastoral ministries was a crowning achievement of *ressourcement* theology. Theologians tend to associate *SC*'s use of the word "liturgy" in this phrase with the Eucharist. The rest of *SC* no. 10 connects the liturgy with the rites of initiation and the Eucharist: "From the liturgy, therefore, and especially from the Eucharist, as from a font, grace is poured forth upon us; and the sanctification of men in Christ and the glorification of God, to which all other activities of the Church are directed as toward their end, is achieved in the most efficacious possible way."[108]

The restoration of the Eucharist as the Church's sacrament of the kingdom was the product of *ressourcement* theology, which contributed to the resetting of the correct relationship between the Eucharist and the Church. Paul McPartlan describes the prevailing relationship between Eucharist and Church from the medieval epoch as "the Church makes the Eucharist," a summary phrase representing

---

107. *SC* No. 10, http:// www.vatican.va / archive / hist_councils / ii_vatican_council / documents / vat-ii_const_19631204_sacrosanctum-concilium_en.html (accessed June 26, 2013).
108. Ibid.

the scholastic theological interpretation of how the hierarchically ordered Church consecrates the bread and wine so that it might become the Lord's body and blood.[109] *Ressourcement* theology reset the relationship to promote the idea that "the Eucharist makes the Church," a notion largely attributable to the work of Henri de Lubac.[110]

Beginning as early as the fourth century, pastors such as Cyril of Jerusalem and Ambrose of Milan taught that specific invocations or words recited during the course of the liturgy resulted in God's consecrating the bread and wine so that it would be the true body and blood of Jesus Christ.[111] Scholars have long believed that the pastors hoped to instill a sense of holy awe or fear in the neophytes who were becoming Christian. The purposes of this message of awe with reference to the Eucharistic species were manifold: first, the mystagogues desired to retain a sense of sacramentality by demonstrating earthly materials such as bread and wine to be worthy vessels of God's presence. Second, they wanted to communicate the reality of God's presence in the covenantal community to which the neophytes now belonged. The reality of God's presence would ideally promote an authentic Christian ethos among those who might have entered Christianity for any number of reasons.

A pastoral emphasis on sacramental reality became one of the most controversial theological issues for the medieval West, perhaps beginning with the famous ninth-century debate between Paschasius

---

109. See Paul McPartlan, *Sacrament of Salvation: An Introduction to Eucharistic Ecclesiology* (Edinburgh: T & T Clark, 1995), and idem, *The Eucharist Makes the Church: Henri de Lubac and John Zizioulas in Dialogue* (Edinburgh: T & T Clark, 1993).

110. "But if the sacrifice is accepted by God and the Church's prayer listened to, this is because the Eucharist, in its turn, realizes the Church, in the strict sense of the words," in Henri de Lubac, *The Splendour of the Church*, trans. Michael Mason (New York: Sheed and Ward, 1956), 151.

111. See, for example, Enrico Mazza, *The Celebration of the Eucharist: The Origin of the Rite and the Development of its Interpretation*, trans. Matthew O'Connell (Collegeville, MN: Liturgical Press, 1999), 151-53.

Radbertus and Ratramnus on the reality present in the Eucharistic species.[112] This controversy escalated with Berengarius of Tours' attempt to mitigate a cannibalistic sacramental reality with reference to the mediation of symbols. The remainder of this history is well-known to historians and systematicians, with the Roman Church eventually embracing the idea that the consecration of bread and wine into Jesus' true body and blood occurs through transubstantiation. For much of Christian history, theologians have attempted to find creative ways to explain how God transforms the bread and wine into the body and blood of Christ. The scholastic synthesis attended to the roles of the priest and the Church in this process of consecration, and thus we can see, through this brief review, how the medieval synthesis concluded with the idea that "the Church makes the Eucharist."[113]

SC's restoration of "The Eucharist makes the Church" was followed by a call for reforming the liturgy so that the people's participation in the liturgy would promote their becoming the Church, the body of Christ in this world. Nos. 49 and 50 of *SC* explicate this vision:[114]

> For this reason the sacred Council, having in mind those Masses which are celebrated with the assistance of the faithful, especially on Sundays and feasts of obligation, has made the following decrees in order that the sacrifice of the Mass, even in the ritual forms of its celebration, may become pastorally efficacious to the fullest degree. The rite of the Mass is to be revised in such a way that the intrinsic nature and purpose of its several parts, as also the connection between them, may be more clearly manifested, and that devout and active participation by the faithful may

112. For a comprehensive summary of the historical progression of this theological problem and its resolution, see Edward Kilmartin, *The Eucharist in the West: History and Theology*, ed. Robert Daly (Collegeville, MN: The Liturgical Press, 1998, 2004), 79-153.

113. Certainly, this synthesis has been retained by the contemporary Catholic Church, as evidenced by the explanation of the consecration of gifts in the Catechism of the Catholic Church.

114. Vatican II, *SC* nos. 49 and 50, http://www.vatican.va/archive/hist_councils/ii_vatican_council/documents/vat-ii_const_19631204_sacrosanctum-concilium_en.html (accessed June 26, 2013).

be more easily achieved. For this purpose the rites are to be simplified, due care being taken to preserve their substance; elements which, with the passage of time, came to be duplicated, or were added with but little advantage, are now to be discarded; other elements which have suffered injury through accidents of history are now to be restored to the vigor which they had in the days of the holy Fathers, as may seem useful or necessary.

Several themes emerge from this passage. First, the Council clearly sought to invigorate the lives of Catholic faithful with the reforms, evidenced by the coupling of "assistance of the faithful" and "pastorally efficacious" in no. 49. Second, the Council sought to illustrate the power of the Mass as a whole by featuring the significance of liturgical components such as the penitential rite, the proclamation of the Word, and Holy Communion. One potential benefit of attending to the relationships between the components of the Mass's structures is that the laity would recognize their value and seek to actively participate in every part of the Mass. The specific reforms promulgated by the Council emphasize components of the Mass bearing the capacity to impact the faithful. These include the proclamation of the Word (no. 51); the requirement of a homily (no. 52); the restoration of the prayer of the faithful (no. 53); permitting the use of the vernacular (no. 54); and the reception of communion consecrated at the Mass (no. 55). In no. 56, the Council connected the umbrella components of the Word and the Eucharist.

The creation of connections between liturgical components is instructive for reflecting on the Council's restoration of the right relationship between Eucharist and Church. When one applies the relationship between the parts of the Mass, one can see that the assembly offers God the gift of bread and wine. God consecrates it and gives it back to the assembly. By eating God's divine food, the assembly receives the power to be transformed and become bearers of Christ, people who steadfastly work for the building up of Christ's body in the world.

Conclusion

This chapter has introduced the historical and theological background to the implementation of liturgical reform in the Catholic and Orthodox Churches. I have discussed the pre-conciliar theological cross-pollination of Catholics and Orthodox and explored the reinvigoration of the royal priesthood of the laity in both Churches. The evidence suggests that Catholic and Orthodox theologians interrogated ancient patristic and liturgical sources to illuminate a muted but living ecclesial priesthood in the Church's sacramental life. An abundance of literary evidence demonstrates that Western theologians began to look to the East as a vast source of liturgical theology for the enterprise of building up the Church. Besides receiving the gift of personal and professional edification, theologians identified significant aspects of liturgical history and sacramental theology that served as potential catalysts for ecclesial *aggiornamento*. Eastern theologians also engaged the West, particularly in adopting scientific methods for rigorous historical study of the liturgy and in connecting the ancient sources of early, late antique, and medieval Christianity that had been largely mute, but bore the capacity to address the challenges posed by modernity. The decision of significant Eastern thinkers to participate in ongoing ecumenical dialogue with Westerners facilitated this ongoing process of gift exchange in the form of sharing theological and liturgical traditions.

The liturgical reform of Vatican II inspired the next step in this dialogue, which proved to be somewhat of a breaking point for the shared ecumenical enterprise. East and West shared much common ground on the theological underpinnings of the liturgy, and Vatican

II retrieved these notions and established them as the foundations for *SC*, the instruction on the liturgy. This chapter has shown that *SC* is known mostly for its teaching on the active participation of the liturgy, but equally substantial is its theology of priesthood. This theology of priesthood establishes Christ as the eternal high priest who presides with the liturgy, with Christ's body, the Church, co-offering the liturgy to God with him. The preceding review of the contributions of ecumenical theologians suggests that *SC* was a product of this theological exchange, manifest especially by the Eucharistic theology of Yves Congar. By articulating this layered theology of priesthood in the liturgy, *SC* showed that the ordained ministers (bishops and priests) and the royal priests (the laity) were all participants in offering the liturgy with Christ. In short, the entirety of Christ's body serves as his concelebrant in the liturgy. The primary task of ordained priests shifted in this renewed paradigm, from functioning as the sole administrators of the liturgy, to presiding in such a way that the laity could participate in the liturgy actively, consciously, and with comprehension, elements necessary to honor its priestly status as Christ's concelebrant. These theological underpinnings were the primary theological elements of *SC*'s liturgical reform, and in this chapter I have argued that both Catholic and Orthodox theologians contributed to the theology of priesthood that underpins *SC*.

Orthodoxy diverges from Vatican II in the manner of implementation. Once *SC* established its theological platform, the council also authorized a surgical reform of the liturgical offices themselves. Many of these reforms are characterized by their integration of Eastern theological features, epitomized by the introduction of three new Eucharistic prayers into the Missal of Pope Paul VI which contain split epicleses, and the revision of the sacrament of Confirmation. These revisions draw from the Eastern repository of pneumatology, and the Catholic decision to strengthen its sacramental pneumatology was one of the key components to encourage ecclesial revitalization. Orthodoxy, however, adopted a different approach to constructing models for liturgical reform. In this vein, Vatican II impacted Orthodoxy because of its stature and the Orthodox perception of Roman liturgical reform in the immediate aftermath of the council.

In the remainder of this study, I will examine the unfolding of liturgical reform in the Orthodox Church in four case studies: the ministry of Alexander Schmemann, the Russian Orthodox Church Outside of Russia (ROCOR), the Church of Greece, and New Skete Monastery. In these chapters, I will illuminate the variegated roles exercised by theologians, bishops, and synods in authorizing and implementing liturgical reforms. I will also attend to the crucial function of creating programs to form clergy who are able to model liturgical renewal and infuse it into the lives of the communities they shepherd. My examination of case studies will also attend to alternatives to liturgical renewal to raise a central point with ecumenical implications: liturgical reform will always have opponents whose liturgical styles and orders depend upon alternative ecclesiologies. While the four Orthodox models for liturgical reform differ, they share two characteristics: first, they tend to view Vatican II as a model to be avoided (with one exception, New Skete Monastery). In this vein, Vatican II impacted Eastern Orthodoxy through a series of perceptions about reform. Second, the Orthodox churches created enterprises for reform that shared the theological foundations underpinning *SC*: the cultivation of a Spirit-laden priesthood of Christ's body that offers service for the life of the world though active and conscious liturgical participation. My analysis of these four models will attempt to clarify misperceptions about the implementation of liturgical reform and rejuvenate the theological foundations for reform, which have been obfuscated by obsessions with surface-level disagreements about specific liturgical elements and aesthetics.

2

———

Alexander Schmemann's Eucharistic Revival

In the previous chapter, I presented the theological rationale for liturgical reform developed by Catholic and Orthodox theologians in the milieu of the ecumenical and liturgical movements. The chapter focused on Vatican II and *SC* as hallmarks of the liturgical movement. Pope John XXIII convoked the council to gather the Catholic bishops for a pastoral response to the impact of modernity on the life of the Church. Vatican II embraced many of the changes proposed by pioneers of the liturgical movement. The council's identification of the liturgy as the source and summit of Church life and its restoration of priestly identity to the laity were major achievements which codified a theological process long in development.

With the Council's proclamation of *SC* and formal approval of broad reforms to be implemented in the liturgy, the liturgical landscape of the Roman Church experienced a radical paradigm shift. The translation of the liturgy permitted parishes to pray in the vernacular, which created an immediate need for new musical settings. The order of the liturgy itself changed; the reinvigoration of ordained ministries revived the role of the diaconate and the presider's role also evolved, reciting prayers aloud and assuming a new position vis-à-vis the people. As the Roman Church authorized and implemented reforms, the people's experience of and engagement with the liturgy was altered. The magnitude of the liturgical reform was broad because of the sheer geographical diffusion of the Roman Church.

Schmemann as Ecumenical Theologian and Teacher

Theologians outside of the Roman communion who were actively engaged in the ecumenical and liturgical movements took note of the immediate scale and impact of Vatican II's reform. In the previous chapter, I identified Alexander Schmemann as a leading Orthodox theologian who contributed to the development of a rejuvenated theology of priesthood in the ecumenical milieu. Schmemann's stature was such in the Orthodox and ecumenical worlds that he became perhaps the most well-known figure of his time for his development of liturgical theology, an articulation of the liturgy as *theologia prima* which was warmly received and further cultivated by Western theologians.[1] Schmemann articulated his definitions of liturgical theology in the English translation of his doctoral dissertation, *Introduction to Liturgical Theology*, in his collection of essays originally titled *Sacraments and Orthodoxy* and later re-released as *For the Life of the World*, and in a series of articles originally

---

1. David Fagerberg, "The Cost of Understanding Schmemann in the West," *St. Vladimir's Theological Quarterly* 53, nos. 2-3 (2009): 179-207. Also see the survey essay by David Bresciani, "La reception de la théologie liturgique du père Alexandre Schmemann dans l'Église catholique romaine," in *La joie du Royaume: Actes du colloque international "l'heritage du père Alexandre Schmemann," Paris, 11-14 décembre 2008* (Paris: YMCA Press, 2012), 196-202.

published by *St. Vladimir's Theological Quarterly* and then published in a collection edited by Thomas Fisch.[2]

In all of these essays, Schmemann traces how liturgy became a scientific sub-field in the larger discipline of systematic theology (a fate he attributes to the hegemony of scholasticism) and explains how participation in the liturgy inspired patristic thinking, since liturgy is essentially an epiphany of the kingdom of God. Furthermore, Schmemann's writings manifest a vibrant ecumenical style, in which he addresses his Orthodox peers, along with his Catholic and Reformed interlocutors. For example, in *Introduction to Liturgical Theology*, Schmemann interrogates both contemporary Western theologians such as Louis Bouyer, Anton Baumstark, Yves Congar, and Olivier Rousseau, and also a sampling of core pre- and post-revolutionary Russian Orthodox thinkers such as N. Glubokovsky, Kyprian Kern, Ivan Mansvetov, and Mikhail Skaballanovich, *inter alia*.[3]

As a professor, Schmemann also exposed his students at St. Vladimir's to the same blend of ecumenical scholarship. One finds diverse authors on the reading list on the syllabus of Schmemann's liturgical theology course taught in 1982-83, including works such as Odo Casel's *The Mystery of Time*, Gregory Dix's *The Shape of the Liturgy*, and Oscar Cullman's *Christ and Time*.[4] We find an even larger selection of Western scholarship in an earlier version of his

2. Alexander Schmemann, *Introduction to Liturgical Theology*, trans. Asheleigh E. Moorhouse (Crestwood, NY: St. Vladimirs Seminary Press, 1986); idem, *For the Life of the World: Sacraments and Orthodoxy* (Crestwood, NY: St. Vladimir's Seminary Press, 1963, fourth printing: 1988); Thomas Fisch, ed., *Liturgy and Tradition: Theological Reflections of Alexander Schmemann* (Crestwood, NY: St. Vladimir's Seminary Press, 1990).

3. Schmemann, *Introduction to Liturgical Theology*, trans. Moorhouse, 9-32. Also see Robert F. Taft, "The Liturgical Enterprise Twenty-five Years after Alexander Schmemann (1921-1983): The Man and His Heritage," *St. Vladimir's Theological Quarterly* 53, nos. 2-3 (2009): 163-64.

4. Alexander Schmemann, Syllabus, Liturgical Theology 22/31A, Spring 1982-83, Fr. Alexander Schmemann Papers at the Father Georges Florovsky Library, St. Vladimir's Theological Seminary, Box 18, Document 8.

Liturgical Theology course taught in 1978, which includes Jean Danielou's *Theology of Judeo Christianity* and *Bible and Liturgy*, Baumstark's *Comparative Liturgy*, and Jungmann's *The Early Liturgy*, among many other selected works.[5] It is clear that Schmemann's liturgical theology was formed in a rich ecumenical context, and that he passed on his method of ecumenical theology to his students.

Schmemann and Vatican II

Reading Schmemann in the immediate milieu of Vatican II leaves one with the impression that he opposed liturgical reform. Schmemann expresses his skepticism about the platform and rationale for liturgical reform inaugurated by Vatican II and espouses a conservative approach to reform for the Orthodox Church. Schmemann notes a fissure between the fruits of the liturgical movement and the result of the liturgical reform inaugurated by Vatican II, stating that some of the practices that appeared in the immediate aftermath of the council contradict the actual liturgical directives:[6]

> On the problem of liturgical reform I can say this: it seems to me that the 'anarchy' mentioned by Dom Botte and which permeates, to a degree, the liturgical scene in the West, is due primarily and precisely to a deep discrepancy between the 'norms' as discovered by the liturgical Movement and a new 'liturgical piety' which claims the authority of Vatican II, yet is in many ways directly opposed to its liturgical directives. Whereas the Liturgical Movement, in its best representatives at least, was oriented towards a recovery of traditional elements of Christian leitourgia, elements which were obscured and even abolished for centuries, the 'liturgical piety' which is behind

5. Alexander Schmemann, Syllabus, Liturgical Theology 57, Winter 1978, Fr. Alexander Schmemann Papers at the Father Georges Florovsky Library, St. Vladimir's Theological Seminary, Box 18, Document 9. It is notable that several of these sources appear under the subheading "History of Orthodox Worship."

6. Alexander Schmemann, "The Role of Liturgical Theology: A Debate," in *Liturgy and Tradition*, 28.

modern 'experimentations' and 'anarchy' is inspired by an altogether different and indeed deeply anti-traditional set of aspirations. This obvious discrepancy between the 'letter' of Vatican II and what is everywhere proclaimed to be its 'spirit' and, thus, the justification for every innovation, is a perplexing mystery for all watchers of the present Roman Catholic scene.

Schmemann's perplexity at the unfolding Western liturgical scene underscores his conservative approach to liturgical reform in the Orthodox Church, which he states must be grounded by proper understanding:[7]

> As for the need for a liturgical 'reform' within the Orthodox Church, it seems to me that this concept must be qualified. For if anything is proved by the hectic reforms and changes in the West, it is that by themselves and in themselves they do not achieve what seems to be their goal. Liturgy is a living tradition, and surgery here is a wrong method. What we need above everything else is the understanding of that tradition, of the 'essence' of liturgy. Once it is achieved it will lead—'organically'—to the necessary purifications and changes and this without any break of continuity, without any 'crisis.' In spite of a deeply rooted common opinion, liturgy always changes because it lives.

These excerpts from Schmemann's response to Bernard Botte, which he originally published in 1968, foreground the analysis below of Schmemann's platform for liturgical reform. Schmemann essentially affirmed the fruits of the liturgical movement and the essence of the liturgical directives of Vatican II (SC), but viewed some of the initial results of the implementation of reform as dissonant with its objectives. When Schmemann describes the possibility of liturgical reform in the Orthodox Church, he emphasizes that the theological rationale must serve as the source for all outcomes. As an observer of the initial effects unleashed by Vatican II's reforms, Schmemann

---

7. Ibid., 29.

encouraged a more conservative and deliberate approach to reform in Orthodoxy.

Schmemann's reluctance to embrace a platform of reform as radical as Vatican II was a cause for criticism within the Byzantine liturgical academy, which was particularly sharp in an insightful article published by Peter Galadza that pinpoints the fissure between Schmemann's elevated liturgical theology and the shortcomings of his own support for the implementation of reforms.[8] Thus, the retrospect on Schmemann is complex and variegated: on the one hand, he is a pioneer of liturgical theology who was the primary figure in shaping a school of liturgical ecclesiology that influenced successors who inherited and expanded Schmemann's work such as Aidan Kavanagh (Roman Catholic), Gordon Lathrop (Lutheran), and David Fagerberg (Roman Catholic).[9] Schmemann's willingness to associate with his ecumenical interlocutors raised doubts about him and his agenda among his own Orthodox peers. On the other hand, some adherents of the Byzantine tradition view Schmemann's scope and contribution as too short-sighted and limited, resulting in a Eucharistic revival but lacking in many other needed dimensions of reform.

Schmemann's status as a modern figure bridging West and East occasions this initial chapter assessing the liturgical renewal attributed to him. The purpose of this chapter is to present and assess Schmemann's model for liturgical reform in its manifestation at St. Vladimir's Seminary in Crestwood, New York. The assessment

---

8. Peter Galadza, "Schmemann Between Fagerberg and Reality: Towards an Agenda for Byzantine Christian Pastoral Liturgy," *Bollettino della Badia Greca di Grottaferrata* 3, no. 4 (2007), 7–32.

9. Michael Aune, "Liturgy and Theology: Rethinking the Relationship, Part 1, Setting the Stage" *Worship* 81, no. 1 (2007): 48. See also a collection of essays originally presented at the international conference honoring the twenty-fifth anniversary of Schmemann's death at St. Sergius Institute titled *La joie du Royaume: Actes du colloque international "l'heritage du père Alexandre Schmemann,"* Paris, 11-14 décembre 2008 (Paris: YMCA Press, 2012).

begins with a review of the inspiration for Schmemann's reforms, namely the deliberations on liturgical reform for the holy council of the Russian Orthodox Church in the period immediately prior to the Bolshevik Revolution. I will show how Schmemann inherited and further cultivated the ideals of the proposed liturgical reforms in his pedagogy and research and began the process of implementing them through his position as professor of liturgical theology and dean at St. Vladimir's. I will also show how Schmemann's platform for reform is supported by the same theological rationale underpinning *SC* and Roman liturgical reform. As a conclusion, I will reflect upon the meaning of the shortcomings of Schmemann's reform and its dependence on clergy infusing a spirit of liturgical renewal in their parish ministries.

Liturgical Renewal in Preconciliar Russian Orthodoxy

In order to understand Schmemann's theological contribution in context, it is necessary to review the Russian Orthodox environment he inherited and attempted to negotiate in the circumstances of immigration. Numerous Russian theologians who settled in Europe in the aftermath of the Bolshevik Revolution continued a dialogue that had commenced in the nineteenth century, as the bishops of the Russian Orthodox Church engaged a rigorous preconciliar process of identifying pastoral issues and developing proposals for addressing them.[10] The celebration of and participation in the liturgy was one

---

10. The literature treating this topic is vast. Two recent monographs update the scholarly literature on the primary Russian figures, their community, and their methods: Antoine Arjakovsky, *The Way: Religious Thinkers of the Russian Emigration in Paris and Their Journal, 1925-1940*, ed. John A. Jillions and Michael Plekon, trans. Jerry Ryan, foreword by Rowan Williams (Notre Dame, IN: University of Notre Dame Press, 2013), and Paul Gavrilyuk, *Georges Florovsky and the Russian Religious Renaissance* (Oxford: Oxford University Press, 2014). Also see Günther Schulz, "Das Landeskonzil der Orthodoxen Kirche in Russland 1917/1918 und seine Folgen für die russische Geschichte und Kirchengeschichte," *Kirche im Osten* 42-43 (1999-2000): 11-28; Martin Corner, "Protection, autonomy and reform : the Russian Orthodox Church 1905-29," *Sobornost* 10, no 1 (1988): 6-21; Irina Papkova, "The Freezing of Historical Memory? The

of the most important pastoral issues addressed. The deliberations on the liturgy were inspired by the original work accomplished by a formidable school of Russian liturgical historians. Most of these theologians were interested in a close examination of liturgical history to promote understanding of Russia's liturgical heritage.[11]

In 2000, Nikolai Balashov of the Moscow Patriarchate published a seminal analysis of the pre- and post-conciliar discussion of liturgical issues.[12] Balashov's study presents a comprehensive overview of the liturgical questions considered by the participants of the preconciliar commission. The bishops and pastors sought to renew Church life in Russia, and turned to the liturgy as a primary pastoral area requiring review and possible reform. Balashov's study treats dozens of issues covered by the preconciliar commission, including the question of introducing vernacular Russian and Ukrainian to liturgical celebration, revising liturgical books, reforming the Typikon, and changing some aspects of the Eucharistic liturgy. Besides Balashov, Marcel Mojzeš has also contributed a scholarly presentation of the proposed liturgical reforms in Russia.[13] One element stands out among the many contributions of Balashov and Mojzeš: their

Post-Soviet Russian Orthodox Church and the Council of 1917," in *Religion, Morality, and Community in Post-Soviet Societies*, ed. Mark Steinberg and Catherine Wanner (Washington, DC: Woodrow Wilson Center Press; Bloomington, IN: Indiana University Press, 2008), 55–84; Dmitry Pospielovsky, *The Orthodox Church in the History of Russia* (Crestwood, NY: St. Vladimir's Seminary Press, 1998), 191–217; Job Getcha, "Les études liturgiques russes aux XIXe-XXe siècles et leur impact sur la pratique," *Les mouvements liturgiques. Corrélations entre pratiques et recherches*, Bibliotheca Ephemerides Liturgicae, Subsidia 129 (Rome: Edizione Liturgiche, 2004), 279–91.

11. For an informative overview of this Russian school and its impact, see Getcha, "Les études liturgiques russes aux XIXe-XXe siècles et leur impact sur la pratique," 279–91. Also see Peter Galadza, "Liturgy and Life: The Appropriation of the 'Personalization of Cult' in East-Slavic Orthodox Liturgiology, 1869–1996," *Studia Liturgica* 28 (1988): 210–31. Also see Paul Meyendorff, "The Liturgical Path of Orthodoxy in America," *St. Vladimir's Theological Quarterly* 40, nos. 1-2 (1996): 44–49, and Taft, "The Liturgical Enterprise Twenty-five Years after Alexander Schmemann," 143–44.

12. Nikolai Balashov, *На пути к литургическому возрождению (On the Path of Liturgical Renewal)* (Moscow: Round Table on Religious Education and Service, 2001).

13. Marcel Mojzeš, *Il movimento liturgico nelle chiese bizantine. Analisi di alcune tendenze do riforma*

presentations on the history of the preconciliar and conciliar deliberations illuminate the collaboration of pastors and academic specialists in the deliberative processes. The preconciliar deliberations and proposals presented to the council of 1917–1918 were informed by academic research and discussed in a series of exchanges between academics and pastors. The Russian preconciliar commission thus established a model of the academy informing the Church on what is possible in liturgy.

The purpose of this chapter is to show how Schmemann addressed particular questions originally raised during the course of deliberation in the preconciliar commission, so I will illuminate a few select issues. Readers should note that many of the proposed reforms were not implemented for several reasons, especially the constant disruption of conciliar proceedings caused by the war and fierce violence waged against the Church.[14]

Despite the council's inability to address the liturgy adequately, discourse on the necessity of injecting new life into the liturgy continued in émigré communities. Schmemann built his legacy of liturgical reform upon his articulation of Eucharistic ecclesiology which would be manifest by the design of sacred space, rites, and texts. The objective of Schmemann's Eucharistic revival was to restore the celebration of the Eucharist so that the people would discover and embrace their identity as priest, prophet, and king, God's servants who gather in communion to bear witness in the world. Schmemann was a central figure in connecting the Church's celebration of the rite of the Eucharist to the vision of who the

---

nel XX secolo, Bibliotheca Ephemerides Liturgicae Subsidia 132 (Rome: Edizione Liturgiche, 2005).

14. For details on the council and the challenges posed to the bishops for deliberation, see the magisterial study by Hyacinthe Destivelle, *The Moscow Council (1917–1918): The Creation of the Conciliar Institutions of the Russian Orthodox Church*, ed. Michael Plekon and Vitaly Permiakov, trans. Jerry Ryan, foreword by Metropolitan Hilarion (Alfeyev) (Notre Dame, IN: University of Notre Dame Press, 2015).

Church's people were to become. When one examines the preconciliar deliberations in Russia, one discovers the threads of Schmemann's Eucharistic ecclesiology in the questions the preconciliar commission deliberated on the Eucharistic prayers, the clergy's performance of the rites, and the design of sacred space.

Example 1: The Recitation of Prayers for All to Hear

For example, during the preconciliar deliberation in pre-revolutionary Russia, several bishops and scholars supported reading aloud the Eucharistic prayers and other prayers of the liturgy traditionally recited quietly.[15] One of the more impassioned pleas came from a layman with the surname of Shvydchenko:[16]

> Strange as it seems . . . the faithful come to the Eucharist for the breaking of the bread and to thank the Lord, but they do not see the performance of the breaking [of the bread], and what is recited at that time—they do not hear. How, then, can they thank the Lord after this? . . . In the early Christian Church at the consecration of the gifts only the catechumens and possessed were forced to leave, but the faithful remained and saw and heard everything done and recited by the presider (the priest). Afterwards the Church—the Greek, and following her, ours, placed the prayers of the priest in secret, and all that remained for the hearers were those excerpts sung by the singers. Why are we laity deprived of these prayers? Are we not the royal priesthood and chosen people, as the apostle says? Why don't the priests recite aloud and openly all the prayers of the liturgy? Why do they conceal them under wraps, and not display them as the light of God, like a brilliant lamp?

Shvydchenko's attention to the combination of ritual and euchology is notable here.

Shvydchenko views the royal priesthood granted to all the Christian faithful as the foundation allowing them to fully participate

15. Balashov, 358–69.
16. Ibid., 359.

in the Eucharistic liturgy. His perspective is quite simple: he wants to see the ritual gestures and hear the prayers recited that mark the most solemn moments of the Eucharist. It is not sufficient to hear the choral hymns: the sensory participation of the faithful people must be consistently present in each part of the liturgy. Without it, Shvydchenko does not see how the faithful can reasonably thank the Lord.

Shvydchenko was not the only proponent of reciting the euchology aloud so that all the faithful could participate in the offering. Balashov notes that the priest Nikolai Kartashev, V. K. Nedels'kyj, Y. A. Karabynov, and Y. Y. Mel'nykov officially supported the reading of the Eucharistic prayers aloud during meetings of the Liturgical commission of the All–Russian Council.[17] The proposition went to a vote at the Russian Council on November 9, 1917, and was soundly defeated. The prohibition of reading the Eucharistic prayers aloud for all to hear was confirmed by directives from Patriarch Tikhon in 1919 and 1921.[18] These prohibitions were not absolute, as the patriarch permitted the Kievan brotherhood of the Sweet Jesus to pray the anaphora aloud; Metropolitan Sergius likewise allowed Hieromonk Theophan (Adamenko) from Nizhny-Novgorod to pray the Eucharistic prayers aloud in 1932.[19]

Example 2: Opening the Gates for All to See

An example which complements our review of the recitation of the Eucharistic prayer is the question of the decoration and arrangement of sacred space, especially the iconostasis and holy gates. The discussions and conciliar decisions on the question of lowering the

17. Ibid., 365–67.
18. Ibid., 366.
19. Ibid., 366–67. Balashov notes that the patriarch's prohibition of reciting the prayer aloud for all to hear represented a change from his original position on the issue.

iconostasis and opening the holy gates for the faithful to see the sanctuary followed the same pattern as the deliberations on the recitation of the Eucharistic prayer aloud. The most vocal opponent of reforming these prominent architectural fixtures was Archbishop Antony Khrapovitsky.[20] In 1917, the All-Russian Council denied the request of those who supported keeping the holy gates open for the liturgy, a decision upheld in 1919 and 1921.[21] The rationale for opening the gates was articulated by Fr. Alexander Hotovytsky:[22]

> The people cannot see the clergy, they cannot hear the mysterious holy prayers, they cannot see the sacred acts which essentially constitute the mystery of the Eucharist, all that remains for them is to prayerfully respond to the frequently incomprehensible exclamation 'singing the triumphant hymn, shouting, proclaiming,' or 'especially for the Immaculate' and so on. It appears that the priest should select a particular time within the limits of the liturgy to explain to the people that which the people would be able to know and see itself.

Hotovytsky observed the incoherence of visual and auditory obstacles with understanding the meaning of the mystery celebrated in the liturgy. His testimony illustrates the concern expressed by many Russian Church leaders and scholars on the need to reform the liturgy to make it engaging and accessible in the lives of the faithful.[23] It is important to note that the proponents of reform recognized a greater benefit in inviting the faithful to participate in the prayers and rituals of the liturgy, the effects being manifested in the lives of the faithful. For example, an anonymous priest from the Vjatsky eparchy

---

20. Ibid., 372-73. On this matter, also see Mojzeš, 138-42. I will elaborate Metropolitan Antony Khrapovitsky's opinions on this matter in Chapter 4.
21. Balashov, 374-75.
22. Ibid., 371.
23. Balashov provides a similar example from another unidentified priest and quoted him as saying: "The Eucharistic gifts are brought in far from the faithful, set down behind a wooden barrier, the one who serves goes there and he performs the sacred activities, invisible to the assembly; there he offers the prayers in a large temple, and due to the server's weak voice those who are praying cannot hear" (ibid.).

recognized the benefits of the faithful hearing the intercessions recited in the anaphora of St. Basil the Great: "We think, that if this prayer would be read for the whole church to hear, she would create many holy and good feelings and that she would greatly strengthen the relationship between the pastor and his flock. His prayer before the throne of God would be quite evident to them."[24]

The majority of the proponents of liturgical reform in Russia were bishops, priests, professors, and lower ranking clergy (such as lectors) who had intimate knowledge of the liturgy and its structures. The testimony from the Russian conciliar environment of the late-nineteenth and early-twentieth century demonstrates the reciprocal relationship between the academic study of the liturgy and its pastoral celebration. The academics valiantly reconstructed and presented historical liturgical structures that suggested the active participation of the laity in the liturgy, whereas the pastors attended to the fissure between a heavily clericalized liturgy and a predominantly disengaged laity. It is important to note that many Church leaders opposed the liturgical reforms, often on account of their sense of the sacred.[25]

The actual Russian council failed to implement the proposed reforms I have treated here. Also, the use of phrases such as "active participation" does not appear in the Russian discourses. However, the examples I have given here are useful for three reasons. First, they illustrate a cooperative discourse on liturgical reform shared by pastors, academics, and laity; second, they attend to the close relationship between euchology and ritual gestures, illuminating liturgy as a sensory experience involving the whole human person; and third, they reveal concern for the lives of the laity and appeal to the possibility that engaging the whole liturgy can generate

24. Ibid., 368n47.
25. Mojzeš, 142.

understanding and impact the lives of the faithful. Mojzeš depicts the Russian deliberative process as a worthy antecedent of the liturgical reforms adopted by Vatican II:[26]

> In our analysis we have seen that already in the early twentieth century, many prominent representatives of the Russian Orthodox Church arrived to the understanding of the needs of that full, conscious and active participation in the liturgy. We can say that in this sense they preceded Vatican II by a good half century.

Liturgical *Ressourcement* in the Russian Émigré Community

Despite the failure of the Russian Council to implement many of the proposed reforms, the immigrants who settled in the West continued the tradition of discourse and interrogation of sources with the academic and pastoral perspectives equally contributing to the conversation.[27] The Bolshevik Revolution caused the shift of the center of liturgical studies from Kyiv to Paris, with Archbishop Gabriel Chepur becoming one of the key figures who shaped the continuing work of the Russian school of liturgical history.[28] Job Getcha states that a paradigm shift in the science of liturgical studies also occurred at this time. Chepur was a disciple of Mikhail Skaballanovich, one of the last masters of the Russian liturgical school who taught in Kyiv, and Chepur was the thinker who closely shaped Kyprian Kern's notion of liturgical theology.[29] Kern cultivated the study of liturgical theology along with Afanasiev at St. Sergius Institute in Paris, completing the paradigm shift from Russia to Western Europe. Kern's and Afanasiev's works on the Eucharist and the Church constituted attempts to elucidate the fullness of Church

---

26. Ibid., 154.
27. Some reforms were implemented. In 1918, the synod of the Russian Church authorized and published several liturgical offices and components related to Patriarch Tikhon's appeal to the Russian people to repent for their sins. See Balashov, 431–34.
28. Getcha, "Les études liturgiques russes," 286.
29. Ibid., 286–87.

by removing the fissure between clergy and laity and promoting a vision of Church that honors the royal priesthood of the laity. Afanasiev completed his work in two studies: *The Church of the Holy Spirit*, his ecclesiological magnum opus, and a shorter but equally prodigious treatise on the Eucharist and its celebration, *The Lord's Supper.*[30]

Background: Nicholas Afanasiev

The chief twentieth-century proponent of a Eucharistic revival in the Orthodox Church was Alexander Schmemann. Before presenting Schmemann's contribution to the Eucharistic revival, it is essential to mention the contributions of his two mentors: Afanasiev and Kern. Afanasiev articulated an early Orthodox position on Eucharistic ecclesiology in *Church of the Holy Spirit* and *The Lord's Supper.*[31] Afanasiev was essentially a *ressourcement* theologian and he developed his ecclesiological model by carefully reading and interpreting early church sources. Afanasiev rehabilitated the priestly ministry of the laity in his work, a contribution I will treat at greater length below. After establishing that the laity is indeed ordained (through Baptism and Chrismation), Afanasiev reads selections from the Eucharistic prayer of St. John Chrysostom to assert that "the people in their entirety" celebrate the Eucharist with the presiders.[32] It is in *The Lord's Supper* that Afanasiev argues forcefully for the identification of the laity as the bishop's Eucharistic concelebrant.[33] In Afanasiev's

---

30. Nicholas Afanasiev, *The Church of the Holy Spirit*, ed. Michael Plekon, trans. Vitaly Permiakov (Notre Dame, IN: University of Notre Dame Press, 2007). Idem, *Трапеза Господня* (The Lord's Supper) (Kyiv: Temple of the Venerable Agapit of the Caves, 2003).

31. For an intellectual profile of Afanasiev, see Michael Plekon, *Living Icons: Persons of Faith in the Eastern Church*, foreword by Lawrence Cunningham (Notre Dame, IN: University of Notre Dame, 2002), 149-77.

32. Ibid., 44.

33. "The concelebration by the laity is effective and real, not ceremonial. In the liturgy the laity are not passive—for those whom God has appointed to the ministry of the royal priesthood cannot

model, laity and bishop are always together, since the bishop is not outside of the Church, and the laity has always had the bishop as the presider over the assembly. Besides his reference to the Eucharistic prayer to illustrate the laity's active liturgical celebration, Afanasiev probes the Russian practice of *govenie* as a symbol of Eucharistic decay.[34] He argues that the Eucharist demands the laity's participation in communion and dismisses the notion of spiritual communion, which legitimizes abstinence from receiving communion since one is unified with Christ by being present in the Eucharistic assembly.[35] Afanasiev refers to the eventual separation of the laity from the reception of communion as "tragic."[36]

Afanasiev's objection has two implications. First, infrequent lay reception of Holy Communion is a historical error and incoherent with the liturgical theology of the Eucharist. Second, that the presider must receive Communion while the laity do not exacerbates the fissure between clergy and laity, described by Afanasiev as "the division of the Church's members into the consecrated and non-consecrated."[37] Afanasiev reads the sources and exegetes the Eucharistic liturgy to arrive at his thesis: the Eucharist is a gathering demanding the full participation of God's priestly people, which includes each order of the assembly.[38] Afanasiev uses the Eucharist

be passive. On the contrary, they participate actively; the liturgical acts are performed by the head of the Church with the con-celebration of the laity" (Nicholas Afanasiev, "The Ministry of Laity in the Church," in William C. Mills, ed., *Called to Serve: Readings on Ministry from the Orthodox Church* [Rollinsford, NH: Orthodox Research Institute, 2010], pp. 8–9). Also see Afanasiev, *Трапеза Господня*, 69-90.

34. *Govenie* is the practice of intense fasting and prayer ranging from one day to a week prior to receiving communion, often for one of the four feasts culminating a fasting period. For a brief overview of *govenie*, see Saint Theophan the Recluse, *The Path to Salvation: A Manual of Spiritual Transformation*, trans. Seraphim Rose and the St. Herman of Alaska Brotherhood (Platina, CA: St. Herman of Alaska Brotherhood, 1996), 269-73.

35. Afanasiev, *Трапеза Господня*, 106-7. Idem, *The Church of the Holy Spirit*, ed. Plekon, 50-57.

36. Afanasiev, *The Church of the Holy Spirit*, 56.

37. Ibid., 57.

38. Among the sources Afanasiev quotes in building a case for catholic participation in the Eucharist are Justin Martyr, Dionysius of Alexandria, Theodoret of Cyrus, the Apostolic

and the other rites of initiation and ordination to promote the rehabilitation of the laity as full-fledged priests, the authentic concelebrants of the liturgy with the presider.[39]

Kyprian Kern

The other figure who influenced Schmemann's Eucharistic theology was Kyprian Kern.[40] Schmemann's work on the Eucharist develops areas of study Kern did not cover. Kern produced an influential historical overview of the Eucharist, a sober engagement employing the historical method of the time. His study includes treatment of multiple Eucharistic prayers, the assignment of prayers to regional families with relationships noted, and a discussion of elements in the Byzantine Eucharistic liturgy that were problematic. A good example of Kern's skill in employing the historical method occurs in his discussion of the interpolation of the Troparion of the third Hour into the anaphora. Kern consults multiple medieval and later manuscripts and examines arguments in favor of and opposed to the inclusion of the Troparion of the Third Hour in the anaphora, and concludes that it was an innovative addition to the anaphora since its grammar is incoherent with the flow, language, and order of the rest of the Eucharistic prayer.

Job Getcha presents an informative study of Kern's ecumenical environment, which formed his employment of the liturgical sciences and ultimately shaped Schmemann's approach to liturgical theology and the Eucharist.[41] Getcha links Kern to the Russian liturgical school

Constitutions, the canons of Antioch and the Apostolic canons, and the liturgies of John Chrysostom and Basil the Great, in ibid., 40-57.

39. For a helpful summary of Afanasiev and a comparison of his ecclesiology with Zizioulas's, see Paul McPartlan, *The Eucharist Makes the Church: Henri de Lubac and John Zizioulas in Dialogue*, foreword by Edward Yarnold, SJ. (Edinburgh: T & T Clark, 1993), 229-35.

40. Kyprian Kern, *Eucharistia* (Paris: YMCA, 1947). St. Vladimir's Theological Seminary Library has an unpublished English translation of Kern's study, and I thank Eleana Silk and Matthew Garklavs for sending me the translation via e-mail on July 23, 2013.

of the nineteenth and twentieth centuries, and also establishes his engagement with Catholic *ressourcement* liturgical theologians.[42] Kern and Afanasiev's inauguration of the Liturgical Weeks tradition at St. Sergius in 1952 continued and sustained a tradition of ecumenical cross-pollination which convened theologians such as Bernard Botte, Louis Bouyer, and Ireneé Dalmais.[43] Getcha highlights Kern's attention to the interdisciplinary requirements of liturgical study, where one consults not only historical development of the rites themselves, but also researches the contemporaneous patristic sources and considers the philological implications of liturgical vocabulary. Getcha views Schmemann as the disciple who continues the work of his master, and credits Schmemann with developing an original notion of eschatology in the study of liturgical theology.[44] Schmemann honored Kern's historical work on the Eucharist by composing a complementary monograph devoted to Eucharistic theology since Kern had presumably completed the historical study of the Orthodox Eucharist.

This brief review of Afanasiev and Kern illustrates the influence the two Russian theologians exercised on Schmemann and his theology. Schmemann develops the ecclesiological agenda established by Afanasiev and explains the meaning of the Eucharist in light of Kern's historical study. But this review of Afanasiev and Kern also demonstrates that they passed on more than agendas and schemes to Schmemann. Afanasiev and Kern demonstrated the value of continuing the work of the late-nineteenth and early-twentieth

---

41. Job Getcha, "From Master to Disciple: The Notion of 'Liturgical Theology' in Fr. Kiprian Kern and Fr. Alexander Schmemann," *St. Vladimir's Theological Quarterly* 53, nos. 2-3 (2009): 251-72.

42. Ibid., 253-59. Getcha refers to Kern's participation in the liturgical movement upon his arrival in Paris. Getcha also mentions Kern's respect for the editors of the Dictionary of Christian Archaeology and Liturgy (DACL) and its most prominent contributors such as Leclerc, Salaville, Duchesne, Cabrol, and others (259).

43. My thanks to Michael Plekon for sharing this insight.

44. Ibid., 263-64.

centuries' Russian liturgical academy while theologizing in dialogue with ecumenical partners.[45] Schmemann's context differed from those of his mentors, but this background clearly places him in a variegated school of liturgical theology populated by nineteenth-century Russian historians and ecumenical *ressourcement* theologians such as Cabrol, Duchesne, Salaville, Casel, Botte, Bouyer, and Congar.

Alexander Schmemann's Eucharistic Theology

Schmemann's identification of the Eucharist as the source and epiphany of the kingdom appears in many of his writings.[46] Schmemann's work is significant because Schmemann is often credited as being the chief catalyst of the restoration of the Eucharist in the Orthodox Church. Michael Plekon outlined Schmemann's chief contributions in his profile of prominent Eastern Church figures and Mills defines Schmemann's Eucharistic foundation in his study of Schmemann's pastoral theology. Here, I will focus on three of Schmemann's contributions to Eucharistic theology that are both original and pertinent to the ecumenical task of this chapter: his unique definition of the Eucharistic as the source of the Church and her worship; his critique of Orthodox and Western perspectives on the Eucharist; and his contribution to the implementation of a Eucharistic reform.

---

45. Getcha notes Kern's robust ecumenical environment and refers to Kern's memoirs where he names Bishop Gabriel and Metropolitan Antony Khrapovistky as his theological mentors Chepure, 254-55. Also see Kyprian Kern, "Reminiscences of Metropolitan Anthony (Khrapovitskii)," trans. Alexander Lisenko, ROCOR Studies: Historical Studies of the Russian Church Abroad, http://www.rocorstudies.org/church-people/lives-of-bishops/2012/10/03/reminiscences-of-metropolitan-anthony-khrapovitskii/ (accessed October 7, 2013). Originally published in *Divine Ascent: A Journal of Orthodox Thought* (2004).
46. For an overview, see Michael Plekon, *Living Icons*, and William C. Mills, *Church World and Kingdom: The Eucharistic Foundation of Alexander Schmemann's Pastoral Theology* (Chicago: Hillenbrand Books, 2012), 100-106.

The Church as Assembly

The first pages of Schmemann's monograph devoted to the Eucharist expose his consistent emphasis on the Church as a Eucharistic assembly. William Mills notes Schmemann's peculiar organization of the book, where each chapter presents aspects of the Eucharist.[47] The first chapter of the book breaks open Schmemann's ecclesiology, since the Eucharist is the sacrament of the assembly. This initial chapter establishes Schmemann's agenda for articulating his Eucharistic theology as he identifies the assembly's gathering as the "first and basic act of the Eucharist."[48] Evidence of Schmemann's advancement of Afanasiev's work appears in his affirmation of Afanasiev's theology of concelebration above. Schmemann affirms the inseparability of the Eucharistic president and the assembly so that the action is one of the body including the head, and not only the head.[49] Later in the same work, Schmemann exhibits his consistent approach to the Eucharist as a sacrament of the assembly when he explores the role of the faithful. Musing on the liturgical components that dismiss everyone who will not or cannot fully participate, Schmemann observes that all of the faithful who remain are ordained and offer the service: "Who is serving . . . is not the clergy, and not even the clergy with the laity, but the Church, which is constituted and made manifest in all fullness by everyone together."[50]

Schmemann's notion of the Eucharist as a sacrament of the assembly is like a refrain, consistent with his earlier writings.

47. Mills, 104.
48. Schmemann, *The Eucharist*, 15.
49. "Any serious study of the Eucharistic ordo cannot but convince us that this ordo is entirely, from beginning to end, constructed on the principle of correlation—the mutual dependence of the celebrant of the service and the people. One may even more precisely define this bond as a co-serving or concelebration, as it was articulated by the late Professor Nicholas Afanasiev in his splendid though not yet fully-appreciated work The Lord's Supper," ibid., 14.
50. Ibid., 88.

Schmemann's emphasis on the Eucharist is evident in *For the Life of the World*, as he begins this collection of essays with the Eucharist.[51] His essay in this volume is brief, and he establishes his distinct agenda by stating that he is writing about the Orthodox Eucharistic liturgy because "one can speak with conviction only insofar as one has experienced that about which one is speaking."[52] Of greater importance is Schmemann's actual exposition of the Eucharist. He presents the Eucharist as a "journey of the Church into the dimension of the kingdom" and also employs metaphors such as "entrance" and ascension."[53] The purpose of this journey, entrance, or ascension is ecclesiological, and Schmemann's simple prose elucidates a rather profound ecclesiology:[54]

> Our entrance into the presence of Christ is an entrance into a fourth dimension which allows us to see the ultimate reality of life. It is not an escape from the world, rather it is the arrival at a vantage point from which we can see more deeply into the reality of the world. The journey begins when Christians leave their homes and beds. They leave, indeed, their life in this present and concrete world, and whether they have to drive fifteen miles or walk a few blocks, a sacramental act is already taking place, an act which is the very condition of everything else that is to happen. For they are now on their way to constitute the Church, or to be more exact, to be transformed into the Church of God. . . . The purpose is to fulfill the Church, and that means to make present the One in whom all things are at their end, and all things are at their beginning.

I describe this theology as profound because Schmemann includes the mundane acts of getting out of bed and driving to Church as the beginning of the sacramental act of assembly. Beyond this, though,

---

51. Schmemann, *For the Life of the World*, 11–46. Schmemann's introductory essay establishes a Eucharistic anthropology which sets the tone for the remainder of the content.

52. Ibid., 26.

53. See, for example, Schmemann's explanation of "entrance" in *Liturgy and Life: Christian Development through Liturgical Experience* (New York: Department of Religious Education, Orthodox Church in America, 1974), 45–46.

54. Schmemann, *For the Life of the World*, 27.

is another point we will flesh out shortly: Schmemann's reference to Eucharistic participation capacitating a vision of the world's reality. Schmemann's remark here hints towards a larger purpose: the Church does not gather as a mere response to a command, but to engage the world in a more meaningful manner.

An important caveat to describing Schmemann's ecclesiology as Eucharistic: it is Eucharistic in as much as the Eucharist completes and fulfills the rites of initiation. Schmemann bemoans treating the Eucharist as a sacrament isolated from the others rather forcefully. In his influential treatise on Baptism, he refers to the rites of initiation as having a threefold structure, belonging to one another.[55] He describes the sacraments as enjoying a type of interdependence, with each sacrament building up the participants into a body, a holistic ecclesiology. Schmemann attributes to the fathers the idea that the Eucharist is the "sacrament of sacraments," and asserts that the Eucharist is the fulfillment of both Chrismation and Baptism.[56] Schmemann juxtaposes the Orthodox understanding of Holy Communion as the fulfillment of the Divine Liturgy to the medieval synthesis of scholastic theology which attended to the question of transforming the Eucharistic species. Schmemann's comments are sharply critical; he claims that Eucharistic practice and piety was Westernized in part due to the doctrine of transubstantiation, "to the exclusion of all other aspects and dimensions of the sacrament."[57]

55. Schmemann, *Of Water and the Spirit*, 115–16.
56. Schmemann's treatment of the relationship between the Eucharist and the other rites of initiation is a bit fragmented. In defining the sacraments as belonging together, he says: "If Chrismation . . . fulfills Baptism, Eucharist is the fulfillment of Chrismation" (ibid., 116). Later, Schmemann says that if Eucharist is truly the sacrament of the Church and not only one of the Church's sacraments, then of necessity to enter the Church is to enter into the Eucharist, then Eucharist is indeed the fulfillment of Baptism" (118). I believe that this is an instance of a stream of consciousness, where Schmemann is attempting to establish the Eucharist as the fulfillment of initiation as a whole. For him, it can be both the fulfillment of Baptism and Chrismation, regardless of their order in the sequence of rites. Also noteworthy is Schmemann's reference to the "Fathers" as a collective entity on 116: Schmemann does not identify which particular "fathers" conceived of the Eucharist as "sacrament of sacraments."

Schmemann defines the Orthodox tradition of Eucharistic transformation accordingly:[58]

> In the Orthodox tradition . . . we find an entirely different approach. Here the metabole itself—the change of the bread and wine into the Body and Blood of Christ—and the communion of the holy gifts are viewed as the fulfillment, the crowning point and climax, of the whole Eucharistic liturgy, whose meaning is precisely that it actualizes the Church as new creation, redeemed by Christ, reconciled with God, given access to heaven, filled with divine glory, sanctified by the Holy Spirit, and therefore capable of and called to participation in divine life, in the communion of the Body and Blood of Christ.

While one could take issue with Schmemann for referring to the reception of communion as the climax of the liturgy, he remains consistent with his ecclesiological thread. The purpose of the Eucharist is to become Church, and as Schmemann tersely reminds the reader, the act of participation is not limited to eating and drinking, but ultimately results in theosis, participation in the divine life of the Triune God.[59] Schmemann's remarks here are striking for two reasons: first, he does not hesitate to make the West solely responsible for the ecclesiological paradigm, "The Church makes the Eucharist." Second, Schmemann is an early and enthusiastic proponent of the opposite, "The Eucharist makes the Church."

In the quote above, Schmemann describes the communion of the holy gifts as actualizing the Church as the new creation. This is a crucial link, as Schmemann's ecclesiology highlights the Church as the frontier of new creation, a creation of human and cosmic unity—the Eucharist, for Schmemann, being the event that actualizes this in the relational folds of ecclesial gathering and communion.

---

57. Ibid., 117.
58. Ibid.
59. See Schmemann's exposition of Chrismation and its inscribing the neophyte into the divine life of God in ibid., 80.

In explaining the etymology of the word "ecclesia," Schmemann describes the first Christians accordingly:[60]

> Their first experience of the Church is not that of an abstraction or idea, but that of a real and concrete unity of persons who, because each one of them is united to Christ are united to one another, constitute one family, one body, one fellowship. The Eucharist, before it is or can be anything else, is thus gathering or, better to say, the Church herself as unity in Christ, his presence among those who believe in Him, love Him and in him love one another; and also because this unity is truly new unity, the overcoming of Christ of 'this world,' whose evil is precisely alienation from God and therefore disunity, fragmentation, enmity, separation.

According to Schmemann, the new creation is a united humanity that has overcome the evil of division and hatred. The new creation lives in a transfigured world, a world that is an icon of the kingdom and suffuses cosmic joy. The newness of creation is discovered in its unity, a unity held together by Christ. The new creation of humanity united in Christ bears the responsibility of proclaiming the narrative of Christian salvation history and announcing the joy of the fruits of the resurrection: humanity's rapprochement with God, symbolized in numerous hymns of the Byzantine Church as the removal of the flaming sword guarding the gates of entrance to Paradise by the wood of the cross.[61] The way of the cross and traditional Christian soteriology thus underpins the unity revealed by the new creation.

Schmemann develops this notion of unity with direct reference to the Eucharist. Schmemann views the exchange of the kiss of peace at the Eucharistic liturgy as the symbolic ritual of unity, along with the reception of Holy Communion. Schmemann occasions his

---

60. Ibid., 118.
61. Here is a representative example: "The middle wall of partition has been destroyed; the flaming sword turns back, the cherubim withdraw from the tree of life, and I partake of the delight of Paradise from which I was cast out through disobedience," from the Feast of the Nativity, in *The Festal Menaion*, translated Kallistos Ware and Mother Maria (South Canaan, PA: St. Tikhon's Seminary Press, 1969, 1990), 253.

explanation of the meaning of Eucharistic unity to condemn egotistical individualized piety:[62]

> Even while standing in the church, we continue to sense some people as 'neighbors' and others as 'strangers'—a faceless mass that 'has no relevance' to us and to our prayer and disturbs our 'spiritual concentration.' How often do seemingly spiritually attuned and 'devout' people openly declare their distaste for crowded gatherings, which disturb them from praying, and seek empty and quiet chapels, secluded corners, separate from the 'crowds.' In fact, such individual 'self-absorption' would hardly be possible in the church assembly—precisely because this is not the purpose of the assembly and of our participation in it.

In the kiss of peace, as a "sacred rite of love" that bears transformative power, Schmemann asserts that the purpose is to transform the stranger into a brother and thus "overcome the horrible alienation that was introduced into the world by the devil and proved to be its undoing."[63] Schmemann's notion of unity is deeply theological: he insists that it is a unity granted "from above," a gift from God. Unity with God, Schmemann argues, originates with a meeting, where one has the opportunity to confess faith in God's divine presence. Christian unity actualized through the Eucharist is a unity with God where Christians confess this faith because of real and living experience with God. It is important to note that Schmemann is not merely retrieving an Eastern accent on eschatology here. Schmemann suggests that many Christians desire human unity but confuse Christian unity with an artificial human unity lacking the power to transfigure the world, which he calls the "unity from below."[64]

---

62. Schmemann, *The Eucharist*, 138.
63. Ibid., 138-39.
64. Schmemann compares these two forms of unity in ibid., 147-58.

Critique of Western and Orthodox Theology

Schmemann's discussion of this issue is complicated by his occasional tangents against certain tendencies in systematic theology. Schmemann creates, perhaps inadvertently, a theological thread connecting "individualistic piety" with "religious feeling" that has contributed to the "degeneration of the original Eucharistic experience."[65] Initially, Schmemann blames Western theology for creating specialized compartments of theology that isolates Church from faith and Eucharist. In his narrative, Schmemann's critique gradually turns inward, addressing his fellow Orthodox. He claims that contemporary Orthodox have replaced the faith of the Church with religious feeling, and asserts that Orthodox decorate a concept of churchliness with this religious feeling while referring to it as conservatism.[66]

One might marvel at Schmemann's voluntary critique of Orthodox culture, but more remarkable is his fidelity to the relationship between the Church's liturgy and her faith, and how a reconfigured understanding of faith has the capacity to promote a healthy ecclesiology. Schmemann's narrative here characteristically fails to cite any sources other than references to New Testament passages, but his argument is grounded by a patristic cosmology, as he attributes the vision of a unified human community without God to the deceit of the devil.[67] Schmemann frequently describes the temptation to subscribe to the idea of a unity from below as originating with the devil and his deceit.[68] In this vein, Schmemann

---

65. Ibid., 142–43.
66. Ibid., 145.
67. See, for example, the explanation of the devil and his deceit in "Homily Explaining that God is not the Cause of Evil," in St. Basil the Great, *On the Human Condition,* trans. Nonna Verna Harrison, Popular Patristics Series (Crestwood, NY: St. Vladimir's Seminary Press, 2005), 75–80.
68. Ibid., 152.

sharply criticizes the confusion of Christian unity with an artificial unity manifested in the human community, a warning directed to all Christians.[69] Schmemann blames the devil for making unity into "an end-in-itself," or an idol. In other words, a human community that views its unity as perfect fulfillment is an idol because true unity depends upon God for life since God is the source.[70] Schmemann's description of the potential consequences of pursuing a human unity torn away from God, or even utopian, is chilling:[71]

> To the degree that it [unity] ceases to be unity with God and in God and is transformed into an end-in-itself and an idol, it becomes not only 'easily transformable,' unstable and easily shattered, but also the generator of every new division, evil, violence, and hated. . . . And nowhere does the truly diabolical essence of this substitution become more apparent than in those utopias of unity that constitute the content and inner motivation of all contemporary ideologies without exception, both 'left' and 'right'—ideologies in which the diabolical lie sells itself as the ultimate dehumanization of man, as the offering of man as a sacrifice to the 'unity' that has become a complete idol.

As if his assessment of the unity from below was not chilling enough, Schmemann offers examples of the impact of unity from below on the Orthodox Church. He claims that it has poisoned church consciousness, and identifies the Orthodox response to secularism, the technological revolution, and ideological utopianism as taking refuge in a "nostalgic attraction" to antiquarianism, which he caricatures as "its own form of a utopianism of the past."[72] Schmemann's assessment concludes on a pessimistic note. He acknowledges that the Church needs only the unity from above since Christ's victory overcomes

---

69. Schmemann describes this problem as "the chief and most frightening danger poisoning contemporary church consciousness," in ibid., 152.
70. Ibid., 153.
71. Ibid.
72. Ibid., 154. Schmemann's critique of western Christians is equally sharp, as he says that they have spontaneously capitulated to the "spirit of our time."

all divisions, but he also states that the church has voluntarily given itself over to serve the unities from below, to sanction every manner of natural, national, ideological, and political agenda.[73] The only hope for the Church is to authentically hear her own confession of faith and acknowledge that this confession is the criterion for her judgment before God's throne, since it contains the terms of the new covenant.

Schmemann often juxtaposes Eastern and Western theological methods and, perhaps uncharitably, attributes the decadence of Orthodox theology to its adoption of Western scholastic theology and its methods.

One of the most jarring juxtapositions is cosmological: Schmemann represents his Orthodox cohorts in projecting a cosmology grounded by salvation history. Schmemann views the contemporary scene through the lens of this cosmology: the devil opposes God, and his work is devoted to deceiving humanity by twisting the meaning of words and ideas. Schmemann does not promote dualism; he states that the devil has no creative power of his own and is capable only of confusing and dividing. For Schmemann, the task of the Church is to retrieve its vertical orientation and seek union with God through the celebration of the Eucharist. The Eucharistic liturgy contains several components that have the capacity to address the conditions of the world exacerbated by the devil's deceit because participating in the liturgy demands that people who have every reason to remain in division rehearse unity. Hence, Schmemann views the ritual act of exchanging the kiss of peace as part of the process of transforming a stranger into a brother.

This community of brothers are united in faith expressed vertically; God nourishes them and grants them Christ and the blessings of the Spirit. Here again, Schmemann is not concerned with musing on

73. Ibid., 156.

a state of spiritual bliss resulting from the liturgy, but in the way the liturgy generates human ability to enact Christ's priesthood. In relation to this, the Eucharist completes the rites of initiation and grants the recipient a vision of the world's reality, to see it for what it is. The ability to see the world is essential to act as its steward before God's throne; in his book on the Eucharist, Schmemann states that the act of thanksgiving results in knowledge of the world (as opposed to knowledge about the world).[74] Moreover, Schmemann draws here the critical connection between the world and the new creation, as the Eucharist—the exercise of Eucharistic ministry and communion—restores Christian kingship over creation. The glorification of humanity in the Eucharist grants this divine gift:[75]

> And thus the knowledge that is restored by this thanksgiving is not knowledge about the world, but of the world, for this thanksgiving is knowledge of God, and by the same token apprehension of the world as God's world. It is knowing not only that everything in the world has its cause in God—which, in the end, 'knowledge about the world' is also capable of—but also that everything in the world and the world itself is a gift of God's love, a revelation by God of his very self, summoning us in everything to know God, through everything to be in communion with him, to possess everything as life in him.

In dismissing the individualistic piety of his time, Schmemann depicts a vision of the Christian vocation manifested by the celebration of the Eucharist. The Christian is to serve God in, to, and for the life of the world. The narrative of salvation history and the patristic image of Christ as the glorified man and divine Son renew access to the life of God. For Schmemann, the Eucharist is the entrance into this life through which participants rehearse the process of becoming

---

74. One might have expected Schmemann to present this glorified vision of humanity in his chapter on the sacrament of communion. Instead, he offered it as a reflection on thanksgiving, whereas his content on communion consists almost entirely of excerpts from the Eucharistic prayers of the Orthodox Church.
75. Schmemann, *The Eucharist*, 177.

like God by serving the world in the capacity of king, priests, and prophets, executing Christ's divine office.[76] The exercise of these Eucharistic offices occurs as a community of holy people, in the sacramental act of assembly.

I have dwelt at length on Schmemann's complex discussion of unity here to illustrate his creative weaving of the world's challenges into the narrative of salvation history and liturgical celebration. Schmemann's agenda is not merely to offer a mystagogical and symbolic explanation of the Divine Liturgy. Schmemann consistently expresses his disdain for such allegorical descriptions of the liturgy.[77] Schmemann retains the patristic vision of the Eucharist as participation in the life of God's kingdom where one receives the divine grace to act as a priest in this world, a journey Schmemann frequently describes as ascension. For Schmemann, the Eucharist is not a source for spiritual reflection, but is the food for daily life. The Eucharist provides the participant with access to God whose life-giving power equips the participant to live a life in coherence with his confession of faith under the conditions of this world.

Schmemann's Liturgical Reform and Eucharistic Revival

One of the longstanding questions about Schmemann's legacy is the role he played in implementing liturgical reform. Schmemann's role in the creation and implementation of liturgical reform is a dense and complex forest containing several crossroads. In an essay profiling Schmemann shortly after his death in 1983, John Meyendorff noted Schmemann's contribution to the liturgical revival at St. Vladimir's Seminary:[78]

---

76. Schmemann, *Of Water and the Spirit*, 107.

77. See Schmemann, *Liturgy and Tradition*, 123-24; also Schmemann's recollection of his debate with Taft at a symposium on Byzantine liturgy at Dumbarton Oaks in *The Journals of Father Alexander Schmemann, 1973-1984* (Crestwood, NY: St. Vladimir's Seminary Press, 2000), 220-21.

During his tenure, it ceased to be simply an academic institution, respected in ecumenical circles, but rather heterogeneous to the life of dioceses and parishes. St. Vladimir's produced priests, and these priests, serving not only within the 'Russian Metropolia' but also in other jurisdictions (particularly the Antiochian and Serbian) were taught the spirit of a universal and missionary Orthodox Church, transcending purely ethnic concerns. Also, St. Vladimir's became the center of a liturgical and Eucharistic revival, which is recognized and praised by both Metropolitan Theodosius and Metropolitan Philip in their homilies at the time of Fr. Alexander's death.

Despite Meyendorff's praise of Schmemann's liturgical contribution, Schmemann resisted the implementation of a diffuse liturgical reform in the Orthodox Church. Schmemann was willing to criticize his native Orthodox tradition and illuminated the absurdity of the positions taken by opponents and proponents of liturgical reforms, referring to polarized issues such as the opening and closing of the royal doors during the liturgy and the use of ancient chants versus congregational singing.[79] Schmemann insinuates that the groups fiercely advocating for a particular liturgical practice do so for the wrong reasons because they find fulfillment in the actual ritual performance. Schmemann condemns this view, which he attributes to both opponents and proponents of liturgical reform, as representing the notion of "the liturgy as an end in itself and not as the 'epiphany' of the Church's faith, of her experience in Christ of herself, the World and the kingdom."[80]

If Schmemann was opposed to broad liturgical reform, he frequently applauded evidence of renewal. In one of his earliest

---

78. John Meyendorff, "Postscript: A Life Worth living," in *Liturgy and Tradition*, 151.

79. A. Schmemann, "Liturgical Theology, Theology of Liturgy and Liturgical Reform," in *Liturgy and Tradition*, 44-45.

80. Ibid., 45. Later in the same essay, Schmemann again criticized the reforms of the Roman Church as having produced confusion, and in the process, Schmemann laments the dismissal of the constructive work of the liturgical movement in favor of the privileging of particular social agendas. Schmemann names these principles as "relevance," "the urgent needs of modern society," "the celebration of life," and "social justice." Ibid., 46.

essays, published in 1960, Schmemann states that even the Orthodox Church is in need of a liturgical revival.[81] Schmemann also spoke favorably of the emergence of a Eucharistic revival, first in terms of the ecumenical liturgical movement and again within the context of the Orthodox Church.[82] Schmemann acknowledges the joyful arrival of the Eucharistic revival in the Orthodox Church as having the capacity to energize the revival of the Church itself.[83] In the concluding remarks to his study of the Eucharist, Schmemann summarizes the Eucharistic defects presented by Kyprian Kern, three in particular, in conjunction with an appeal for renewal. The three defects Schmemann highlights are the hegemony of an allegorical symbolism on the meaning of the Eucharist; the recitation of secret prayers which deprives the laity of hearing the "priceless treasure" of the Eucharistic texts; and the distinction between clergy and laity during communion.[84] Schmemann also offers a model of for the celebration of Baptism with the Eucharistic Liturgy.[85] Schmemann's model calls for the fusion of Baptism with the liturgy as a restoration of the unified celebration of entrance into the Church. He identifies Saturday as the preferred day for such baptismal liturgies as an adaptation of the obviously baptismal character of the Vesperal Liturgy of Holy Saturday. Schmemann carefully insists that only the Church hierarchs have the authority to implement such a reform, but this did not prevent him from suggesting it.

Despite Schmemann's reservation of advocating specific liturgical reforms, there is ample evidence to suggest that he was the chief catalyst not only for liturgical reform, but also for an entire

---

81. Schmemann, "The Liturgical Revival and the Orthodox Church," in *Liturgy and Tradition*, 101.
82. See Schmemann, *Introduction to Liturgical Theology*, 45, for the reference to the liturgical movement.
83. Schemann, *The Eucharist*, 242.
84. Ibid., 243.
85. Schmemann, *Of Water and the Spirit*, 169-70.

generation of clergy whose pastoral service marked a paradigm shift in the liturgical life of American Orthodoxy.[86] Besides Schmemann's own references to a Eucharistic revival, there are three specific sources demonstrating his direct impact on Orthodox liturgical life: Paul Meyendorff's testimony on liturgical practices in America, Schmemann's surprising letter addressed to his metropolitan on liturgical directives, and Schmemann's own assessment of the liturgical problem in America.

Schmemann's Impact on Liturgical Practices in America

In his report on liturgy in American Orthodoxy, Meyendorff shared the report of the Liturgical Commission of the Orthodox Church in America, based on a survey of clergy.[87] Meyendorff described the results as "striking," and they included the following outstanding facts: 80% of priests read the anaphora aloud; 95% of priests encouraged frequent Communion; 39% celebrated a variant of a baptismal liturgy; and 21% celebrated evening Eucharistic liturgies. As for the implementation of the reform, Meyendorff unveils the mystery by attributing it to Schmemann's influence as a teacher and dean at St. Vladimir's:[88]

> Many of the changes in American liturgical practice are attributable directly to the work of Fr. Alexander Schmemann. Many of the priests now serving in America have studied under him, and it would be difficult to find a priest who has not at least read his works. Through both the spoken and the written word, Schmemann always stressed the ecclesial dimension of worship. The liturgy, he insisted, must be an action of the entire church, clergy and laity together.

The graduates of St. Vladimir's who studied under Schmemann

---

86. Taft, "The Liturgical Enterprise Twenty-five Years After Alexander Schmemann," 167, 174.

87. Paul Meyendorff, "The Liturgical Path of Orthodoxy in America," *St. Vladimir's Theological Quarterly* 40, nos. 1-2 (1996): 52.

88. Ibid., 53.

employed the liturgical theology and models studied at seminary and implemented them in Orthodox parishes of North America. Meyendorff's data indicates that the changes are largely Eucharistic, which is consistent with the emphasis of Schmemann's liturgical theology.

Schmemann's Open Letter to Metropolitan Ireney

In 1972, Schmemann wrote an open letter to his bishop, Metropolitan Ireney (Bekish), on liturgical practices.[89] Schmemann's letter was a response to liturgical directives issued to the clergy of the Diocese of New York and New Jersey attributed to Metropolitan Ireney. This open letter provides precious insights into Schmemann's thoughts on pastoral liturgy, and also demonstrates his command of the contributions of the liturgical movement. Schmemann's letter confirms Meyendorff's thesis that Schmemann continued the work commenced by his Russian forefathers prior to the Russian revolution.[90] The letter opens with Schmemann's overview of the reforms proposed by the preconciliar deliberations of the Russian Church as an illustration that the very people who had established the Metropolia in America were in the process of reforming the liturgy. This process was interrupted on account of the tragic and unprecedented consequences of the Bolshevik Revolution.[91] Schmemann points out that the challenges the Russians were attempting to address had migrated to America:[92]

These problems did not originate in America, although they certainly acquired here new dimensions and a new degree of urgency. Their

---

89. Alexander Schmemann, "Notes and Comments: On the Question of Liturgical Practices, A Letter to my Bishop," *St. Vladimir's Theological Quarterly* 7, no. 3 (1973): 227-38.

90. See Meyendorff, "The Liturgical Path of Orthodoxy in America," 49-50.

91. Schmemann, "One the Question of Liturgical Practices," 229, and Meyendorff, "The Liturgical Path of Orthodoxy in America," 49.

92. Schmemann, "One the Question of Liturgical Practices," 230.

existence was acknowledged in Russia and is being acknowledged today in virtually all Orthodox Churches. Therefore what saddened me more than anything else in the instruction is the total absence from it of any such acknowledgement, of any recognition that problems do exist which are not solvable by decrees which have never solved any real problems and are not likely to solve any in the near future.

Schmemann then identifies the causes of these problems, which include the influence of Western piety and sacramental theology on Orthodoxy, resulting in a chilling diagnosis: the Orthodox Church is sick.[93] The sickness of the Church in Schmemann's time was manifest in bankruptcy, apathy, petty rivalries, parochialism and secularism, to name a few.[94] Schmemann exposed the hypocrisy of his Church's bishops who seemed concerned about issuing liturgical directives while quietly condoning dubious practices of divorce and remarriage and fundraising.[95] Schmemann's preamble to his response to the liturgical directives is clear: the liturgical directives are grounded by a hopeless and empty goal, the achievement of liturgical uniformity, which will not have the capacity to build up the kind of Church able to withstand the paramount challenges of the time. Schmemann dismisses the ideal of liturgical uniformity as a dream which never existed, especially since the Church "never considered it to be the condition and expression of her unity."[96]

A close reading of Schmemann's responses to the liturgical directives attributed to Metropolitan Ireney discloses his underpinning liturgical theology, and his belief that the rapprochement of liturgy with theology and eschatology would most effectively build up the body of Christ into an icon of the kingdom in the midst of a turbulent society. Several examples illustrate this point.

93. Ibid.
94. Ibid., 230-31.
95. Ibid., 231.
96. Ibid., 232.

First, Schmemann challenges the instruction's demand that no litanies be omitted from the liturgy. Schmemann argues that the omission of the little litanies belonging to the antiphons of the liturgy of the Word might be advantageous if they allow "the celebrant to read the beautiful and deeply corporate prayers of the antiphons."[97] Schmemann then proposes that saying all of the litanies while omitting the secret prayers is a much greater abuse. He offers a similar defense of shortening the litanies of the faithful preceding the offertory: "If, however, the practice of reading aloud the prayers, which in both orders—Chrysostom and Basil—are extremely meaningful and beautiful, were to be reintroduced, the corporate preparation of the Church for the offertory would acquire its full significance."[98]

Schmemann's remarks on a non-euchological aspect of the liturgy confirm his advocacy of corporate worship. The directive instructs churches to install a curtain behind the holy doors within two weeks and to close the holy doors at three points in the liturgy: during the litany of the catechumens and the first and second litanies of the faithful, after the Great Entrance and during the litany of the Prothesis, and during the communion of the clergy. Schmemann dismisses these instructions as an attempt to absolutize rubrics that are elusive.[99] Schmemann then exposes what appears to be one of the motivations of the instruction: the desire to retain the sharp distinction between clergy and laity.[100] Schmemann openly advocates

---

97. Ibid., 233.
98. Ibid., 234.
99. He makes a humorous reference to one of the standard books of Russian liturgy presented by Ireney as a model, published in Moscow in 1904, which does not even mention the curtain, in ibid., 237.
100. "Personally I am convinced that the contemporary Greek practice of not closing the doors at all during the entire Liturgy is much more faithful to the true spirit of the Eucharist an the Orthodox understanding of the Church than the one adopted in the Russian Church which seems to constantly stress the radical separation between the people of God and the clergy," in ibid.

for keeping the royal doors open for the entirety of the liturgy (following the Greek practice) as representing "the Orthodox understanding of the Divine Liturgy as corporate prayer, corporate thanksgiving, and corporate communion."[101] Schmemann concludes by saying that promoting practices (such as reciting prayers aloud and keeping the royal doors open during the liturgy) that symbolize the liturgy as an act of the entire Church will mark a "return to the genuine Orthodox tradition clearly revealed in our liturgical texts and patristic commentaries."[102] The practices of Schmemann's day—high iconostases, curtains, and the silent recitation of prayers—made the laity "attendants" rather than participants of the divine services.[103]

Schmemann's response to the liturgical directives attributed to Metropolitan Ireney represents his hope that a healthy sense of liturgical theology could authentically build the Church into a holy people capable of witnessing to and bearing Christ in the turbulence of modernity. Schmemann's instructions demonstrate the penetration of liturgical theology into the very fabric of liturgical celebration. Every liturgical component has a purpose, and a proper understanding of liturgical history reveals how a component functioned in its native form. Schmemann's essay also provides precious insight into his respect for the scientific method of liturgiology. His references include attributions to prestigious Russian scholars such as Dmitrievsky, Kern, and Skaballanovich, and also mention of his contemporary Byzantine liturgical historians like Panagiotis Trempelas and Mateos. Methodologically, Schmemann follows the path laid out by historians such as Mateos and Robert Taft

101. Ibid., 238.
102. Ibid.
103. Ibid.

by using history to inform his bishop on how the liturgy formed and what reforms might be gleaned from reflection.

Schmemann's Vision of Pastoral Liturgy in America

Schmemann openly challenged his bishop to recognize two crucial historical realities: the formation of a liturgical movement in Russia that anticipated reform, and the reality of challenges facing Orthodoxy in America. Schmemann observed that the problems Russian reformers had begun to address had migrated to America with the people who constituted the parishes. But Schmemann, as an observant student of history, was quite sensitive to the reality of Orthodoxy in America. In ecumenical circles, Schmemann is known for his contributions to liturgical theology, but within Orthodoxy, an equally impressive achievement was Schmemann's role as one of the chief architects of autocephaly for the Orthodox Church in America.[104]

Schmemann's letter responding to Metropolitan Ireney was published after the Moscow Patriarchate granted autocephaly to the Orthodox Church in America (in 1970). Above, I mentioned Schmemann's preference for the Greek practice of opening the holy doors for the entirety of the Divine Liturgy. Schmemann's dismissal of the fantasy of liturgical uniformity was also a nod to the need for a cooperative and organic development of a local liturgical tradition in America.[105] Schmemann's sense of the world around him was acute,

---

104. See John Meyendorff, "A Life Worth Living," in *Liturgy and Tradition*, 151–53. Also see Thomas FitzGerald, "Le père Alexandre Schmemann, l'autocephalie de la Métropole de l'OCA et la réponse du Patriarche œcuménique Athénagoras," in *La joie du Royaume: Actes du colloque international "l'heritage du père Alexandre Schmemann," Paris, 11–14 décembre 2008* (Paris: YMCA Press, 2012), 243–51.

105. "If the Orthodox Church in America is to be the sign of Orthodox unity in this country, it will never achieve that unity by imposing on all one tradition—be it Russian, Greek, Serbian, Romanian, or any other. It will achieve it only by searching, on the one hand, for that which is truly universal in the Orthodox Tradition, and, on the other hand, for that which will incarnate that Tradition in our own situation. Yet even then, I am sure there will remain an inescapable

and he constructed a liturgical program with the capacity to address the immediate situation of that world. In his case, the reality was complex; a small but now autocephalous Orthodox Church facing the challenges of modern American life and attempting to demonstrate its legitimacy alongside parallel Orthodox jurisdictions. Schmemann's letter to Ireney was not the admonition of an academic specialist, but a challenge issued by a subordinate to the leader for the leader to take account of the holistic situation of the Church he oversees.

It is reasonable to assume that Schmemann shared this holistic vision of liturgical theology and its capacity to shape the future of the Church with the seminarians at St. Vladimir's who would be charged with leading its parishes. These students were exposed to not only the labyrinthine history of the Byzantine Rite, but also to the penetration of liturgical theology and its consequent ecclesiology into the fabric of the liturgy's details. So students who weighed the possibility of reading the anaphora aloud for all to hear would learn that exposing the text of the anaphora to the laity would facilitate a process of formation where the anaphora was free to shape people. The students also observed a teacher whose conviction in the truth and its relevance for contemporary ecclesial life fueled the courage to challenge his immediate superior in the Church. Given the number of students who learned from Schmemann, one can see how he was viewed as a liturgist who implemented a radical liturgical reform.

An earlier and somewhat famous article by Schmemann sets the stage for summarizing his program for liturgical reform and demonstrating his thesis that liturgical theology is the key ingredient for a contemporary ecclesiology equipped to navigate the challenges

and healthy diversity for, as Church history shows, it disappears only when a Church begins to die and her worship, rather than being life and the source of life, is progressively touched by rigor mortis," in Schmemann, "An Open Letter to my Bishop," 232-33.

of modernity.[106] Schmemann's overview of the liturgical problem echoes much of what we have reviewed in his letter to Metropolitan Ireney.[107] Schmemann performs a diagnosis of the problem and identifies one chief cause for Orthodoxy in America: secularism.[108] Schmemann observed that secularism has distorted liturgy so that liturgy is no longer viewed as the sanctification of life.[109] His observation raises the question of the value of liturgy in a secularized parish community. If liturgy is not the gathering of God's people to enter the kingdom and deepen the covenant with God, then it becomes something else entirely. Schmemann's writings include numerous references to the decay of liturgy so that it becomes, for example, a rite affirming one's solidarity in ethnic identity. His most keen insight on liturgical decay occurs in this assessment:[110]

> The liturgy is still the center of our Church life, unquestioned, unchallenged, unopposed. But it is in fact a center without periphery, a heart with no control on blood circulation, a fire with nothing to purify and to consume, because that life which had to be embraced by it, has been *satisfied with itself* and has chosen other lights to guide and to shape it.

A parish community can be satisfied with itself when it accomplishes measurable objectives. Meeting or exceeding expectations on baptisms, receptions, financial income, and even the number of divine services celebrated during the course of a year seems to indicate parish community success. Schmemann infers that Orthodox parish culture began to measure success in such terms in his assessment. One can see why Schmemann bemoans the displacement

---

106. Alexander Schmemann, "Problems of Orthodoxy in America: The Liturgical Problem," *St. Vladimir's Seminary Quarterly* 8, no. 4 (1964): 164-85.
107. In ibid., Schmemann treats language, rubrics, and the Western Rite.
108. Schmemann, *For the Life of the World*, 117-34. Also see Plekon, *Living Icons*, 194-97.
109. Schmemann, "Problems of Orthodoxy in America: The Liturgical Problem," 174.
110. Ibid., 175. Emphasis in the original text.

of liturgy in parish life because liturgy is just one thing (among many) that a given parish does.

Schmemann's notion of liturgical decay has another related layer: the celebration of liturgy itself becomes an end so that the clergy, servers, and singers are satisfied when they celebrate a liturgy in accordance with its requirements. This sense of satisfaction is ecumenical, quite real, and spiritually dangerous. Parish workers experience the satisfaction for job performance at the conclusion of solemn liturgical seasons. Priests and choir directors are relieved when the Christmas and Easter services are concluded. In Orthodox culture, this is particularly true for demanding liturgical services, such as the hierarchical liturgy. Relief is a common sentiment experienced by performers who "did their job" and sang the required pieces during a bishop's visit. This affective sentiment tends to prevail, but it cannot account for the range of related possibilities that occur during a bishop's archpastoral visit: was the assembly edified and inspired by the bishop's visit? In parishes afflicted with liturgical decay, the only truth that would matter is that they fulfilled the requirements of the hierarchical liturgy. Fulfilling these requirements could signal success in Schmemann's caricature of a secularized parish, whereas the actual outcome could differ.

Schmemann offered some reflections on the path to liturgical restoration that could edify and build up the parish community. He calls these hints of a blueprint, and his actual agenda for change is not surprising. Schmemann calls for the restoration of Baptism "as the liturgical act concerning the whole Church," he advocates for a "proper understanding of communion," and he proposes that liturgical experience of time must be understood in its relationship with the time people experience in daily life.[111] Schmemann confesses that his approach is ultimately pastoral. He sought a paradigm shift

111. Ibid., 178–80.

from the notion of liturgy as an end-in-itself to liturgy as "concerned primarily with the life of man, with its churching."[112] Schmemann's anthropological maximalism appears here, as he positions the liturgy as shaping and forming its celebrants into holy people as opposed to an event a community must have in order to achieve its objectives. In applying this to Schmemann's actual agenda, one can outline how the paradigm shift would impact the reception of communion. In the Orthodox Church of Schmemann's time, communion was received once a year as an obligation of membership in the church and a symbol of individual piety.[113] Schmemann proposes that the act of receiving communion is experienced as communion with God where God enters the life of the participating community. But the greatest blessing of a liturgical restoration is one that Schmemann believes is most needed in a secularized America:[114]

> What we have to do is neither accept nor reject but simply face the world in which we live, and face it as Orthodox Christians. This means: we see everything in it and the whole of it as related to our faith, as an object of Christian evaluation and judgment and as capable of being changed and transformed. . . . And it is here that the liturgical problem acquires its true significance, for it is primarily in and through worship that the Church acts upon the lives of her members and through them—upon the world in which they live . . . it is the liturgy, in short, that is the power, given to the Church, top overcome and destroy all 'idols'—and secularism is one of them. But liturgy is all this only if we ourselves accept and use it as power.

This excerpt from one of Schmemann's earliest essays on liturgical restoration aptly summarizes his chief contribution to the implementation of liturgical reform. A healthy understanding of liturgy's power to build up a body of individuals into a holy people

112. Ibid., 178.
113. Ibid., 179–80.
114. Ibid., 184–85.

122

who worship God corporately can lead to the transformation of the world itself. Schmemann's comments were directed to the turbulent Orthodox Churches in America, and he addressed them in a pastoral manner, calling upon them to embrace what they experience at liturgy as an encounter with the living God who touches them. In this essay (and earlier), Schmemann identifies spiritual vision of the world as the gift God grants to the Church in liturgy. This vision of the world removes its distortion and allows Christians to see it for what it really is. For Schmemann, vision is not the end; it must translate into action, but he does not say what that action is, because the act is a commission of God given to the holy people. Schmemann's pithy conclusion to his study of the Eucharist demonstrates his model of humans carrying out God's will in the world as emanating from the Eucharist itself (commenting on the dismissal from the liturgy): "We depart into life, in order to witness and to fulfill our calling. Each has his own, but it is also our common ministry, common liturgy—'in the communion of the Holy spirit.'"[115] Schmemann views daily life as a common liturgy, energized by the communion of the Holy Spirit he so frequently cites from the Eucharistic liturgies, an indication that he viewed God as the source of corporate ministry in the world.

In sum, we can offer the following assertions on Schmemann's role in inaugurating the implementation of liturgical reform in the Orthodox Church:

- Schmemann was hesitant to call for an overhaul of Orthodox liturgy and insisted that liturgical reform needed a rationale;

- Schmemann developed a sophisticated rationale for liturgical reform. His rationale consists of the following components:

115. Schmemann, *The Eucharist*, 245.

- The liturgy has been divorced and isolated from theology, eschatology, and piety on account of the scholastic compartmentalization of distinct theological areas as sciences;

- The most pressing need for liturgy is rapprochement between liturgy, theology, and eschatology, with liturgy functioning as the source for all theology since liturgy is an epiphany of the divine-human encounter and the irruption of God's kingdom in the world;

- The Eucharist is the source of liturgical theology and celebration, and the Eucharist governs Christian notions of time. The Eucharist is also inherently ecclesiological; every aspect of the Eucharist is sacramental, even the act of gathering, which is an act of people gathering for a journey to God;

- The point of liturgical celebration is to sanctify one's life, which is lived in community and in the world. Views of liturgy resulting in individual sanctification or religious feeling are distortions exacerbated by the prevalence of secularism. Liturgy is wholly cosmological, and in liturgical participation, God imparts the blessing of vision to the people who can behold the world and its reality, and have the divinely-given power to transform it into an icon of the kingdom;

- Liturgical participation is inherently corporate. Participants in community are called to overcome the divisions promoted by the prince of this world and join in unity with one another as citizens of God's heavenly realm. Liturgical forms that divide the clergy from the laity or obfuscate aspects of the liturgy from the people are decadent and distorted;

- The key ingredient for liturgical reform is to promote a healthy understanding of this liturgical theology. Schmemann believed that it was possible for liturgical participants to gain access to the power of the liturgy without completely overhauling the Church's liturgical structures and contents;

○ Even liturgical reform can be corrupted by idolatry, so that liturgy serves any number or type of reductions. Liturgical reforms that promote the inherently Eucharistic and ecclesiological worldview should open the power of the liturgy to the people, which requires liturgy to be corporate;

○ The reforms directly attributable to Schmemann emphasize the fine-tuning of liturgy so as to make it corporate and participatory.

Schmemann's rationale for liturgical reform, the notion of liturgy as the power source for gathering people and transforming them into God's holy people who perform this service in and for the world, is arguably the more important achievement of his legacy. A close reading of Schmemann's works strongly supports Paul Meyendorff's assertion that Schmemann continued the work commenced by the pioneers of the Russian liturgical movement before the 1917 revolution. Kyprian Kern and Nicholas Afanasiev, *inter alia*, were the theologians who most profoundly shaped Schmemann's vision. In this vein, we might depict Schmemann as one of many contributors to liturgical renewal, as other figures of the Russian religious renaissance shared and expounded his profoundly Eucharistic perspective of the world.

Towards an Assessment of Schmemann's Liturgical Reforms

The pioneers of the liturgical movement professed faith that a potent liturgical theology that supported accessible liturgical structures could result in the transformation of people and structures. Schmemann supported the liturgical movement and recognized its potential fruits, and as we have seen above, was the most prominent catalyst of the implementation of liturgical reform through St. Vladimir's Seminary. In assessing Schmemann's liturgical reform, we should note its limitations. Schmemann's reforms caused reverberations throughout the Orthodox churches in America, but they were limited, particularly to aspects of Eucharistic celebration. After hailing Schmemann's contributions to liturgical reform, Paul Meyendorff notes that the process of renewal was far from complete and outlines three specific areas requiring emphasis in the years to come: the participation of the laity in the liturgy, the reinvigoration of daily prayer (the Liturgy of the Hours), and the reform of the lectionary.[116]

Schmemann actually instigated the process of reinvigorating the tradition of praying the Saturday evening Vigil by creating a model for a parish Vigil called "The Lord's Day," a cause Meyendorff himself supported and continued under the title of "Parish Vigil."[117] More recently, Peter Galadza criticized Schmemann for failing to call for a more comprehensive reform of the Byzantine liturgy.[118] In doing so, Galadza also forwards an agenda for liturgical reform, including the promotion of congregational singing, the development of a Byzantine version of the RCIA, the expansion of the diaconate (beyond liturgical decoration), the renewal of the artoclasia, the reading of the anaphora aloud, the restoration of the Old Testament

---

116. Paul Meyendorff, "The Liturgical Path of Orthodoxy in America," 57–63. Meyendorff suggestions include the encouragement of congregational singing, promotion of the liturgy of the hours in families and small groups, and for the lectionary, both expanding the assigned lections after Pentecost and restoring the Old Testament reading to the Sunday liturgy.

117. For an assessment of this model, along with the Vigil used by New Skete Monastery, see Nicholas Denysenko, "The Revision of the Vigil Service," *St. Vladimir's Theological Quarterly* 51, nos. 2-3 (2007): 221-51. Schmemann's role in beginning this process originated from his tenure as the chair of the Liturgical Commission of the Orthodox Church in America. The Lord's Day scheme for Sunday liturgy (which includes the Saturday Vigil) occurred in 1979-80.

118. Galadza, "Schmemann Between Fagerberg and Reality," 7-32. For a response to Galadza's critique, see Nicholas Denysenko, "Towards an Agenda for Byzantine Pastoral Liturgy: A Response to Peter Galadza," *Bolletino della Badia Greca di Grottaferrata* 7 (2010): 45-68.

reading, the revision of the Augmented Litany, and the daily celebration of the Liturgy of Presanctified Gifts during Lent.[119] The process of reform, of course, is still ongoing, so any assessment of Schmemann's liturgical reforms is provisional.

Schmemann's Critique of Clericalism and Reductions

Schmemann's own evaluation of the Eucharistic revival attributed to him elucidates the reality of its reception in the Church. A mark of Schmemann's humility is his own ongoing assessment of Church life recorded in many of his writings, especially his journals. I present some of these excerpts here as an illustration of the environment in which Schmemann attempted to implement liturgical reform. Above, I noted Schmemann's deep frustration with reductions in Church life to achievement of specific objectives belonging to programs. In an entry from December 23, 1976, Schmemann expressed concern over students' perceptions of the Church and her ministry:[120]

> The situation at the seminary is worrying me. I have the feeling that we are not doing what we should; not heading where we could; something is wrong! We had a three-hour faculty meeting about it, but without a consensus, neither about an analysis of the situation, now how to deal with it. My point of view is that a good half of our students are dangerous for the Church—their psychology, their tendencies, a sort of constant obsession with something. Orthodoxy takes on a different, ugly aspect, something important is missing, and the Orthodoxy that these students consciously or subconsciously favor is distorted, emotional—in the end, pseudo-Orthodoxy. Not only at the seminary, but everywhere, I acutely sense the spread of a strange Orthodoxy. . . . Everywhere, some anxiety, and unbalanced search, as if there was no joy from God's presence, joy from faith.

The immediate question here is what are these students seeking?

---

119. Galadza, 25–32.
120. Schmemann, *The Journals of Father Alexander Schmemann*, 139.

What are they seeking in Church life and pastoral ministry? Schmemann seems to bemoan the absence of recognizing joy in being together, in belonging to a community committed to sharing and living the good news of the Gospel. Over two years later, Schmemann makes the same juxtaposition of obsession and joy in a passing comment on seminarians, and he seems to attribute the absence of joy to an obsession with clericalism, particularly with presiding at long and frequent services.[121]

Schmemann is sensitive to particular models of the Church, and his concern with clericalism stems from his observation that seminarians wanted to fulfill a particular image of the priesthood where priests help people and perform the divine services because this was in the priest's job description, as it were. From Schmemann's perspective, this is a reduction, alien to gathering as Church because God has called all into one gathering for the privilege of worshiping him. Instead, alternative variants of Church exist for the purpose of fulfilling a particular vision. Schmemann openly criticized a favored model of Church for Orthodox, what we might call the monastic variant. For Schmemann, proponents of the monastic variant had succumbed to yet another reduction of Orthodoxy, as he writes in an entry from 1980:[122]

> At this time, there's a triumph of monasticism both in theology and in piety. In Serbia, every revival is connected with a monastic experience, trend or teaching. I'm worried about this trend becoming identified with Orthodoxy. In America, we often see the reduction of Orthodoxy to icons, to ancient singing, to Mt. Athos books about spiritual life. Byzantium is triumphing without a cosmic dimension. I can't avoid thinking that it is all a sort of romanticism—a love for that Orthodoxy, love because that image is radically different from the images of the contemporary world. Escape, departure, reduction of Orthodoxy. What

121. Ibid., 218.
122. Ibid., 268.

is very significant for me is that wherever this trend is triumphant, the Eucharist, Communion, the meaning and the experience of the Church are lost. This meaning and experience are needed now more than ever. The Eucharistic Church identifies itself as 'in this world, but not of this world.' The monastic trend of the Church is that the parish, community, etc., give this world only an opposition, while departure from this world is shown as the Orthodox answer and the true Orthodox way.

In the same entry, Schmemann notes John Meyendorff's expressed puzzlement at why the people of the Church were so enchanted with the fathers. Schmemann believed that this enchantment was due to favoring a style; he stated that the people are "charmed by a melody."[123] Schmemann's concern on the danger of favoring the monastic variant of Church discloses his displeasure over renouncing the world. For Schmemann, the Eucharist recapitulates the world to God and the original goodness of the world given to it by God in creation is revealed to humanity. Schmemann's critique of the monastic variant is also a rejection of the outer layers representing this model of Church, namely the absolute identity of liturgy with fulfilling all of the requirements of the Typikon. From Schmemann's perspective, this was nothing but another reduction of the Church to a particular variant. Theologically, Schmemann identified the danger inherent in this variant as a dualism of sacred and profane, where the world itself is profane and not worthy of the Church. Hence, the outer layers of Church life, especially liturgical celebration, are decorated with all the trappings of monastic vesture, to create a sacred space providing refuge from the evils and temptations of this world.[124]

Schmemann essentially collected the various reductions he

123. Ibid., 269.
124. Note that Schmemann did not limit his reduction to the monastic variant. He also critiqued an institutional variant of Church in ibid., 328-29. Schmemann's applied the same critique to the Roman Church's reduction of Church and liturgy to a particular message in ibid., 229-30.

consistently identified and named them as dangers to the Eucharistic revival he witnessed in the life of the Orthodox Church. He described the chief of these as the "sacralization" of the Church, where the Church becomes an institution separating the world from the Church instead of enfolding it.[125] This is an implicit rejection of any type of sacralization, be it monastic, lay, or one of social justice. Schmemann affirms what the Church is:[126]

> The Church is not an organization but the new people of God. The Church is not a religious cult but a liturgy, embracing the entire creation of God. The Church is not a doctrine about the world to come but the joyous encounter of the kingdom of God.

Schmemann and the Formation of Parish Clergy

Besides his writings, one can obtain a sense of Schmemann's concern for his students' ability to implement liturgical reform by referring to select lectures. On February 4, 1980 (late in his career), Schmemann delivered a class lecture titled "Liturgical Changes."[127] Schmemann structured the lecture around three fundamental questions: "why change," "what to change," and "how to change." At the beginning of his lecture outline, Schmemann notes that this is a practical aspect of the liturgical enterprise. Schmemann notes that one must be able to address these three questions to avoid failures. His sensitivity to the pastoral dimension is evidenced by his depiction of what parish priests encounter in the parish:

> A priest comes to a new parish, sees all kinds of 'differences' from the seminary, from his previous parish . . . and simply 'jumps' into changing.

125. Schmemann, *The Eucharist*, 242.
126. Ibid.
127. Alexander Schmemann, "Liturgical Changes," Lecture Outline, February 4, 1980, Fr. Alexander Schmemann Papers at the Father Georges Florovsky Library, St. Vladimir's Theological Seminary, Box 18.

Schmemann attributes such actions to clericalism and pride on the part of the priest, which creates conflict and ultimately results in failure.[128] Schmemann then states that changes are only partial and are made "without reference to the whole," and without a plan; changes made without reference to the whole are incapable of transformation. Schmemann affirms this point when he states that "nothing deep is possible without liturgical education," especially preaching liturgy on the basis of being "what you are." Preaching and teaching with retreats are the core ingredients of a "restoration of meaning," along with "endless patience." Schmemann also notes that cooperation with the choir is essential. His concern for clericalism contributing to failure is evident in his appeal for a conciliar process for implementing liturgical change in the parish, which entails answering questions as opposed to adopting a confrontational stance rooted in clerical authority.

The reader will note the emergence of several themes we have already identified in Schmemann's platform for liturgical reform. Schmemann views careful teaching and preaching as the primary mechanisms for implementing liturgical reform in the parish. But his construction of this lecture for his seminarian students exposes his concern to guide them towards success in implementing reform: Schmemann observed clericalism and an obsession with authority as the primary obstacle to reform taking root in a particular parish.

Schmemann's hope that clergy would implement a Eucharistic revival in the local parish for the building up of its life emerges from a lecture he offered in 1971 on the transformation of the parish.[129] In this lecture, Schmemann caricatures the stereotypical concerns parish

---

128. "A conflictual situation is created, which will make it virtually impossible to change without hatred," ibid.
129. Alexander Schmemann, "Transformation of the Parish," Lecture at St. Andrew's parish, 1971, Fr. Alexander Schmemann Papers at the Father Georges Florovsky Library, St. Vladimir's Theological Seminary, Box 17, Document 12.

leaders tend to occupy themselves with, and insists that the only source for authentic parish transformation is the the Eucharist. For Schmemann, this is not solely a matter of adhering to the correct Eucharistic doctrine, but for the parish itself to become a communion of the Holy Spirit. Schmemann attempts to illustrate how such a real body might emerge in his lecture:[130]

> We should restore, first of all, the ecclesiological dimension of communion and that means the divine liturgy, the Eucharist as the sacrament which builds up the church. . . . The second one is . . . to balance the spirituality of Holy Communion. That means what we are looking at is not only the healing of soul and body, but first of all, that participation in that which 'the eye has not seen, the ear has not heard and hasn't entered the heart of man without God has prepared for those who love him'—the ecclesiology, the spirituality. And finally, that belt of communication: the Eucharist and the parish meeting, the Eucharist and theological education, the Eucharist and the budget for the year 1971–72, the Eucharist and everything.

Schmemann acknowledged that it was difficult and even impractical for parish people to see how the Eucharist can connect with the banal activities of fundraisers and paying bills. For Schmemann, the point was to emphasize that the Eucharist unites the entire community in Christ. Schmemann placed the onus of responsibility for energizing parish transformation upon the clergy. Schmemann makes it clear that the clergy are the gatekeepers and key figures who can facilitate transformation through their leadership:[131]

> What is required? How can this transformation be originated? I would say it must be originated first of all by the clergy—the priests who stand at the altar. They can add to their vocation whatever they want in addition to being priests—fine with me. But they are ordained, first of all, to stand at the altar to be the ministers of the holy mysteries. If the priests would agree on that, if the priests would be at the centers of their

130. Ibid., 29.
131. Ibid., 30–31.

preoccupations, this common mind, which constitutes really what all of us sitting here . . . experienced when we were ordained and stood for several minutes holding the Body of Christ in our hands and heard the Bishop say, 'receive that token on which you will be judged at the last coming of Christ.' Now if priests . . . do not reach that agreement on what is communion, what is for example the connection between communion and life in the parish, then everything will go down the drain. And the first and last chance of the regeneration of the parish will be lost.

Schmemann's own observations on the process of transformation capacitated by the implementation of liturgical reform are illuminating. Clearly, Schmemann recognized the popularity of variant models of Church, be they monastic, lay, theme-oriented, or clericalism. It seems that Schmemann would not have accepted the adoption of particular liturgical practices that co-exist with the prevailing spirit of people who prefer an ecclesiology of Church as refuge from the world.

Schmemann used his position as Dean of St. Vladimir's to influence the Synod of Bishops of the OCA by encouraging them to normalize frequent participation in Communion in parishes. Schmemann's report to the Holy Synod of bishops on "Confession and Communion" was presented and approved in 1972.[132] The synod approved the practice of general confession to encourage more frequent participation in the Eucharist. Schmemann's advocacy of general confession is another instance of his rehabilitation of a practice that had specific historical antecedents along with some support among progressive theologians in the milieu of the revolution in early-twentieth-century Russia.[133] In Schmemann's

---

132. For the complete text in English, see Alexander Schmemann, "Confession and Communion," http://www.schmemann.org/byhim/confessionandcommunion.html (accessed July 23, 2015).

133. For details, see Nadieszda Kizenko, "Sacramental Confession in Modern Russia and Ukraine," in *State Secularism and Lived Religion in Soviet Russia and Ukraine,* ed. Catherine Wanner (Oxford: Oxford University Press, 2012), 195-97.

proposal, the general confession included the reading of the prayers before Confession, a silent prayer of repentance, a general confession offered by the priest for the assembly, with the people receiving absolution of their sins at the end. Anyone who desired private confession was able to do so after the dismissal of the general confession.

In his report, Schmemann referred to the relationship between the Eucharistic revival in America and the improvement in the health of parish life, and stated that there was no justification for infrequent Communion when one consults Church tradition.[134] Schmemann identified the perception that Confession was required before Communion as an obstacle to encouraging liturgical and ecclesial renewal, and thus proposed the establishment of general confession as a way to open the doors for frequent Communion while honoring the need for repentance in preparation for the Divine Liturgy. Schmemann asserted that general confession would inaugurate a school of repentance and result in improved individual confessions.[135] The Synod's acceptance and implementation of Schmemann's proposal demonstrates the power of his influence on the Church in America, a vision rooted in a liturgical renewal with the capacity to truly transform people and their parish communities.[136]

---

134. In his report, Schmemann cites John Cassian and John Chrysostom as proponents of frequent communion, and "Russian liturgiologists" as those who demonstrated the problem of liturgical and ecclesial decay in Orthodoxy, in Schmemann, "Confession and Communion."

135. "Experience shows, that those who take part in such a general confession begin to have a much better individual confession. For the whole point here is precisely that the general confession is under no circumstances meant simply to replace individual confession, is not and must not be a substitute. It is only for those and those alone who, receiving communion often and regularly confessing their sins, realize the self-evident need for purifying their conscience, for repentance, for that spiritual concentration and attention, which is so difficult to achieve in our modern life," ibid.

136. Despite the Synod's affirmation of general confession, the practice of general confession as preparation for communion at the Divine Liturgy is not normative within the OCA.

The Reception of Schmemann in Orthodox America

The evidence appears to indicate that Schmemann's reform was received and implemented by some of the Orthodox clergy in America who either studied with him or were exposed to his teaching. The data from the Liturgical Commission of the Orthodox Church in America presented by Meyendorff indicates that many clergy and parishes were actively encouraging corporate liturgical participation and desired to find additional ways to draw people into the liturgy with their bishop's permission. We can consider this data as evidence indicating partial success for the implementation of Schmemann's reform. This success is in spite of the fact that some clergy and parishes did not positively receive or implement Schmemann's proposed reforms. The rejection or passive ignorance of a Eucharistic revival is not an indication of its failure, but an instance of a preference for an alternative liturgical or ecclesial ethos. Schmemann himself consistently argued that liturgical uniformity was futile and could not achieve the kind of healing needed by the Church, so by his own criteria, the proliferation of alternative liturgical forms is not necessarily problematic. In fact, liturgical history clearly demonstrates that regional liturgical diversity prevails even when a particular order, style, or innovation is promoted by a prominent liturgical center.

St. Vladimir's Seminary was the center for the development and implementation of Schmemann's liturgical reforms, but many clergy in North America did not learn liturgical theology and ecclesiology at St. Vladimir's. Parish priests of Schmemann's Orthodox Church in America also studied at St. Tikhon's and St. Herman's seminaries, and Schmemann did not have any direct influence on liturgical pedagogy at seminaries such as Holy Trinity in Jordanville (ROCOR), Holy Cross Greek Orthodox Theological School, and St. Andrew's

Ukrainian Orthodox College, among others. In Schmemann's era and today, Orthodoxy in North America has multiple variants of liturgical theology and ecclesiology which occasionally compete with each other. Schmemann's acknowledgement of these variant ecclesiologies and their attachment to specific styles of worship is instructive for us because they are coherent with liturgical history, which does not offer instances of absolute liturgical uniformity. From this perspective, the fact that dozens of clergy and parishes followed the lead of an established liturgical center and implemented its practices demonstrates some success of the implementation.

Conclusion

In conclusion, we can identify two concrete areas where Schmemann's enterprise for liturgical reform has had a tangible impact. The first area is Schmemann's impact on the broader liturgical academy. Taft presented an eloquent and accurate assessment of Schmemann's real contribution in his essay published on the occasion of the twenty-fifth anniversary of Schmemann's death. Taft credits Schmemann with going "right to the heart of things by defining liturgy in new and exciting ways," which resulted in a paradigm shift for liturgical studies, from explaining how liturgy works to what liturgy is.[137] Schmemann was the pioneer who elucidated a theology "that rejoined ecclesiology, eschatology, and spirituality: a theology that did not explain the liturgy, but rather a theology that was the liturgy."[138] The following excerpt from Taft's essay explains why students and scholars of liturgy and sacramental theology remain engrossed by Schmemann and his writings despite his deficiencies:[139]

---

137. Taft, "The Liturgical Enterprise Twenty-five Years After Alexander Schmemann," 166.
138. Ibid.
139. Ibid., 174.

Fr. Alexander was the one who finally succeeded in putting Humpty-
Dumpty together again. He took a decomposed and fragmented vision
of liturgy, known by the code-name 'theology of the liturgy,' and
transfigured it . . . into a 'liturgical theology' expressive of what Christ
and his Church is, the 'Sacrament of the Kingdom' inchoatively present
among us now, in mystery, 'For the Life of the World.'

Taft concludes his essay by stating that the so-called "Schmemann-
Kavanagh-Fagerberg-Lathrop" school of liturgical theology is more
needed than ever within the liturgical academy.[140] The inspiration
for this kind of praise can only be Schmemann's consistent reference
to the transformation of the community made possible by active
participation in the liturgy. Despite the formidable challenges of
Schmemann's Christian era, a community of believers could truly
become a new creation bestowed with the gift of seeing the world
through the fourth dimension, where the unity from above becomes
the model for the unity people experience in the world.

Schmemann's vision of sacramental theosis experienced primarily
through the Eucharist was quite appealing to both his Eastern and
Western audiences. Schmemann's rejection of reductions prevented
an academic or pastoral hijacking of the Eucharist for a particular
theological or social cause. Reducing the Eucharist to a gathering
devoted to seeking solidarity with the poor was just as deficient as
presenting the Eucharist as a moment of consecration or defining the
rite of communion as a private union between the individual and
God. Schmemann's critiques of theme-based reductions in both East
and West permitted the liturgy to be what it is: the eschatological
encounter of the Church with God, in Christ, for the life of the
world. We agree with Taft that Schmemann's insistence on the
liturgy as theologia prima continues to nourish his scholarly and
pastoral disciples.[141]

140. Ibid., 176.

It is ironic that Schmemann's legacy has impacted Western Christianity more than his own Orthodox Church, manifested by the fact that Catholic and Lutheran theologians have continued his work in liturgical theology. The inconsistent reception of Schmemann in the Western and Eastern churches seems complicated, but is consistent with his own life experiences. In this chapter, I have shown how Schmemann drew richly from both Western and Orthodox sources in his scholarship and teaching. Schmemann was truly an ecumenical theologian, shaped by the liturgical movement yet faithful to his native tradition. Schmemann's reluctance to embrace the liturgical changes introduced by Vatican II is simultaneously ironic and appropriate. On the one hand, Schmemann approved of the theological rationale underpinning the liturgical reform of Vatican II, viewing it as consistent with the fruits of the liturgical movement. In this sense, we can conclude that Schmemann adhered to the same core principles of SC's theological rationale, principally the restoration of a layered priesthood grounded by Christ the high priest, from which the ordained and lay priesthoods derive. Schmemann's Eucharistic ecclesiology is stridently faithful to this notion of the priesthood, which inspired him to declare that the laity is the Eucharistic concelebrant, a precept originally iterated by Afanasiev.[142] Schmemann also consistently insists on the necessity of corporate worship, a notion identical to the teaching of the active participation of the laity in the liturgy iterated by SC. Again, in promoting corporate worship and emphasizing liturgical catechesis and understanding in his writings, Schmemann shaped a liturgical enterprise that would permit people to engage the liturgy without obstructions from verbose explanations or clerical obstruction.

141. Ibid., 177.
142. Schmemann, *The Eucharist*, 14. Here, Schmemann attributes this notion of Eucharistic concelebration to Afanasiev.

With regard to *SC* and Vatican II, Schmemann essentially held the theological rationale for the liturgical reform in common with the Roman Catholic Church, and he was correct in attributing the reform to the fruits of the liturgical movement. In this sense, Schmemann's liturgical renewal and *SC* were both products of the liturgical movements, albeit with vastly different degrees of scope and impact. Schmemann's hesitance with the liturgical reform of Vatican II concerned its spirit and his perception that its implementation was haphazard. Schmemann's observation of the impact of *SC* on the Catholic Church in the first few years of its implementation may very well be the most significant impact of Vatican II on Schmemann's liturgical renewal. Schmemann understood that the extant divisions within Orthodoxy, which were exacerbated by the pain of immigration and the persecution of large Orthodox populations in the Soviet bloc, constricted a pan-Orthodox process of deliberating liturgical reform. As a faithful priest who desired increased Church unity, Schmemann adopted a more conservative approach to liturgical renewal within Orthodox that emphasized the clear articulation of a theological rationale, the active participation of the people in the liturgy, and the people's discovery and interiorization of their priestly identity. Schmemann believed that it was entirely possible and desirable to fine-tune the received liturgical tradition in such a way that the liturgy would invite the people's active participation and enable them to hear the invitation to become God's priests and servants.

While Schmemann rejected surgery as a method for liturgical reform, he was a consistent and serious proponent of quality liturgical catechesis and the revision of select liturgical elements to encourage active liturgical participation. Schmemann's 1972 letter to Metropolitan Ireney demonstrates his awareness of the extant liturgical scholarship pastors could draw from the fine tune the existing liturgical tradition. Schmemann's liturgical priorities are elements we will see appear again in our other three Orthodox models for reform, especially his emphasis on catechesis and fidelity to the received liturgical tradition.

Schmemann's most significant contribution to our examination of liturgical reform is his own assessment of its impact in the Church. Schmemann viewed clericalism as the most formidable threat to the Eucharistic revival, the worst of all the possible reductions he identified in his writings. Schmemann spent the bulk of his career teaching liturgical theology and serving as dean at St. Vladimir's Seminary. A generation of clergy learned under Schmemann, pastors who served parishes in the OCA, the Serbian and Antiochian, and many other Orthodox churches. Some clergy who did not attend St. Vladimir's were exposed to Schmemann's teachings on account of his frequent lectures throughout North America and his writings. Schmemann also impacted the liturgical life of the Greek Orthodox Archdiocese of America by contributing to the liturgical theology of Alkiviadis Calivas. Schmemann invested much of himself into forming clergy who would presumably implement what they learned at St. Vladimir's in their parishes. In this vein, Schmemann was the primary architect of a liturgical center at St. Vladimir's that established a pattern for liturgical renewal for Orthodox in North America.

On the other hand, Schmemann's frequent and sobering lament about seminarians and their expectations of their studies and his critique of the clericalism prevalent among Orthodox clergy explains why the impact of liturgical renewal has been limited. Schmemann provides an insight that is simultaneously simple and profound: many people enroll in seminary studies because they desire power in a pastoral appointment and have reduced ministry to exercising authoritarian administration over a community of people in accordance with a dated rule for Church life. Despite the best efforts of Schmemann and his colleagues at the seminary, some graduates rejected his teaching on liturgical renewal in favor of alternate ecclesiologies that emphasized clerical privilege. Schmemann's sober awareness of this phenomenon in his journals and lectures is remarkable. His identification of the clergy as the primary gatekeepers of liturgical renewal is the key to understanding his goal. Without clergy who are willing and able to work with the people of their parishes and patiently instruct them on the liturgy, even the best-conceived surgical liturgical reform is doomed to failure.[143]

Schmemann's identification of the problem and diligent attempts to encourage the clergy to embrace change and work hard at implementing it in parish ministry are evidenced by his direct instructions to his students in his lecture on "Liturgical Changes" and the transformation of the parish. In other words, the clergy must exercise their priesthood in accordance with the priesthood of Christ by being with and for the people in their parish ministry. Without a strong company of clergy leading the way, the impact of liturgical renewal will be limited. One might add that the reform of the clergy was a constituent staple of Schmemann's liturgical renewal enterprise.

Alexander Schmemann was a pioneer in liturgical theology and renewal. This chapter has elucidated Schmemann's contributions to liturgical renewal and has demonstrated his fidelity to the liturgical movement, his consonance with the principles underpinning Vatican II and *SC*, and his furtherance of the program of liturgical renewal belonging to the Russian religious renaissance. I have also assessed the

---

143. Schmemann concluded his proposal for a baptismal Divine Liturgy with these words: "It must be clear, however, that such liturgical restoration would bear no fruits unless it is properly prepared by appropriate teaching and preaching, i.e., by the deepening of the Church's mind. The liturgy must reveal the Church's faith, make it a living one. Thus no liturgical changes will fulfill anything if they are not the expression and the fulfillment of our own reconversion to the true meaning and power of our Orthodox faith," *Of Water and the Spirit*, 170.

impact of Schmemann's liturgical reform by emphasizing his creation of a liturgical center at St. Vladimir's Seminary, his illumination of the potential transformation of the parish into a communion of the Holy Spirit through Eucharistic participation, and have discussed how the appeal of alternative ecclesiologies and the problem of clericalism limited the impact of his teaching. Schmemann's emphasis on liturgical catechesis, the active participation of the laity in the liturgy, the laity's priestly identity, and the formation of quality clergy are themes that will appear variably in our next three models of modern Orthodox liturgical reform.

3

A Russian Alternative

Liturgical Maximalism in ROCOR

"What I have always admired in the Russian Church Abroad is its faithfulness to the liturgical and ascetical spiritual traditions of Russian Orthodoxy in particular and Orthodoxy in general. I was always impressed by their faithful performance of the church services and their re-printing of the liturgical books, at a time when they were very difficult to obtain. . . . I also admired the faithful presentation of liturgical piety at a time when other Orthodox, like the Greeks in America, were making changes in the services. I had not visited Russia at that time though of course there too the services were properly performed."

–Metropolitan Kallistos (Ware)[1]

When Deacon Andrei Psarev published the interview he conducted with Metropolitan Kallistos (Ware) on his experience with the Russian Orthodox Church Outside of Russia (ROCOR), links to the

---

1. Andrei Psarev, "Metropolitan Kallistos Ware: 'ROCOR's Emphasis on Ascetic and Liturgical Tradition is very much Needed Today," ROCOR Studies website, http://www.rocorstudies.org/interviews/2014/03/27/metropolitan-kallistos-ware-rocor-emphasis-on-assetic-and-liturgical-tradition-is-very-much-needed-today/ (accessed October 6, 2014).

interview went viral on social media and were exchanged via e-mail. Metropolitan Kallistos's remarks about ROCOR's preservation of the liturgical tradition canonized a common perception of ROCOR as a Church steadfastly preserving tradition and promoting liturgical maximalism. In many ways, an examination of ROCOR's liturgical traditions does not fit a scholarly assessment of liturgical reform in the Orthodox Church because ROCOR has not implemented an initiative of liturgical reform comparable to that of the Church of Greece or Alexander Schmemann. Furthermore, of all the Orthodox models of liturgical reform belonging to this study, ROCOR was certainly influenced less by Vatican II than any other Church because ROCOR does not, in general, encourage ecumenical dialogue with the Roman Catholic Church.

In fact, the common perception of ROCOR is that it is a profoundly conservative Church devoted to upholding the way of the fathers and the traditions of the pre-revolutionary Orthodox Church in Russia. Numerous elements support this perception. For most of its existence, ROCOR followed a staunchly monarchist and anti-communist trajectory, being the first Orthodox Church to glorify Tsar Nicholas II and members of the Romanov family as new martyrs while rejecting modernism, the influence of Western theology on the Orthodox Church, ecumenism, Sergianism, and innovation within the Orthodox Church as unwelcome developments.

All of these matters within ROCOR deserve research and analysis by experts, but the topic for this chapter is ROCOR's liturgical theology and its contribution to our examination of Orthodox liturgical reform in light of Vatican II. I am examining this topic here because ROCOR's devotion to the received tradition of the liturgy, particularly the style of liturgy prevalent in pre-revolutionary Russia, helps us understand the diversity of approaches to the liturgy within

Orthodoxy and the theological rationale underpinning the liturgy. Furthermore, a particular ecclesiology accompanies ROCOR's liturgical tradition, one that depends on the leadership of the bishop, his cultivation of clergy who are devoted to liturgical excellence (particularly in the *ars celebrandi*), and calls for a kind of episcopal collegiality bound, at least in part, by liturgical like-mindedness. This chapter will examine the liturgical theology of ROCOR by discussing ROCOR as a direct inheritor of pre-revolutionary Russian liturgical traditions, by analyzing the notion of liturgical maximalism promoted by ROCOR clergy, and by exploring the special care maintained to the cultivation of liturgical music within ROCOR. In presenting this history, I will consult components from the debates on liturgical reform in pre-revolutionary Russian Orthodoxy, episcopal directives and instructions on the liturgy, and the mechanisms employed by ROCOR to preserve and cultivate tradition. The reader will find that liturgical maximalism is much more than fierce fidelity to maintaining the received tradition: in ROCOR's case, liturgical maximalism views liturgy as apostolic and a gift to be received and handed down without distortion, a perspective on the liturgy that impacted the clergy's responsibility in the milieu of persecution, immigration, and a strong sense of apocalypticism.

In the Beginning:
Metropolitan Antony Khrapovistky and the Liturgy

In the previous chapter, I presented selections from the pre-revolutionary deliberations on the liturgy in the Russian Orthodox Church as an important source for Schmemann's liturgical reforms. I noted that most of the proposed reforms were not approved and implemented, which is partially attributable to the environment of the Russian Council, which met sporadically and hastily during and following the revolution. Historians identify the restoration of the

Moscow Patriarchate as the council's most renowned accomplishment, and there is no doubt that this was probably the primary topic occupying the bishops.[2] However, it is equally clear that the liturgical discussions were also of interest to the bishops.

In the previous chapter, I identified specific topics that were integral to the reformers' agenda, especially the participation of the people in the liturgy. Metropolitan Antony Khrapovitsky, one of the central figures in the Russian Church of this time, emerged as a figure who consistently opposed reforms. Antony's opposition to reforms has resulted in his reputation as a liturgical conservative, but his theological thinking about the liturgy proposes a more profound understanding representing a critical mass of Russian Orthodoxy to the present day, particularly on the priest's role as presider and caretaker of the received tradition. Metropolitan Antony's role is of particular importance to our discussion of ROCOR as he is deeply venerated as the central figure who founded ROCOR and shaped its mission to the present day.

Metropolitan Antony was born in 1862, in Vatagyno, near Novgorod.[3] After attending the theological academy in St. Petersburg, Antony attained a reputation as a talented and smart young man, ascending to the position of rector of the Moscow Theological Academy at the age of 27, moving to the Kazan Academy in 1895-7, and ordained as a bishop in 1897.[4] His

2. Hyacinthe Destivelle, *The Moscow Council (1917-1918): The Creation of the Conciliar Institutions of the Russian Orthodox Church*, eds. Michael Plekon and Vitaly Permiakov, trans. Jerry Ryan, foreword by Metropolitan Hilarion (Alfeyev) (Notre Dame, IN: University of Notre Dame Press, 2015); Dimitry Pospielovsky, *The Orthodox Church in the History of Russia* (Crestwood, NY: St. Vladimir's Seminary Press, 1998), 134-35; James W. Cunningham, *A Vanquished Hope: The Movement for Church Renewal in Russia, 1905-1906* (Crestwood, NY: St. Vladimir's Seminary Press, 1981), 256-65.

3. Metropolitan Laurus (Shkurla), "Наследие митрополита Антония (Храповицкого)" ["The Legacy of Metropolitan Antony (Khrapovitsky)"], in *Metropolitan Antonii (Khrapovitskii): Archpastor of the Russian Diaspora*, ed. Vladimir Tsurikov (Jordanville, NY: Foundation of Russian Culture, 2014), 11.

4. Ibid., 12.

ecclesiastical career witnessed his time as the bishop of Volhyn' and Zhitomir, Metropolitan of Kyiv and Galich, imprisonment and confinement in a Uniate monastery, and ultimately, his sojourn to Belgrade, where ROCOR held a synod in Karlovci that established it as the successor to the Russian Church until the Fall of the Soviet Union and the eventual reunion of ROCOR with the Moscow Patriarchate in 2007.

Antony was an active theologian, a promoter of good pastoral theology who was well-versed in canon law and experienced with conversation and exchange with non-Orthodox Christians. Scholars have examined Antony's Slavophilism, monarchism, rejection of Anselm's soteriology, patriotism, and the role he played in the restoration of the Patriarchate.[5] But Antony was deeply invested in the liturgy as well. Upon reading Antony's remarks on the liturgy, it is tempting to hastily categorize him as a conservative who was opposed to change, but a careful reading of his rationale for retaining the liturgy discloses his conviction that people simply need to engage it more actively, beginning with the clergy.

Metropolitan Antony on the Church Interior

Several examples illustrate Antony's approach to the liturgy. During the course of the deliberations on liturgical reform, some clergy and people observed that the traditional Russian iconostasis functioned as a barrier between the people and the clergy and enhanced the people's passive participation in the liturgy. These observations led to proposals that the iconostasis be modified or even removed from churches. Antony referred to contemporary examples of Orthodox

5. The following essays present an overview of the relevant topics: Nikolai Artemov, "О сотериологии митрополита Антония (Храповицкого)" ["On the Soteriology of Metropolitan Antonii (Khrapovitsky)"], in *Metropolitan Antonii* 19-68; and Samuel Nedelsky, "Archbishop Antony (Khrapovitskii), Imiaslavie, and Hesychasm," in *Metropolitan Antonii (Khrapovitskii): Archpastor of the Russian Diaspora*, 69-91.

church buildings in Petersburg and Sergiev Posad that did not have iconostases.[6] Antony states that churches like these have a "purely western character," complete with statues and decorated in a rococo style. Antony states that the churches have open altars with the liturgical activities of the clergy visible to all, and asks, "is this good?"[7]

Antony then reflects on the people's desire to petition God for his divine mercy throughout history, and how the faithful have traditionally followed the path of repentance and humility, gifts granted to them from the martyrs and ancient venerable fathers.[8] Antony focuses on the faithful Christian's sense of unworthiness to justify the practice of separating the laity from the mystical aspects of liturgical celebration occurring in the sanctuary:[9]

> Here is that consciousness of unworthiness, that repentant attitude and separation of the holy of holies of the Christian temple from the praying people, the mystery of the holy activities of the altar concealed from his eyes (except for Bright Week), just as the radiant face of Moses was concealed from the people.

Antony advocates for a healthy separation of the people from the mystical liturgical celebration at the altar for their own good. He was aware of the question that would naturally follow such a teaching, and he attributes the laity's questioning of the holiness of their contemporary clergy, in comparison with saints such as Athanasius the Great. He asserts that "even more difficult restrictions are placed on priests," who are required to fulfill obligations such as reciting the entrance prayers before the liturgy, performing prostrations and penances, calling upon the Holy Spirit before performing the mysteries, and prostrating and requesting forgiveness before Holy

---

6. Archbishop Antony (Khrapovitsky), "Преданіе или произволъ?" ("Tradition or arbitrariness?") Вера и разумъ (p. 414) (1914), 157.
7. Ibid., 157.
8. Ibid., 158.
9. Ibid.

Communion.[10] Antony assures the reader that such requirements are not to be found in ancient liturgical books; their purpose is to "gradually remove the spirit of the priest from sin and from the world and to lift him up to God."[11]

Metropolitan Antony on the *ars celebrandi*

The spiritual burden carried by the priest is efficacious; his role as the mediator for the community cannot be compromised in any way, which requires his complete attention and concentration on liturgical presidency. Antony was thoroughly devoted to cultivating clergy who approached liturgical presidency with gravitas. Antony viewed the prospect of an open altar as a temptation for the priest to forsake his sacred duty of liturgical presidency to please the people instead:[12]

> Aware that all of their prayerful actions are visible to the people, priests will no longer be concerned with the fact that the Lord God, and the angels, and the saints see them, but will think about how to pray affectively, and like the Polish Catholic priests, gradually convert from prayerful men into actors, into affected people, and in this way make their service loathsome before God.

Antony states that this style of liturgical presidency was adopted among the Latins and was akin to religious theater, resulting in the people's boredom and consequential decision to leave the Church.[13] Antony expressed thanks that the churches of Rus' had preserved canonical forms of the temple, and a purely ecclesial spirit of iconography, singing and chanting, and the possibility of observing the entirety of the liturgical requirements of the office. In short, there

---

10. Ibid.
11. Ibid., 159.
12. Ibid.
13. Antony claimed that five-hundred thousand Parisians did not attend church for Sunday Mass on account of the liturgical style adopted by their priests in ibid., 159.

is a significant difference between the ecclesial style of architecture and music and that belonging to the world.

Antony's cultivation of clergy who were devoted to excellent liturgical presidency emerges in one of his lectures.[14] Again, he appears to promote a conservative approach to the liturgy in this lecture. In commenting on the theological debates of his times, he dismisses the notion that Christianity can be reduced to loving one's neighbor. Antony argues one first has to learn how to love God through tradition (the liturgy), and only then can one love one's neighbor. He then goes on to criticize those who depict the Typikon as having a particular provenance belonging to a monastery, namely the Palestinian monastery of St. Sabbas—he states that the entire Church has received the Typikon and views it as holy, divine, and required for the whole Church. He also states that for one-thousand years many bishops and priests have vowed to observe it.[15] Antony sharply criticizes clerical ignorance on the Typikon, especially the failure of so many clergy to read slowly, to sing the holy stichera, to perform the prostrations, to make the sign of the cross properly. He complains that the presider becomes an actor, concerned with entertaining the people as opposed to attending to the service, or to infuse an individualistic style into his celebration.[16]

Metropolitan Antony on the Priest as Celebrant and Teacher

The onus of responsibility for good liturgical celebration in the parish obviously falls on the clergy. Antony compares two models of clergy: one that is obsessed with his own individualistic piety, and the other who works closely with the people of the parish to

14. Metropolitan Antony, *О Пастыре, Пастырстве, и объ исповеди* (On the Pastor, Ministry, and on Confession), ed. Archbishop Nikon (New York: East American and Canadian Eparchy, 1966), 285-91.
15. Ibid., 286-87.
16. Ibid., 288.

competently perform the required liturgical elements. Priests who distort the significance of liturgy are guilty of falling prey to false delusions, and the first of these is vanity. Antony's caricature of the inattentive priest who dishonors the Typikon concentrates on clergy who perform private prayers during the liturgy:[17]

> The second delusion is extreme solitude (individualism) in prayer, when the priest-celebrant gazes during public worship, as if it was personally essential only for him. This often happens with Great Russian priests: they disregard the words of the Apostle (Paul): 'you are giving thanks well, but your brother is not edified.' I precisely identify the kind of priests who through essentially all of worship think about the commemoration of the living and the dead and for most of the duration of Orthros and liturgy putter at the table of oblation, not following or hearing the service, but muttering to themselves during the third hour and more: 'Maria, Daria, Simeon' and so on. Others often read the canons for Holy Communion in the altar with zeal, but themselves do not pay attention to the prescribed canon and how it is to be performed on the kliros.

Antony's critique illuminates his sense of the clergy's lack of engagement with the liturgy: they are so preoccupied with their own private devotions that on some occasions, they are not even following the order of service. For Antony, the problem of clergy succumbing to their own individualistic style of liturgical leadership violates the whole purpose of the Typikon, which establishes order for the services.[18] Like his uncharitable description of Catholic liturgy in his discourse on the iconostasis, here Antony attributes these aspects of liturgical individualism to Latin influence.[19] The Latin

17. Ibid., 289.
18. Ibid., "These two deviations from Christian piety exhaust almost all deviations from the Church's Typikon, if one does not consider again laziness, carelessness and ignorance."
19. Ibid., 290. Here, Antony identifies several glaring omissions from liturgical life as particularly nefarious, such as the absence of observing the Praises of the Theotokos and the Liturgy of Holy Saturday, and even the burial of children without the rite of burial ("допущеніе погребать детей безъ отпеваніе").

influence also results in the selection of poor music for worship; Antony presents parishes that cultivate Church chant traditions as modular, as opposed to those that rely on the music of "contemporary composers."[20]

Antony briefly describes the model of priest who disavows individualism and approaches liturgical presidency in an appropriate manner:[21]

> Priests are doing well when they review the entire service with the cantor and choir director on Friday or Saturday, following the Octoechos and Menaion or the Triodion, pointing out the combination of Troparia at Vespers, Orthros and Liturgy, telling them to check the appointed tones of the Octoechos and Menaion at rehearsal, and to permit (if possible) to instruct the singers at rehearsal and the laity at Orthros the difficult phrases in the heirmoi, stichera, and Troparia.

Antony suggests that attention to the interpretation of central ecclesial hymns and prayers such as "Gladsome Light," the Cherubikon, and the Creed at seminary will plants the seeds of love for ecclesial chant in seminarians, who are (presumably) the shepherds of parishes.[22] For Antony, learning and teaching the beauty of Orthodox worship is the catalyst for igniting faith and love in parishioners. Antony establishes high expectations for parish clergy and their task is manifold. They are to rediscover authentic Orthodox liturgy untouched by Western influences, which begin with the Typikon and its order of divine services and are expressed primarily through traditional liturgical aesthetics. Clergy themselves are the models for observing the rules of the Typikon: if clergy disavow their own individual piety and attend to the liturgy while teaching its

20. Ibid. Antony's disdain for the use of contemporary music in the Russian church is manifested by his identifying Greeks, Georgians, Arabs, Southern Slavs, and Moldovans who perform "angelic chants" ("ангельскіе напевы") as opposed to Petersburg, which moved liturgical practices in conformity with "western heretics."

21. Ibid., 291.

22. Ibid.

structures and nuances to the singers and people with the same zeal, then they will provide the people with the spiritual sources of faith and love.

Metropolitan Antony's Liturgical Example

Antony's career as an archpastor and instructor was marked by several instances illustrating his conviction that the key to building up the life of the Church resided in cultivating clergy devoted to excellence in liturgical presidency. Sophia Senyk elucidates Antony's admiration for the steadfast observance of liturgical traditions in Pochaiv during his tenure as archbishop of Volyn' and Zhitomyr.[23] Antony idealized the liturgical practice of the Lavra of St. Job of Pochaiv, remarking that "church services even in our times constitute nine tenths of the forces building up the Church" in a letter to V. K. Sabler.[24] Senyk reports that Antony's admiration for the monastery's practice did not extend to the parishes and cathedrals, where pastors adjusted the liturgy to make it suitable for their communities.[25] Following a seemingly universal episcopal tradition, Antony embarked on an enterprise to establish liturgical uniformity in his diocese:[26]

> One of Antonij's first undertakings was to correct this, beginning with what was to set an example, his own cathedral. The first all-night vigil he celebrated at the cathedral, without any omissions, he wrote to the ober-prokuror, almost killed the cathedral rector.

Antony's undertaking included an instruction to diocesan clergy, monastics, and chanters to carefully read the Typikon and its

23. Sophia Senyk, "Antonij Xrapovickij in Volyn': 1902-1914," in *Metropolitan Antonii (Khrapovitskii): Archpastor of the Russian Diaspora*, ed. Tsurikov (Jordanville, NY: Foundation of Russian History, 2014), 249-54.
24. Quoted from Senyk, ibid., 250.
25. Ibid.
26. Ibid. Senyk cites a letter from Antony to the Ober-Prokurator of the Russian Church holy synod written in 1902.

instructions for the celebration of the vigil and the performance of bows and prostrations; the Typikon was the primary source of liturgical learning for the clergy.[27] Antony established the model for liturgy himself, as he and his vicars "celebrated the liturgy four times a week" during Lent, with Antony instructing priests to follow their example and attempt to hold services every day.[28] Metropolitan Laurus asserted that Antony exerted the most influence during his tenure in Volyn' though his devotion to building up the liturgical life, setting the example during Lent by serving "every Wednesday, Saturday, and Sunday, and serving every day beginning with Lazarus Saturday until Thomas Sunday . . . without failure, he preached at every liturgy."[29]

This brief review of Metropolitan Antony's teachings on the liturgy yields several threads which will prove to be influential in the life of ROCOR. First and foremost, there is no doubt that Antony did not support a surgical approach to liturgical reform. Antony perceived the received liturgical tradition as pristine. The problem in Russian liturgical praxis did not lie with the order of services listed in the Typikon, which Antony interpreted as a repository of holy tradition that warranted reception with thanksgiving. Antony was convinced that the clergy's neglect of the received tradition was the chief catalyst causing decay and the absence of understanding the liturgy among the people. The clergy's unwitting reception of Western influences in the liturgy, especially in liturgical aesthetics, caused a domino effect in parish life. The people simply mirrored the clergy's approach to the liturgy: if the clergy exuded extreme individualism in the liturgy, preferring to ignore the order of services

27. Ibid.
28. Ibid.
29. Metropolitan Laurus (Shkurla), "Наследие митрополита Антония (Храповицкого)" ("The Legacy of Metropolitan Antony Khrapovistky") in *Metropolitan Antonii (Khrapovitskii): Archpastor of the Russian Diaspora*, ed. Tsurikov, 14.

and attending to their own private devotions, then it followed that the people would do likewise, ignoring the offices while engaging private devotions. Antony identified the delusion of such individualism as the chief cause of the problem, which explains why he attempted to establish chief models. His model was the strict observance of the monastic Typikon, exemplified by the pattern he established for liturgy during his episcopal tenure in Volyn', idealizing the liturgy of the Lavra of St. Job of Pochaiv and frequently presiding himself with during the Lenten period.

However, it is not accurate to hastily label Antony as a liturgical conservative who desired to impose monastic liturgical maximalism on the people. While he was a proponent of liturgical uniformity, he was also keenly sensitive to the need to encourage the faithful to actively participate in the liturgy. For Antony, diocesan clergy were responsible for modeling active liturgical participation, and it was this deep engagement in the liturgy that would lead one to discover and interiorize love for God and for one's neighbor. Antony's repetitive references to cultivating a musical life and encouraging priests to instruct the singers on the significance of the Church's hymnography discloses his awareness of the thin distinction between entertainment and authentic engagement in the liturgy.

Metropolitan Antony on Confession and Communion

Furthermore, Antony's liturgical theology is somewhat complex. On the one hand, he repeatedly referred to existing structures of the liturgical tradition as the paths to salvation for the faithful. On the other hand, he encouraged the faithful to deepen their engagement with the liturgy, including more frequent participation in Holy Communion. Antony's instruction to priests on the mystery of Confession illustrates the fusion of his devotion to the order and rules of the Typikon with his desire for frequent participation in the liturgy. Antony instructs priests to enforce the following juridical elements of confession inscribed in the Orthodox liturgical books:[30]

> Each time you must precede confession with a detailed and inspiring sermon, or even more than one. In the first one, exhort people to sincere repentance before God and to a sincere confession of sins before their spiritual father. In the second one, which you will deliver at the reading of the prayers of the rite of confession, recall what penances were prescribed by the Church at the Ecumenical Councils and read out several of them from the Trebnik. . . . Then read the words of the Nomocanons in the Trebnik by which it is permitted to reduce the penances on account of tearful repentance, fasting, almsgiving, or tonsure into the monastic order, and explain that without these conditions—without great contrition of heart and ascetic struggles—the sins of perhaps the majority of those standing before you would prevent them from being allowed to take Communion . . . remind those standing before you of the self-evident truth, that, even if a priest has the great daring to admit great sinners to Communion when they have offered sincere repentance, he still has absolutely no right to do the same for those Christians who do not admit some notorious sin of their to be sinful, or even admit that it is sinful but do not express any determination to stop it, desiring to continue in their sinful state—for example, of illicit cohabitation.

I have cited this text at length to elucidate Antony's pastoral initiative of reinvigorating the liturgical tradition to build up the Church into a body of holy people. In this lecture, Antony refers the priest-confessor to his liturgical book as the source for everything he needs to explain the gravity of repentance in the life of the Christian. The Trebnik (literally "book of needs") contains both the liturgical and the canonical sources needed by the priest to exhort the faithful to repentance. This small excerpt from a series of lectures on confession shows that Antony was devoted to cultivating outstanding clergy

---

30. Metropolitan Antony (Khrapovitsky), *Confession: A Series of Lectures on the Mystery of Repentance*, trans. Father Christopher Birchall (Jordanville, New York: Holy Trinity Monastery, 1983), 24–25.

who would serve as the models for equally outstanding Christians: he wanted the clergy to set the bar high for the people.

His reference to observing the canons exudes ecclesial conservatism, but he promotes this conservatism through a reinvigorated sacramental life. His instruction that the priest preach about confession, more than once, demonstrates his commitment to reconstructing a liturgical ecclesiology; in this instance, the priest exhorts the faithful to receive confession within the liturgical assembly itself. Antony's admonition to clergy on admitting faithful to communion responsibly coheres with his instructions on learning the Typikon. He was infusing accountability into the culture of the clergy under his pastoral leadership. The model the faithful are called to emulate is certainly monastic, and the clergy are responsible for demonstrating it to them. Most important, Antony wants the people to receive confession; his liturgical program disavows minimalism, which would permit the people to partake of confession once a year during Great Lent or another fasting period.

Antony's attempt to reinvigorate the liturgical life through more frequent participation in Holy Communion is communicated in this same lecture on Confession:[31]

> Try to give Christians Communion not only in the Great Lent, but also in the others, and in the Great Lent, not only on Saturdays, but also on Wednesdays, Fridays, and Sundays, and on the Annunciation and on Polyeleos days when the Presanctified is appointed. Either do it this way, or else persuade them to confess not only on the eve of Communion but also on the preceding days.

This excerpt again demonstrates Antony's attempt to subvert liturgical minimalism in the Russian Church, which would permit the Christian to receive Confession once during Lent. Here, he attempts to expand the priest's ministry so that faithful can approach

---

31. Ibid., 26.

both sacraments on all the days the Liturgy of Presanctified Gifts can be celebrated on the weekdays of Lent. Antony does not compromise the austerity connected with Orthodox notions of sanctity; his initiative directs clergy to infuse a sense of desire among the people to seek lives interiorizing and exteriorizing such sanctity, beginning with seeking repentance, engaging it in truth, and as a result, participating in Holy Communion.

Metropolitan Antony sought to build up the Church by encouraging the people to deepen their engagement in the liturgical life of the Church. The most important component of Antony's mechanism was the cultivation of clergy who would observe the Typikon in its fullness and model the blessings one will reap from participation in good liturgical presidency and modeling a life of sanctity. Earlier, I stated that the platform for liturgical reform in the Russian Church failed on account of the Bolshevik Revolution. The inheritors of this platform cultivated and implemented it in immigration, namely Kyprian Kern and Alexander Schmemann. The cultivation of this alternative approach to the liturgy was also implemented in immigration, when Orthodox Russians established ROCOR under Antony's leadership when it became clear that the Moscow Patriarchate would never enjoy freedom under Soviet rule.

Antony's liturgical theology conforms to Thomas Pott's notion of converting the faithful to the liturgy in his taxonomy of reform.[32] In the remainder of this chapter, I will elaborate the unique features of ROCOR's liturgical legacy by pursuing the most salient threads of Antony's liturgical platform. Antony's legacy is not unique on account of his originality; he was one of many conservatives in Russia who believed that the clergy's irresponsible ignorance of the Typikon

32. Thomas Pott, *Byzantine Liturgical Reform: A Study of Liturgical Change in the Byzantine Tradition*, trans. Paul Meyendorff, Orthodox Liturgy Series, Book 2 (Crestwood, NY: St. Vladimir's Seminary Press, 2010), 96.

was the chief catalyst to liturgical and ecclesial decay. Antony's legacy is important because his Church, ROCOR, upheld it with unusual fidelity. The mechanisms employed by ROCOR in upholding this liturgical tradition are informative for our understanding of liturgical reform in all of its variants. In the remainder of this chapter, I will present the following aspects of ROCOR's liturgical reform which hearken back, in some way, to Antony's leadership: the role of the bishop in cultivating clergy who model liturgical maximalism (especially Saint John Maximovich of Shanghai and San Francisco), the meaning of liturgical maximalism in ROCOR and the Church's resilience to external pressures in a new cultural environment, and the cultivation of liturgical aesthetics through education in liturgical music.

Liturgical Maximalism

Above, I introduced the liturgical legacy of ROCOR by reviewing Metropolitan Antony's liturgical theology. Antony's conviction that an authentic observance of the received liturgical tradition was the best possible catalyst for the building up of the life of the Church and leading the faithful to love God and their neighbor lays the foundation for a sophisticated definition of liturgical maximalism. This maximalism is manifold: it is fiercely anti-minimalist, viewing the haphazard omission of services and liturgical elements as the primary cause of liturgical decay in the Church. The minimalist approach also promoted individualism among the people and the clergy, creating a vicious cycle of liturgical disengagement that caused problems permeating society as a whole. Antony was a vocal proponent of maximalism during his tenure in Russia, and his maximalist approach accompanied him abroad and into ROCOR, along with other like-minded Church leaders. In this section, I will review select approaches to the liturgy promulgated by other

ROCOR figures, and will show how this maximalism resulted in an approach to the liturgy promoted within the Church by its clergy and teachers.

St. John Maximovich

Numerous sources present the narrative story of St. John Maximovich.[33] St. John was a disciple of Metropolitan Antony and his cultivation of the Synodal-era Russian liturgical ethos. Because the story of St. John's life has been narrated in association with his glorification, many of his teachings on the liturgy have been published and provide precious insight into his own liturgical initiatives in Harbin and San Francisco.

St. John was particularly beloved in San Francisco by the immigrants who arrived there from Shanghai and Harbin. After his ordination to the episcopacy in 1934, he was assigned Bishop of Shanghai and arrived there in 1935.[34] His ministry was energetic, beginning by resolving conflicts and brokering peace between immigrant Serbs, Greeks, and Ukrainians.[35] He devoted special energies towards helping children and performing frequent hospital visits. Protopresbyter Elias Wan stated that St. John founded an orphanage and prioritized visiting people: "because Vladika John was very busy from morning till night, he was almost always late to

---

33. St. John's official title is John, Archbishop of Shanghai and San Francisco, the Wonderworker. The principal source is the hagiography in its third edition by Peter Perekrestov, *Владыка Иоанн—Святитель Русского Зарубежья, 3d ed., Серия "Житиа святых"* (Vladyka John—A Saint of the Russian Diaspora) (Moscow: Strentensky Monastery, 2009). A shorter version of the hagiographical narrative appears in Peter Perekrestov, *Man of God: Saint John of Shanghai and San Francisco* (Richfield Springs, New York: Nikodemus Orthodox Publication Society, 2012). Also see *Святитель Іоаннъ (Максимовичъ) и Русская Зарубежная Церковь* (Saint John (Maximovich and the Russian Church Abroad) (Jordanville, NY: Holy Trinity Monastery, 1996), and *Service and Akathist to Our Father Among the Saints John, Archbishop of Shanghai and San Francisco, The Wonderworker* (San Francisco: Russkiy pastyr, 2013).
34. *Святитель Іоаннъ (Максимовичъ) и Русская Зарубежная Церковь*, 11.
35. Ibid.

services. He ran about all day long, visiting hospitals and homes. He had no concept of time; he didn't even wear a watch."[36]

St. John was a promoter of liturgical and ascetical austerity. Wan offered a precious glimpse into St. John's devotion to maintaining the order of divine services in two memorable quotes:[37]

> Vladika John served Liturgy every day, all year round. Different priests would assist him in rotation. The services were very long. With his arrival, Vespers took place in the evening together with Compline. During Compline, at the very beginning of the service, there were always readings from one of the three canons to the saints. At six o'clock in the morning was the Midnight Office, followed by Matins and Liturgy. Vladika John . . . insisted that all verses appointed to be sung, be sung and not read. . . . He was very strict with the clergy. . . . Many people didn't like the fact that the services lasted so long. . . . In Shanghai there were pastoral meetings every Thursday. If someone was absent, he demanded a full explanation. At these meetings, most of the time was spent on questions of how to serve. Vladika would ask the priests about certain unique aspects of some of the upcoming services, testing their knowledge.

St. John's emphasis on preserving the fullness of the liturgical cycle is remarkable for an émigré Orthodox community and testifies to his liturgical ethos. Above, I mentioned that Antony concentrated his efforts on cultivating fidelity to strict liturgical observance among the clergy, and this was a pastoral quality shared by St. John. St. John reiterates the fact that the clergy must always serve as a model for their flock in an exhortation reflecting on the relationship between pastoral ministry and engagement in public affairs for clergy. St. John distinguishes the clergy's roles from those of the laity, stating that the laity attends to worldly affairs while the pastor concentrates on spiritual matters, especially personal and communal prayer.[38]

---

36. Quoted by Fr. Perekrestov in *Man of God*, 65.
37. Ibid., 63–65.
38. Ibid., 232.

St. John's vision of clergy echoes Antony's, but St. John's strictness was not limited to the clergy. Father Peter Perekrestov explains a dilemma St. John confronted while in San Francisco in 1949 when the Russian community organized a concert on the eve of the Sunday of All Saints.[39] St. John admonished the people to refrain from attending the concert and instead attend the Vigil for this important feast of the liturgical year. The following morning, during the course of his homily, he admonished those who attended the concert and refused to permit them to receive Holy Communion until they repented. St. John read the prayer of absolution over them himself.

Zealous advocacy for a longsuffering flock and liturgical maximalism shape the narrative of St. John's life before he became bishop of San Francisco, and the arrival of thousands of immigrants from Shanghai to San Francisco bridge this gap. The problem of parishes scheduling social events on the eves of great feasts was widespread. In 1951, ROCOR's Synod of Bishops instructed pastors to convince the faithful to avoid scheduling such events on the eves of feasts and on Saturday evenings as these are the most intense preparatory liturgical offices for participation in the Divine Liturgy.[40]

After the cathedral in San Francisco was erected, St. John again directed his attention towards promoting education, establishing required theological courses for clergy and laity, arguing that the laity must be acquainted with Orthodoxy in order to teach it to their children.[41] He was also consistent in exhorting the people to sustain a rigorous liturgical life. In his life, he issued several liturgical

---

39. Perekrestov, *Владыка Иоанн—Святитель Русского Зарубежья*, 120-21.

40. See the resolution of the ROCOR's synod titled "Об увеселениях в канун воскресньіх и праздничньіх дней" ("On Amusements on the eves of Sundays and Feasts Days") in D. P. Anashkin, ed., *Законодательство Русской Православной Церкви Заграницей (1921-2007) (Legislation of the Russian Orthodox Church Outside of Russia, 1921-2007)* (Moscow: Foundation of Russian History, Publication of St. Tikhon's Orthodox University, 2013), 17-18.

41. Perekrestov, *Владыка Иоанн—Святитель Русского Зарубежья*, 239.

directives. In a homily delivered before Lent, St. John exhorted the people to receive Holy Communion frequently:[42]

> Communing of the body and blood of the Risen Christ unto life eternal—this is the aim of the holy Quadragesima (Forty Days). Not just on Pascha does one commune. On the contrary, on Pascha those people should commune who fasted, confessed and received the holy mysteries during Great Lent. Just before Pascha itself there is little opportunity for a proper and thorough confession; time and the priests are occupied with the Passion services. One must prepare ahead of time.

St. John's instruction is similar to Antony's; he calls upon the people to engage actively in the appointed services of Lent. Like Antony, St. John sought to eliminate minimalism among the clergy and laity, and in this instance, minimalism is limiting the reception of Communion to Pascha. For St. John, increased liturgical participation would permit the repentant Christian to receive Communion during Lent and again on Pascha. In another liturgical directive concerning the reception of Communion on Pascha, St. John remained consistent with his encouragement of lay Communion by exhorting the people to receive, which required them to stay for the full duration of a long order of services.[43]

He also issued a directive prohibiting faithful from enjoying entertainment on the eves of feast days: "those who attend a dance or similar form of entertainment and diversion may not participate in the choir the next day, may not serve in the altar, enter the altar or stand on the kliros."[44] He created a rule for all acolytes on proper behavior and disposition during church services, and the twentieth rule stated that those who "violate the 'Church rule for acolytes' will

---

42. Perekrestov, *Man of God*, 130.
43. "No one should leave the Church prematurely, rushing away to eat the meat of animals instead of receiving the most holy body and blood of Christ," from "Concerning the Reception of the Holy Mysteries on Pascha," (n. d.), Perekrestov, *Man of God*, 233.
44. Ibid., 234.

stand on the left kliros until the conclusion of the divine service," meaning that they would be prohibited from serving.[45]

St. John also issued rules for Church wardens and other adult parish leaders prohibiting them from entering the altar area and distracting the clergy from their prayers regardless of the reason, and instructing them to stand before the royal doors with the collection plates until they receive a blessing from a bishop or priest to commence the collection of donations.[46] St. John exhibited sensitivity to proper church singing in a short directive addressed to clergy and singers.[47] St. John's directive employs generic language concerning the singing, but one can detect his sensitivity to distinguishing between styles reminiscent of Antony, as he dismisses music which is only a "delight to the ear."[48]

St. John's teaching on church singing is remarkably coherent with Antony's disdain for music that entertains and preference for the use of traditional chant in the service. Antony had instructed clergy to lead both singers and the faithful in using the correct music and understanding it, a theme clearly present in St. John's statement. In his remembrance of St. John, Archimandrite Ambrose stated that St. John was both strict and forbearing, and was especially concerned about the order of divine services.[49] But St. John occasionally contradicted his own liturgical maximalism: another witness spoke of St. John's refusal to chastise a priest who abbreviated a Vigil so that it would last only 45 minutes.[50]

45. Perekrestov, *Владыка Иоанн—Святитель Русского Зарубежья*, 557-58.

46. St. John Maximovich, "О денежныхъ сборахъ во время богослужений" ("On monetary collections during worship"), in Anashkin, ed., *Законодательство Русской Православной Церкви Заграницей*, 12.

47. "Ukase addressed to clergy and church singers," in Perekrestov, *Man of God*, 238.

48. Ibid.

49. Perekrestov, *Man of God*, 30. Archimandrite Ambrose also said that St. John could be equally forgiving and understanding of mistakes.

50. Ibid., 53, quoting E. G. Chertkov.

St. John's instructions on the liturgy are less direct than Antony's. Antony's remarks are clearly directed towards diagnosing the problem with the celebration of the liturgy and providing a prognosis for a remedy, which resides primarily in the formation of clergy who are faithful to the Typikon. From this brief consideration of the evidence, we can conclude that St. John shared with Antony the same concern for preserving the received liturgical tradition. It is possible that St. John inherited this concern from Antony as well, but drawing such a conclusion would amount to conjecture, since many Russian bishops held the same opinion on this matter. It is clear that St. John promoted a priority of ROCOR in his liturgical austerity. By carefully selecting and cultivating clergy who would implement this program of liturgical maximalism, St. John contributed to Holy Virgin Cathedral's formation as a liturgical center exercising influence on ROCOR.

Michael Pomazansky and Liturgical Maximalism

Other representatives of ROCOR express the value of liturgical maximalism. In a collection of essays addressing a variety of topics, Father Michael Pomazansky delivers a sharp critique of Alexander Schmemann's liturgical theology.[51] Pomazansky was a native of Volyn', and came to know Antony, who assisted Pomazansky's career as a teacher of theology. Pomazansky taught at Holy Trinity Seminary in Jordanville in 1949, teaching there until his death in 1988. Pomazansky's critique of Schmemann is manifold: he is concerned with Schmemann's method and perceives Schmemann as having accepted the notion that the Typikon itself became an amalgamation of liturgical practices resulting in the loss of the ecclesiastical key one needs to interpret it. Pomazansky strongly

---

51. Michael Pomazansky, *Selected Essays* (Jordanville, NY: Holy Trinity Monastery, 1996).

disagrees with Schmemann here, and his explanation of the correct view of the Typikon is instructive:[52]

> The Typikon, in the form which it has come down to our time in its two basic versions, is the realized idea of Christian worship; the worship of the first century was a kernel which has grown and matured to its present state, having now taken its finished form. We have in mind, of course, not the content of the services, not the hymns and prayers themselves, which often bear the literary stamp of an era and are replaced one by another, but the very system of divine services, their order, concord, harmony, consistency of principles and fullness of God's glory and communion with the Heavenly Church on the one hand, and on the other the fullness of their expression of the human soul—from the Paschal hymns to the Great Lenten lamentation over moral falls. The present rule of divine services was already contained in the idea of the divine services of the first Christians in the same way that in the seed of a plant are already contained the forms of the plant's future growth up to the moment when it begins to bear mature fruits, or in the way that in the embryonic organism of a living creature its future form is already concealed.

Pomazansky argues that the received tradition is like a mature plant, having developed organically over time. The services themselves are authentic, and because the plant is a living organism, the liturgy is suitable for the contemporary Church.

Pomazansky states that attempts at development within liturgics—particularly aesthetics—symbolizes the approach of the end times for humankind.[53] Pomazansky is suspicious of Schmemann's method, musing that Schmemann sought to comment on the Typikon in such a way that would free it from the Western captivity, and concluding that Schmemann's work is indeed Western. More important for our purposes is Pomazansky's response to the caricature of the Typikon as irrelevant, since parishes cannot realistically

52. Ibid., 84–85.
53. Ibid., 85.

observe it.[54] Pomazansky uses the word "maximalism" to describe the liturgical ideal Orthodox should observe "based on the commandment, *pray without ceasing.*"[55] Pomazansky states that the complete order of services is retained even if a community does not observe it, and he expresses disappointment in the tendency of parishes to shorten or abbreviate the offices.

Pomazansky echoes the values we find in Antony and St. John. While Pomazansky acknowledges shortcomings in parish celebration, their purpose is to manifest the failures of clergy and laity to observe the rule of prayer. He repeats the problem of minimalism in his brief essay on encouraging children to participate in the life of the Church. Pomazansky asserts that adults who are responsible for the preparation and order of divine services should bear in mind the impact they have on children, asserting that attempts to tinker with the service in any way can impact children's attitudes towards church.[56]

Pomazansky emphasizes the need to provide children with opportunities for active participation in the actual services: "There is one thing that must not be forgotten: human nature requires at least a minimal degree of active participation. In church this can take the form either of reading, or of singing, serving in the altar, or of decorating and cleaning the church, or of some other activity, even if it is only indirectly connected with the services."[57] For Pomazansky, this responsibility requires attentiveness on the part of the adult to permitting an opportunity for young people to serve, beyond perfunctory activities such as handing the censer to a cleric.[58]

Like Antony and St. John, Pomazansky embraced the pastoral

54. Ibid., 86.
55. Ibid.
56. Ibid., 20.
57. Ibid., 21.
58. Ibid., 22.

impetus to create a liturgical environment that engages everyone. His discussion of liturgical maximalism is not limited to the notion of blind obedience to the forms of the Typikon the Church has received: he simply elaborates the notion of liturgical asceticism prevalent in ROCOR, that liturgy should be hard work, it should be authentic toil where one experiences the sensations of praying without ceasing in body, soul, and mind, because such vigilance is required for people who are striving for entrance into God's kingdom.

Valerii Lukianov on the Observance of the Typikon

ROCOR prioritized liturgical maximalism throughout its history by assiduously encouraging the clergy to observe the fullness of the liturgical services, even when they were discouraged when the laity did not attend divine offices. Protopresbyter Valerii Lukianov's compilation of "Worship Notes" ("Богослужебныя заметки") presents practical explanations on liturgical matters which were published in the ROCOR periodical "Православная Русь" over the course of many years.[59] The book is essentially a manual for clergy and musicians on how to perform elements of a variety of liturgical rites, from the Divine Liturgy to the special offices of the liturgical year.

The book begins with a brief bibliography of works the pastors can consult as a guide to liturgical questions, most of which concern the Typikon.[60] Lukianov then cites Pomazansky on the significance of the Typikon and how it is oriented to shape the daily life of the faithful.[61] The next question addresses the matter of "worship

59. Protopresbyter Valerii Lukianov, *Богослужебныя заметки: Опытъ разъясненія практической стороны богослуженія Православной Церкви (Liturgical Notes: Expert Explanations of Practical Aspects of the Liturgy of the Orthodox Church)* , third ed. (Jordanville, NY: St. Job of Pochaev, Holy Trinity Monastery, 2006).
60. Ibid., 15-17.

in the temple in the absence of worshippers."[62] Lukianov's remarks demonstrate a reflection on a common pastoral challenge, with the encouragement to observe the fullness of the appointed liturgical order without compromise:[63]

> In our days of spiritual decline, when in some parishes it is difficult for worshippers and singers to assemble for Vespers, priests, justifying this impoverishment to themselves, cease serving the Vigil of Sunday, and, at best, restrict the service to an abridged Matins before the liturgy.

After explaining the absence of the people from Matins as a result of their unfamiliarity with a new order for worship, Lukianov upholds the value of observing the fullness of the prescribed order by referring to a conversation between a parish priest and Igumen Nazari from the Valaam monastery, where the priest claimed that he did not offer services for an empty temple. According to Lukianov, Igumen Nazari stated that "the temple cannot be empty . . . an angel who is the guardian of the altar of the Lord is found there. And then, if worshippers do not come forth, angels come forth, the protectors of their souls, for at every doxology of God angels are present first . . . and they would fill your church."[64] In other words, the angels populate the church on behalf of the people, even if the faithful are absent from liturgy. The pastor's duty is to offer the liturgical doxology to God in its fullness without taking attendance into account.

Metropolitan Laurus's Remarks on Liturgy to Seminary Graduates

The liturgical maxmalism of ROCOR is threaded throughout its whole history and continues to thrive today. In a more recent

61. Ibid., 21.
62. Ibid., 22.
63. Ibid.
64. Ibid.

document, the address of Metropolitan Laurus to graduates of Holy Trinity Seminary in Jordanville, Laurus champions similar notions of liturgical maximalism.[65] Laurus iterates the notion of the Typikon as a repository for the Orthodox way of life, a school of piety and a "real theological school, instructing us in all our theological sciences through live, colorful images and highly inspired, prayerful expressions."[66]

After a description of the riches offered by the liturgy for the salvation of the Christian, Laurus painfully diagnoses the problem:

> What do we observe in actuality in our times? For the significant majority of believers, this greatest of spiritual riches has become unapproachable, it seems to be hidden under a bushel; it remains completely unused. The reason for this . . . lies in the secularization of life, in the departure from the Church, which began long ago among our Russian society . . . as a result of an imprudent rapprochement with the West and a flippant enthusiasm for anti-Christian, Western pseudo-culture. In society different secular interests and aspirations, as opposed to spiritual ones, began to dominate. Genuine, living faith began to weaken and people became weary of true services conducted according to the actual Typikon. Services were shortened. As a result of this process, as can be observed in contemporary parishes, only the skeleton of the services remains.[67]

Laurus goes on to critique the abbreviations of the services and the adoption of "complicated, concert pieces" in the singing of the services, which results in monotony at liturgy.[68] The people "lose interest," and people no longer attend all-night Vigils.[69] The similarity of Laurus's diagnosis in the late-twentieth century with Antony's almost one-hundred years ago, separated not only by time,

---

65. Metropolitan Laurus (Shkurla), "The Significance of the Practical Study of Liturgics," *Orthodox Life* 45 (1995): 42–48.
66. Ibid., 43.
67. Ibid., 44–45.
68. Ibid., 45.
69. Ibid.

but also by region and culture, is remarkable. The problem for liturgy remains the same: the decay is caused by carelessness and laziness and is most manifest in the liturgical aesthetics (music and iconography), leading to the people's disengagement with the liturgy. It is clear that the same thread of thought concerning the liturgy was maintained among the leaders of ROCOR.

It is prudent to add Laurus's prognosis for the liturgy, keeping in mind that this speech was delivered to graduates of the seminary, many of whom would embark on parish assignments:[70]

> The divine services should cultivate in the faithful the spirit of Orthodoxy and not the *prelest* of the West. Unlawful Western chant and realistic art invading our churches obviously can only foster the spirit of Western ecstatic, seducing *prelest*, destructive to souls but in no way in the spirit of genuine Orthodox piety. . . . Thus, Liturgics should be the inspiring study of the living richness of the Church, which is to be found in our divine service books and, besides, should not be separate from external expression in Church chant and art. Such a mission we at Holy Trinity Seminary try to fulfill, according to our abilities and strength.

Laurus also noted that non-Orthodox who express interest in Orthodoxy in the diaspora are drawn to the Church on account of its chant and iconography. Clearly, for Laurus, the key to reinvigorating authentic Orthodoxy in ROCOR was to cultivate clergy who were faithful patrons of liturgical aesthetics. The similarity of his message with Antony's delivered over one-hundred years ago in imperial Russia is much more remarkable for our purposes.

Archbishop Averky on Retaining Liturgical Tradition

The late Archbishop Averky (Taushev) also encouraged the steadfast observance of liturgical order and traditions in ROCOR as the authentic Orthodox way. Archbishop Averky's teaching on the

---

70. Ibid., 47.

significance of the liturgy is relevant on account of his tenure as rector of Holy Trinity Seminary in ROCOR, which began in 1952, and the hope expressed by the late Metropolitan Laurus that future generations of seminarians would use the text as a primary source for understanding the liturgy.[71]

Archbishop Averky made frequent speaking appearances in parishes in addition to his teaching ministry at Holy Trinity Seminary, and his book on the liturgy was intended to serve as a textbook for seminarians and clergy. His book is somewhat similar in the collection of essays by Lukianov in that it emphasizes the practical dimension of liturgical celebration, but Averky's monograph also has a systematic presentation on worship as liturgical theology as well as an explanation of various aspects of Russian Orthodox liturgiology.

Archbishop Averky's book is a demonstration of ROCOR's adherence to liturgical maximalism in the inclusion of two appendices to the book. The first appendix discusses the history of the Typikon and the possibility of reforming it to simplify parish liturgy.[72] This section refers to the work of the All-Russian Council of 1917–1918 which considered the possibility of taking on Church reforms. This appendix republishes the lecture of Ivan Karabinov titled "Concerning the Typikon: the Church Order." The decision to include this essay serves two purposes: first, it is an homage to Averky's consistent appeal for students and clergy to attend to liturgical history, since Karabinov introduces the Constantinopolitan and Jerusalemite elements of the Typikon in his essay. Second, Karabinov asserted that the history of the Typikon yielded historical information that one cannot ignore in considering a reform of the Typikon, including the fact that the Typikon is neither purely nor

---

71. Archbishop Averky (Taushev), *Литургика* (*Liturgics*) (Jordanville, NY: St. Job of Pochaev Press, Holy Trinity Monastery, 2000).
72. Ibid., 491–507.

solely of monastic provenance, and that the regional contributors to the Typikon—Constantinople and Jerusalem—offered elements that are both ancient and of immeasurable value.[73] Karabinov's caution against hurrying to reform supports ROCOR's general liturgical conservatism, especially the prevailing notion of the liturgy as a living organism bearing apostolic elements that are precious.

Of equal relevance is Averky's description of the Orthodox liturgy as humanity's encounter with God, a definition Averky presents in juxtaposition with the decadence of Roman Catholic and Protestant worship. Averky states that the Catholic Church has adopted the course of reform following Vatican II, and the liturgical reform introduced new vestments, the placement of the altar in the middle of the church, and the positioning of the clergy with their back to the altar, facing the people.[74] Averky describes the sources and motives for Roman Catholic liturgical reform:[75]

> In this way, Roman Catholicism went on the path of Protestantism. Now Roman Catholics can create the breaking of worship at any time depending on the circumstances. We are aware of the encounters of the Roman Pope with leaders of other faiths, he participated in prayers of non Christians, for example with those who pray in tongues, Jews, and Muslims.

In describing Protestant worship, Averky follows a similar trajectory by arguing that Protestant worship has a strong ecumenical character, evidenced by Protestant participation in the World Council of Churches, which has permitted non-Christian elements to permeate Protestant worship.[76] Averky depicts Orthodox liturgy as differing from Catholic and Protestant on account of Orthodoxy's unbroken connection to the ancient Church.[77] The changes in and additions to

73. Ibid., 506-7.
74. Archbishop Averky, 17.
75. Ibid., 17-18.
76. Ibid., 18.

Orthodox worship are attributable to the "Church living her gracious life," which required "new services for newly-glorified saints, [and] the appearance of new offices and prayers for various needs."[78] Averky asserts that "it is necessary for each Orthodox Christian to know the history and development of worship (even a little), so that participating in public worship, he might clearly comprehend its mystical meaning, for with this he will not know how and why it is celebrated, nor will he understand its meaning."[79]

ROCOR's concern for upholding the fullness of the divine services was associated with the use of liturgical books. The idea that an officially published liturgical book bears the full authority of the Church is quite common in Christianity, and ROCOR follows this pattern. ROCOR's synod of bishops prohibited ROCOR clergy from publishing their own local liturgical books from local use; the directive included a reference to "new prayer books" and "other liturgical texts."[80]

ROCOR consistently encouraged clergy to use the texts published by ROCOR's St. Job of Pochaev Press in Jordanville: the Synod instructed clergy to maintain a library of liturgical books published "in-house" while discouraging them from adding books from non-Orthodox publishers or dubious jurisdictions.[81] The use of liturgical books published by ROCOR promotes simultaneous observance of ROCOR's preference for liturgical fullness and its privileging of

---

77. Ibid., 20. In fact, Averky attributes the idea that contemporary Orthodox worship differs from that of the ancient church to the influence of people of other faiths who "have an unfriendly disposition towards our Orthodox worship."

78. Ibid., 20.

79. Ibid., 20-21.

80. ROCOR Synod of Bishops, "О самовольном составлении церковных служб" ("On the unauthorized compilation of Church services"), in Anashkin, ed., *Законодательство Русской Православной Церкви Заграницей*, 21.

81. See "Руководственные правила для священнослужителей Русской Православной Церкви Заграницей" ("Guiding Rules for the Clergy of the Russian Orthodox Church Outside of Russia"), in Anashkin, ed., *Законодательство Русской Православной Церкви Заграницей*, 161.

the chant tradition of liturgical music, evidenced by the Synod's encouragement of clergy to use the book of chants published by Jordanville's St. Job of Pochaev Press for correct church singing.[82]

Archbishop Averky's description of the meaning and purpose of Orthodox liturgy is consistent with Antony's, Pomazansky's, Lukianov's, and Laurus's. First, Averky views the Orthodox liturgy as the natural continuation of apostolic liturgy, with additions occurring on the basis of practical necessity. Second, Orthodox liturgy differs from Catholic and Protestant worship the latter are inspired and shaped by ecumenical dialogue and break tradition by permitting reform. Third, the study of Orthodox liturgical history is necessary before the consideration of any reform, as demonstrated by Karabinov's conclusions on the history of the Typikon presented at the 1917 council. Averky's remarks on the liturgy confirm our hypothesis on ROCOR as an adherent of liturgical maximalism because of the consistency of his opinion with those of other major figures and his influential position as rector and teacher at Holy Trinity Seminary in Jordanville.

John Townsend on Observing the Full Order of Services

The retention of liturgical maximalism in ROCOR evokes the possibility of promoting maximalism as theological medicine that can be given the Church uniformly. ROCOR conceives of the received tradition as suitable for all environments and times, as evidenced by a lecture delivered by Father John Townsend on the topic of prayer and worship at the Southern Orthodox Conference in 1998.[83] Townsend condemns the prevalence of minimalism introduced by

---

82. See the Synodal directive "О церковном пении" ("On Church Singing" (1959)), in Anashkin, ed., *Законодательство Русской Православной Церкви Заграницей*, 38-39.

83. John Townsend, "Order of Prayer and Worship for Orthodox Faithful," *Orthodox Life* 48 (1998), 29-39.

secular culture, and depicts the liturgy as having an eternal character that warrants its strict observance by contemporary Orthodox Christians:[84]

> Are we today less in need of unceasing prayer than were our ancestors? Are we less in need of worship than the holy martyrs? Do we have some right or obligation to shorten the Services of the Church to make them more acceptable to men of our day, to keep people from thinking that we have completely lost our minds? Do we accede to the complaint that people simply will not attempt to fulfill the ancient discipline of prayer and worship? Is our world substantially different from theirs? The answer to all these questions is a completely logical and practical 'no!'

Townsend engages the arguments for adjusting the Church Typikon that depend on contemporary socio-economic conditions. For example, he acknowledges that people no longer live close to church and are busy with work and school, but he dismisses these choices as a voluntary reduction of the Church as "just one aspect of our busy lives."[85]

Townsend argues that Orthodox are obliged to view the maximalist character of liturgy, and when one acknowledges the possibility of attempting to observe it, the shortening of services results in a deficiency because "the order was established for the salvation of souls."[86] Townsend then argues that the "the content of the Services is scriptural and dogmatic in essence, and not cultural. They were not modeled on cultural paradigms."[87] Christians have adopted the wrong approach in cherrypicking aspects of the liturgy they will draw from for spiritual edification; instead, Orthodox should make it "our business to determine how we can receive the grace from the treasury of the Church's ongoing worship."[88] The

84. Ibid., 32.
85. Ibid., 33.
86. Ibid., 34.
87. Ibid.
88. Ibid.

onus of responsibility for converting the faithful to the liturgy (Pott's taxonomy) lies on the clergy:[89]

> We clergy must stop making the excuse that no one will attend the services even if we serve them, and begin to have the services necessary for our own salvation and the salvation of our people, whether anyone decides to come or not. . . . Truly, this is a matter of being faithful. We clergy must lead the way and provide the services even when we think that not one person will attend in the flesh, knowing that the saints and angels will be there to encourage us.

This brief review of ROCOR documents on the liturgy demonstrates that the notion of liturgical maximalism is threaded through ROCOR, echoed by bishops such as St. John Maximovich, Metropolitan Laurus, and Archbishop Averky, and repeated by other influential teachers such as Fathers Michael Pomazansky, Valerii Lukianov, and John Townsend. Our examination of these texts yields ROCOR's diagnoses of and prognoses for the remedy of the problem.

First, liturgy itself is in a constant state of growth that is not determined by culture, but is a primary aspect of tradition, a theological repository that communicates to the faithful the salvation history and the way to the kingdom of God. Second, the secularization of culture and the permeation of Western thinking, music, and art into Orthodox societies have resulted in the disengagement of the people from the liturgy.[90] The clergy have

---

89. Ibid., 35–36.
90. A notable collision of East and West has existed in ROCOR among Orthodox parishes that celebrate the Western Rite (communities that observe Western liturgical rites but are in communion with the Orthodox Church). ROCOR's policies on the Western Rite have varied. In 2013, the Synod of Bishops adopted several actions aimed towards rooting out the existence of Western Rite parishes in ROCOR, including the instruction not to ordain clergy for the Western Rite, and most significantly, the establishment of a commission which would integrate Western Rite parishes into the liturgical life of the Orthodox Church. For the full text, see "An Extraordinary Session of the Synod of Bishops is Held," ROCOR Synodal web site, http://www.synod.com/synod/eng2013/20130712_ensynodmeeting.html (accessed January 26, 2015). Note that this decision is consistent with the 1978 ROCOR synodal statement, "O

recognized the people's tepid engagement of the liturgy and, in an attempt to address their boredom, have shortened the services and adopted aesthetical models that are not engaging, but entertaining, which has only increased the magnitude of the crisis. The solution to the problem begins with the clergy, who must be converted to the existing liturgy so that they will be equipped to teach the laity how the liturgy functions as their entrance into the life of God.

The content of this life is austere and ascetic by nature: faithful Christians are called to lives of sanctity and thus must rehearse repentance in this life through frequent and long liturgy that shapes and forms them into the repentant people who can worthily belong to the communion of the Holy Spirit. The clergy's first priority is to shape the liturgical environment so that it is authentically Orthodox; the existence of Western themes and music in Orthodox buildings creates a dissonance and distortion that contributes to decay.

It is essential to emphasize that the history of this diagnosis of the liturgical problem, the narrative has remained unchanged: it opposes the values of the Church to secular society and appraises the West suspiciously and dismissively. The existence of the World Council of Churches and the reforms of Vatican II illuminate a model Orthodox should avoid, since these break with tradition and permit the integration of non-Christian elements into liturgy. The retention of all the primary features of this liturgical theology in ROCOR's

так называемом Западном обряде" ("On the so-called Western Rite"), in Anashkin, ed., *Законодательство Русской Православной Церкви Заграницей*, 30. An analysis of the history and significance of the Western Rite in Orthodoxy is outside of the scope of this study. For the complete background on the Western Rite, see the following articles by Jack Turner: "Journeying Onwards: An overview of the Liturgical Books in Western-rite Orthodoxy," *St. Vladimir's Orthodox Theological Quarterly* 56, no. 1 (2012): 93-112; "The Journey thus Far: A Review of the Literature of Western-rite Orthodoxy," *St. Vladimir's Orthodox Theological Quarterly* 53, no. 4 (2009): 477-505; "Western Rite Orthodoxy as an Ecumenical Problem," *Journal of Ecumenical Studies* 47, no. 4 (2012): 541-54.

history, from imperial Russia to the contemporary diaspora, is remarkable, and I will address this matter in my conclusion.

The Primary Mechanism of Liturgical Renewal: Aesthetics

The most important mechanism for creating an authentically liturgical environment in ROCOR is the cultivation of the liturgical arts, especially music and iconography. To this point in the analysis, we have noted a consistent steadfast insistence within ROCOR on fidelity to the received tradition. ROCOR's most influential leaders have not diagnosed liturgical order, form, and content as the problem causing liturgical decay: poor leadership on the part of the clergy was the chief issue. ROCOR's leaders also attested to the need for better liturgical music. In the nineteenth century, Antony was already juxtaposing a variety of chant traditions as superior to the contemporary style of music prevalent in Petersburg, and Metropolitan Laurus repeated the significance of cultivating a strong musical tradition in his address to the graduates of Holy Trinity Seminary.

Historical Survey of Liturgical Music in Russia

In the history of the Russian Church, liturgical music has made a central contribution to liturgical style for about 500 years. When the city-states of Rus' embraced Christianity in the tenth century, they inherited the liturgical traditions of Byzantium, including the musical heritage of chant.[91] As liturgical practices developed in dialogue with the local cultures of Rus', each region developed its own native chant

---

91. See Johann von Gardner, *Russian Church Singing*, vol. 2: *History from the Origins to the Mid-Seventeenth Century*, trans. and ed. Vladimir Morosan (Crestwood, NY; St. Vladimir's Seminary Press, 2000), 28–37. Gardner suggests that singing in liturgical Kyivan Rus' may also have been shaped by non-Byzantine sources. Also see Vladimir Morosan, *Choral Performance in Pre-Revolutionary Russia*, Russian Music Studies no. 17 (Madison, CT: Musica Russica, 1986): 3–13.

tradition. Two of the primary chant traditions of Rus' were the Kyivan and Znamenny traditions. Cathedral and monastic musicians who sang the services tended to write signs near the liturgical texts, which provides an etymological source for the adjective "Znamenny," as the sign (znak') indicated the melodic motif the chanter employed at various portions of a given text.

A new era began for the liturgical arts in general towards the end of the sixteenth century. At this point in history, the city states of Rus' had evolved in accordance with different trajectories. After the disastrous Mongol invasion of 1240, Kyiv became part of the Polish-Lithuanian Commonwealth whereas Muscovy became the most prominent center. As Moscow grew in prominence, it eventually became the most powerful ecclesial center among the Orthodox churches, achieving the status of a Patriarchate in 1589. Kyiv, however, increasingly fell under the influence of Poland in particular. In 1596, the bishops of the Kyivan Metropolia entered into Eucharistic communion with Rome as a result of the political influence exercised by Poland. The majority of the Orthodox laity refused to accept union with Rome, and the Orthodox held their ground by establishing schools administered by lay brotherhoods which established continuity with Orthodox while employing the pedagogical methods and topics prevalent in Poland, particularly Jesuit ones. In 1620, Patriarch Theophanes of Jerusalem consecrated a new Orthodox hierarchy for Kyiv, where he stopped en route to Moscow for the enthronement of Patriarch Joachim.

The restoration of an Orthodox hierarchy in Ukraine created a situation where the Orthodox majority had successfully resisted absorption into the Catholic Church while still finding themselves under the political and cultural influence of Poland. This situation continued for quite some time, and for the topic of liturgical reform, it became increasingly influential when a Moldovan became the

Metropolitan of Kyiv, Peter Mohyla. Mohyla implemented a program of liturgical reform for the Orthodox that centered on the publication of new liturgical books.[92] These books contained several Latinisms, which provided evidence of Roman Catholic practice permeating Orthodox liturgy. The books also contained much longer introductions to the celebrations of various mysteries, representing Mohyla's attempt to cultivate liturgical uniformity through the clergy.

This brief historical survey is crucial for discussion of music in ROCOR because it is during this time period and in this environment when other Westernisms began to penetrate the Orthodox Church, all the way to Moscow via Kyiv.[93] The influx of Western musical and iconographic styles was part of the education program administered by the lay brotherhoods. Kyiv became a center of evolving liturgical aesthetics, with Kyivan published in books in square notation, and the entrance of Western polyphony into Orthodox liturgy, which included the training of Ukrainian composers under Italian masters. The metamorphosis of liturgical music had already occurred in Poland, where the Jesuits encouraged

92. On this topic, see Ronald Popivchak, "The Life and Times of Peter Mohyla, Metropolitan of Kiev," *Logos: A Journal of Eastern Christian Studies* 43-45 (2004), 339-59; Frank E. Sysyn, "The Formation of Modern Ukrainian Religious Culture," in *Religion and Nation in Modern Ukraine*, ed. Serhii Plokhy and Frank E. Sysyn (Edmonton and Toronto: Canadian Institute of Ukrainian Studies Press, 2003), 1-22; Ihor Ševčenko, "The Many Worlds of Peter Mohyla," *Harvard Ukrainian Studies* 8, nos. 1-2 (1984): 9-40 (this issue is devoted to the study of the Kyiv Mohyla Academy); Peter Galadza, "Seventeenth-century Liturgicons of the Kyivan Metropolia and Several Lessons for Today," *St. Vladimir's Theological Quarterly* 56, no. 1 (2012): 73-91; and Paul Meyendorff, "The Liturgical Reforms of Peter Moghila: A New Look," *St. Vladimir's Theological Quarterly* 29, no. 2 (1985): 101-14. Mohyla was glorified as a saint in the Ukrainian Orthodox Church in 1996.

93. For an overview of the role of music in the education program implemented by the brotherhoods, see Morosan, *Choral Performance in Pre-Revolutionary Russia*, 37-55. Also see Frank E. Sysyn, "The Formation of Modern Ukrainian Religious Culture: The Sixteenth and Seventeenth Centuries," in *Religion and Nation in Modern Ukraine*, ed. Serhii Plokhy and Frank E. Sysyn (Edmonton and Toronto: Canadian Institute of Ukrainian Studies Press, 2003), 13-16; Vera Shevzov, "The Russian Tradition," in *The Orthodox Christian World*, ed. Augustine Casiday (London and New York: Routledge, 2012), 20-23; and Pospielovsky, 84-100.

contemporary composition as part of the counter-Reformation efforts; Reformed traditions had effectively engaged the people in liturgical participation through the Chorale tradition.

The Orthodox offered a response similar to the Jesuits: they adapted the musical styles of the most influential culture as one of the many ways to engage the people in the liturgy. Moscow was not immune to the Western metamorphosis of the liturgical arts. In fact, Tsar Alexis Mikhailovich was so enamored with the Western-influenced liturgical aesthetics flourishing in seventeenth-century Kyiv that he began to import Ukrainian musicians and iconographers to Moscow to introduce the new styles there.

This was not the final step in the process of the gradual Westernization of Russian Orthodox liturgical aesthetics, but it was a central one. The process became somewhat permanent as Ukraine was annexed to Russia in 1654, and the Kyivan Metropolia was absorbed by the Moscow Patriarchate in 1686. The Westernizing policies of the Russian crown continued the process of Western aesthetics permeating Orthodox liturgy. The native chant traditions were gradually displaced by polyphonic singing in the cathedrals, which had many consequences for liturgy as a whole. Georges Florovsky, the famous Orthodox theologian to whom the neo-patristic revival is largely attributed, invented the notion of the Western captivity from which Orthodox theology needed to be liberated.[94] The time period under discussion here is perhaps the primary source of this Western captivity, and there are numerous studies devoted to its analysis.[95]

---

94. See Georges Florovsky, *Collected Works*, vol. 4: *Aspects of Church History* (Belmont, MA: Nordland Publishing Co., 1975), 177-82. See Paul Gavrilyuk's analysis of Florovsky's discussion of pseudomorphosis in *Georges Florovsky and the Russian Religious Renaissance: Changing Paradigms in Historical and Systematic Theology* (Oxford: Oxford University Press, 2014), 172-91.

95. The best recent source is George Demacopoulos and Aristotle Papanikolaou, eds., *Orthodox Constructions of the West* (New York: Fordham University Press, 2013). Robert Taft offers an informative presentation on this topic in "Between Progress and Nostalgia: Liturgical Reform

For the purposes of this study, liturgical music and aesthetics takes on a thick layer of importance in the Orthodox attempt to free itself from the Western captivity. Liturgical music is important because the liturgical structure requires the liturgy to be sung in its entirety, and in the Eastern Slavic tradition, there is no instrumental accompaniment. This, the musicians perform a central liturgical ministry by singing all of the responses to the liturgy, and leading the singing in instances when the assembly joins in the responses. One's entire experience of the liturgy is shaped by the music; this simple fact explains why music is at the center of all contemporary liturgy "wars," and the complaints about music made by Metropolitans Antony and Laurus demonstrate their understanding that good music is inseparable from good liturgy. In ROCOR's case, scholars and musicians collaborated to offer an evaluation: the Western-style music detracted from liturgy because it was entertaining; the reform of the liturgy would be primarily implemented through the restoration of canonical chant, which is engaging.

Liberation from Western Captivity: the Moscow Synodal School

ROCOR's reform of liturgical music continued a process that originated in Russia in the eighteenth and nineteenth centuries. The process of turning to chant traditions to revive native choral singing flourished at the Moscow Synodal school, which became the primary center of chant study under the leadership of Stepan Smolensky.[96] The scholars involved with the project endeavored to research the

---

and the Western Romance with the Christian East; Strategies and Realities," in *A Living Tradition: On the Intersection of Liturgical History and Pastoral Practice*, ed. David Pitt, Stefanos Alexopoulos, and Christian McConnell (Collegeville, MN: Liturgical Press, 2012), 19-42.

96. Nicolas Schidlovsky, "Sources of Russian Chant Theory," in *Russian Liturgical Music Revival in the Diaspora: A Collection of Essays*, ed. Marina Ledkovsky and Vladimir von Tsuripov, Readings in Russian Religious Culture, vol. 4 (Jordanville, NY: Foundation of Russian History, 2012), 45-46.

whole history of Russian chant and consulted medieval sources, including traditions that had been maintained by the Old Believers following their schism with the Orthodox in the seventeenth century.[97] Nicolas Schidlovsky describes the research as bearing the potential to foment change in choral singing, with larger pastoral concerns the primary motivation driving the research on liturgical music.[98]

Schidlovksy notes that the interest in Russian chant became the domain of secular musical analysis, which is not surprising, given that the Church's capacity to sustain major research undertakings was compromised during Soviet persecution.[99] In reference to future areas of research, Schidlovsky notes that "it is the Liturgy that holds the clues to many inherent processes of this repertory—and the liturgical environment is inseparable from its appreciation."[100] Vladimir Morosan asserts that the Moscow School distinguished "liturgical singing" from "sacred music," and referred to chant as the preserver of "the symbiotic relationship between text and music," a relationship which adherents of the school sought to restore in their common enterprise.[101]

Johann von Gardner and Congregational Singing

Another scholar who exercised considerable influence on reforming the tradition of liturgical singing in the Russian Church was Johann von Gardner, whose two-volume series on chant has become a classic

---

97. Ibid., 49–54. On the Old Believers Schism and liturgical practices, see Paul Meyendorff, *Russia, Ritual, and Reform: The Liturgical Reforms of Nikon in the 17th Century* (Crestwood, NY: St. Vladimir's Seminary Press, 1991).

98. Schidlovsky, "Sources of Russian Chant Theory," 57.

99. Ibid.

100. Ibid., 62.

101. Vladimir Morosan, "Liturgical Singing or Sacred Music? Understanding the Aesthetic of the New Russian Choral Music," in *The Legacy of St. Vladimir: Byzantium, Russia, America*, ed. John Breck, John Meyendorff, Eleana Silk (Crestwood, NY: St. Vladimir's Seminary Press, 1990), 75.

in Orthodox theology.[102] When the pre-revolutionary Russian bishops engaged the deliberation process on liturgical reform, singing was one of their primary interests, and the traditions maintained by Orthodox and Greek-Catholic in the Carpathian churches were modular in many respects because they had not adopted the polyphonic Italianate musical styles, but had maintained native chant traditions.

Gardner integrated his observations of congregational practices from this region into his research and presented the chant tradition as modular for a potential wholescale Russian reform that would encourage the people to participate actively in the liturgy by becoming the choir. Gardner's observations are significant because he compares research he conducted in Carpathian Rus' towards the beginning of the twentieth century with the practice he observed in a Russian émigré parish in Belgrade between 1924 and 1927.[103] He states the purpose of his article accordingly: "the question which occupies us now concerns the active participation of the faithful in the performance of the divine services and the form of that participation."[104]

Gardner establishes that the practice of congregational singing was not only rare, but even discouraged among Russians, though the practice was introduced to some Great Russian churches at the end of the nineteenth century.[105] The practice of having the entire

---

102. Johann von Gardner, *Russian Church Singing, Vol. 1: Orthodox Worship and Hymnography*, trans. Vladimir Morosan (Crestwood, NY: St. Vladimir's Seminary Press, 1980), and idem, *Russian Church Singing*, vol. 2., trans. Morosan.

103. Johann von Gardner, "Several Observations on Congregational Chanting During the Divine Services," in *Russian Liturgical Music Revival in the Diaspora: A Collection of Essays*, ed. Marina Ledkovsky and Vladimir von Tsuripov, Readings in Russian Religious Culture, vol. 4 (Jordanville, NY: Foundation of Russian History, 2012), 263-71.

104. Ibid., 263.

105. Ibid., 267.

assembly chant the entire liturgy was particular to Carpathian Rus', as described by Gardner:[106]

> In Carpatho-Russia, in all village churches (both Uniate and Orthodox), congregational chanting at all the services in their entirety has been practiced exclusively, including singing the hymns of the 'proper,' utilizing the full range of tones and melodies. The people chant from the Great Anthology (Velikii Sbornik), which contains all the necessary texts. The chants, which are quite diverse . . . were well-known to all, even to schoolchildren. The cantors . . . who stood on the kliros began the chanting. As soon as those present recognized the melody, the whole church sang: they sang all the stichera, all the troparia, all the irmoi—in a word, everything that the Typikon indicated was to be sung.

Gardner remembers this experience as one of "extraordinary power."[107] Gardner explained his sense of the profundity of a singing congregation when he reflects on the deeper significance of an assembly that performs the singing. He acknowledges that it is difficult for a typical observer to receive because of the absence of trained choristers, but once one has been exposed to the singing and has a sense of its unitive power, one experiences singing not only with one mouth, but also one heart.[108] This kind of active participation is not limited to performance, but also concerns the process of receiving and understanding Church doctrine, since the peasants' ability to sing all of the chants exposed them to the theology communicated by the hymns.[109]

Gardner had the Russian diaspora in mind as the community that would retrieve the tradition of congregational singing. In his reference to the parish in Belgrade, he shows how the assembly sang the *litia* hymn, with the assistance of the chanters.[110] Because

106. Ibid., 264.
107. Ibid.
108. Ibid., 266-67.
109. Ibid., 267.
110. Ibid., 265.

of the intricate responsorial singing, the amount of time needed for the chanting with the congregation was significantly longer than is customary at the litia, but Gardner notes that the "hymnody held an extraordinary attraction for those present," which mitigated the usual problem of hurrying through the texts.[111]

Gardner's thesis was clear: chant was the path to restoring a liturgical ecclesiology that had been obscured, it was not a matter of privileging a particular aesthetical style belonging to one culture or region. In punctuating his thesis on the ecclesiality of congregational singing, Gardner says that "there is a vast difference between one who passively views and listens to the services, and one who takes part in it," noting that all of those who sing "perform the service together" with the clergy, rendering them the liturgy's concelebrants (as it were).[112]

In this essay, Gardner refers to the liturgical practices of living parishes to demonstrate his thesis that all the people are capable of singing chants and in the act of singing become the concelebrants with the clergy of the divine services. His essay also distinguishes between entertainment and engagement, which was mentioned by Antony: Gardner's identification of extraordinary power in the liturgy was not inspired by a master choir, but the extraordinary power of an entire assembly singing together. In a follow-up article, he offers a four-step process for implementing the reform, directed to his readers in the Russian Orthodox diaspora: to establish chanting itself as liturgy, the actual performance of the divine service; to extend the performance of chanting beyond the clergy and to the people; to concentrate all attention on the melody for congregational singing; and to introduce correct, canonical chants, which would exclude the court Common chant.[113]

111. Ibid.
112. Ibid., 271.

This brief survey is designed to illustrate how Russian musicologists diagnosed the problem of liturgical music while mentioning the sources they consulted in proposing remedies to the problem. We learn that the work of the Moscow Synodal School was designed to research chant traditions and through the publication of scholarly works, to demonstrate the role of chant in the celebration of the liturgy. The work of Gardner leads us to a concrete proposal on how restoring chant which can be performed by the entire assembly as the key to renewing the existing, received liturgical tradition. Gardner provides a viable distinction between entertainment and engagement in liturgical music, and his explanation of assembly singing refers to a potent liturgical ecclesiology enabled by music. In this next section, I will discuss how ROCOR continued the work of the Moscow Synodal School and other pioneers in cultivating liturgical music excellence.

Boris Ledkovsky and Canonical Singing

Marina Ledkovsky provides a survey of ROCOR's approach to liturgical music in several essays. She reviews the history of Russian music and the creation of the Synodal school up until the revolution, and shows how the school's influence continued at St. Sergius Institute in Paris, beginning in the 1920's, and cultivated in particular by the work of Michel and Nicolas Ossorguine.[114] Marina Ledkovsky attributed special importance to Gardner, whose scholarship and practical examples of "traditional ancient Russian Orthodox chants" was disseminated to several leading Russian Orthodox musicians and

---

113. Johann von Gardner, "Still More on Congregational Chanting of the Divine Services," in *Russian Liturgical Music Revival in the Diaspora: A Collection of Essays*, 272-77.

114. Marina Ledkovsky, "The Renaissance of Russian Orthodox Liturgical Music in the Russian Diaspora," in *Russian Liturgical Music Revival in the Diaspora: A Collection of Essays*, ed. Marina Ledkovsky and Vladimir von Tsuripov, Readings in Russian Religious Culture, vol. 4 (Jordanville, NY: Foundation of Russian History, 2012), 66-68.

also many non-Orthodox communities and music lovers in the West.[115] Ledkovsky identified her late husband, Boris Ledkovsky, as an important figure in the dissemination of the liturgical school in the diaspora.[116] A graduate of the Moscow Conservatory, Boris Ledkovsky was a member of the choir led by Alexander Kastalsky and "an observer of the teaching methods at the renowned Synod Choir School."[117] Boris Ledkovsky's legacy was the most important of all the contributors because his work permeated not only ROCOR, but other Orthodox churches as well.

Boris Ledkovsky's experience in ROCOR took shape when he was appointed to conduct the choir at the Synodal cathedral in New York at the invitation of Metropolitan Anastasy (Gribanovsky).[118] Boris Ledkovsky's appointment was motivated, in part, by Metropolitan Anastasy's desire to continue the Muscovite liturgical tradition he cultivated during his tenure at Moscow's Dormition Cathedral. Ledkovsky implemented the precepts of correct, canonical singing propagated by the Moscow school by purifying "choral church singing from those popular banal compositions that predominated in the worship practice of the last centuries."[119]

An example of this initiative can be identified in Boris Ledkovksy's arrangements for the eight liturgical tones: the foundations for these chants were Znamennyi and Kyivan chants, and also Greek, Valaam, and other monastic melodies.[120] Another objective was to eliminate completely the prevalent use of the Bakhmetev obikhod, which held hegemony among Russian and Ukrainian parishes (and still does to

115. Ibid., 68–69.
116. Ibid., 72.
117. Ibid.
118. Marina Ledkovsky, "Dedication to the ROCM Foundation," in *Russian Liturgical Music Revival in the Diaspora: A Collection of Essays*, 21.
119. Ibid.
120. Ibid.

this day).[121] Boris Ledkovsky sought to create new harmonies that could be used in almost any parish, as Marina Ledkovsky attests:[122]

> Ledkovsky arranged the chants and compositions compactly in close harmony, thus making them accessible for performance by contemporary, frequently small émigré choir, even quartets. His goal was to have any church choir perform in strict observance of the ecclesiastical mode of the given pieces, by all means avoiding inappropriate 'operative effects.'

Marina Ledkovsky also mentioned Boris Ledkovsky's prioritization of the melody while subordinating the music to the text and not vice versa, to maintain the theological integrity of the structure. Ledkovsky's legacy permeated the life of the Metropolia (now the OCA), as he taught liturgical music at St. Vladimir's Seminary from 1952-1968 with many of his compositions transposed into English.

Marina Ledkovsky mentions the high musical standards maintained at St. Vladimir's, cultivated in English, with the tradition he established carried out by his protégé and successor, David Drillock. Boris Ledkovsky's contribution extended to his teaching of a conducting style: Marina Ledkovsky states that he preferred refined and sparing gestures, and did not take the liberty to eccentricities that were popular among maestros in the convert hall, yet another distinction between entertainment and engagement.[123]

Boris Ledkovsky's Legacy in the OCA

David Drillock also testifies to Ledkovsky's contribution to the pedagogy of liturgical music at St. Vladimir's Seminary.[124] Drillock

---

121. Ibid.
122. Ibid.
123. Ibid., 26.
124. This information is taken from David Drillock's lecture titled "My Life in Liturgical Music," delivered at the Institute of Liturgical Music and Pastoral Practice at St. Vladimir's Seminary, Crestwood, NY, June 2004. Professor Drillock shared this essay with me in an e-mail on November 20, 2014. I am grateful to Professor Drillock for sharing these insights.

discusses the context of the Russian Metropolia in his youth, describing the church as enduring a transition, with parishes beginning the process of integrating English into the liturgy by necessity.[125] Drillock became Ledkovsky's assistant, and attests to Ledkovsky's implementation of the objectives of the Moscow Synodal School via his teaching at St. Vladimir's:[126]

> Professor Ledkovsky had a profound influence on changing the direction of church singing in the Orthodox Churches in America. He was an ardent follower of the Moscow School of Music and strove first and foremost to purify choral singing from the popular compositions of the so-called Italian school of Russian church composers. This is what predominated in most of the churches following the Slavic musical tradition. . . . Boris Ledkovsky's compositions, on the other hand, attempted to convey what he so often referred to as 'tserkovnost,' i.e., churchly. And, like the teachers of the Moscow Synodal School, Ledkovksy believed that such 'tserkovnost' can be found in the old Russian chants. Like his teacher Kastal'sky, Ledkovsky helped to establish a new tradition here in America in church music by returning to the indigenous Russian church unison melodies and using those melodies as the basis for the composing of church music, very much in the way that Palestrina and others used the Gregorian chant melodies as cantus firmi for their polyphonic compositions. However, here Ledkovsky was also influenced by Ivan Gardner, who maintained that the church chants are the 'canonical' melodies that are acceptable for use in church and these follow more stringent rules regarding text and music. At no time should music predominate over text. Repetition of words, not found in the chant settings, distorts the meaning of the text and should not be tolerated. In his harmonized settings of church chants, Ledkovsky followed such precepts.

Drillock became a disciple of the Moscow Synodal School through his association with Boris Ledkovsky, further study with Serbian

125. "The reason for the introduction of English is that the children of the Russian immigrants, being trained in American schools, are not capable of speaking, reading, or understanding the language of their parents and grandparents," Drillock, "My Life in Liturgical Music," 3.
126. Ibid., 10.

musicologist Velimirovic, and the encouragement of musicians such as Alfred Swan and Johann von Gardner, along with the support of Schmemann and other faculty at St. Vladimir's. In the early 1960's, St. Vladimir's Seminary produced multiple recordings of liturgical music in English and Church Slavonic, with the chorus directed by both Drillock and Boris Ledkovsky.[127]

The primary purpose of such recordings and the creation of a travelling octet was to promote "liturgical music done well in English that was more conducive to worship than the concert stage."[128] Drillock became a central figure in inaugurating and planning the programs for an annual summer institute hosted at St. Vladimir's that was devoted to developing choral leadership skills and enhance pastoral practice.[129] Thus, the legacy of the Moscow Synodal School impacted not only ROCOR, but also the Metropolia and OCA on account of Boris Ledkovsky's tenure as professor of music at St. Vladimir's, with Drillock continuing and advancing his legacy during his teaching career. The reader should note the transferable quality of the principles of the Moscow Synodal School: Drillock applied the same principles to composing and leading liturgical music in English.

In the small émigré church of ROCOR, Boris Ledkovsky was the primary figure who implemented the vision established for liturgical singing by the Moscow Synodal school. His leadership of the Synodal choir in New York caused it to lead the singing at numerous events throughout the United States, including the glorification of St. John

127. Ibid., 17-18.
128. Ibid., 17.
129. "It was with the purpose of relating Orthodox liturgical theology with Orthodox practice that the first summer Institute of Liturgical Music and Pastoral Practice was organized by the Seminary in 1968. I remember planning the program together with Fr. Alexander, and Fr. Glagolev whom we co-opted to organize this first summer Institute. The Summer Institute has been held continuously for over 30 years and has brought several thousand Orthodox pastors, choir directors, singers, and simply lay persons interested in theology to the seminary campus for one week of intensive study, prayer, and fellowship," ibid., 20.

Maximovich in San Francisco.[130] Boris Ledkovsky was the living representative of the Moscow School, continuing the work inaugurated by Smolensky, Razumovsky, and Gardner, *inter alia*, and while his work impacted ROCOR, it was also cultivated by musicians of the Metropolia at St. Vladimir's seminary, an educational institution preparing seminarians and musicians for service in many Orthodox jurisdictions of America.

Marina Ledkovsky has established the formation and continuation of a living school of liturgical music within the Russian Diaspora that was authorized to renew liturgy by ROCOR. Her own words testify to the continuation and proliferation of this school, particularly through annual summer seminars aimed at developing skilled liturgical musicians:[131]

> The truly rewarding proof of the revival of Russian Orthodox church music in the Russian Diaspora is the present activity of several highly talented young descendants of émigré parents. The third and fourth generations in exile, who, following in the footsteps of their predecessors successfully carry on and further develop the best traditions of Russian liturgical singing. . . . During these sessions old church chants are investigated and participants are shown how to use them in actual church services. These seminars serve as an invaluable tool for promoting the practice of authentic church singing.

The summer seminars are well-known throughout the Orthodox diaspora, as choir directors receive first-rate training from masters in the filed who belong to the Moscow school. Marina Ledkovsky avers her preference for the Moscow style, yet acknowledges that the so-called Petersburg school of music has a place in the liturgy of the Russian Church.[132]

130. Ibid., 28.
131. Marina Ledkovsky, "The Renaissance of Russian Orthodox Liturgical Music in the Russian Diaspora," 74.
132. Marina Ledkovsky, "The Dispute Between Moscow and Petersburg about Canonical Singing

The references to contemporary writings of church leaders discussing the problems with liturgical music show that not all clergy and parishes have embraced the Moscow style of singing. For example, Krassovsky states that Michael Konstantinov was a key contributor to establishing the Kyiv liturgical tradition at Holy Virgin Cathedral in San Francisco, which became a liturgical center in its own right.[133] Krassovsky noted that Konstantinov and Ledkovsky were friendly, and agreed to preserve the traditions of their native cities in San Francisco and New York respectively, until the Russian Church would be able to break free of Soviet oppression and retrieve its own native traditions. Thus, the cathedral in San Francisco functioned as a liturgical center representing the traditions of Kyiv, and the New York Cathedral served as the repository for Muscovite tradition.

Both cathedrals steadfastly preserved their traditions through episcopal patronage and primarily communicated them through the local musical traditions which were passed on to the next generation. In New York, Alexander Ledkovsky continued his father's work, whereas Krassovsky continued Konstantinov's work in San Francisco. Schidlovsky and Gardner both attested to the prominent role played by music in communicating liturgical tradition and theology, so one can argue that a diversity of approaches to liturgical tradition exists within ROCOR, while its leaders stated their clear preference for the proliferation of the Moscow style.[134]

---

in the Middle of the Nineteenth Century," in *Russian Liturgical Music Revival in the Diaspora: A Collection of Essays*, 147.

133. Per phone conversation with Vladimir Krassovsky on February 12, 2014. I am grateful to Mr. Krassovsky for sharing his knowledge of the aesthetical traditions of ROCOR.

134. Marina Ledkovsky, "The Renaissance of Russian Orthodox Liturgical Music in the Russian Diaspora," 75. In addition to the testimony of Metropolitans Antony and Laurus offered above, ROCOR's preference for chant-based singing is manifested by the Synodal directive "О церковном пении" ("On Church Singing" (1959)), in Anashkin, ed., *Законодательство Русской Православной Церкви Заграницей*, 38–39.

Musical Diversity within ROCOR

Marina Ledkovsky's reference to musical diversity within ROCOR is confirmed and elaborated by the ethno-musicological contributions of Natalie Zelensky. Zelensky examined the musical repertoires and attitudes towards liturgical music of several ROCOR parishes.[135] Her examination of select New York ROCOR parishes led Zelensky to conclude that "the predominant ROCOR repertoire also entails music of the 'Italian' school." Characteristics of this kind of liturgical singing include "the inclusion of solos, duets, and trios, lyrical melody, [and] affective qualities of music that do not always coincide with the meaning of the text."[136]

Zelensky contrasts the Italian-influenced repertoire of the New York parishes with the objectives of Boris Ledkovsky and the Moscow School, exposing the musical "worship wars" that continue to occur within ROCOR.[137] Zelensky notes that parishioners resisted the efforts of Ledkovsky and other adherents of the Moscow School who sought to reform liturgical music within ROCOR. She concludes that the tendency to retain an older strand of liturgical music was "an adaptive strategy of survival," one that permitted the people to sustain a "psychological bond" to the church of their homeland through a "perceived semblance of continuity."[138]

Zelensky criticizes the proponents of the Moscow School who sought to introduce musical reform within ROCOR, referring to their project as a claim to "an archaic past bound to a pre-Western

135. Natalie Zelensky, "Chanting the Homeland: Discourses of Authenticity and Sacrality in Competing Styles of Church Music in the Russian Orthodox Diaspora of New York," in *The Oxford Handbook of Music and World Christianities*, ed. Jonathan Dueck and Suzel Ana Reily (Oxford: Oxford University Press, January 2015, online version), DOI: 10.1093/oxfordhb/9780199859993.013.18. I am grateful to Dr. Zelensky for directing me to her work on October 13, 2014.
136. Ibid.
137. Ibid.
138. Ibid.

Russia,'" or a "mythologized past." Time has healed some of these divisions in the post-Soviet era, especially as ROCOR has reestablished communion with the Moscow Patriarchate. The gradual healing has permitted a transition from internal worship wars manifested in music to "increasing diversity of music within ROCOR."

Zelensky's examination of musical repertoire in four ROCOR parishes brings our analysis full circle. Zelensky's description of parishes that retain an Italian-influenced musical repertoire and resist the influence of the Moscow Synodal School shows just how challenging it is to implement liturgical reform. The principles underpinning the reform of the Moscow School include numerous elements, including the desire to excise Western elements and to restore a balance between music and text to make the latter more comprehensible and thus more engaging for the liturgical assembly.

The people's resistance to the implementation of reform is largely based upon their identity: the retention of the musical practices of their native regions, cities, and parishes took on greater significance in the diaspora for the sake of cultivating their ethno-religious identities. The introduction of new practices, even those ostensibly grounded in a canonical, pre-Western past, is perceived by some constituencies within ROCOR as dubious threats because they would ultimately change one's worship experience.

The internal collisions of principles and musical styles in ROCOR mirror those we reviewed in Schmemann's liturgical renewal program in the previous chapter. These contrasts and battles are multi-layered and complex; they are not only matters of ecclesiological preference and aesthetical flavors, but are personal issues of identity that are clothed in aesthetics. Most important is the fact that the conflict of aesthetical styles described by Metropolitan

Antony accompanied immigrants into their new communities in the diaspora.

Despite the existence of disagreements over musical styles within ROCOR, one cannot understate the multidimensional purpose of ROCOR's support for a strong program of liturgical music.

The bishops assigned the parish clergy a crucial role in cultivating musicians whose musical leadership would energize the body of faithful into active liturgical participation with understanding. Metropolitan Antony briefly alluded to this pastoral task in his lectures on the pastorate, and the same notions remained vibrant throughout ROCOR's history. In the pastoral handbook adopted by ROCOR's synod in 1956, the bishops remind parish clergy that they are to instruct parishioners on the fundamentals of church reading and singing, along with the Typikon.[139]

One can identify a thematic thread of liturgical catechesis of the people facilitated by the clergy through liturgical music in ROCOR's history: by raising up competent musicians in the local parish, clergy would introduce the people to that comprehensible and active participation in the liturgy to which they are called.[140] The attempt to build up the body of Christ through an improved program of liturgical music remains a work-in-progress, and while prominent bishops and musical leaders prefer the principles of the Moscow Synodal School, significant segments of ROCOR continue to refuse to receive and adopt it.

139. See "Руководственные правила для священнослужителей Русской Православной Церкви Заграницей" ("Guiding Rules for the Clergy of the Russian Orthodox Church Outside of Russia"), in Anashkin, ed., *Законодательство Русской Православной Церкви Заграницей*, 161.
140. Elizabeth Ledkovsky highlighted this pastoral priority in a phone conversation on October 22, 2014. I am grateful to Ms. Ledkovsky for sharing her knowledge of ROCOR's musical heritage with me.

Conclusion

Marina Ledkovsky's meticulous presentation on the achievements of the Moscow school and its dissemination in the diaspora, particularly through the efforts of her late husband, Boris, establishes that ROCOR intentionally continued the alternative approach to liturgical reform propagated by Metropolitan Antony Khrapovitsky in the late-nineteenth century. The central features of this reform are steadfast fidelity to the received liturgical tradition grounded by the belief that the liturgy is a gift given by God to humankind which is not subject to cultural adaptation. The reform seeks to build up loyal and educated clergy who excel at liturgical presidency by focusing on God and eschewing all individualism while mastering their own knowledge and understanding of the contents of the divine services.

Hypothetically, clergy who preside well will edify and inspire the people to pay attention, which results in the desired objective, which is the active and conscious celebration of the people in the liturgy. The key mechanism to implementing the conversion of the people to the existing liturgy (Pott's taxonomy) is through the liturgical arts, especially music, since singing is the primary activity engaged by all liturgical celebrants, including the people. The bishops play an important role in advocating for such a conversion to the liturgy: besides cultivating clergy, the bishops also support educational programs that have the capacity to have impact within the church.

Has ROCOR's approach to the liturgy resulted in reform? The testimony of a theologian with the stature of Kallistos Ware suggests that ROCOR has been faithful to preserving the liturgy and has thus achieved the objective of tradition, to pass on to others what one has received. However, when one reads the remarks of figures such as Metropolitan Laurus and Father John Townsend, it is obvious that the same problems identified by Metropolitan Antony, including inadequate liturgical music ministry and the preponderance of individualism and arbitrariness among the clergy, continue to cause problems within the Church today. If the attempt to implement reform had been successful on a large, churchwide scale, there would be less evidence of leaders exhorting clergy to have the services and avoid abbreviating them.

Marina Ledkovsky's useful survey of the implementation of musical reform in the Church is quite persuasive, especially in her identification of a vibrant school carrying out the precepts and traditions established by the Moscow Synodal School.

Marina Ledkovsky shows how church life was impacted in a profound way, by establishing a school of music leaders who promoted the restoration of chants that served the text and consequently opened the theological contours of the texts they accompany to the people. The arrangement of texts that can be sung by a choir of any size makes the enterprise churchwide, so that even the smallest community can reap the blessings from the reform. Gardner had identified the most profound area of reform in his discussion of congregational singing, and the evidence does not discuss how ROCOR has embraced the scholarly suggestions of creating music that people can sing which would transform passive assemblies into a singing church with the capacity to live out what it prays. In this vein, perhaps Gardner's challenge to implement the principles of congregational singing he discovered in Carpathian Rus' is best equipped to achieve the larger objectives of people engaging the liturgy and thus being converted to it, as opposed to seeking entertainment at church.

In many ways, our discussion of ROCOR's enterprise of liturgical reform is similar to the one implemented by Schmemann at St. Vladimir's Seminary, because Schmemann was also an inheritor of the Russian liturgical tradition and its pre-revolutionary study, as was

Boris Ledkovsky. There is, however, a significant difference between the two approaches, with one obvious similarity. Schmemann's and ROCOR's approaches to the liturgy are similar in their fidelity to the received tradition. Schmemann adopted the approach of most Orthodox liturgical theologians by viewing some restoration of the liturgy as possible, whereas ROCOR's appraisal of the liturgy as a living tradition that evolved by the will of God for the sake of the people made it unchangeable.

Schmemann believed that certain liturgical structures and elements could be restored so that they would manifest the underpinning theological foundation of a priesthood of all believers that called all the people to engage the structures. Metropolitan Antony's distinction between clergy and the people called for the people to pursue repentance and divine forgiveness in the nave and outside of the sanctuary while the priest focused on God, which was manifest in his more strict and petitionary bodily postures at the altar. In other words, an ecclesiology that makes more of a distinction between the priesthoods of the laity and the clergy limits the amount of liturgical reform that can occur without revising the ecclesiology.

Gardner's observation on the role of the people's singing as an exercise of their concelebration of the liturgy conforms to the ecclesiology of Afanasiev and Schmemann, which is perhaps one of the reasons St. Vladimir's Seminary invited Boris Ledkovsky to teach music to seminarians. This divergence between Schmemann and ROCOR confirms our thesis that preferred liturgical styles tend to manifest preferred ecclesiologies, and vice versa. Diverse and even colliding ecclesiologies exist in every church body. In the case of ROCOR, it is likely that the retention of particular musical styles in defiance of those privileged by teachers such as Boris Ledkovsky illustrates the power of the parish to receive or reject some teachings. To be sure, the Moscow style bears sophistication by emphasizing the relationship between text and music, the capacity of chant motifs to communicate meaning, and the possibility of offering musical harmonizations rooted in chant that can be sung by any community. However, as Zelensky persuasively demonstrates, there is no mechanism that can enforce the appropriation of a particular chant on a given parish, which manifests a local community's freedom to receive musical traditions. The power to receive, reject, or create a local hybrid is not surprising nor is it particularly innovative. The diverse musical preferences of parishes represent the local selection of musical styles that have implications beyond one's experience of and engagement with music in the parish. As the Moscow tradition implies, particular musical styles can promote robust lay participation that has the capacity to inform the notion of a shared priesthood of the ordained and lay. The selection of a different musical style not only enhances the distinction between entertainment and engagement, but also encourages the laity to observe the liturgy, which has ecclesiological implications.

In this vein, the primary area of liturgical reform within ROCOR has serious ecclesiological implications that are relevant to our discussion of the traditional theological foundations of liturgical reform. The theological foundations underpinning *SC* are the priesthood and active participation, and participation depends on the reformation of the ordained and lay priesthoods. We see a similar dynamic at play in ROCOR, where the attempt to reform the priesthood was designed to provide a model for the laity to adopt. The clerical model was elevated: the laity is called to ascend to a life of sanctity of extraordinary characteristics. ROCOR's emphasizes the clergy in its program of liturgical renewal, which is also designed to excise Western elements from the liturgy and create a barrier that prevents their permeation of the Church and her liturgical celebration. So unlike Schmemann's model, Vatican II has had very little impact on ROCOR's liturgical reform, other than providing a model to be avoided.

Despite the absence of a relationship between the two phenomena, we can make two comparative observations about Vatican II and ROCOR. First, ROCOR's tendency to excise Western ideas as unwelcome notions that have polluted Orthodox worship is in direct contrast to Vatican II which sought to enrich Roman worship by integrating Eastern ideas in the spirit of ecclesial catholicity. Second, the stature and reputation of Vatican II's reform in *SC* caused a reactionary response among all Orthodox (as we will see). ROCOR's notable retention of anti-Western verbiage in its contemporary analysis of the liturgy probably represents the general Orthodox perception of *SC* as radical.

The more significant difference between the reforms of Schmemann and ROCOR is manifest in divergent approaches to liturgical reform within its natural habitat. In both Schmemann's and ROCOR's cases, the deliberations on liturgical reform that began in Russia accompanied the immigrants to their ultimate destinations, such as Paris, Belgrade, and New York. As an observer of culture, Schmemann was motivated to find a way to build up the body of Christ in dialogue with North American idioms, while desiring to excise secularisms particular to American culture that had permeated the Church.

For Schmemann, the Orthodox Church in America had to become a church that could flourish in an authentically American environment. The liturgical culture we see unfolding in ROCOR treats the liturgy just as it was in its original cultural habitat, epitomized by various centers of imperial Russia. The implementation of liturgical renewal through the Moscow Synodal musical school simply continues the work inaugurated in Moscow. It was natural for the immigrants to carry out the initiatives that accompanied them in immigration, especially when the Church perceived the liturgy itself as unchangeable; this notion of the liturgy entails that the received tradition can be reasonably uniform, permitting variations one might find within the historical received tradition, such as the distinctions between Moscow and Kyiv, or New York and San Francisco, as it were.

Had such an implementation of reform occurred in Moscow, without the interruption of the revolution, it is entirely possible that the Church would have adopted this approach because the liturgy would have evolved within its natural habitat. However, the immigrants of ROCOR brought their liturgy to the diaspora and cultivated it in dialogue with a surrounding culture that was distinctly European or North American. The liturgy itself was removed from its natural habitat, which contributes to the appeals of conservative thinkers who continue to view Westernisms as threats to traditional liturgy, even though the people who cultivate the liturgy are Western, by definition. ROCOR's reforms occurred outside of the liturgy's natural habitat, in immigration, which isolated the liturgy from discourse with its native worship traditions (Kyiv, Moscow, and so on).

Furthermore, the point of comparison for liturgy was now the celebration of the Byzantine Rite by other Orthodox communities who were considering varying degrees of reform, which impacts the mindset of communities, as liturgy becomes a more powerful marker of identity and belonging in émigré culture. ROCOR desired to implement liturgical reform without consideration of cultural paradigms, and the consequences of such an implementation are significant, even with music, because consideration of musical evolution in the surrounding culture would characterize a liturgical reform in its natural habitat.[141]

ROCOR's liturgical reform constitutes an alternative to the forms we have investigated here because of the community's steadfast fidelity to carrying on native traditions in immigration. I refer to the liturgy as an alternative ecclesiology because ROCOR maintained the episcopo-centric ecclesiological paradigm from the imperial Russian period. The ecclesiology they sustained through fidelity to the liturgy is the same as its parent in imperial Russia: faithful to the unchangeable nature of the liturgy, anti-Western, and supportive of the liturgical arts. Its most notable features are the role of the clergy in modeling liturgy for the faithful and the identification of the liturgical arts as the appropriate element for encouraging active participation in and of the liturgy without performing any surgery to its structures, components, and interpretation.

141. Note that Boris Ledkovsky's music translated into English occurred in the Metropolia-OCA, which was more open to cultural paradigms than ROCOR.

4

Contemporary Liturgical Renewal in the Church of Greece

In this chapter, we will examine our third model of Orthodox liturgical reform: the Church of Greece. As an inheritor of the traditions of the Patriarchate of Constantinople, the Church of Greece traces its liturgical history to the Byzantine Empire. Historically, the Church of Greece began to chart its own independent course when it declared autocephaly in 1833 and received recognition from the Patriarchate of Constantinople in 1850. In the post–Byzantine period, an episode of liturgical renewal emerged in the context of the eighteenth-century philokalic movement on Mount Athos.[1] Among the elements of renewal

---

1. Stefanos Alexopoulos, "The State of Modern Greek Liturgical Studies and Research: A Preliminary Survey," in *Inquiries into Eastern Christian Worship*, Selected Papers of the Second International Congress of the Society of Oriental Liturgy, Rome, 17-21 September 2008, ed. Bert Groen, Steven Hawkes-Teeples, and Stefanos Alexopoulos, *Eastern Christian Studies* 12 (Leuven: Peeters, 2012), 376. I am grateful to Fr. Stefanos for introducing me to the seminal literature on liturgical renewal in the Greek Orthodox tradition.

highlighted at Mount Athos was an impetus to encourage faithful to receive Holy Communion with greater frequency. The proponents of liturgical reform on Mount Athos in this period are known as the "kollyvadic fathers," a description assigned to them on the basis of their insistence that the blessing of wheat (kollyva) should be restricted to Saturdays only.[2]

Its ecclesial independence from Constantinople notwithstanding, the Church of Greece refers to the liturgical reforms implemented by the Constantinople Patriarchate in the late-nineteenth and early-twentieth centuries as part of their tradition.[3] The Patriarchate of Constantinople recognized the need for a distinctly parish liturgical celebration and modified the Typikon.[4] The first revision of the Typikon was primarily the work of Constantinos Protopsaltis and was published in 1838, with a refreshed edition revised by Geroge Violakes in 1888. Stefanos Alexopoulos states that the publication of a new Typikon "brings forth the incompatibility between a monastic Typikon and a parish" and "points to the need to design a Typikon suitable for parish use."[5]

The Violakes version of the Typikon is essentially the one used in modern Greek liturgical celebration. The changes made in this Typikon do not represent a radical change in liturgical order, but pastoral revisions implemented to simplify the liturgy within the received tradition.[6] For example, the order of the All-night Vigil was

---

2. Cyril Hovorun, "Kollyvadic Fathers," in *The Encyclopedia of Orthodox Christianity*, vol. 2, ed. John McGuckin (Chichester, West Sussex: Wiley-Blackwell Publications, 2011), 365. For an English translation of the text encouraging frequent participation in communion by the Kollyvades, see Hieromonk Patapios and Archbishop Chrysostomos, *Manna from Athos: The Issue of Frequent Communion on the Holy Mountain in the Late Eighteenth and Early Nineteenth Centuries*, Byzantine and Neohellenic Studies, vol. 2, ed. Andrew Louth and David Ricks (New York: Peter Lang, 2006), 95-173.

3. Alexopoulos, "The State of Modern Greek Liturgical Studies and Research," 375-92.

4. Ibid., 376-77. Also see Amfilohije Radovic, "Reformes liturgiques dans L'Église de Grec," in *Liturgie de l'Église particuliére, Liturgie de l'Église universelle*, Bibliotheca ephemerides liturgicae subsidia 7 (Rome: Edizione liturgiche, 1976): 261-74.

5. Alexopoulos, "The State of Modern Greek Liturgical Studies," 376.

suppressed, with Orthros abbreviated and moved to Sunday morning. Also, the reading of the resurrection Gospel was moved from its original position following the Prokeimenon and preceding Psalm 50 to the end of the canon, after Ode 8 and just before Ode 9 (The Magnificat Canticle).

The Patriarchate's recognition of the need to revise the Typikon and make it suitable for parish liturgy discloses the pastoral nature of liturgical reform. Earlier, we reviewed the internal processes of study and deliberation exercised by the pre-revolutionary Church in Russia for the purpose of building up the body of Christ. The liturgy was a central factor in reflection on ecclesial reform because the liturgy constitutes the faithful's primary and most frequent experience of Church. That said, the liturgy was not the only topic of the deliberative process: it was a central issue of reform, but still belonged to a larger enterprise. The same holds true for the role of liturgy in the reform process of the Roman Catholic Church leading up to Vatican II. In Russia, the primary task of pre–revolutionary liturgists was liturgical archaeology: liturgists employed the same sciences used by Western scholars and began the process of narrating liturgical history by publishing medieval Byzantine liturgical texts.

Numerous Greek scholars took up this work of *Liturgiewissenschaft* by publishing editions of manuscript texts and narrating their history. The study of liturgical history and its capacity to inform pastors on what is possible in liturgical celebration impacted modern Greek liturgical studies, particularly through the contributions of scholars such as Panagiotis Trempelas and Ioannis Fountoulis.[7] Alexopoulos notes the influence exercised by the historical work of Juan Mateos,

6. For brief descriptions of these changes, see Job Getcha, *Le Typikon décrypte: manuel de liturgie byzantine*, pref. Hieromonk Macarius (Paris: Cerf, 2009), 52-53, and Alkiviadis Calivas, *Essays in Theology and Liturgy*, vol. 3: *Aspects of Orthodox Worship* (Brookline, MA: Holy Cross Press, 2003), 90-91.
7. Alexopoulos, "The State of Modern Greek Liturgical Studies and Research," 380-82.

Robert Taft, and Miguel Arranz (among others) on Fountoulis's scholarship and teaching.[8]

Greek Theologians on the Task of Theology in Modernity and Postmodernity

The contemporary enterprise of liturgical rebirth in the Church of Greece fuses the method and contributions of liturgical history with an honest pastoral assessment of conditions in the Church. In an article reflecting on the future trajectory of Greek Orthodox theology, Petros Vassialidis notes that Greek theologians transitioned from a scholastic academic approach to a patristic one in the twentieth century.[9] Vassiliadis stated that the most influential Greek theologians adopted the theological approach of Russian theologians in the diaspora, where patristic thinking emphasized looking ahead with the fathers as opposed to remaining in the past.[10] He refers to three developments in Greece that manifested this new theological creativity: the creation and publication of a theological periodical (*Synaxis*), an endeavor to engage "a wider circle of intellectuals, . . . especially the Athonite community, in the shaping of the Greek Orthodox theological thought of the next generation"; the establishment of Theological Syndesmos "as a response to the increasing alienation of modern Greek society from the values and the authentic spirit of Orthodoxy"; and the translation of the New Testament into modern Greek.[11]

---

8. Ibid., 381. In "Did the Work of Fr. Alexander Schmemann Influence modern Greek Theological Thought? A Preliminary Assessment," *St. Vladimir's Theological Quarterly* 53, nos. 2-3 (2009): 273-99, Alexopoulos presents Schmemann's contribution to Greek liturgical and theological thinking. One item of interest is the observation of Petros Vassialidis that Schmemann was too brazen in calling for renewal, and that a more careful and deliberate process of study and reflection was needed, as opposed to surgery (290-91).

9. Petros Vassialidis, "Greek Theology in the Making: Trends and Facts in the 80's—Vision for the 90's," *St. Vladimir's Theological Quarterly* 35 (1991): 34.

10. Ibid., 36.

11. Ibid., 36-45.

The objective motivating the Greek theologians was to engage modern society with traditional Orthodox theology.[12] Of course, not all theologians and Church leaders joined the bandwagon for finding creative ways to engage modernity. Vassiliadis notes that the hierarchy of the Greek Church remained steeped in conservatism, manifested by a synodal decision to remove the agenda item on increasing the laity's participation in the liturgical life of the Church from the Synod's 1971 meeting.[13]

Vassiliadis composed a second essay on the task of Orthodox theology in the twenty-first century, essentially an update to his initial analysis.[14] In this essay, Vassiliadis adopts an ecumenical perspective to performing the contemporary task of theologizing and refers to the liturgy explicitly as the chief criterion for theology. He supports this bold assertion comparatively:[15]

> The Roman Catholics have Vatican II to draw from; the Orthodox do not. The Lutherans have an Augsburg Confession of their own; the Orthodox do not, and the latter also lack the equivalent of a Luther or Calvin, to mention just two from the Reformation movement, who could give a theological identity.

For Vassiliadis, then, the liturgical tradition is the primary course for theologizing and also provides Orthodox with their theological identity.[16]

The primary task for Orthodox theology is to shift the theological paradigm from the monastic interpretation of the liturgy as an ascent resulting in the salvation of one's soul to an earlier eschatological emphasis, where the Church will be.[17] For Vassiliadis, Orthodox

---

12. Ibid., 38–39.

13. Ibid., 40–42.

14. Petros Vassiliadis, "Orthodox Theology Facing the Twenty-First Century," *Greek Orthodox Theological Review* 35, no. 2 (1990): 139–53.

15. Ibid., 143.

16. Here, Vassiliadis quotes Florovsky and links right faith with right worship, ibid.

17. Ibid., 149. I will return to Vassiliadis's treatment of this matter later in the chapter.

theology's primary source is the liturgy: "The Orthodox understanding of the liturgy goes far beyond the ritual; it is rather an authentic expression of the relation of the people of God to the Creator, to humanity, and to the entire cosmos."[18]

Several other theologians commented on problems within the life of the Church that needed to be addressed. Pantelis Kalaitzidis presented initiatives for renewing and reforming the Orthodox Church in a recent comprehensive essay.[19] Kalaitzidis asserts that Orthodoxy has become frozen in time and needs to address the dilemma of the collision between globalization and fundamentalism.[20]

After surveying the development of Orthodox theology through history, Kalaitzidis offers several desiderata for updating the Church in postmodernity.[21] His bold agenda calls for evangelizing and doing mission in the world without attempting to dominate it, engaging in anthropological reflection consonant with scientific discoveries and insights, welcoming difference and diversity in the church, and adopting the following liturgical platform:[22]

> Extending and deepening the liturgical renaissance movement, bringing God's people—the lay community—back into active participation in the Eucharistic celebration. As this movement develops greater depth, and as theological education is revived, these will lead lay people into taking an active part in the life of the Church. . . . Even more importantly, they will lead to the reestablishment of Eucharistic communities and to the authentic, real-world expression of the vision of the church as the body of Christ, the communion of the Holy Spirit.

---

18. Ibid., 144.
19. Pantelis Kalaitzis, "Challenges of Renewal Facing the Orthodox Church," *The Ecumenical Review* 61, no. 2 (2009): 136-64.
20. Ibid., 160: "Today we live in a completely postmodern world, and yet Orthodox Christianity still has not come to terms with modernity."
21. Ibid., 158-60.
22. Ibid., 158-59.

Kalaitzidis's agenda identifies liturgical renewal as a central initiative in building up the body of Christ, creating a strong link between liturgy and ecclesiology.

Soteris Gouneras discussed fractures within the Greek Church, highlighting a general condition among the people where there is scant sense of love for one's neighbor.[23] Gouneras bemoans the triumph of individualism which permeates ecclesial life by promoting self-indulgent groups of people who mingle only on account of their shared interests. He asserts that the Church has lost her identity, succumbing to secularization and modernization that makes the ecclesial body indistinguishable from society at-large.[24] Gouneras does not spare the theological elite from criticism, accusing their propensity towards self-aggrandizement as one of the causes of the decline of concern for one's brother or sister in the Church.[25] Gouneras views the redemption of Greek society as possible through living engagement with the mystery:[26]

> Today, more than any other time, Greek society and the Greek Orthodox Church needs to rediscover the significance and the meaning of the Logos, not through the formulations of an abstract, theoretical or professional theology, but through a total personal experience of the mystery of the Incarnation which becomes action or materialized in action. To do this we must subject ourselves to a self-examination

23. Soteris Gouneras, "Notes on Urgent Issues Concerning Orthodox Christians in Greece and in the World," in *Synaxis: An Anthology of the Most Significant Orthodox Theology in Greece Appearing in the Journal Synaxe*, vol. 3: *Ecclesiology and Pastoral Care*, trans. Peter Chamberas, ed. John Hadjinicolaou (Montreal: Alexander Press, 2006), 203-13.

24. "Today, in the name of 'acceptance,' which is always like a phantom banner, the modernization of the Church is promoted, instead of attempting a more profound and authentic experience of her mystery, or at least, a new 'discovery' of her mystery. The theological or the ecclesial body is divided into tendencies, groups, factions, companies, or as they may otherwise be called, or even as 'parish centers,' where each one lives the mystery of the Church in their own way and where often each group appears as the guardian of the truth in contrast to the others. This condition in which individualism reigns tends to break up the ecclesial body, which is essentially kept united by the grace of the order of the Typikon of the Liturgy and by the help of the saints, and not by any other reasons of spiritual affinity," in ibid., 206.

25. Ibid.

26. Ibid., 210.

in order to confess to what extent we theologize 'in spirit and truth,' and to what extent we theologize 'according to the traditions of men,' structured and dependent upon activities and processes that have been nurtured by the alienation of man from God.

Gouneras's prognosis for the Church of Greece necessitates the conversion of the theological academy which is called upon to engage the mystery of the Incarnation as the first order of theology. In advancing this argument, Gouneras's diagnosis and prognosis for ecclesial renewal shares a common theme with Vassiliadis's.

A similar sentiment about the state of affairs in Greece was iterated by Philotheos Faros, who critiqued the failures of the theological academy a bit more forcefully.[27] Faros looks at the question of religious instruction in Greece at the macro level and views the established custom of secular, religious instruction in schools as an ugly symptom of the deterioration of church life. Faros speaks openly about the point of education in modern Greek life, as it promotes "the general aspiration of the modern Greek to deal with the problem of earning a living by getting a job in the public sector."[28] The child's experience of receiving religious education outside of the ecclesial environment is a threat to the Church in Faros's view: "it gives the child and the adolescent the impression that the word and the contribution of Christ and the Church to mankind is a lot of hot air; that Christ and the Church do not offer love, but definitions of love."[29]

Faros expresses deep frustration on the untenable situation of the

---

27. Philotheos Faros, "Ecclesial Life and Theology: From Mutual Fulfilling to Mutual Undermining," in *Synaxis: An Anthology of the Most Significant Orthodox Theology in Greece Appearing in the Journal Synaxe*, vol. 1: *Anthropology, Environment, Creation*, trans. Peter Chamberas, ed. Liaidan Sherrard (Montreal: Alexander Press, 2006), 213-19.
28. Ibid., 215.
29. Ibid.

contemporary Greek Orthodox academic,[30] but one element of his diagnosis is particularly relevant to our examination here:[31]

> A second factor that has contributed to the creation of the subject of religious studies in state schools is the aberration of ecclesiastical life generally and particularly of the liturgical life of the Church which, instead of being the new way of approaching the human situation through Christ, has become a kind of magic ritual, showing no disposition to infuse ecclesiastical principles into everyday life, and creating no bond in the ecclesial community between its members or with the clergyman.

Faros's grave diagnosis and forceful commentary on the state of the Church and the study of theology is unique, and several other Greek thinkers echo a similar sentiment a bit more gently.

Metropolitan John Zizioulas, one of the most celebrated Orthodox theologians, picks up on the tension between symbols in ritual and the perception of liturgical celebration as magic tricks in a seminal essay on liturgical symbology.[32] Zizioulas comments on Orthodoxy's preference for retaining rich symbols, such as ornate episcopal vestments, and states that the popular piety of the laity facilitates an interpretation of liturgical symbols as magical manifestations, yielding a grave problem for the Church.[33] This brief presentation of Greek Orthodox theologians reflecting on the contemporary theological enterprise and its role in drawing from the Church as the primary source of theology, engaging the world, and speaking

---

30. "The contemporary Orthodox theologian is forced either to commit himself to the lived ecclesial experience and to function as a teacher of it, or to confine himself to the study of written texts and to become a scholastic, which means that he ends up accepting one of the most serious of Christian heresies," ibid., 216. Faros adds that academic theology is concerned with 'abstract themes," and not "relationships with persons" (216–17).

31. Ibid., 214.

32. Metropolitan John Zizioulas, "Symbolism and Realism in Orthodox Worship," trans. Elizabeth Theokritoff, *Synaxis: An Anthology of the Most Significant Orthodox Theology in Greece Appearing in the Journal Synaxe*, vol. 1: *Anthropology, Environment, Creation*, trans. Peter Chamberas, ed. Liaidan Sherrard (Montreal: Alexander Press, 2006), 251–64.

33. Ibid., 252.

clearly to society sets the stage for the chief feature of this chapter: the program of liturgical rebirth authorized by the Synod of bishops of the Church in Greece.

Liturgical Rebirth in the Church of Greece

The situation leading up to the contemporary platform for liturgical rebirth in Greece is a fusion of received tradition and a consideration of pastorally responding to the Church's environment. The Church of Greece inherited the reforms of the Byzantine Rite, including the legacy of the kollyvadic fathers and the modest reforms implemented by the Ecumenical Patriarchate in the nineteenth and twentieth centuries. There were also grassroots movements within the modern Church of Greece that influenced its activities. The most notable of these is the so-called "Zoe" movement, which originated in 1907 as a lay brotherhood which sought to inaugurate a spiritual reawakening among the Greek people.[34] Towards the end of the 1930s, a number of sisterhoods joined the movement.

Marcel Mojzeš presents the salient points of Zoe's influence on liturgical renewal in the Church of Greece and states that the movement impacted pastoral liturgy by requesting a shortening of the duration of the liturgy, appealing for clergy to read prayers aloud, calling for the faithful to actively participate in the liturgy, petitioning for a closer connection between the New Testament and the mysteries of confession and the Eucharist, encouraging more frequent communion, and enhancing catechesis for confession.[35]

---

34. For an overview, see Demetrios Constantelos, "The Zoe Movement in Greece," *St. Vladimir's Theological Quarterly* 3 (1959), 11-25, and Spyridoula Athanasopoulou-Kypriou, "Emancipation through Celibacy? The Sisterhoods of the Zoe Movement and the Role in the Development of 'Christian Feminism' in Greece, 1938-1960," in *Innovation in the Orthodox Tradition? The Question of Change in Greek Orthodox Thought and Practice*, ed. Trine Stauning-Willert and Lina Molokotos-Lierman (Aldershot, Burlington: Ashgate, 2012), 101-21.
35. Marcel Mojzeš, *Il movimento liturgico nelle chiese byzantine. Analisi di alcune tendenze do riforma*

In engaging a discourse on renewing the Church, the theologians of the Church of Greece also observed environmental conditions of the Roman Catholic and other Orthodox churches. We have already noted Vassiliadis's references to post-revolutionary Russian theologians and his appeal to look the future with the fathers as opposed to waiting. Vassiliadis also differentiated Orthodoxy from Catholics and Protestants, asserting that Catholics have Vatican II and Lutherans the Augsburg Confession as theological identities, leaving Orthodoxy with the liturgy.

Vassiliadis's terse reference to Vatican II and the Augsburg Confession should not be overlooked in our analysis, as it displays the degree to which Greek theologians were not only looking inwards, but also attending to developments in sister Orthodox communities and the Roman Catholic Church.

Ioannis Fountoulis, a giant among Greek liturgical theologians, cautioned Orthodox readers against following the lead of the liturgical reform implemented by Vatican II, especially since the attitudes of Roman clergy toward the reforms became more negative when clergy began the process of implementing them.[36] Fountoulis promoted a series of discussions on liturgical reform that would occur within Orthodoxy's unique ecclesiological systems, ranging from local, diocesan discussions, to synodal discussions within autocephalous churches, to the possibility of deliberation at the long-awaited great and holy synod.[37] Apparently, Fountoulis was confident that Orthodoxy's ecclesiastical apparatus could

---

nel XX secolo, Bibliotheca Ephemerides Liturgicae Subsidia 132 (Rome: Edizione Liturgiche, 2005), 161-64. Mojzeš also notes that Trempelas was associated with Zoe for many years.

36. Ioannis Fountoulis, "Η ΛΕΙΤΟΥΡΓΙΚΗ ΑΝΑΝΕΩΣΗ ΣΤΗΝ ΟΡΘΟΔΟΞΟ ΕΚΚΛΗΣΙΑ ΔΥΝΑΤΟΤΗΤΕΣ ΚΑΙ ΕΜΠΟΔΙΑ" ("Liturgical Renewal in the Orthodox Church: opportunities and Obstacles") *Kleronomia* 21 (1989): 325-34. For details on other pioneers of liturgical studies in the Church of Greece, including a survey of the contributions of Panagiotis Trempelas and Evangelos Theodorou, see Alexopoulos, "The State of Modern Greek Liturgical Studies and Research," 379-83.

37. As of this writing, the great and holy synod is scheduled for 2016.

accommodate necessary discussions on liturgical renewal within the Church.[38] Fountoulis also reflected on the possibility of liturgical reform in the Church of Greece by expressing an affinity for the freedom of the Orthodox presider to adjust the liturgy for pastoral purposes, which was contrasted by the absolute episcopal authority demanded in the liturgical reform of the Greek Melkite (Catholic) Church.[39]

Additional discussions on the nature and form of liturgical rebirth occurred among theologians of the Church of Greece via a proposal for liturgical renewal published by faculty from the seminary in Tinos in 1968 and an inter-Orthodox symposium on liturgical reform in Thessalonica in 1972.[40] Mojzeš identifies the revision of liturgical texts, the distinction between the monastic and parish Typica, the placing of the Eucharist at the center of liturgical life, the improvement of the communitarian nature of the liturgy, and liturgical formation as the chief priorities of the proposal.[41] Advocates of the proposal referred to problems caused by the received tradition as necessitating reform, such as the negative impact caused by the complicated rubrics of special services on the prayerful liturgizing of presiders, and the absurdity of Orthros superseding the Divine Liturgy on Sundays.[42] The 1972 symposium gathered an international representation of Orthodox theologians on the topic of tradition, and featured Alexander Schmemann, who presented some of his research on the distinctions between the monastic and cathedral Typica while also emphasizing the eschatological nature of liturgy.[43]

---

38. Fountoulis's deference to the pan-Orthodox council occurred during a period of intense preparation for the convocation of the council, which commenced in 1959 and lasted until 1976. See Mojzeš, 169-71, 176-81 for details on the liturgical topics taken up by the preconciliar commissions.
39. See Mojzeš's analysis of Fountoulis's generally conservative approach to liturgical renewal in 171-76.
40. Ibid., 183-202.
41. Ibid., 185.
42. See ibid., 183-84, 188.

In 2000, Dimitrios Tzerpos of the University of Athens published a seminal essay on liturgical renewal which demonstrates how the deliberation on the liturgy in the twentieth century arrived at a point for more serious consideration by the synod of bishops.[44] Tzerpos interprets the enterprise of liturgical renewal by examining the tension between the legacy of renewal in Orthodox tradition and the current environment of the Church. Tzerpos affirms Fountoulis's caution against adopting the method and mechanism of Vatican II, but he also states that doing nothing is not an option.[45] Tzerpos refers to the contributions of the Kollyvades movement and Trempelas's enormous historical work, but his most keen insight is his comparison of society with the liturgy.

Tzerpos discusses the radical paradigm shifts endured by Greek society, beginning with the Ottoman yoke and monastic privilege in church life to the phenomenon of modernism, which ushered in the era of national churches and the increasing irrelevance of ancient liturgical languages in the life of the Church. Tzerpos points out that the liturgy remained inert while people's lives evolved rapidly, resulting in a disjunction between liturgy and life that is unnatural. Having depicted the Vatican II reform as impossible for the Orthodox, he states that the essential inactivity on liturgical evolution in Orthodoxy has led the church to the opposite extreme. In many ways, Tzerpos's essay reflects on the same themes of renewal that had been sources for reflection among Greeks throughout the twentieth century.

43. Ibid., 192-96.
44. Dimitrios Tzerpos, "ΠΡΟΣ ΜΙΑ ΑΝΑΝΕΩΣΗ ΤΗΣ ΕΚΚΛΗΣΙΑΣΤΙΚΗΣ ΜΑΣ ΛΑΤΡΕΙΑΣ" ("Towards a Renewal of Our Ecclesiastical Worship") Church of Greece website, http:// www.ecclesia.gr / greek / holysynod / commitees / liturgical / liturgical-0001.htm (accessed September 15, 2014).
45. Ibid., Tzerpos does not contribute a new perception of Vatican II reforms; he is content to cite Fountoulis and to say that a reform on the scale of the Roman one is "impossible, futile, and dangerous to the Orthodox East."

The dual reflection on the state of the liturgy and the Church among Greek theologians finally resulted in decisive action on the part of Church leadership. The action resulted in a partnership between the academic and pastoral enterprises, which had been in tension, as we have seen from our survey above. The diverse movements within the Church of Greece that encouraged reforms in various aspects of liturgical life, especially the Zoe movement, reflection on liturgical reform in other traditions, the proposal of the seminary faculty of Tinos, and the symposium in Thessalonica set the stage for a more concentrated enterprise of liturgical rebirth.

The most important development in liturgical renewal for the Church of Greece was the creation of the Synodal Committee for Liturgical Rebirth at the initiative of the late Archbishop Christodoulos.[46] The committee deliberated the agenda items for liturgical rebirth in a series of symposia from 1999-2008.[47] The symposia treated numerous topics, including the celebration of the sacraments, the revision of liturgical books, promoting liturgical rebirth, and encouraging the Eucharist. Table 5.1 lists the symposia in chronological order:

---

46. Alexopoulos, "The State of Modern Greek Liturgical Studies and Research," 383-85. Mojzeš views the contemporary symposia on liturgical rebirth as the natural result of the pattern of intense interest in the liturgy (200).

47. Pavlos Koumarianos, "Liturgical Rebirth in the Church of Greece Today: A Doubtful Effort of Liturgical Reform," *Bolletino della Badia Greca di Grottaferrata* 3 (2007): 119-44. In his abundantly informative and excellent article, Koumarianos presents an assessment of the entire process of liturgical rebirth from the perspective of a participant. See his article for a detailed report of the process of liturgical rebirth. Also see Pantelis Kalaitzidis, "Challenges of Renewal and Reformation Facing the Orthodox Church," *The Ecumenical Review* 61, no. 2 (2009): 158.

Table 5.1: Chronological list of Symposia Hosted by the Synodal Committee for Liturgical Rebirth:

Year	Symposium Theme
1999	Baptism
2000	Liturgical Rebirth
2001	Eucharist
2002	Marriage
2003	The Holy Scriptures in Orthodox Worship
2004	Orthodox Worship and Idolatry
2005	The Mystery of Priesthood
2006	Heortology
2007	The Mystery of Death
2008	Health and Illness
2009	Mystagogia and Teaching
2010	People and Places that Contributed to the Development of Divine Worship
2011	Contemporary Liturgical Language
2012	The Liturgical Arts
2014	On the Night Offices

The work of the synodal commission on liturgical rebirth is an ongoing process; the commission holds annual or semi-annual meetings to deliberate on a particular theme. The commission is designed to bridge the academic and pastoral; at every symposium, experts in particular fields of liturgical studies and sacramental theology deliver papers, and the symposia include discussion among panelists and worship. The Church of Greece publishes many of the papers on their web site and also provides a report on the central conclusions of the symposia. The symposia themselves are largely academic in nature because the format engenders learning and discussion, and while the symposia can suggest actions for the bishops, it is up to each individual bishop or the Synod as a whole to communicate directives on the liturgy. The process of liturgical rebirth in the Church of Greece has the appearance of following an ideal model, the one preferred by liturgical historians since the task of liturgical history is to inform, and not reform.

In 2004, the Synod of Bishops of the Church of Greece issued twelve encyclicals on topics the symposia addressed. Table 5.2 lists the encyclicals published online:[48]

Table 5.2: Liturgical Encyclicals from the Synod of Bishops of the Church of Greece:

- On the Method for Reading the Prayers of the Divine Liturgy[49]
- On the Participation of the Faithful in the Divine Eucharist[50]
- The Time of the Divine Liturgy and the Possibility of Celebrating it in the Evening[51]
- The Hagiographical Reading and Teaching at the Divine Liturgy[52]
- The Sacramental Life of the Church and Broadcast Media[53]

48. I was unable to obtain the encyclicals that the Church of Greece did not publish online.
49. Synod of Bishops of the Church of Greece, "Περὶ τοῦ τρόπου ἀναγνώσεως τῶν εὐχῶν τῆς Θείας Λειτουργίας," Church of Greece website, http://www.ecclesia.gr/greek/holysynod/egyklioi/egkyklios2784.html (accessed September 15, 2014).
50. Synod of Bishops of the Church of Greece, "Περί τῆς συμμετοχῆς τῶν πιστῶν εἰς τὴν Θείαν Εὐχαριστίαν," Church of Greece website, http://www.ecclesia.gr/greek/holysynod/egyklioi/egkyklios2785.html (accessed September 15, 2014).
51. Synod of Bishops of the Church of Greece, "Ὁ καιρός τῆς Θείας Λειτουργίας καί ἡ δυνατότης τελέσεώς της τό Ἑσπέρας," Church of Greece website, http://www.ecclesia.gr/greek/holysynod/egyklioi/egkyklios2786.html (accessed September 15, 2014).
52. Synod of Bishops of the Church of Greece, "Τά Ἁγιογραφικά ἀναγνώσματα καί τό κήρυγμα εἰς τήν Θείαν Λειτουργίαν," Church of Greece website, http://www.ecclesia.gr/greek/holysynod/egyklioi/egkyklios2791.html (accessed September 15, 2014).
53. Synod of Bishops of the Church of Greece, "Ἡ Μυστηριακή ζωή τῆς Ἐκκλησίας καί τά Ραδιοτηλεοπτικά Μέσα Ἐνημερώσεως," Church of Greece website, http://www.ecclesia.gr/greek/holysynod/egyklioi/egkyklios2792.html (accessed September 15, 2014).

• Ekphonetic Notation in Orthodox Liturgical Practice[54]

In the following section, I will present selections representing some of the central contributions of the symposia, highlights from encyclicals from the Holy Synod, and an analysis of the theological foundations threaded through the liturgical rebirth symposia and underpinning the Greek Church's approach to liturgical reform. My analysis is designed to parse out the theological rationale for liturgical rebirth, so I am organizing the presentation according to the following thematic subheadings: catechesis; promoting the active and conscious participation of the laity in the liturgy; and mechanisms for implementing the program of liturgical rebirth.

Catechesis

Catechesis constitutes the preferred method of liturgical rebirth for the Church of Greece. One can find references to catechesis in numerous documents connected with the synodal commission. The symposia emphasized catechesis because the drive for liturgical rebirth was going to occur from within the received liturgical tradition. This strategy for liturgical rebirth differs from the method of deconstructing and rebuilding liturgical offices. In principle, explaining the meaning of the liturgy to the faithful helps them to engage it in a new way. Encouraging catechesis also means that the people's experience of the liturgy has been historically limited.

The symposia provide several references to the need for strong catechesis of the liturgy to the people. The first symposium on

---

54. Synod of Bishops of the Church of Greece, "Ἐκφωνητικὴ σημειογραφία ἐν τῇ πράξει τῆς Ὀρθοδόξου Λατρείας," Church of Greece website, http://www.ecclesia.gr/greek/holysynod/egyklioi/egkyklios2793.html (accessed January 22, 2015). This encyclical concerns the place of chant in various aspects of worship such as the recitation of prayers and how to properly employ vocal inflections in the proclamation of the Word of God.

Baptism in 1999 mentions the need to remedy problems in the sacrament's liturgical celebration:[55]

> This sacrament [of Baptism] constitutes the first-fruits of man's rebirth in Christ, and the gateway through which he enters into the communion of the Church . . . the nature of the problems that arise during its [liturgical] celebration demand the taking of immediate measures for the restoration of the harm done to its liturgical and pastoral practice . . . the first priority amongst the existing problems is to put forth the soteriological significance of the Sacrament of Holy Baptism as man's participation 'through water and the Spirit' in the mystery of the Cross and the Resurrection of Christ.

The summary report on Baptism also calls for the creation of catechetical materials for adult candidates for Baptism, the creation of an Orthodox Catechism on Baptism, and the printing and free distribution of catechetical texts. The laity is not the only order of the Church to receive instruction on Baptism: the clergy also requires instruction, as the symposium recommended regular gatherings of clergy for "the formation and sensitization of the clergy in dealing with all the problems that arise today during the celebration of Holy Baptism."[56] The thrust of the symposium was the deepening of understanding the meaning of Baptism. The symposium made some original recommendations for the liturgy of Baptism, but the primary focus of the symposium was to draw out the meaning of Baptism and equip leaders to educate the faithful on its meaning.

A similar emphasis on catechesis emerges from the sixth symposium held in 2004 on Orthodox worship and idolatry. The references to catechesis in this symposium's report are implicit, with one proposal calling for improved liturgical instruction of the clergy

---

55. "The First Pan-Hellenic Liturgical Symposium," Church of Greece website (English version), http://www.ecclesia.gr/English/holysynod/committees/liturgical/symposium_1999_1.html (accessed September 15, 2014).

56. Ibid. The symposium also recommended increased collaboration with seminaries and theological schools to improve the education of priests in baptismal celebration.

and laity.[57] The entire thrust of the symposium was to inculcate a proper understanding of the meaning of Orthodox worship and its relationship with the teachings and beliefs of other religions and philosophies. For example, the symposium concluded that "Christian doctrine . . . far exceeds ancient Greek thought in importance within the framework of God-man relations."[58] The symposium stressed that Orthodox worship is theocentric, and thus distinct from the symbolic approaches of mystery cults and other religions.

The symposium stated that "the liturgical symbolism of the Church's rites of worship is not a simple typology, but a depiction of the eschata, the kingdom of God," and "the Eucharistic sacrifice is a continuation of our Lord's sacrifice on the Cross and possesses not a symbolic, but a real and realistic character."[59] The pastoral impetus of the symposium was to clarify the meaning of a liturgical symbol, and the gathering seemed to address problems in Greek society on how believers perceive liturgical symbols and compare them to ritual enactments in Greek mythology and other religions.[60]

The symposium's primary initiative of deepening understanding of liturgical symbology shares several similarities with Metropolitan John Zizioulas's seminal essay on liturgical symbols discussed earlier in this chapter. Zizioulas's essay also seeks to distinguish liturgical symbols from magical rituals and to aid pious faithful in avoiding the pitfalls of idolatry.[61] Zizioulas argues that symbols refer the beholder

57. Sixth Pan-Hellenic Symposium, Church of Greece website, http://www.ecclesia.gr/English/holysynod/committees/liturgical/symposium_2010_2.html (accessed September 15, 2014).
58. Ibid.
59. Ibid.
60. On the relationship between Greek folk traditions and the liturgy, see Dimitrios Tzerpos, "Η ΟΡΘΟΔΟΞΗ ΛΑΤΡΕΙΑ ΣΤΑ ΗΘΗ ΚΑΙ ΕΘΙΜΑ ΤΟΥ ΕΛΛΗΝΙΚΟΥ ΛΑΟΥ" ("Orthodox Worship in the Customs of the Greek People"), Church of Greece website, http://www.ecclesia.gr/greek/holysynod/commitees/liturgical/latreia_ethima.html (accessed September 15, 2014).
61. "It is in consequence a dangerous view (shared by many Orthodox) that the divine energies somehow reside in the nature of these sacred objects, if we do not simultaneously stress the

to the personal presence of the one depicted who is not in his or her natural state through the medium of the symbol, the core of a definition he encapsulates in the term "iconic ontology."[62] Zizioulas asserts that rationalism and individualism contributed to the corrosion of Orthodox iconic ontology which results either in outright dismissal of the symbol's significance or the reduction of the symbol to appeal to a particular need.[63]

I have placed the symposium's attempt to rehabilitate the meaning of the liturgical symbol under the heading of catechesis because the symposium did not make any explicit recommendations for revising the liturgy to disclose the meaning of liturgical symbols with greater clarity. In his essay, Zizioulas merely refers to pious faithful who continue to observe the Church's ritual customs of liturgical symbology as beacons of hope for the revival of iconic ontology in Orthodox worship.[64] Zizioulas points to numerous examples of liturgical revisions as betrayals of authentic iconic ontology, such as the decision to move the sermon to communion, the preference expressed for small chapels over cathedral churches, and the appeal to clergy to abandon ornate vestments for simple ones.[65] It is clear that Zizioulas views the received liturgical tradition as containing appropriate symbols that do not require purification: this is an instance of pastorally encouraging proper catechesis to invigorate

personal quality of the divine energies," John Zizioulas, "Symbolism and Realism in Orthodox Worship," 259.

62. Zizioulas defines iconic ontology gradually throughout his essay. The premise of his definition is that icons denote personal presence, but nature is secondary. Zizioulas elaborates: "Given that iconic symbolism in the liturgy is . . . a matter of personal presence and not of natural presence, nature participates in it only in a secondary way and to the degree that it is hypostatized in the person. Thus place, time, matter, colors, speech, smell, hearing, . . . are used in symbolism; not, however, as the source of the symbol—the sources are always personal and historical-eschatological—but as borrowings express the personal presence," in ibid., 257.

63. Ibid., 261. Zizioulas essentially argues that moral messages addressing contemporary societal needs have become the purpose of liturgical symbols, which guided the Church "to participate in the communion in the last times" in their original state.

64. Zizioulas, 261.

65. Ibid.

understanding of the received tradition of the liturgy without revising this version of the liturgy itself.

The symposium on Orthodox worship and idolatry does not present desiderata on revisions to the liturgy. The symposium's proposals are entirely catechetical and designed to educate the faithful to the point of an interior awakening to and acceptance of the iconic ontology of symbols. Besides the general appeal for developing liturgical instruction for clergy and laity, the symposium also proposed a program of careful instruction of the faithful on the significance of offering gifts in the liturgy, on the distinction between the mysteries (sacraments) of the Church and pagan rituals, and on the theological repository of the liturgical year.[66]

The catechetical approach occurs within the received liturgical tradition, and the approach to liturgical reform is to revive dormant aspects of the tradition that have fallen into disuse as opposed to purging liturgical elements and replacing them with new ones. The catechetical strategy is directed to two audiences: clergy, as the primary educators of the faithful, and the faithful themselves. The Greek Church's Synod of bishops took concrete steps to implement a more catechetical approach in 2004, particularly with the encyclical on hagiographical readings at the liturgy. The Synodal encyclical reserves the larger task of reforming the lectionary to the future great and holy synod while offering several suggestions for preaching. First and foremost, the bishops refer to the biblical character of Orthodox worship itself and their relevance to the entire Divine Liturgy, which is an implicit attempt to demonstrate the significance of hearing the Word of God at the Eucharistic assembly.[67]

66. Sixth Pan-Hellenic Symposium, Church of Greece website, http://www.ecclesia.gr/English/holysynod/committees/liturgical/symposium_2010_2.html (accessed September 15, 2014).

67. "The biblical character of Orthodox worship highlights the great importance of the readings for the sacramental Synaxis and interpreting these unbreakable attachment after the whole mystery of the Divine Liturgy," Synodal Encyclical, "The Hagiographical reading and Teaching at

The bishops' primary concern in the encyclical is to illuminate the liturgical function of preaching to both the clergy and the faithful. The encyclical's content exposes homiletics as enduring a state of crisis in the Church of Greece. The bishops refer to the sermon as an "essential component of divine worship," and bemoan the omission of preaching as unjustified, especially since lay theologians can fill the preaching gap when clergy are unable to preach.[68] The encyclical stipulates several requirements for preaching. For example, the sermon must occur after the Gospel (and not after the liturgy); the duration of the sermon must be around twelve to fifteen minutes; the content must be Christocentric and draw from the dogmatic deposit of the Church, and not be reduced to moralizing. The homilist must employ a preaching style and speak in a language people can understand, for the ultimate purpose of unveiling the mystery of the biblical texts and guiding the people more deeply into sacramental participation.[69]

The encyclical on hagiographical reading and preaching was not explicitly catechetical, but I have placed it under this subheading because its content is consistent with the general catechetical imperative of the liturgical rebirth enterprise. The clergy are responsible for exercising their presidency of the liturgy of the word to evangelize the people and deepen their participation in the sacred mystery. An intersection between evangelization and catechesis occurs here because of the encyclical's references to mystagogy and concern that the content of preaching is grounded in dogmatic truths and not reduced to moralizing. The encyclical continues the

---

the Divine Liturgy," http://www.ecclesia.gr/greek/holysynod/egyklioi/egkyklios2791.html (accessed September 15, 2014).

68. Ibid.

69. Note that the encyclical does not use the words "sacramental participation," but the bishops do view the homily as a mystagogy of biblical texts, which suggests a view of the liturgy of the Word as sacramental.

pattern of catechizing both the clergy and the laity. Clergy are to deepen their own understanding of the liturgy of the word and the purpose of preaching; by strengthening this ministry, the laity will be nourished by the word and attain understanding.

An essay on the priest as a teacher of the Gospel by C. Filia elaborates this aspect of the encyclical.[70] Filia explains that the teaching ministry of the priest stems from his role as presider at the altar, and sacramental catechesis is designed to ignite deep faith among the baptized.[71] The teaching does not stop at imparting intellectual knowledge, but is designed to arrive at divine illumination. Filia's essay coheres with the synodal encyclical by emphasizing catechesis as an integral function occurring through the liturgical sermon and capacitating the faithful deeper entrance into covenant with Christ.

To be sure, the encyclical also contains specific liturgical instructions: certain assigned pericopes can be revised if they are repeated at another time in the liturgical year (pending the examination of the lectionary by a pan-Orthodox synod); the sermon must draw from the biblical readings of that day; homilists are to preach either from the ambon or from the holy gates. The bishops' primary concern in the encyclical is catechesis, to restore the purpose of the liturgical function of preaching; liturgical reforms are either deferred to the pan-Orthodox synod or discussed as apparatuses supporting the larger catechetical enterprise.

The final issue for consideration under the catechetical heading is the question of introducing modern Greek into the liturgy. The first such attempt at using modern Greek was introduced by no other than

---

70. C. N. Filia, "Ο Ιερέας ως διδάσκαλος του Ευαγγελίου" ("The Priest as a teacher of the Gospel"), Church of Greece website, http://www.ecclesia.gr/greek/holysynod/commitees/liturgical/z_symposio_3.html (accessed September 16, 2014).

71. Ibid.: "Within the Divine Liturgy, the task of teaching the Gospel is interwoven with the performance of the mystery."

the late Archbishop Christodoulos himself, who instructed churches in Athens to read the appointed lessons from the New Testament in modern Greek in 2004.[72] The modern Greek readings would follow the readings in the much older liturgical Greek, which would seem to offer a pastoral approach of gently introducing a new practice to the Church. Among the changes proposed, it would seem that the introduction of modern Greek would be among the most innocuous reforms, but observers have noted the failure of this initiative.[73]

Vassiliadis has addressed the question of using modern Greek texts in the liturgy at some length.[74] Vassiliadis states that the Orthodox churches that pray primarily in Greek have been deliberating on this matter for decades, and have largely avoided using a vernacular translation because the champions of vernacular tended to use the language as a crucial element of an argument "to promote phyletistic and nationalistic secessionist movements."[75] Also, some Greeks perceived using a translation of the Bible as "an inclination toward the Protestant tradition," or "an imitation of the measures taken by the Vatican II Council."[76] The debate on the use of translated texts in the liturgy discloses the positions adopted by divided ecclesial parties and their perceptions on the relationship between elements of liturgical renewal and its spurious origins.

This section presents various elements from the synodal symposia on liturgical rebirth and supporting documents that illustrate

72. "Athens Churches told to use Modern Greek," *Christian Century* 121, no 4 (October 5, 2004), 18.

73. See, for example, the comments of Alexopoulos in "The State of Modern Greek Liturgical Studies," 390. Alexopoulos asserts that "the use of modern Greek in worship is a matter of time," and calls for the establishment of a project that would translate liturgical texts into modern Greek. Since the 2011 symposium took up the theme of liturgical language in general, it seems that this process is unfolding as Alexopoulos predicted.

74. Petros Vassiliadis, "The Liturgical Use of the Bible in Greek Orthodoxy: An Orthodox Critical Approach in 12 Steps," Unpublished Essay. Published by Professor Vassiliadis on his academia web page, https://www.academia.edu/3852656 (accessed January 22, 2015).

75. Ibid., 9.

76. Ibid.

catechesis as the preferred method for igniting liturgical rebirth in the Church of Greece. I have noted that the symposia and the bishops do occasionally suggest more concrete liturgical reforms. The catechetical strategy is directed towards the clergy whose role as liturgical presiders is clarified; they, in turn, are to catechize the people through the received liturgical tradition, not as religious instructors who impart definitions of Christianity, but as pastors whose orderly and solemn exercise of their ministry leads the faithful more deeply into the covenant with Christ.

The Active and Conscious Participation of the Faithful in the Liturgy

Our section treating catechesis provides an appropriate segue for addressing the active participation of the people in the liturgy, because the conceptual model of liturgical rebirth entails forming clergy who are equipped to preside in such a way that the liturgy evangelizes and catechizes the people. The question of lay participation in the liturgy was raised in multiple symposia. For example, the second symposium which occurred in Volos in October 2000 addressed liturgical renewal, and provided the following definition:[77]

> The Symposium's target was to define the meaning of the term 'Liturgical renewal' on the one hand, while on the other, to examine whether or not such a renewal is possible or desirable, and to specify the possible changes, improvements and adaptations of certain elements of Divine Worship. Special effort was made to make clear that by the use of the term 'Liturgical Renewal' is meant: a) the conscientious participation in Divine Worship and the development of Liturgical formation in the Church's faithful (pleroma) so that they will not be

77. "Special Synodical Committee for Liturgical Rebirth; THE SECOND PAN-HELLENIC LITURGICAL SYMPOSIUM: Volos, 22-25 October 2000; Findings and proposals of the 2nd Liturgical Symposium," The Church of Greece, Official Website, http://www.ecclesia.gr/English/holysynod/committees/liturgical/symposium_2010_1.html (accessed July 9, 2013).

passive participants and isolated from the liturgical action, but rather be initiated, through theology and Divine Worship into what transpires in the Church. b) the understanding of the words, types and symbols employed in Divine Worship, since Divine Worship is characterized as 'reasonable' or 'logical' Worship. c) the unity of the liturgical act through the various traditional liturgical types and forms, i.e., the use of a single liturgical form, a single rite or Typikon.

It is impossible to ignore the verbiage of "conscientious participation," "liturgical formation," and "understanding." Like *SC*, the aim of this special synodal commission was the laity. The symposium's summary report stated the discussions occurred around two "poles": a clear understanding of the Church's liturgical treasures and the maximizing of the people's participation in the liturgy for their sanctification.[78] The symposia were gatherings of academic specialists and pastors with knowledge of the pulse of parochial life. The gathering of academics and pastors illustrates the cooperation of two crucial organs to improve the life of the Church.

The point of the symposia was not to illuminate the Greek Church's historical liturgical treasury as an artifact to be venerated. The symposia kept in mind the needs of today's Church, as illustrated by multiple references to coupling the Church's millennial traditions with her pastoral needs of today.[79]

The Greek Church's emphasis on lay participation in the liturgy and promoting liturgical understanding appeared again in the third symposium on the theme, "The Mystery of the Holy Eucharist."[80]

---

78. Ibid.

79. This is particularly emphasized by two passages from the report of the second symposium in 2000: "It was found that the subjects were developed by the speakers on the basis of the scientific data from each section of Theology but at the same time taking into consideration present-day circumstances and the pastoral needs and demands of the body of the Church"; "Up to the present the two thousand year old liturgical tradition of our Church constitutes a source of inspiration and a sure and guiding factor for the dealing with contemporary problems of Orthodox worship. At the same time, the serious needs of today's Christians and especially the new prevailing circumstances of urban life for the Church's faithful must be kept in mind," in ibid.

Five of the twelve points of emphasis are directed, at least in part, to the sanctification of the faithful. Point no. 6 explicates the participation of the faithful and repeats the language of the previous symposium on liturgical rebirth:[81]

> The active and conscious participation of the people during the celebration of the Holy Liturgy was one of the main points of the Symposium's concern. Thus, the need for further understanding of the elements that highlight the communal nature of the Divine Liturgy was emphasized, e.g., the 'decent and pious' attitude of the faithful at the Liturgy, their participation in the chanting, the audible reading of the holy prayers by the celebrant and focusing upon the dialogic manner in which the Eucharistic *anaphora* is to be expressed.

The commission emphasizes the words "active and conscious participation," and also locates the laity's participation in the dialogical components of the liturgy, especially the anaphora. Also, one should note the similarity between this point and the teachings of *SC* nos. 14 and 30 on the active participation of the laity. The Roman Church had identified psalms, acclamations, and gestures as appropriate places for the people to actively participate. Similarly, the Greek synodal commission identifies chanting, the audible reading of the prayers, dialogical structures and components, and the decent and pious attitude of the people. Point 7 further develops the audible reading of prayers mentioned in point 6 by calling upon the clergy to render audibly all of the petitions and prayers.[82] Point 7 also discouraged clergy from chanting the prayers, and called upon parishes to use simpler music, which would enable the people to join in the chanting and singing of responses and refrains.[83]

80. Special Synodal Committee for Liturgical Rebirth, "The Mystery of the Holy Eucharist," Church of Greece Official Web Site, http://www.ecclesia.gr/English/holysynod/committees/liturgical/symposium_2010_1_1.html (accessed July 10, 2013).
81. Ibid.
82. Ibid., Point 7.
83. Ibid., "Further, the variety of liturgical modual tones used should be limited, the traditional

Point 9 refers to the laity by calling upon pastors to "take all measures necessary to facilitate the faithful in attending the Eucharistic synaxis."[84] Point 10 addresses Holy Communion and calls for the faithful to frequently partake while cautioning that participation must be orderly. Point 12 called upon the Synod of the Greek Church to continue its work in providing liturgical formation to both the clergy and the laity in the spirit and method of mystagogy.[85]

The impetus to encourage the active and conscious participation of the people in the liturgy was one of the central elements of the Greek Church's liturgical rebirth enterprise, and echoes of this desire are found in synodal encyclicals. The encyclical "On the Method for reading the Prayers of the Divine Liturgy" is primarily concerned with "the salvation of the people through conscious participation in the Divine Liturgy."[86] The bishops emphasize that the method used by presiders in reading the prayers of the liturgy is for the purpose of enabling the people to enter into the mystery with the priests.

A similar theme emerges in the seemingly esoteric synodal decision to restore the position of the resurrection Gospel ("eothina") read

ones being preferred in rendering the musical parts of the Liturgy, which in any case should be executed simply, so that the people's participation in the chanting is facilitated."

84. Ibid.

85. The commission delivered other points not specifically pertaining to the life and ministry of the laity, but illuminating a Eucharistic theology coherent with Schmemann's and SC. Point 1 states that the Eucharist is a manifestation of the mystery of the Church, in other words, the source of ecclesiology. Point 2 repeats this idea by asserting that history demonstrates the role of the Eucharist in shaping the body of the Church. Point 3 discusses the biblical and eschatological dimensions of the Eucharist and calls for a revision of the lectionary so that it could be "expounded for the edification of the faithful." Point 4 stressed the integrity and centrality of the sermon in the liturgy. Point 5 called for the avoidance of "disorderly and exaggerated ceremonial practices" and anticipated that the publication of the next hieratikon (euchologion or sacramentary) would provide an outline for the ceremonial order of liturgical celebration. See Koumarianos, 129-39, for his assessment of the hieratikon that was published during the course of liturgical rebirth.

86. Synod of Bishops of the Church of Greece, "Περὶ τοῦ τρόπου ἀναγνώσεως τῶν εὐχῶν τῆς Θείας Λειτουργίας," Church of Greece website, http://www.ecclesia.gr/greek/holysynod/egyklioi/egkyklios2784.html (accessed September 15, 2014).

at Orthros. In the late-nineteenth century reforms of the Greek Typikon, this Gospel had been moved to a later point in the resurrection Orthros service, immediately anterior to the ninth ode of the Canon, the Canticle of the Theotokos. The purpose of this reform was to enable the "entire Church, the people of God, to hear the joyful message of the Resurrection and to venerate the Holy Gospel."[87]

Because Orthros itself had been returned to Sunday morning immediately before the liturgy, there was very little time in between the two Gospel readings, namely the "eothina" resurrection Gospel of Orthros and the appointed Sunday Gospel from the lectionary. The synod decided to restore the eothina Gospel to its original position in Orthros, between the Prokeimenon and the chanting of Psalm 50. The bishops directed presiders to wear a white phelonion during this Gospel reading, so the priest would symbolize the angel who was present at the tomb of the risen Lord, which would enhance the ritual complement to the reading of the resurrection account. This directive is an attempt to illuminate the Paschal nature of Sunday and the directive to wear a white phelonion is an implicit way of inviting the people's participation since the people know that white vestments are worn on the highest ranking feasts of the liturgical year.

The synod's most significant encyclical concerned the people's participation in the Divine Liturgy.[88] The encyclical reviews the history of patristic and canonical teaching on the Eucharist and

87. "Ἡ μετάθεσις αὕτη τῆς ἀναγνώσεως τοῦ Ἑωθινοῦ Εὐαγγελίου, καθιερώθη προφανῶς, διά νά δίδεται ἡ δυνατότης εἰς μεγαλύτερον μέρος τοῦ πληρώματος τῆς Ἐκκλησίας, "τοῦ λαοῦ τοῦ Θεοῦ", νά ἀκούῃ τὸ χαρμόσυνον μήνυμα τῆς Ἀναστάσεως καί νά ἀσπάζεται τὸ Ἱερὸν Εὐαγγέλιον," Synod of Bishops of the Church of Greece, "Ἐπαναφορά τῆς Τάξεως τοῦ Ἑωθινοῦ Εὐαγγελίου εἰς τήν κανονικήν αὐτοῦ θέσιν," Church of Greece website, http://www.ecclesia.gr/greek/holysynod/egyklioi/egkyklios2794.html (accessed September 15, 2014).

88. Synod of Bishops of the Church of Greece, "Περί τῆς συμμετοχῆς τῶν πιστῶν εἰς τήν Θείαν Εὐχαριστίαν," Church of Greece website, http://www.ecclesia.gr/greek/holysynod/egyklioi/egkyklios2785.html (accessed September 15, 2014).

suggests that the Orthodox tradition consistently favors the laity's frequent reception of communion. The bishops refer to the Eucharist as "the source and center of the spiritual life in Christ, the manifestation of the Church as the body of Christ and the communion of the all-holy Spirit."[89]

Receiving the gift of communion results in salvation and redemption of sins for people who participate consciously.[90] But the bishops are aware of the prevailing culture of abstaining from communion among Greek Orthodox faithful, as they refer to limiting communion to great feasts such as Pascha or Christmas as an "obvious loss," and frown upon the usual ritual sequence of the priest inviting the people to communion ("in the fear of God with faith draw near") only to return to the altar without having imparted communion.[91] A sense of betraying the mystery of the Eucharist occurs when the faithful abstain from receiving communion.

Regular and frequent reception of communion in the Divine Liturgy is a priority for liturgical rebirth promoted by several theologians involved with the liturgy enterprise in the Church of Greece. Archimandrite Elias Mastrogiannopoulos offered a brief essay outlining the Orthodox theological foundation and pastoral approach to the faithful's participation in Eucharistic communion.[92] The similarities between Mastrogiannopoulos's essay and the synodal encyclical are numerous and striking, and it appears that his essay was the basis for the encyclical.[93] The Greek bishops affirmed a

89. Ibid: "ἡ Θεία Εὐχαριστία θεωρεῖται καί εἶναι ἡ πηγή καί τό κέντρον τῆς ἐν Χριστῷ πνευματικῆς ζωῆς, ἡ φανέρωσις τῆς Ἐκκλησίας, ὡς Σώματος Χριστοῦ καί ὡς κοινωνίας τοῦ Παναγίου Πνεύματος."

90. Note the reference to "participating consciously" in the text ("συνειδητῶς μετέχοντας").

91. Ibid.

92. Elias Mastrogiannopoulos, "Περί συμμετοχῆς των πιστών στην Θ. Κοινωνίαν" ("On the Participation of the Faithful in Holy Communion"), Church of Greece website, http://www.ecclesia.gr/greek/holysynod/commitees/liturgical/z_symposio_11.html (accessed September 17, 2014).

93. One noteworthy item is Mastrogiannapoulos's description of the Eucharist as the "source and

tremendous chorus of voices calling for the people to actively and consciously participate in the liturgy. The desiderata for liturgical rebirth iterated by prominent Greek theologians punctuate active participation in the liturgy as the most desired outcome of the liturgical rebirth enterprise. In his influential essay on Orthodox liturgical renewal, Petros Vassiliadis proposes the following tactics for liturgical renewal:[94]

> The restoration of the catholic participation in the eschatological table of the kingdom; this means participation of the entire community to the Holy Communion (not just frequent communion) with no juridical or legalistic preconditions (such as worthiness, or strict preparation of the individual faithful), without any subordination of the sacrament par excellence of the Church (Eucharist) to other sacraments (repentance, priesthood, etc.). . . . Return to the early Christian status of full and inclusive participation of the entire people of God . . . to the actions, processions and singing in our liturgy . . . , and of possible rehabilitation of the 'Cathedral office.' . . . Emphasis on all processional, liturgical and participatory elements of our Orthodox liturgy.

Vassiliadis's repetition of attending to frequent participation in the liturgy demonstrates his emphasis on this tactic. The reader will also note the dissonance between his proposal for Eucharistic communion and that of the synod of bishops, as Vassiliadis calls for catholic participation without legal obstacles, while the synodal encyclical stated that laity should partake frequently as long as they prepare with confession and repentance.[95]

In his essay explaining the role of the priest as liturgist, Dimitrios

---

center of the spiritual life in Christ, the manifestation of the Church as the body of Christ and as communion of the All-holy Spirit" ("ἡ πηγὴ καὶ τὸ κέντρον τῆς ἐν Χριστῷ πνευματικῆς ζωῆς, ἡ φανέρωσις τῆς Ἐκκλησίας ὡς Σώματος Χριστοῦ καί ὡς κοινωνία τοῦ Παναγίου Πνεύματος"), language evoking the Roman Church's conciliar teaching on the liturgy in SC.

94. Petros Vassiliadis, "Liturgical Renewal and the Orthodox Church," unpublished essay taken from Professor Vassiliadis's academia web page, https://www.academia.edu/3581957 (accessed January 22, 2015).

95. "The conditions for the existential participation of our faith in the great mystery are the unity of faith, love, repentance and mutual love, all accomplished through repentance and confession,"

Tzerpos discusses the presider's role in encouraging the active participation of the people in the liturgy.[96] He refers to minor liturgical elements, such as reciting the Lord's Prayer as a community at the liturgy, or encouraging the people to confirm the Eucharistic Prayer with the final "Amen," actions which manifest the fullness of the priesthood of the laity in the liturgy.[97] Tzerpos reminds priests that the common practice of saying appointed prayers silently keeps them hidden from the people, and this practice facilitated the phenomenon of covering ritual actions with long, melodious chants, which discouraged the people from active participation and instead transformed them into passive observers of the liturgy.[98]

Perhaps one of the most underdeveloped objectives of the symposia was to restore the eschatological emphasis of the liturgy and one's participation in it. Several of the symposia refer to restoring the eschatological dimension of the liturgy, most notably the symposium on the Eucharist. However, the critique of liturgical decay offered by Vassiliadis refers to the disappearance of the eschatological nature of liturgy as the greatest loss suffered by the Byzantine Rite in its history. Zizioulas's essay on liturgical symbology also concentrates on eschatology, speaking of how symbols refer to the future state of glorified humanity in the kingdom of God.[99] Vassiliadis's critique is particularly startling:[100]

Synodal encyclical, "On the Participation of the Faithful in the Divine Eucharist," accessed September 17, 2014.

96. Dimitrios Tzerpos, "Ο Ιερεύς ως Λειτουργός" ("The Priest as Liturgist"), Church of Greece Web Site, http://www.ecclesia.gr/greek/holysynod/commitees/liturgical/z_symposio_6.html (accessed September 17, 2014).

97. Ibid.

98. Ibid.

99. Zizioulas, 255: "Typological symbolism never refers to the past, but always to the future. Thus Baptism is not a type of the Flood, but the Flood is a type of Baptism, etc. In worship, nothing leads us to the past, except to refer us through the past to the future."

100. Vassiliadis, "Liturgical Renewal and the Orthodox Church," 9-10.

The Church ceased to be an icon of the eschaton and became an icon of the origin of beings, of Creation, resulting in a cosmological approach to the Church, to its liturgy, and to its mission, instead of a historical one, as in the Holy Scriptures. Naturally, therefore, the close connection between liturgy and mission disappeared, together with interest in the institutional reality of the Church, whose purpose is now characterized, at best, as a sanatorium of souls. The Church's mission—and the purpose of liturgy—is now directed not in bringing about synergically the Kingdom of God, but toward the salvation of the souls of every individual Christian.

Of the liturgical reforms advanced by the synod, two communicate the eschatological dimension of the liturgy most urgently: the appeal to the faithful to receive Holy Communion and participate in the liturgy, and the instruction to the presider to wear a white phelonion. The synod's actions do not communicate the same degree of urgency or emphasis as Vassiliadis conveys in his attention to this matter in his essays.

It is clear, then, that the symposia on liturgical rebirth in the Church of Greece prioritized encouraging the active participation of the people in the liturgy. Their recommendations were based upon academic deliberations that were in continuity with the pastoral work accomplished by figures and organizations such as Trempelas, Fountoulis, and Zoe, along with the Tinos seminary proposal of 1968 and the 1972 international Orthodox symposium on tradition. The driving motivation towards active participation was the continuing and troublesome detachment of Church from society along with the perception that the Church's ability to shape people was diminishing. Pastors and theologians observed the people's disinterest in liturgy and their passive participation in it.

The theological rationale for liturgical reform was manifold: primarily, it was to enable the people to become the Christians God had invited them to be by actively engaging the liturgy. Reforming select aspects of the liturgy, such as saying some prayers aloud for the people to hear, improving preaching, and reading the resurrection Gospel with the celebrant vested in white pointed to liturgical celebration as paschal: when the people participated in the liturgy, they became witnesses of and participants in Jesus Christ's saving death and resurrection. The symposia privileged the removal of obstacles to understanding the liturgy. As long as central liturgical elements remained inaccessible to the people, they would be unable to actively engage them in the liturgy.

The symposia's preference for catechesis was designed to remove the primary obstacles and capacitate the people to understand the liturgy. The catechesis followed the Orthodox tradition of mystagogy so the people were not necessarily obtaining intellectual knowledge about the liturgy, but were receiving training to enter more deeply into its mystery, the eschatological encounter with the Triune God through Jesus Christ. The emphasis on catechesis would open the door to active liturgical participation, so the two tactics are inseparable. Finally, it is important to note that the symposia suggested numerous liturgical reforms, while the synodal encyclicals authorized limited reform. Reform was limited because the Greek Church's notion of liturgical rebirth is that it can occur within the framework of the received tradition.

Implementing Liturgical Rebirth

The symposia contributed a treasury of observations and recommendations for liturgical rebirth in Greece grounded by academic study and pastoral guidance. However, the symposia had no authority on their own, and they were the result of a special synodal commission charged with studying and deliberating the possibilities of liturgical rebirth. The mechanism for liturgical change in the Church of Greece comes from either synodal instructions, which would be mandated for the entire Church, or directives issued by diocesan hierarchs.

The mechanism adopted by the Church of Greece follows a pattern established by Fountoulis in his essay on liturgical reform, where he expressed reluctance to adopt a reform on the scale of Vatican II (a sentiment echoed by Tzerpos) and articulated confidence in the Orthodox ecclesiological framework to deliberate and implement reform. The framework envisions dialogue occurring at every level of the Church on liturgical matters, including parishes, deaneries, dioceses, synods, and reserving the most grave matters for the great and holy synod.

Our examination of the symposia has already shown that the dialogue was enriched by encounters between academics and pastors. These encounters produced a thick collection of rich scholarship, including papers examining various aspects of global and local liturgical histories, and examinations of attempts at liturgical renewal in other Orthodox churches. The process of liturgical reform is informed by academic research, which shows what is possible, along with pastoral evaluation, which illuminates problems in the Church's liturgical life. The decision to implement reform is reserved for the highest rank of Church order, the bishop, an honor that conforms with Schmemann's approach to the implementation of reform. We must note that the situation in the life of the Greek Church rendered the expectation that the synod would adopt all of the suggested reforms implausible, given the conservative tendencies of the bishops supported by constituencies in the Church which do not want change.[101]

Let us begin with a selective description of prescriptions for reform; we have mentioned some of these earlier in our discussion of the chief features of reform in the Greek Church, and we will

101. See the insightful comments by Koumarianos, 139–43.

add to this list here. The symposium on Baptism included numerous suggestions for liturgical reform including the establishment of baptismal days in the Church calendar, permitting occasions where large numbers of people could receive baptism, and a proposal for creating an architectural model for contemporary baptisteries and for renovating existing spaces so that a liturgically-suitable space for Baptism could be added. We have also noted the minor reform concerning the position of the reading of the eothina resurrection gospel at Orthros authorized by the bishops, accompanied by the presider wearing a white phelonion. The symposium on the Eucharist suggested the reform of the Lectionary, a task the synod deferred to the great and holy synod of the global Orthodox Church. This symposium also suggested that a new edition of the hieratikon would resolve deficiencies in liturgical celebration and encourage priests to celebrate in an orderly fashion.

Pavlos Koumarianos was a central participant in the symposia and offered an assessment of the process and its subsequent implementation.[102] He chronicled the symposia and analyzed the adoption of the recommendations and the ensuing implementation of rebirth by hierarchical authority. In addition to the synodal encyclicals presenting directives on the liturgy, Archbishop Christodoulos, the presiding bishop of the Church of Greece at the time of liturgical rebirth, issued twelve encyclicals on liturgical matters directed to the clergy of his diocese (Athens).[103] The encyclicals include recommendations, and some aspects of reform

---

102. Pavlos Koumarianos, "Liturgical Rebirth in the Church of Greece Today: A Doubtful Effort of Liturgical Reform," 123-24.

103. For an assessment of Archbishop Christodoulos's attempt to renew the Church of Greece, see D. Oulis, G. Makris, and S. Roussos, "The Orthodox Church of Greece: Policies and Challenges under Archbishop Christodoulos of Athens (1998-2008)," *International Journal for the Study of the Christian Church 10, nos. 2-3* (2010): 192-210. These scholars criticize Christodoulos for sustaining a conservative status quo, though they do not cover liturgical renewal. For an opposing view, see Alexopoulos, "The State of Modern Greek Liturgical Studies," 383-84.

were implemented by metropolises of the Greek Church. Koumarianos's assessment begins by identifying eight points emphasized by the encyclicals. Most of these points cohere with the priorities of the synodal commission. For example, the encyclicals strive to restore the Eucharist as the center of the Church's being; they aim for the laity to actively participate in the liturgy by having the celebrants read most of the priestly prayers aloud; they call for priests to offer sermons and instructions on liturgical history and theology; and they seek to remove distortions and exaggerations from the chanted portions of the liturgy, so the texts would be not only audible, but also comprehensible.

The liturgical directives tended to emphasize the activity and symbolism of the clergy and laity, and they instruct particular ministers on the way they are to engage the liturgy.[104] Bishops are to use traditional vestments and avoid fancy and decorated ones; simple vestments are preferred (nos. 10 and 23). Most of the directives apply to parish priests. Priests are to read the prayers of the Eucharist aloud, read other prayers at the correct place in the liturgical structure, give sermons, lectures, and seminars on the liturgy, use all of the loaves brought by the people for the Eucharist, avoid infusing their own styles into liturgical celebration, preach the sermon after the Gospel, use simple vestments, distribute the antidoron, distribute Communion at the appointed time (not after liturgy), and refrain from scolding the people during the liturgy. Chanters are to avoid exuberant musical decoration when reading the Scriptural lessons and chanting hymns and are prohibited from laughing, joking, or loitering at the chanter's stand. The laity are to hear the Eucharistic prayers and respond with "Amen," learn from seminars and other instruction designed to promote active participation, bake and offer bread for the Eucharist, partake of communion frequently, and

---

104. This section follows Koumarianos's summary of the directives.

preach (for those who have the required education). Bishops, priests, chanters, and the laity share the responsibility for promoting active participation in the liturgy.

This organization of the directives according to order and ministry is both deliberate and accurate, because the encyclicals address various orders of the Church. The directives have an innate ecclesiological character: the chief priority of the enterprise was to fine-tune the received liturgical tradition of the Church, and not radically reform its shape and order. In determining the objectives of the synod and individual hierarchs, it is evident that the implementation sought to restore order to the liturgy by removing abuses, and also sought to reinvigorate the dialogical character of liturgy. Most of the directives pertain to priests, but almost all of these directives envision the primary outcome: the laity's active participation in the liturgy. For example, while instructing the priest to read the prayers in their proper liturgical place, the objective also concerns the laity, since the liturgical act of reading the prayer will presumably benefit the laity who will now have access to the prayers.

Likewise, the instruction to preach the Gospel after the sermon as opposed to the end of the liturgy is a way of promoting the power of proclaiming God's word in its natural sequence within the liturgy. Priests who preach the Gospel after the sermon keep good order, but they also offer a better service to the laity who hear the moral message of the sermon immediately following the actual lessons from the bible. The instruction to simplify the vestments is yet another instance of promoting comprehensibility. If the audible components of the liturgy of the Word are to be in their proper places, the visual liturgical symbols should likewise be comprehensible for the laity, which follows the platform established by the seminal essay of Metropolitan John Zizioulas. The instructions are essentially ecclesiological.

Like Schmemann's reforms, the encyclicals of the Church of Greece attempt to emphasize the integrity of the received liturgical tradition by allowing each component to properly function. The bishops seemed to understand that the first step in building a strong Church in Greece was to encourage those who constitute the Church—the people who gather for the Sunday Eucharist—to fully engage the liturgy so that the liturgy might form them into God's holy people. One of the most significant aspects of this liturgical reform is the realization that the laity belongs to the Church and can only become Church through liturgical participation.

Koumarianos notes that many opposed the implementations proposed by the encyclicals, which coheres with the tensions between progressives and conservatives in the Church mentioned by Vassiliadis in his essay.[105] Koumarianos's assessment offers several insightful remarks on the process and mechanism of the reform. Most significant for our purposes is his insight on the relationship between the preparatory phase, the deliberative process where liturgical rebirth was formed and offered recommendations, and the actual implementation of the reforms by the synod and individual bishops:[106]

> A listing of the topics covered by the reform shows that there is neither a coherent sequence nor a well-defined axis of liturgical arrangements, restitution of the worship tradition, or settlement of liturgical pending issues. The course so far has been a little bit of everything. There is too much haste. The Synod or archbishop pass their verdict on issues that require further investigation although they are aware more research is needed, whose outcomes will call for changes to such verdicts. It is still uncertain how the Holy Synod and the Holy Metropolises assess and make good use of the conclusions reached at the Symposiums. Until today the Holy Synod has released no communication or made any reform on the basis of Symposium results. . . . Many of the suggestions

---

105. Koumarianos, 132–33.
106. Ibid., 139.

and recommendations by the Holy Synod and the Archbishop have turned dead letters and remain unapplied today. There is also this regrettable impression that a certain number of these recommendation were doomed to remain in documents. . . .

Koumarianos's final comments on the fissure between the recommendations and the actual implementation illuminate the mechanism for liturgical reform. The bishops inaugurated the process of liturgical reform by appointing a commission of experts (academic and pastoral) to study and deliberate the process. The commission studied and deliberated these points over a lengthy period of time, almost ten years, and offered recommendations to the bishops. The bishops then implemented reform by issuing a variety of encyclicals and publishing a new hieratikon for liturgical use. There are fissures between the deliberative process and the actual reform because some opposed the reform, while others did not fully receive it.

Perhaps most important is the apparent absence of ongoing implementation after the encyclicals have been issued and the new hieratikon published. It is hazardous to assume that clergy immediately follow the instructions they have received. There is no evidence in the process of training for clergy on how they were to change their style and process of liturgical celebration to conform to the teachings and recommendations of the encyclicals. Koumarianos also points out that there appears to be no ongoing consultation on the part of the bishops.

Clearly, the bishops carefully selected the agenda items warranting implementation. When one considers the recommendations for liturgical renewal advanced by Tzerpos, the Greek Church's progress in liturgical reform is adequate.

Tzerpos's recommendations include the following: consulting the contributions already made by Greek and other liturgical scholars; establishing programs for identifying problems in Orthodox worship;

disseminating synodal directives aimed to create order and unity in Greek liturgical practice; editing and updating liturgical books; investing in liturgical formation of priests; consideration of permitting the celebration of certain sacraments with larger groups.[107] We have seen that the symposia addressed many of these issues with an emphasis on encouraging the creation of quality catechetical programs and materials for the laity and in the formation of priests.

The Greek Church's decision to authorize rebirth within the received liturgical tradition precluded a more radical liturgical reform. The synodal decision to defer larger questions (such as the revision of the lectionary) to the forthcoming great and holy council demonstrates the theologians' perception of the received tradition as adequate. Vassiliaidis was the one theologian who envisioned a bolder enterprise of liturgical reform for the Church of Greece. Above, we referred to two of his suggestions for liturgical reform (which, incidentally, apply to all of Orthodoxy, and not just the Church of Greece): catholic participation in the Eucharist without the prerequisite of confession and repentance and the full engagement of the assembly in the liturgy. When we examine some of the details of Vassiliadis's proposed reform, we shall see why some voices in the Greek Church are disappointed in the implementation and the disagreement on the approach to liturgical form will also become evident.

Vassiliadis also proposed the following reforms:

- Replacement of the normal choir . . . by the entire laos.

- Intensive care that the Eucharist, as well as other connected to it

---

107. Tzerpos, "Towards a Renewal of Our Ecclesiastical Worship" Church of Greece website, http://www.ecclesia.gr/greek/holysynod/commitees/liturgical/liturgical-0001.htm (accessed September 15, 2014).

liturgical services . . . are celebrated in a form profitable to the grass root faithful and understood by the entire community, the natural co-celebrants of the Holy Mysteries of the Church.

- Complete abolishment of all the secretly read by the presiding celebrant common prayers, especially those of the anaphora to its entirety. . . .

- Return of the Orthodox Church building technique to its original form.[108]

- Emphasis on all processional, liturgical and participatory elements of our Orthodox Liturgy, starting with the re-establishment of the ambo . . . the return of the Great Entrance to its original form. . . .

- [The] abolishment of the iconostasis, a development that has had an unfortunate effect and has further intensified the existing barrier between the clergy and the rest of the people of God.

- Underlining of the exclusively eschatological character of the Sunday Eucharist . . . by the return to the sabbaitic Typikon, attaching the Sunday matins to the Saturday evening Vespers.

Vassiliadis presents a brief summation of the purpose of liturgical renewal: "the transformation of the world, the Liturgy after the Liturgy."[109] Vassiliadis's bold proposal and the approach adopted by the symposia and bishops share two themes in common: first, liturgical renewal is needed; second, a variety of problems exist within Orthodoxy and its worship that need to be addressed for the sake of the people. The bishops adopted a slower and more deliberate approach to liturgical renewal that seeks to fine-tune the

---

108. Vassiliadis adds here that interior spaces should be illuminated for the purpose of "directing the community toward the light and joy of the Kingdom," in "Liturgical Renewal and the Orthodox Church."

109. Ibid., 15.

received tradition, clarify the role of clergy as liturgical presiders and leaders, and catechize the people to inspire them into a more robust engagement of the liturgy.

In his essay on the state of modern Greek liturgical studies, Stefanos Alexopoulos also iterated desiderata for the liturgical rebirth enterprise in the Church of Greece, calling for the following additions to the agenda: the expansion of course offerings (in colleges and universities) to include electives on Byzantine liturgical history; a new emphasis on liturgical inculturation; the continuation of the liturgical symposia; the permeation of liturgical renewal, especially among the clergy; revision, correction, and editing of liturgical books, including pew editions; translation of texts into modern Greek; and the establishment of an institute for liturgical study and research.[110] Alexopoulos stated a poignant recommendation representing a critical mass of Greek theologians: "changes that affect the everyday liturgical life of the Church should be implemented gradually and slowly, only after the clergy and lay representatives of each parish have been exposed to the nature and reason for each change."[111]

The distance between Vassiliadis's proposed reform and that adopted by the Greek bishops is vast and occasions a critique of the reform, whereas Alexopoulos's recommendations call for intense study of the liturgy with sensitive pastoral implementation. Koumarianos offered a sharp critique of the liturgical rebirth enterprise. Koumarianos lamented the hastiness of the process and appealed for the assignment of more time, which attests to the preference for a deliberate pace among some participants. He also presented a list of proposals for change, all directed towards the

---

110. Alexopoulos, "The State of Modern Greek Liturgical Studies," 387–92.
111. Ibid., 390. Alexopoulos refers to the failure of Archbishop Christodoulos's directive that the Apostle and Gospel should be read in modern Greek at each liturgy, as the clergy was not convinced of the rationale for the measure.

primary goal of the symposia: "the communion of life and the living communion of the believers with each other and with God."[112]

The mechanism adopted by the Church of Greece coheres with the deliberative, cautious approach to liturgical renewal favored by some Greek theologians. A central element in the process of liturgical renewal in Greece was the theologians' attention to liturgical thoughts in the Orthodox and Catholic worlds. The symposia on liturgical renewal included consideration of the historical context of liturgical development in Greece, but also pondered approaches to renewal in other Orthodox churches. My introduction to the work of Greek theologians earlier in this chapter illustrated their attention to the so-called Russian religious renaissance and the contributions of Russian émigré theologians. As we saw in chapter 3, Alexander Schmemann was a product of this Russian religious renaissance, and Stefanos Alexopoulos has carefully examined Schmemann's influence on liturgical theology in the Church of Greece.[113]

Alexopoulos demonstrates that Schmemann was a prominent figure in liturgical and ecclesial discourse in Greece given the tendency to translate and distribute his books and articles. Schmemann's approach to Eucharistic ecclesiology and liturgical renewal were not without criticism, however. Alexopoulos notes that most Greek theologians critiqued Schmemann's approach to liturgical renewal as too bold:[114]

> Most Greek Orthodox liturgists . . . adopt a more careful approach toward liturgical reform. This reserved approach does not mean they deny the existence of a liturgical crisis that, as Schmemann described it, is real and dangerous. Rather, it indicates a non-surgical approach to liturgical renewal moving around three axes: 1) the systematic study of

112. Koumarianos, 143-44.
113. Stefanos Alexopoulos, "Did the Work of Fr. Alexander Schmemann Influence Modern Greek Theological Thought?," 273-99.
114. Ibid., 290.

liturgical history; 2) the rediscovery of the meaning of liturgy; 3) the extensive liturgical education of the people.

Alexopoulos refers to the liturgical scholarship of Fountoulis, Filias, and Tzerpos as blazing the path for liturgical renewal in Greece:[115]

> The liturgical crisis is acknowledged, but the mending of the problem needs to be done carefully, slowly, with much study, together with diligent work in educating and catechizing the people, convincing them that what is done is not a betrayal of the tradition, but its rediscovery—a tradition that is vital, living, and relevant today.

Alexopoulos's description of the prevailing Greek approach to liturgical renewal confirms what we have discovered in our examination of the liturgical rebirth enterprise in this chapter. The central point is that the received liturgical tradition is adequate and one can reinvigorate it from within, without surgery. Vassiliadis constitutes one Greek voice who believes that the Church needed to adopt a more aggressive platform for reform which requires significant surgery. Had the Church adopted Vassiliadis's suggestions, clergy and faithful would experience a radical change from their customary experience of liturgy, especially with the restoration of the ambo and the sung cathedral office.[116]

Alexopoulos's implicit comparison of the prevailing Greek approach to Schmemann needs to be revisited, however. In his

---

115. Ibid., 291.
116. Another notable advocate for reform is the most prominent Greek liturgiologist in North America, Alkyviadis Calivas, professor emeritus of Holy Cross Greek Orthodox School of Theology in Brookline, Massachusetts. Calivas's approach to liturgical renewal fits the paradigm of the other Greek theologians described in this chapter. His book, *Essays in Theology and Liturgy*, vol. 3: *Aspects of Orthodox Worship* (Brookline, MA: Holy Cross Press, 2003), provides a rich presentation on how the academic study of liturgical history and sacramental theology can inform pastoral practice. Calivas writes for a North American audience, but his message is relevant for all Orthodox Churches attempting to navigate modernity and postmodernity. Particularly relevant is his final chapter on invigorating liturgical life in the parish, where Calivas presents several suggestions for invigorating the received liturgical tradition of the Church as a way of transforming North American Orthodoxy from a "Sunday-only" assembly to a body praying corporately throughout the daily, festal, Lenten, and Paschal cycles.

teaching on liturgical renewal, Schmemann deferred significant reforms to the Church hierarchy and disavowed the surgical approach to reform. The fruits of Schmemann's work are primarily more frequent participation of the laity in the liturgy, especially by partaking of Holy Communion, reciting select prayers aloud for the people to hear (especially the anaphora), designing the interior sacred space of the Church to mitigate the physical barriers between the clergy and the people, and establishing a seminary curriculum that encouraged a musical program involving significant assembly participation. Schmemann was quite cautious in working within the received liturgical tradition and largely continued the work inaugurated by the pre-conciliar deliberations on the liturgy in Russia. The mechanism for liturgical reform in Schmemann's program was through education, primarily St. Vladimir's Seminary as the progressive liturgical center of North America; the theological rationale for liturgical renewal was ignited by forming clergy who would implement renewal in their pastoral assignments, to the best of their ability.

A review of Schmemann's mechanism for renewal yields a striking similarity with that of the Church of Greece, especially given the shared emphasis on working within the received tradition and catechesis of clergy and laity. One difference in the mechanism for reform stands out: the platform adopted by the Church of Greece is much more comprehensive and attempts to implement the reform through the Orthodox ecclesiological structure, noteworthy for its deference to the long-delayed great and holy synod.

The Greek Church's attempt to implement liturgical renewal through the extant ecclesiological structure also distinguishes it from Vatican II's liturgical renewal. Vatican II initiated liturgical reform for the Latin Church; the Eastern churches retained the competence to address their own liturgical issues from within. Vatican II impacted the process of liturgical renewal in Greece in many ways. It is obvious that scholars such as Fountoulis, Tzerpos, and Zizioulas paid attention to Vatican II and its implementation. Fountoulis referred to Vatican II as a model of liturgical renewal the Orthodox should avoid, perceiving Vatican II as having unleashed too radical a reform, one that would result in dangerous consequences for Orthodoxy if it adopted a similar path. This negative view of Vatican II is based on the resistance of some Catholic clergy to its implementation, which suggests that the Church should have some sense that the clergy and laity will receive a liturgical reform when it is introduced. Vatican II thus contributed to the Greek Church's more deliberate and careful approach to liturgical reform, especially its preference for working within the received liturgical tradition.

I am confident, however, that Vatican II impacted the liturgical reform of the Church of Greece in another, more implicit manner. The ubiquitous appearance in the various documents of the symposia referring to the active and conscious participation of the people in the liturgy is an adoption of the now-famous phrase from *SC*. This study has demonstrated that Orthodox scholars established initiatives for the active participation of the people in the liturgy as early as the eighteenth century, with the Kollyvades movement in Greece. Vatican II did not invent active and conscious participation in the liturgy. However, Vatican II permanently inscribed the active and conscious participation of the laity in the liturgy into ecumenical theological vocabulary on a universal scale. Vatican II's canonization of this initiative created an environment where its communication of the phrase rendered it a cliché to be copied throughout the world. The active and conscious participation of the people in the liturgy became a universal refrain, easily memorized and repeated, which explains its frequent appearance in the proceedings on liturgical rebirth in the Church of Greece. The Church of Greece followed a theological trajectory well-established in the Eastern tradition and popularized in modernity, particularly among Russians. When Vatican II adopted this phrase and communicated it in conciliar teaching, it obtained a new stature and prestige which contributed to the misleading notion that it was a Roman Catholic invention. Thus, Vatican II enabled the Church of Greece to promote a popular liturgical initiative that had become prestigious because of its adoption by the Catholic bishops.

An Example of Liturgical Renewal: Metropolitan Meletios of Preveza

At this point it is crucial to note a different perspective on liturgical renewal within the Church of Greece. Metropolitan Meletios of Preveza promoted liturgical renewal as a way of steering his diocese of Nikopolis out of a period sullied by scandals.[117] Metropolitan Meletios also insisted that the clergy dress appropriately in public, by wearing the *rason* (a large black robe) and the *skoufos* (clerical headware).[118] Stephen Lloyd-Moffett asserts that the rules governing external appearance were designed to shape internal spiritual discipline of the clergy.[119]

Metropolitan Meletios's liturgical reforms were derivatives of his attention to cultivating spiritually robust clergy. His initial reform was to encourage priests to "hold daily services, especially morning matins and afternoon vespers," and to add "occasional vigils to their liturgical calendar so that today nearly every major feast has at least

---

117. See Stephen Lloyd-Moffett, *Beauty for Ashes: The Spiritual Transformation of a Modern Greek Community* (Crestwood, NY: St. Vladimir's Seminary Press, 2009). Also see Nicholas Denysenko, "Liturgical Maximalism in Orthodoxy: A Case Study," *Worship* 87 (2013): 355-57.
118. Ibid., 83.
119. "The priests would demonstrate with their outward appearance and behavior their inner devotion, dedication, and resolve. As respect grew for the clergy, so would their spiritual authority," ibid., 83-84.

one vigil connected with it somewhere in the Metropolis."[120] Lloyd-Moffett underscores Metropolitan Meletios's sensitivity to translating the requirements of the liturgical practices to cohere with the realities of modern life:[121]

> The liturgical practices introduced by Bishop Meletios were not novel; rather, they represented a return toward an ancient rhythm of worship. However, Meletios has adjusted them for modern life. As one of the hieromonks noted, 'for the liturgical program, effort was made to take in mind the way in which people live today and make it easier for them to participate...we changed hours, chanters, the atmosphere of the Church...' Accessibility without compromise became the key. For example, the vigils, known for being sometimes ten hours long in the monasteries, are not long—three to four hours—and they begin at a reasonable hour (at least for Greeks) so that even families can attend.

Lloyd-Moffett notes that the transformation Metropolitan Meletios hopes God will achieve in Preveza is a work-in-progress, with many problems persisting.[122] His most notable observation is that the key to the ongoing transformation is in no way attributable to a particular program or strategy, but is grounded by "the character of the bishop and the example he sets."[123]

Metropolitan Meletios's program of liturgical renewal did not belong to the period of study and deliberation authorized by Archbishop Christodoulos and the synod of Greek bishops, but it is instructive for the reader. First, we emphasize that the bishop's priority in renewal was to cultivate clergy who would be exemplary pastors and models of holiness for their people. Second, we should note the increase in liturgical celebration: the bishop noted the problem of moral decay among the people and called for an increase in exposing them to liturgy, with the confidence that increased

120. Ibid., 90-91.
121. Ibid., 91.
122. Ibid., 113.
123. Ibid.

opportunities for prayer would facilitate the shaping and forming of the people.

Meletios's program also demonstrates an assumption in the implementation of liturgical renewal in traditional Churches: the primary beneficiaries of increased liturgy and its intensity are the clergy. The clergy's more frequent and intense engagement of liturgical prayer would presumably equip to minister more effectively. Meletios's program of liturgical renewal is directed primarily towards cultivating a strong school of disciples through strict liturgical discipline. The program did not account for the distinction between the monastic and parish life rhythms to which the Constantinopolitan patriarchate attended in the nineteenth century in its initial simplification of parish liturgy. In the quote above, the hieromonk opines that Meletios adjusted the liturgy to make it more accessible to the laity.

In postmodern culture, it is hard to fathom how mainstream laity can attend vigils lasting three to four hours long, much less attend the Sunday Eucharistic liturgy. Meletios's program of liturgical renewal thus illuminates the variegated nature of liturgical reform: for some bishops, monasteries are models for liturgical renewal and should set the pace for the Church's liturgical rhythm. Also, the key to implementing liturgical renewal is by developing excellent clergy who will model good liturgy to their people and catechize them on it. In some ways, Meletios's approach to liturgical reform previewed the larger scale process of liturgical rebirth in the Church of Greece: seeking to enliven the clergy and invigorate liturgical life within the received tradition, yet conservative and non-surgical.

Conclusion

This brief examination of the case study in the Church of Greece is outstanding for other obvious reasons. The Church's objectives enjoy a strong coherence with those of Vatican II and Alexander Schmemann. Building up the Church into the holy people of God was the chief objective of the reform in Greece, and the path to achieving this objective is through the Eucharist, the primary and regular occurrence of the Church's gathering. In the case of the Church of Greece, on the one hand, its ecclesiological priorities are similar to both those of *SC* and Schmemann, but its language and content shares an even stronger parallel with *SC*. On the other hand, their selected approach to liturgical renewal depicts Vatican II as too bold. The similarity between the reforms is evidenced by their shared emphasis and language on the active and conscious participation of the laity in the liturgy, their appeals to restore the Eucharist as the source and summit of the life of the church, and also their desire to remove liturgical practices that exaggerate gestures, hymns, actions, and texts which result in distortions that prohibit comprehension.

The outstanding features of liturgical rebirth carried out by the Church of Greece are as follows:

- The process continued a gradual historical process of liturgical rebirth that began to take shape with the kollyvadic fathers, the Zoe movement, the *Liturgiewissenschaft* cultivated by figures such as Trempelas and Fountoulis, and the proposals for liturgical renewal put forward by the preconciliar commission, the Tinos seminary faculty, and the 1972 international symposium in Thessalonica;

- The process embraced a dialogue between academics and pastoral leaders, in which the Church consulted the academic to shape the pastoral;

- The process engaged the Orthodox ecclesiological mechanism, operating under the auspices of an autocephalous church, with broad representation from individual dioceses and clergy;

- The process referred central liturgical matters to the great and holy synod, where the autocephalous churches would deliberate collaboratively, adding a universal dimension to the local;

- The Church viewed rebirth as occurring within the received liturgical tradition, so renewal would occur within the extant structure and order of the Church;

- Comprehensive liturgical and sacramental catechesis of both clergy and laity were the primary objectives of the enterprise;

- Igniting the active and conscious participation of the people in the liturgy was the other primary objective;

- The Synod approved some minor liturgical reforms, such as permitting the clergy to read some prayers aloud for the laity to hear;

- Vatican II was perceived as a model of liturgical renewal not suitable for Orthodoxy and to be avoided;

- The liturgy is presented as a central event equipping the Church to engage the postmodern world.

In addition to these features, we can also make some remarks about the theological foundations of the liturgical rebirth enterprise in the Church of Greece. First, it is clear that the Church of Greece shared the same ecumenical sense of viewing the liturgy as the divine-human encounter that results in the outpouring of the spirit on the royal priesthood of the people. The reforms of Vatican II and Alexander Schmemann connected the liturgy with this notion of priesthood more explicitly, but the framework of reform within the Church of Greece illustrates concern for priesthood. The Church of

Greece places the onus of responsibility on the ordained pastors to lead liturgy in such a way that the people can engage it and engage the world as citizens of God's kingdom. Many figures recognized that the liturgy needed revision for pastors to preside in a prayerful manner, without focusing solely on observing complicated rubrics. The liturgy equips an ongoing process of transformation among the people, and the responsibility of manifesting God to the world belongs to the people.

The Church of Greece has a unique mode of liturgical rebirth within the Orthodox world: the process of reform is somewhat conservative and deliberate. Koumarianos's remarks on the movement for liturgical rebirth are a sober reminder that the Greek view this process as one in infancy. The bishops' decision to follow the path of liturgical rebirth within the ecclesiological framework of the Orthodox Church is not surprising. There are opponents to liturgical reform within the Church of Greece, hence the decision to proceed with caution. In this sense, the context of the Church is Greece shares a similarity with the reform authorized by Vatican II, which was also implemented despite opposition among the bishops and the rank and file clergy and laity. The careful and deliberate process of reform may very well ease the laity into a process where their perception of the symbols, rites, and rhythm of the liturgy becomes more comprehensible. What remains unknown is whether or not foregoing the opportunity to embrace a more bold approach to liturgical reform will stifle the ecclesial renewal the bishops in Greece hope for. It is quite possible that theologians within the church will urge the bishops to adopt more surgical measures of reform if the Church does not engage with and respond to contemporary culture in a dialogical manner.

5

Liturgical Scholarship and Monastic Reform

New Skete Monastery

Our survey of approaches to liturgical renewal in the Orthodox Church has illuminated a reverence for the received liturgical tradition. One school of thought identifies catechesis and fine-tuning as the best methods for engaging the people in the liturgy. The renewal programs ascribed to Alexander Schmemann and the Church of Greece represent this first perspective. The other school of thought representing by ROCOR promotes liturgical maximalism as the optimal approach to invigorating ecclesial life. In this chapter, we will examine our fourth and final model of liturgical renewal, New Skete Monastery in Cambridge, New York. New Skete's model of liturgical renewal is unique within Orthodoxy because the communities consulted the academic analysis of Byzantine liturgical history in developing liturgical offices appropriate for a small monastic community in North America. The result of the liturgical reform was radical in comparison with our three earlier models. In this chapter, I will present the theological rationale for liturgical reform articulated by the community and will demonstrate the mechanism they employed for implementing reform by examining the structure of their Divine Liturgy, the rite of Holy Communion, and selections from the offices of Holy Week and Pascha.

Introduction

New Skete Monastery in Cambridge, New York, began as a community of Byzantine Franciscans in 1966.[1] The community desired to live an "authentic Eastern Christian monasticism for our day, inspired by the vision of the early monastic fathers."[2] The monks express their vision for community life in their own words:[3]

> They also had a passion for liturgy, seeking to infuse new life into Eastern Catholic worship. In that spirit, they took the name 'New Skete,' after one of the first Christian monastic settlements in northern Egypt, in the desert of Skete. From the very beginning, their intention was to incarnate the simplicity of the original principles of monastic life, unencumbered by the institutionalized accretions of the centuries, and to do this in a way that made sense for twentieth-century America.

Several episodes in the life of the community, especially encounters with key figures, shaped the future course of New Skete Monastery. Dom Damasus Winzen, OSB, a prior at Mount Saviour Benedictine Monastery near Elmyra, New York, and a pioneer in monastic and liturgical renewal, provided lodging for the community, initially in Pennsylvania.[4] After searching for a suitable location, they landed in Cambridge, New York, and were firmly established in an idyllic setting on three-hundred plus acres of dense woodland on Two

---

1. The Monks of New Skete, *In the Spirit of Happiness* (Boston: Little, Brown, and Company, 1999), 8-23.
2. Ibid., 9.
3. Ibid.
4. Ibid.

Top Mountain, performing the heavy manual work of building the community themselves.[5] New Skete expanded with the addition of a community of contemplative nuns in 1969; the nuns occupied a space on a hilly pasture across the road two miles from the monastery, and the community "acquired the unusual characteristic of being a modern male and female monastic community."[6] A married couples' community that embraced the life and vision of New Skete began in 1982. New Skete concluded their journey through Eastern Christianity by being received into the Orthodox Church in America in 1979.

As a community devoted to principles of *ressourcement* and *aggiornamento* and in search of the authentic spirit of Eastern liturgy, New Skete exercised the freedom traditionally belonging to Eastern monastic communities in creating a suitable liturgical *ordo* (Typikon). Several members of the community remarked that their experience of the liturgical movement and the energy surrounding the liturgical reforms authorized by Vatican II contributed to their motivations to adopt a Typikon that would be suitable for their community. The ordo they adopted is grounded in the desire to live an authentic Eastern Christian life in the contemporary conditions of the world. Another key figure who contributed to the shaping of New Skete liturgy was the Jesuit liturgical historian Juan Mateos.[7] In 1965, Mateos led a seminar on Eastern liturgy for the soon-to-be-Monks of New Skete, which resulted in additional consultations with Mateos, who gave them his lecture notes from courses he taught at the Pontifical Oriental Institute in Rome.[8] New Skete also consulted

---

5. Ibid., 8–10.
6. Ibid., 13.
7. Brother Stavros Winner, "Liturgical Renewal: Have We Missed the Boat?" Unpublished essay. Mateos wrote the first volume in the seminal and meticulous history of the liturgy of St. John Chrysostom, succeeded in this endeavor by Robert Taft and Sister Vassa Larin.
8. Via e-mail with Brother Stavros Winner, March 30, 2014.

other scholars who specialized in Byzantine liturgiology at the Pontifical Oriental Institute (PIO), including Miguel Arranz and Robert Taft. New Skete's version of the Divine Liturgy illuminates their passion for consulting the fruits of academic research in constructing an appropriate order of worship for the contemporary Church:[9]

> The celebration of the divine liturgy envisioned by this book finds its principles, for the most part, in the research that was and still is being done in the field of Byzantine worship over the last fifty to one-hundred years, especially by scholars associated with the Pontifical Oriental Institute in Rome. . . . We have listened carefully to the scholars and devoured every word of theirs, written and spoken, that was within our reach, so that, in the light of their findings, we might find the ways and means of liberating the treasures of Byzantine worship from the paralysis that has tried to suffocate it over the last several centuries, and to do this that they might be more eloquent for our contemporary American monasticism.

New Skete consistently expresses gratitude to the liturgical scholars of the PIO in its publications, while also extending thanks to other familiar liturgists such as Alexander Schmemann, Alkiviadis Calivas, Gabriel Bertoniere, and Sebastian Janeras. The monastic community researched ancient models of the liturgy that would be suitable for their realities. New Skete is a working monastery: the monks raise and train dogs and market gourmet foods, and the sisters support themselves by baking cheesecakes.[10]

New Skete's selection of principles that serve as the foundation for their liturgical scheme likewise shapes their architecture. Their devotion to their work, necessary for their financial stability, limits

---

9. Monks of New Skete, *The Divine Liturgy* (Cambridge, NY: New Skete Monastery, 1987).

10. Brother Stavros Winner, "The Monastery and Applies Liturgical Renewal," in *Worship Traditions and Armenia and the Neighboring Christian East: An International Symposium in Honor of the 40th Anniversary of St. Nersess Armenian Seminary*, ed. Roberta R. Ervine (Crestwood, NY: St. Vladimir's Seminary Press, St. Nersess Armenian Seminary, 2006), 311.

the number of liturgical offices they can pray in community each day. They gather for Orthros before the workday begins and Vespers in the evenings, which rendered the Athonite monastic liturgical model ill-suited for their life.[11] Instead, they turned to the now–extinct cathedral offices of Jerusalem and Constantinople, revising them into modern forms suitable for monastic life in contemporary America.[12]

The Rationale for Liturgical Renewal

In the beginning, the rational for liturgical renewal at New Skete was pragmatic. When the monastery formed in 1966, the brethren observed the received Byzantine liturgical tradition (praying in Church Slavonic) while engaging their passion for liturgical history. The community constructed a traditional temple that was suitable for their liturgical life, the Holy Transfiguration Church. As the community worked and prayed, they realized the challenges of observing the fullness of the monasticized Byzantine liturgy while attending to their tasks. As committed students of Byzantine liturgical history, the monks recognized an opportunity to construct a new liturgical life that was both faithful to tradition and possible in their contemporary environment.

The community's commitment to liturgical renewal was emboldened by two primary sources: first, their experience as Franciscan friars exposed them to the liturgical reforms unleashed by Vatican II which essentially followed the same paradigm of consulting liturgical history for the purpose of constructing a liturgical ordo suitable for the contemporary Church. Second, the monks also appealed to the freedom monasteries traditionally enjoyed in Byzantine history in cultivating a healthy liturgical life suitable to the place and context.[13] The monks first diagnosed the contemporary

11. Ibid.
12. Ibid.

liturgical problem by attributing inertia to monasteries and then defined their task as retrieving the original monastic role of cultivating and reinvigorating tradition:[14]

> For the past several hundred years, however, it has been the monasteries ... that have been the cause of the freeze in Orthodox (and, we might add, Eastern Catholic) Church life; it has been the monasteries that have entrenched themselves and shown others in the church how to entrench themselves in the impregnable fortress of self-righteousness and stubbornness, refusing to countenance any change whatever, no matter how good, how necessary. . . . The monasteries have been the biggest culprits in the process of stagnation that has paralyzed the liturgical life of the church, always with the intention and under the guise of preserving the totality of the church's tradition. . . . It is in the tonality of the previous, healthier, and really ageless monastic dynamism in the church that our New Skete communities struggle to exist and function. It is the primordial spirit of monastic creativity and independence that fuels our attempt to live more deeply rather than on the surface of things, to add creatively to church life on all levels by being open to the Spirit of God, and to refuse to accept distorted and falsified history.

This excerpt from the monastery's introduction to its book of prayers offers a snapshot of the community's diagnosis of the problem and proposal for resolving it. The problem is that Byzantine liturgical development became quite stagnant for a number of reasons, and the churches adhering to Byzantine tradition adopted a veneration of the liturgy as fixed, unchangeable, and unchanged through several centuries of Church history, a perception that became prevalent among many Orthodox populations.

In their experience of the liturgy of the received tradition, the monks observed that the services are simply too long. They define the problem as "widespread disenchantment with church attendance and

13. See Monks of New Skete, *Sighs of the Spirit* (Cambridge, NY: New Skete Monastery, 1997), xxix.
14. Ibid., xxix-xxx.

the lack of interest in, not to mention love for, the worship of God among so many people."[15] The monks then identify the two factors primarily contributing to the problem: the "interminable length of so many of our offices," and the inadequacy of the clergy in presiding, celebrating, and catechizing. New Skete attributes the length of the offices to their monastic origins, an abbreviation of the fusion of the monastic and cathedral offices of the Byzantine tradition. This synthesis is symbolized primarily by the expansion of hymnography which populated Byzantine liturgy to such a degree that the hymns overtook Scripture. New Skete observes that the multiplication of the hymns impacted liturgy to such a degree that the offices are "beyond the capacity of even the most able parish communities to utilize."[16]

Since many parishes struggle to fulfill the requirements of the offices, pastors make adjustments in their celebration. New Skete observes that there is no standard for fine-tuning Byzantine liturgy and making it coherent with the contemporary life of the Church, so as a result, clergy adopt varying approaches to adjusting the liturgy so that it is possible to observe it in parish life:[17]

> As a response to the unreasonable length of the services, the offices sometimes are either entirely suppressed or they are abbreviated in a haphazard way. This is done without due recognition of their essential structures and the coherence and cohesion of their internal elements and rationale, as well as their original themes and purposes. . . . Another way of coping with the length of the services is to rush through them, racing through word and action so that the symbolism they employ and the dignity and transcendence they would manifest are hopelessly eroded.

Rushing through the celebration is problematic because it betrays the natural rhythm and pulse of the liturgy, especially the proclamation of the texts. The monks observed that the Byzantine offices are

15. *The Divine Liturgy*, xxiii.
16. Ibid., xxiv.
17. Ibid., xxiv–xxv.

normally sung, so they emphasize the musical quality of Byzantine liturgy. The hurried liturgical celebration alters the perception of the proclamatory liturgical element in its structural context, which "prevents the faithful from hearing the word in its fullness, enunciated with the clarity and reverence that are its due."[18] The monks underscore the negative impact incompetent celebration has on the faithful with strong words:[19]

> It prevents them [the faithful] from perceiving the psychological and psychic overtones . . . of the word in its context. Consequently, people miss the whole thrust and purpose of the worship of God. What good is it to serve in the language of the people if the way that language is enunciated and handled is itself a detriment to understanding it! So, people are not edified; they are not inspired. On the contrary, many end up bored, perhaps even those undaunted souls whim, it would seem, nothing can dissuade from attending church.

The monks attribute the errors of fine-tuning to the absence of knowledge and a subjective approach to revising the received tradition. The monks complete their diagnosis of the problem by illuminating the problem of liturgical celebration on the part of the clergy. They are sensitive to the *ars celebrandi* and comment on the presider's hypothetical concern that the people are bored. The proclamation of the word is not the only liturgical element subject to distortion through incompetent liturgical presidency; ritual actions are also compromised.[20] New Skete thus exercised the spirit of Eastern monastic freedom in constructing their own liturgical order and created a constructive method of appealing to tradition as presented by the leading liturgical scholars in the field.

New Skete's proposed remedy for this liturgical malaise was to

18. Ibid., xxv.
19. Ibid.
20. "Thus, we race through the celebration in such a way that our movements lack all grace," ibid., xxvi.

create offices that conform to the lives of contemporary communities, and the revisions are sensitive to the problem of time.[21] The monks summarize their method for constructing the order of the Divine Liturgy they observe in their community:[22]

> In this edition of the Eucharistic liturgies, we attempt to obviate the textual and structural length by a return to more ancient, less complex forms. Within reason, a great deal of the repetitions accumulated through the centuries has also been eliminated, and the ceremonial, too, is simpler, less cluttered by baroque accretions. All in all, if celebrated at a reasonable pace, these forms of the Divine Liturgy will require about an hour and a half for their celebration.

The monks state with clarity that the liturgy is important and that the intent is not to teach the faithful that God is not worth their time:[23]

> We ought to note that while we have already agreed that most of the offices of the received usage, including the Divine Liturgy, are unnecessarily long, the solution to this problem does not lie in the opposite extreme, e.g., in some sort of exaggerated brevity; God, after all, does deserve our time and attention! So, the structures and general plan of the liturgies in this volume are sufficiently brief to allow a dignified celebration without undue haste and the inevitable sloppiness that goes with it.

The monks add that the offices might be longer if there are more communicants; their priority is to create structures and elements that will engage each participant and render the temptation to hurry through the service unnecessary. The monks communicate their concern for the *ars celebrandi* as they discuss the crucial elements of preparing and celebration:[24]

---

21. The author of the introduction states, "The traditional length of the services, then, as well as the pace of life today are two of the many considerations behind the publication of the present edition," ibid.
22. Ibid.
23. Ibid., xxvi–xxvii.
24. Ibid., xxvii–xxvii.

Each of us must consider his own personal way of celebrating. Each must reassess his physical bearing at the holy table, the way he moves about during the service or as he participates simply as a member of the congregation. We must reexamine our conduct and eradicate from ourselves all mannerisms and ways of acting foreign to the liturgical rites and to whoever would lead the people in the celebration of those rites. . . . It is not enough to abide by the letter of the rubrics; we must strive to interiorize as well as exteriorize their true meaning and purpose.

One cannot understate the monks' attention to developing an ethos of good liturgical celebration that edifies and inspires the people without calling attention to one's self.[25] They identify proper proclamation, and enunciation of texts and devotion to singing as two impoverished skills requiring improvement, calling upon presiders to seek professional consultation as needed to develop these skills.[26] The monks are careful not to depict the significance of singing so that it could be misconstrued: the entire purpose of the liturgical renewal enterprise is to "help our faithful come to a better comprehension of our worship."[27] Ultimately, the responsibility of instructing the faithful in worship and leading to an encounter with the living God lies with the clergy:[28]

Our people are willing to learn, so it is incumbent on us not only to teach them, but, even more crucially, to provide them with the proper example of our own lives. It must be our conduct, first and foremost, that demonstrates to all that our worship is the sacred drama wherein we mystically encounter God. Our concrete example, then, will further their growth in the understanding that leads to greater devotion and, ultimately, the kingdom of God. However, all the examples in the world will not suffice if unaccompanied by a catechesis that is fully profound, clear, and convincing.

25. Ibid., xxviii.
26. Ibid., xxix: "We would not be losers were we to seek out the advice, counsel, and assistance of professionals capable of helping us to improve our singing."
27. Ibid., xxx.
28. Ibid., xxx–xxxi.

This examination of the "practical word" introducing the reader to the New Skete's publication of the Divine Liturgy unveils the core principles of the theological rationale underpinning their liturgical renewal enterprise. The monks were exposed to the possibilities of liturgical history in their experience as Eastern Catholic Franciscans, enriched by the relationship they cultivated with Juan Mateos of the PIO. Their attempt to observe the requirements of the received Byzantine liturgical tradition while living an authentic contemporary monastic life led them to realize the challenge of following a monasticized office that had not been significantly revised due to its canonization through printing and distribution and the rapidly increasing perception of the liturgy as unchangeable.

Their encounter with liturgical history exposed this view as historically dubious, and they were emboldened by a monastic heritage that valued independence and freedom in cultivating good liturgy. Thus, the monks began a process of developing a liturgy that conforms to the environment of contemporary North American life, a work that is still in progress. In undertaking this task, the monks envisioned a liturgy that was purified of complex additions and simple, so that the people could behold and hear it with understanding. It is notable that the forewords to many of the monastery's liturgical publications communicate a promotion of the same ideals: quality liturgical leadership, simplicity, the purging of repetitions and unnecessary accretions, and the reconstruction of elements into simple structures more faithful to their historical origins, all for the purpose of engaging the people in a liturgy that is both comprehensible and also leads them into the kingdom of God.

In implementing liturgical renewal, New Skete enacted a bold style of liturgical reform that differs from the other three models examined earlier and is more similar to that of Vatican II, with the significant exception of scale and impact. The New Skete model of reform shares the principles of catechesis of clergy and laity with the three Orthodox models while employing a surgical approach to liturgical revision. In the following sections, I will offer several examples of New Skete's liturgical renewal from the actual offices of celebration and will analyze them in light of their historical antecedents and the monastery's stated approach to liturgical renewal.[29]

The Divine Liturgy: Revised Liturgy of the Word

Perhaps the most apparent revision to the Divine Liturgy occurred in the Liturgy of the Word. In the received Byzantine liturgy, the proclamation of the Word is preceded by several prayers and ritual actions, illustrated by Table 6.1 below:

Table 6.1: Liturgy of the Word in the Received Byzantine Liturgy:

- Entrance Prayers (recited quietly by clergy)
- Orthros (Greek/Antiochian) or reading of the Third/Sixth Hour(s)
- Prothesis (Liturgy of Preparation)
- Ritual Censing of Sanctuary and Temple
- Opening Prayers: Blessed is the Kingdom
- Great Synapte (litanic biddings)
- First Antiphon
- Small synapte (short litanic biddings)
- Second Antiphon/Monogenes
- Small Synapte (short litanic biddings)

29. There are dozens of examples of liturgical revision in New Skete's order, and a thorough examination and analysis of all of them is beyond the scope of this study.

- Third Antiphon
- Little Entrance with Gospel
- Troparia and Kontakia (Hymnody)
- Trisagion Hymn
- Prokeimenon (responsorial psalmody)—first offering of peace by presider
- Epistle Reading
- Alleluia (responsorial reading)
- Gospel reading

Several elements precede the actual liturgy of the Word, in the received Byzantine tradition, namely a number of preparatory elements, including the apologetic prayers of purification by the clergy and the three antiphons with accompanying prayers. In the received rite, the first significant ritual action is the little entrance, which usually begins while the people are singing the third antiphon. The little entrance consists of the clergy venerating the altar, and processing to the solea (or bema) with the Gospel book. In contemporary practice, it is customary for the presider to say the prayer of the entrance quietly during the procession, though in some parishes, the deacon intones "Let us pray to the Lord" aloud, and the presider says the prayer of the entrance for all to hear. The clergy stop before the doors of the iconostasis, and the deacon says to the presider, "bless, master, the holy entrance"; the presider blesses the entrance, venerates the Gospel book, and the deacon lifts the Gospel and chants, "Wisdom! Attend!" The deacon makes the sign of the cross with the Gospel and places it in its place on the holy table, as the presider venerates the two icons of Christ and the Theotokos on both sides of the door, stopping to bless the servers to return to the sanctuary, which he himself does, venerating the Gospel and altar table upon entering.

In the received tradition, the little entrance is a small movement that begins and ends in the same place: the sanctuary. The entrance rite's function of gathering the people and preparing them to hear the word of God is obscured by the collection of liturgical elements preceding it (the litanies and antiphons) and following it (the hymnody and Trisagion hymn). A review of an earlier version of the entrance rite's function from the eighth century illustrates its original function of gathering and preparing the people to hear the word of God.

Liturgical history demonstrates that the current order of the received tradition experienced several revisions in the history of the Byzantine Rite. One of the oldest Eastern witnesses to the beginning of the liturgy in Antioch is by John Chrysostom, writing in the fourth century. Chrysostom reports that the liturgy began with the presider processing to the synthronon and offering the peace, followed by the appointed readings for the day. John Baldovin, Mateos, Taft, and Vassa Larin have contributed to the reconstruction of the history of the beginning of the liturgy in the Byzantine Rite.[30] Baldovin's research on the stational liturgy in Constantinople, based largely on an examination of the so-called Typikon of the Great Church, shows that faithful in the imperial city would sing the antiphons on their way to the stational church appointed for that day. Robert Taft describes the performance of the office of three antiphons on the nonstational days:[31]

---

30. The most recent scholarship on the beginning of the liturgy in the Byzantine tradition is by Vassa Larin, "The Opening Formula of the Byzantine Divine Liturgy, "Blessed is the kingdom," among Other Liturgical Beginnings," *Studia Liturgica* 43 (2013): 229-55; Juan Mateos, *La célébration de la parole dans la liturgie byzantine*, Orientalia Christiana Analecta 121 (Rome: Pontifical Oriental Institute, 1971): 34-71; See Robert F. Taft, "The Liturgy of the Great Church: An Initial Synthesis of Structure and Interpretation on the Eve of Iconoclasm," *Dumbarton Oaks Papers* 34 (1980-81): 45-75.

At nonstational liturgies, before the entrance of the patriarch and his entourage at least one presbyter and one deacon would have gone in before the chancel to lead the gathering congregation in the office of the enarxis, a simple rite of three antiphons, each preceded by an oration and its customary oremus. Neither the opening blessing nor the great synapte ("litany of peace") were part of the enarxis at that time.

Taft's description of the actual entrance illustrates its original function as the first ritual action of the liturgy:[32]

> The patriarch is seated in the narthex before the royal doors, awaiting the signal for the introit. When the psalmists in their chamber beneath the ambo intone the Monogenes, traditional refrain of the introit psalm—the third antiphon of the enarxis on nonstational days—the patriarch goes before the royal doors to say the introit prayer. . . . Upon arriving at the throne in the apse, the patriarch greets and blesses the congregation with the traditional 'Peace to all' and is seated. There follow immediately the gradual psalm or prokeimenon, epistle, alleluia psalm, and Gospel.

Taft notes that the people sing the Introit—Psalm 94—with the Monogenes ("Only-begotten Son and Word of God") the hymn functioning as the refrain of the psalm. During the singing of the introit, the patriarch and his entourage would process through the church into the sanctuary. This primary rite of gathering led immediately to the proclamation of the word of God.

New Skete's reconfiguration of the beginning of the Divine Liturgy attempts to remove some of the clutter that obscured the function of the entrance rite. In their reconstruction of this portion of the Divine Liturgy, New Skete consulted historical research and established an order for gathering and preparing to hear the word of God that reflects earlier historical paradigms without copying them. New Skete's reconstruction of the beginning of the Divine

---

31. Taft, "The Liturgy of the Great Church," 50.
32. Ibid., 50–52.

Liturgy is notable because they have privileged the cathedral tradition for their ordo. New Skete has three variants of the liturgy of the word: in version 1, the antiphons are sung in procession outside; in version 2, the antiphons are sung in the narthex, and in version 3, the community gathers outside the doors of the temple for the entrance prayer, which is taken from the earliest extant Constantinopolitan euchologion, Codex Barberini 336.[33]

In New Skete's order, each prayer is recited aloud by the presider for the people to hear, a departure from the customary practices where the presider recites the prayer quietly during the chanting of the litanies. The architecture facilitates a sense of liturgical progression in the Eucharistic liturgy. In New Skete's restoration, the Church sings the psalmody outside of the nave in front of the small fountain: upon entering, everyone takes their proper place with the presider and assistants in the center of the ambo, the assembly in the seats, and the choir positioned to the left. When everyone has entered the church and taken their proper place, the presider recites the prayer of the Trisagion, the people sing the Trisagion hymn, and the proclamation of the Word commences.[34] The architecture facilitates a sense of communal prayer, as everyone is gathered in the nave with the clergy on the ambo. The ambo is not a replica of the impressive structure of the Hagia Sophia. At New Skete, it is a bema formed by the large carpet in the nave, and it contains the lectern for proclaiming the Scriptures and seats for the presiding clergy.[35] The

---

33. "O maker and benefactor of all creation, receive your church which approaches you. Bring about all that is best for us, lead us to perfection and make us worthy of your kingdom. By the grace and mercy and love for mankind of your only son, with whom you are bless'd, together with your all-holy, good, and life-giving Spirit: now and forever, and unto ages of ages," *The Divine Liturgy* (Cambridge, NY: New Skete, 1987), 79, from the Liturgy of St. John Chrysostom. The current practice of singing the office of the antiphons is based on e-mail dialogue with Brother Stavros Winner.

34. Brother Stavros notes that New Skete occasionally sings the Trisagion as one of the entrance hymns, via e-mail exchange on December 2, 2014.

35. New Skete has undertaken a serious revision of its lectionary, a process which has been ongoing

clergy remain on the ambo until it is time for the prayers of accession before Great Entrance.

This example illustrates New Skete's method of reconstruction: they consulted liturgical history without duplicating it. The point was to restore the entrance rite as one of gathering and preparing the assembly to hear the word of God. The assembly's gathering at the fountain where the antiphons are sung, gradual procession to the door of Holy Wisdom temple, introit prayer, and procession into the church all facilitate the assembly's entrance into the Church—clergy and laity together—to hear the word of God. While much of the entrance is reminiscent of the Constantinopolitan cathedral tradition described by Mateos, Baldovin, and Taft, New Skete did not follow every detail from the historical blueprint of the cathedral tradition. The clergy remain on the ambo with the laity until the time for the offering arrives which illustrates New Skete's commitment to mitigating the distinctions between clergy and laity at the liturgy by intermingling them from the outset. The assembly hears the word of God together, in the same place, at the ambo. New Skete's consultation of liturgical history to reconstruct the entrance rites and liturgy of the word illuminates several principles of their liturgical renewal: the consultation of scholarly research to shape contemporary practice; the removal of complex liturgical accretions to simplify the liturgy; and the privileging of an order that contributes to the faithful's participation in and understanding of the liturgy. This

and unfolded gradually over a period of thirty-five years. The Sunday lectionary has been revised in two ways: first, the community added an Old Testament reading for each Liturgy, based on the appointed Gospel lection. Second, the Sundays after Pentecost, which constitute the bulk of the liturgical year (similar to ordinary time in the Western tradition) observe a two year cycle (A and B). In both years A and B, the Gospels draw primarily from Matthew and Luke; the epistles begin with Romans in year A and follow the canonical order of the New Testament. The community drew heavily from the various lectionaries of Jerusalem dating from the fourth through the seventh centuries. I will discuss some of the revisions applied to the lectionary of Holy Week later in this chapter. This information is based on an e-mail exchange with Brother Stavros Winner, January 23, 2015.

change also exhibits a notable consequence of the reconstruction: the selection of elements from cathedral liturgy. We should also note that New Skete preserved some elements of the received tradition. For example, the Monogenes is sung as the refrain on the second antiphon, and not on the Introit, which demonstrates the community's impetus to promote the restoration of principles, and not liturgical details.

The Rite of Holy Communion

New Skete's rite of Holy Communion at the Divine Liturgy also demonstrates their commitment to reconstructing liturgical rites that communicate the principles of engagement, understanding, and the full participation of the laity in the life of the Church. In this instance, the revision of the rite of Communion is less obvious upon initial observation, because there are no changes to the order of preparing Communion. In the received tradition, Communion begins in the sanctuary with the clergy. The clergy begin by consuming the holy bread. After each cleric has partaken of the bread, they drink from the cup. The laity receive Communion via intinction, from a spoon in the chalice, a retention of the received tradition.

After fracturing the Lamb and preparing the particles for communing clergy, the presider begins communion by inviting any concelebrating bishops, priests, and deacons to come forward and receive a particle. The senior cleric takes a particle and communes himself, and concelebrating priests also take a particle and commune themselves. The senior cleric imparts a particle to the deacons. The clergy follow the same process for partaking of the chalice, beginning with the senior cleric, who communes himself. Again, only the deacons receive Communion from the presider (or his delegate).

New Skete's revision occurs in the order of imparting and receiving Communion. There is no change in the order of preparing the elements, but the revision occurs in their distribution. The monks explain the method for distributing and receiving with a rationale:[36]

> Since the Eucharist is a gift given to each member of the church, no one should simply take communion, but each communicant should receive it, including the clergy. Therefore, when more than one priest serves, or when there is more than one priest who wishes to receive, the main celebrant and one of the other priests approach the gifts, making three reverences before them. Then the priest who is not the main celebrant gives a particle to the one who communicated him. Other priests who intend to receive come around the altar counter-clockwise one by one and approach the gifts from the north side, making the usual reverences, and then receiving a particle from the main celebrant. When all the presbyters have received, the main celebrant gives a particle to the deacon. After partaking of the lamb, the clergy go back around the holy table clockwise along the north side and all partake of the chalice in the same way as they shared in the lamb, but from the south of the holy table.

The most significant change that occurs in this paradigm is that all the communicating priests receive Communion from the hand of another. In this revision of the rite of Holy Communion, the monks applied the historical research of Robert Taft, whose descriptions of the rite of Communion in the eleventh century showed that even bishops received Communion from the hand of another.[37] In this restoration, the monks have emphasized that the presider belongs to the assembly and is a recipient of the gift, just as everyone else. The revision is somewhat limited to a particular aspect of the ritual act, but the change has ecclesiological implications that venerate the teaching that Christ is the high priest who presides at the liturgy.

We should note the limitations of this revision. The New Skete variant of Holy Communion is written for communities with

---

36. Monks of New Skete, *The Divine Liturgy*, 120-21.
37. Robert F. Taft, *Through Their Own Eyes: Liturgy as the Byzantines Saw It* (Berkeley, CA: InterOrthodox Press, 2005), 105-12.

multiple priests; there is no provision for a priest presiding without concelebrants, nor is there discussion of a single priest serving with a deacon.[38] Second, the rite retains the received tradition almost intact, which means that the method for imparting communion to the laity differs. The clergy receive the holy gifts separately; the laity receive via intinction, spoon-fed from a chalice. The monks permit the rite of communion to occur according to the order of the liturgy of St. James, where the laity receive the bread and cup separately, and the formula differs.[39] Otherwise, the distinction in the method for imparting and receiving communion remains faithful to the received tradition. In this example, one should note some conservatism on the part of the monks, especially since Taft's research on communion shows that the laity once partook of the bread and cup separately. This is another example of the monks revising the liturgy to restore a theological principle; they consulted liturgical history, but did not adopt every detail from the historical pattern in their restoration.

Holy Week and Pascha

If there is a high point in the liturgical year for Orthodox, it is Holy Week and Pascha.[40] This is true for most Christians, and especially so for adherents of the Byzantine Rite, especially the clergy and

---

38. Brother Stavros notes that the on the few occasions a priest served with a deacon, the priest received communion from the deacon (via e-mail, December 2, 2014).
39. Monks of New Skete, *The Divine Liturgy*, 123.
40. See Mark Morozowich, *Holy Thursday in Jerusalem and Constantinople: The Liturgical Celebrations from the Fourth to the Fourteenth Centuries*, forthcoming in Orientalia christiana analecta; Sebastià Janeras, *Le vendredi-Saint dans la tradition liturgique byzantine: structure et histoire de ses offices*, Analecta liturgica, Studia Anselmiana 99 (Rome: Abbazia S. Paolo, 1988); Gabriel Bertonière, *The Historical Development of the Easter Vigil and Related Services in the Greek Church*, Orientalia christiana analecta 193 (Rome: Pontifical Oriental Institute,1972); Robert F. Taft, "A Tale of Two Cities: The Byzantine Holy Week Triduum as a Paradigm of Liturgical History," in *Time and Community: Essays In Honor of Thomas Julian Talley (NPM Studies in Church Music and Liturgy)*, ed. J. Neil Alexander (Washington, DC: The Pastoral Press 1990), 21–41; Pavlos Koumarianos, "Liturgical Problems of Holy Week," *St. Vladimir's Theological Quarterly* 46, no. 1 (2002): 3-22.

singers, for whom this week is the most demanding of all in the liturgical year. The Byzantine liturgical synthesis is most manifest at this time of the year, when parishes schedule several services for each day. The parish community that attempts to observe the entirety of the liturgical requirements will find it challenging, even if it is equipped with capable singers and committed clergy. Holy Monday, Tuesday, and Wednesday call for the Liturgy of Presanctified Gifts and Bridegroom Orthros at minimum. Holy Thursday introduces Vespers with the Liturgy of St. Basil in remembrance of Jesus' supper with his disciples. Holy Friday has several offices, beginning with Orthros and twelve Gospel readings, an office filled with hymnography that is quite demanding for clergy and singers. The Royal Hours and Vespers follow, and Holy Saturday has both Orthros with Lamentations and the Vespers with the Liturgy of St. Basil, including fifteen Old Testament readings. Pascha begins with the chanting of the canon at Nocturne, followed by Orthros, the Divine Liturgy of St. John Chrysostom, and Vespers. All of these offices include special rituals pertaining to the themes of Holy Week and Pascha, including the ritual mimesis of Jesus' burial and processions with his shroud (epitaphios) around the Church.

In short, the services are quite intense and require considerable musical competence and attention on the part of the clergy and singers. Clergy and faithful of the Byzantine Rite are well aware of the preparation and energy required by the offices. For many, this is the most anticipated part of the liturgical year, evoked in part by the solemnity of the services, but also the domestic traditions of the Church, including the breaking of the strict fast of Great Lent with savory foods, meat and dairy products.

In reality, Holy Week and Pascha is also a season of challenge for parish communities that struggle to fulfill the liturgical requirements. These offices are the most prone to liturgical revision, especially the kind of adjustments the monks of New Skete deplored in their introduction to the Divine Liturgy, where priests excise texts to abbreviate the services so that their celebration is possible in the typical parish. The monks describe the particular challenges posed by Byzantine Holy Week in the introduction to their ordo for these offices:[41]

> All the received practices, but most especially the Holy Week celebrations, are a mish-mash of the usages of Constantinople and Jerusalem, not to mention a host of other places, many perhaps now long-forgotten. This has resulted in the accumulation of a seemingly unlimited number of texts, some of them extremely beautiful and useful. Another bulk of texts contains material that is mediocre and therefore not even desirable, let alone necessary. . . . The lectionary, too, is a jumble of repetitious and overlapping pericopes that must be reduced and reorganized. . . . Given this overabundance, then, we have determined to reduce it.

In short, the monks' diagnosis of the problem of Holy Week is that it is too demanding. In presenting their version of the offices, the monks begin with a detailed rationale for each part of Holy Week and Pascha. They begin by repeating their emphasis on music: all of the offices are to be sung so as to highlight the "critical points of the week" and remove any possibility of "boredom or routine setting in on those present."[42] The monks also address the problem identified by Pavlos Koumarianos in his diagnosis of Holy Week, namely that the morning offices are celebrated in the evening, and evening offices in the morning.[43] At New Skete, "there is no anticipation of offices": they celebrate evening offices in the evening, and morning offices

---

41. Monks of New Skete, *Passion and Resurrection* (Cambridge, NY: New Skete, 1995), xxxix-xl.

42. Ibid., xliv.

43. See n. 40 above. Also see Alkiviadis Calivas, *Great Week and Pascha in the Greek Orthodox Church* (Brookline, MA: Holy Cross Orthodox Press, 1992), 9n32. Calivas refers to New Skete as a model for drawing from the cathedral tradition in forming their own Typikon.

in the morning in contrast to the actual practice of the received tradition.

New Skete treated all of the offices of Holy Week, and I will limit my analysis to the popular offices that begin on Holy Friday to illustrate how their liturgical revisions promote the underpinning theological and pastoral rationale. In the received tradition, Holy Friday is the busiest liturgical day, beginning with the long Orthros and Passion Gospels (customarily sung in parishes in Thursday evening), and including the Royal hours, Vespers, and concluding on Friday evening with the Orthros of Holy Saturday.

New Skete performed several revisions for Holy Friday. The most significant revision is in the reduction of Gospel readings: at Orthros, there are twelve readings, and New Skete has reduced this number to three, based on the following rationale:[44]

> [Holy Friday Orthros is] heavily farced with twelve gospel readings, each followed by extensive troparia in the form of antiphons (fifteen in all). These more than sixty troparia reiterate and embellish what has already been repeatedly described in the course of the gospel narratives . . . we reduce the gospel pericopes to three, though not at the expense of covering the whole passion narrative that pertains to the historical events of Holy Friday. The antiphons that follow these gospels are also severely abbreviated.

The monks' sensitivity to oversaturation of the senses and the body with the abundant accumulation of liturgical material underpins their abbreviation and simplification of the office. They refer to the received tradition as "a veritable endurance test" and a "marathon."[45] In addition to pruning material from the office, they celebrate it on Friday morning in deference to the elderly, providing them with an opportunity to hear a service during a more convenient time of day.

44. Ibid., liii–liv.
45. Ibid., liv.

The decision to revise the service is not only to make it more bearable, but also to reduce the sheer amount of repetition.[46] Orthros contains a significant ritual element: the monks celebrate an office of the procession of the cross following the Troparion of the day, based upon the hagiopolite veneration of the cross mentioned by fourth- and fifth-century Jerusalemite sources.[47] The monks express their fidelity to the office's solemnity by stating that about two hours are needed to celebrate their variant, especially since everything is sung at an appropriate pace. The actual Gospel readings are arranged in a two year cycle (A and B) illustrated by table 6.2:

Table 6.2: Holy Friday Orthros Gospel Readings:

Year A	Year B
John 18:12–27	Mark 14:53–72
Luke 22:66–23:35	Mark 15:1–20
Luke 23:26–49	Mark 15:21–41; Luke 23:26–49; Mk. 15:29–41

New Skete does not repeat any Gospel pericopes in its Holy Week lectionary, which explains most of the twelve Gospel lessons are not taken at Orthros. For example, the first gospel of the received tradition (the longest), John 13:31–18:1, is appointed for New Skete's Thursday tersext office in abbreviated form.[48] The second gospel of the received tradition (John 18:1–28), becomes the first gospel in cycle A, though some of the text has been removed.[49] The fifth gospel (Matthew 27:3–32), is included in the Friday evening composite

46. Ibid.: "The cost in distractions and the energies lost in struggling to pay attention to what one has already heard over and over again—all this takes its toll, and only the Lord knows the truth of it. Fewer people seem to be attending from year to year."
47. Ibid., lv.
48. Ibid., lxvii. Note that this office also includes the rite of washing of the feet.
49. Ibid.

reading, so it is not included here. The ninth gospel (John 19:23–37), Jesus' death, is appointed to Friday tersext; and the tenth and eleventh gospels which report the burial of Jesus are suppressed.[50] The revised lectionary has the following goal, according to the monks: "to lead us through the events of Holy Friday morning, up to and including the death on the cross."[51]

This revision of the Holy Week lectionary simultaneously corrects the historical accident of a growing accumulation of readings that occurred through the fusion of hagiopolite and Constantinopolitan liturgical traditions while restoring a sense of gradual commemoration through the cycle of services. The lectionary of the received tradition repeated many passages from Gospel pericopes read previously in the cycle. New Skete's removal of these passages provides a much cleaner and sensible lectionary with the assumption that the community will follow the evangelistic narrative throughout the week. A consequence of the biblical repetition in the received tradition of Holy Week is that people can hear a portion of a lesson proclaimed at an earlier service.

This small detail demonstrates New Skete's creation of a lectionary suitable for a monastic community that assumes participation in each office. The implications of correcting a liturgical error that remained stagnant throughout history is perhaps more notable for our purposes. By reconfiguring the lectionary in such a way that repetition is removed with the word performing its function of proclaiming the story, New Skete has taken a crucial step in restoring a proper sense of pulse and sequence in the commemoration of events during Holy Week. Furthermore, it has liberated pastors from the

---

50. Ibid., lxviii. The twelfth gospel is also surpressed because it is the same one taken at Holy Saturday Orthros.
51. Ibid.

obligation of justifying the repetitions as an opportunity to hear what was proclaimed during the previous evening.

Holy Saturday

New Skete performed significant revisions for the offices of Holy Saturday as well. The most striking excision is the removal of the liturgy of St. Basil from the day's offices.[52] The order for the day begins with Jerusalem Orthros, followed by Vespers, and a short office with the removal of the shroud from the tomb and its placement on the holy table (instead of the Paschal Nocturne). The revisions fulfill the principle of establishing a simple office that communicates the theme and character of the day without repetition and complexity. The result is, again, a seamless and sensible order of services that are notably distinct from those of the received tradition.

The Orthros is celebrated on Saturday morning, not Friday evening as is customary in Byzantine Rite churches. The community sings the "famous" hymns of lamentation on Psalm 119, and has reduced their number.[53] Vespers includes the hymnography of the received tradition, but the community reads only three of the appointed fifteen readings.

The explanation for these surgical revisions is twofold: first, the revisions are supported by a weighty theological rationale, the observance of a sequential remembrance of Jesus' death, burial, and resurrection. The monks also corrected the accidents of liturgical history in this revised order. The monks explain their theological rationale for simplifying the services of Holy Saturday:[54]

---

52. Ibid., lviii.
53. Also noteworthy is New Skete's singing of the Canticle of Moses from Exodus after Psalm 51, and the restoration of the Canticle of the Theotokos (Magnificat) in the canon, with the ninth irmos from the received Triodion sung as a refrain, ibid.
54. Ibid., lviii.

The whole character of Holy Saturday, it should be sharply noticed, is not one of celebrating what has yet to happen liturgically—i.e., the resurrection—but, rather, of spending this day in waiting together with Christ, who takes his Sabbath rest in then tomb. Historically, this was the way Constantinople originally preferred to observe the whole week, i.e., to watch and pray, celebrating the daily offices without much more solemnity than during the rest of Lent, and this certainly applied to Holy Saturday.

The monks' expressed preference for restoring the Constantinopolitan liturgical principle of Holy Week discloses a deeper meaning to limiting the liturgical offices on Holy Saturday: as a Christian community, they join Jesus in his Sabbath rest in quiet prayer and vigil. The decision to excise the liturgy of St. Basil has the appearance of a radical innovation, but it demonstrates the community's commitment to living the liturgical principle while also correcting an accident of liturgical history.

In the received tradition, the liturgy of St. Basil celebrated on the evening of Holy Saturday is the original cathedral liturgy announcing the resurrection. The replacement of Alleluia with Psalm 81 accompanied by vesting in white and reading the Gospel from St. Matthew on the resurrection was the cathedral way of beginning Pascha. The monastic hymnography composed for the Vespers of Holy Saturday meditates on Jesus' Sabbath rest and descent into Hades, which has resulted in pastoral attempts to explain this celebration as an intense anticipation of the resurrection still to come. The cathedral celebration was also baptismal, which is why fifteen readings were required.

Historically, the readings were proclaimed in the Great Church while the patriarch baptized neophytes in the baptistry. If the number of people receiving Baptism was large, then more readings were required in the church. Once the baptisms were finished, the clergy came vested in white, representing all the faithful in wearing their baptismal garments, and the neophytes entered the church to the Trisagion processional hymn, "as many as have been baptized into Christ." In their first partaking of the Eucharistic liturgy in its fullness, the neophytes would hear the announcement of the resurrection through the proclamation of Psalm 81 and the Matthean resurrection Gospel. In the received tradition, the popular piety associated with Paschal Nocturne, Orthros (and the canon of St. John Damascene), and the Divine Liturgy has resulted in the displacement of the original Paschal vigil so that it is typically celebrated on the morning of Holy Saturday.

Pastorally, this is a time when many faithful come to church to fulfill the annual obligation of a Lenten confession, so for some clergy, it is a busy Saturday. It is thus convenient to explain this office as distinct from Pascha, an anticipatory liturgy that is in the liminal stage between Jesus' Sabbath rest and resurrection. The problem with such explanations is that they contradict the Paschal nature of the Vigil now delegated to some time on Holy Saturday: it is delusional to begin a celebration of the resurrection only to reverse course and mourn at Jesus' tomb.

New Skete corrects this historical accident by removing the liturgy of St. Basil. They explain their rationale accordingly:[55]

> It should thus be clear that we do not observe this Holy Saturday by the celebration of the Eucharistic liturgy—neither in the morning with Vespers as is traditionally done, nor at any other time. The received use of celebrating vespers with this liturgy is properly the vigil service that actually initiated the paschal celebration. The only full liturgy that we celebrate at New Skete during this entire week is the one for Holy Thursday in the late afternoon, with vespers. There will be no other Eucharistic celebration until the day of the Pasch itself. The entire time intervening is strictly aliturgical and infinitely more in keeping with the events being commemorated. The character of the 'great vigil' observed

55. Ibid., lviii–lix.

throughout Christendom on this day thus becomes ever clearer and considerably more sober in tonality and texture when we observe it minus the necessarily festal celebration that the Eucharist is.

By adopting this practice, New Skete has taken a bold step towards living out the theological rationale underpinning their Holy Week practice in the face of potential criticism, given Christianity's general reluctance to revise practices during solemn seasons of the Church year. Above, I mentioned the theological absurdity of explaining the vespers of Holy Saturday as an intense anticipation of Christ's Pascha. Others have approached this as a pastoral opportunity to restore the baptismal character of Holy Saturday by preparing catechumens for Baptism and Chrismation throughout the Lenten period and baptizing them during this liturgy. The liturgy of the Word for Holy Saturday supports this practice. Some pastors have erred in their attempt to restore the baptismal character of this liturgy by scheduling Baptisms and Chrismation before the liturgy, so as to avoid interrupting the flow of the office with its fifteen readings. Such practices ignore the history leading up to appointing fifteen readings, which are all about Baptism. New Skete's explanation for their reduction of the readings offers another element supporting their theological rationale for the order of Holy Saturday:[56]

> The cluster of fifteen readings in the traditional lectionary was obviously assembled to hold the attention of the congregation during the numerous baptisms that took place on this day. (Note, again, the parallel of the immersion of the baptismal candidates with the immersion of Christ in the tomb). Here at the monastery, we obviously seldom have baptisms, least of all scheduled for Holy Saturday, so the number of readings used at this office is drastically reduced.

New Skete's reduction of the Holy Saturday readings is pragmatic: their reading of history indicated that the fifteen readings were

---

56. Monks of New Skete, *Passion and Resurrection*, lix.

baptismal in content and designed to cover the ritual baptisms. The fusion of the monastic and cathedral liturgies and the prevalence of infant Baptism in the East led to the decline of cathedral baptisms on Holy Saturday. As the monastic variant of the liturgy became normative in Byzantium, performing baptisms on appointed days of the liturgical year such as Pascha and Theophany declined. The baptismal elements of these festal liturgies are remnants of the cathedral elements of liturgy which do not manifest the same meaning when baptisms are not actually celebrated in the liturgical context. New Skete's revision is thus bluntly honest: as a monastic community, they do not anticipate many baptisms in the course of the liturgical year. Hence, they adjusted the liturgy to represent the present historical reality, as opposed to offering a creative explanation that justifies fidelity to the received tradition.

New Skete is remarkably consistent in following this approach, evidenced by their elimination of the Paschal Nocturne (midnight office).[57] In parish practice within the received tradition, Nocturne may be the most sensational aspect of the liturgical office because of its drama. In the received tradition, the faithful gather in a dark church before midnight, typically dressed in their finest clothing, in anticipation of the announcement of the resurrection. The office consists almost entirely of the singing of the canon, a short office of hymnography fusing the themes of lamentation at the tomb, Christ's defeat of Hades, and the imminent discovery of the empty grave with the announcement that he is risen.

The details on the ritual component vary within the Byzantine tradition. Some clergy celebrate the office before the tomb in the

---

57. A consultation of Passion and Resurrection suggests that the midnight office is a simple monastic chanting of the canon. According to Brother Stavros, the community no longer observes the Nocturne. The hymns from Paschal Nocturne are sung while the faithful come forward to venerate the shroud on the evening of Holy Friday. (Per e-mail exchange with Brother Stavros, December 2, 2014).

middle of the church, while some remain in the sanctuary. In the Slavic custom, the epitaphios (icon of Jesus buried) is carried in procession from the tomb and laid on the holy table, a ritual action which accentuates the idea that one will find the tomb empty at this present time. In the Greek custom, the epitaphios is moved from the tomb to the holy table at Jerusalem Orthros. After the conclusion of the office, the presider lights a candle, intones the troparion of the resurrection, and shares the light with all of the people, who then process around the church bearing their candles. Orthros begins outdoors, outside of the church, and when the people re-enter the church for Paschal Orthros, it is the custom to illuminate it completely with flowers and white vestry decorating the entire interior. The transition from darkness to illumination suggests a powerful moment in time when sorrow is pierced by the joyous news of the resurrection. The experience of this dramatic moment is certainly one of the factors motivating faithful to attend the Paschal services, which often results in people leaving before the Divine Liturgy.

New Skete favors a spirit of austerity in its observance of the offices of Holy Saturday, which coheres with New Skete's themes of vigil and watchfulness throughout the week. The element of drama occurs at Paschal Orthros where the monks follow the received tradition by vesting in white, distributing the lighted tapers, processing around the church while singing the troparion, then gathering at the church door with a gospel reading, and beginning Orthros with the canon of St. John Damascene.[58] The beginning of the service certainly has a dramatic element, but the revision loses the sense of stark transition from the darkness of Nocturne to the illumination of the resurrection. By applying this revision, the monks have addressed the temptation

58. Order for Pasch in *Passion and Resurrection*, 225–43.

to reduce Pascha to a single strong moment: for the monks, the watchful vigil continues even after Nocturne, as they are instructed to retire until they gather for Orthros at the appointed time.[59]

New Skete's liturgical offices of Holy Week and Pascha correct accidents of liturgical history, seek to engage the faithful in a liturgical ordo that is possible, and emphasize the themes of vigil and watchfulness while reducing the amount of overt drama currently infused in the received tradition. Furthermore, the revised offices remove numerous repetitions, simplify the services, and generate a pulse of liturgical remembrance much more coherent with the historical events. Their application of the yields from liturgical history to their revised offices is selective: their revision is significant and generally prefers the cathedral tradition, but monastic elements remain.[60] Perhaps the most notable result of the revision is the boldness of the change: Holy Week and Pascha constitute the most solemn season of the liturgical year, so the undertaking of a significant revision of these offices elucidates the community's conviction that change was needed to enable a theological restoration that captured the spirit of Holy Week and Pascha more effectively.

Creativity

In my analysis of liturgy at New Skete, I have identified select components from the Divine Liturgy, Holy Week, and Pascha as examples communicating the theological rationale for renewal. For each aspect of their liturgical life, the monks carefully explain the process they employed in transitioning from the received tradition to their monastic ordo. I have described this transition using diverse

---

59. Ibid., 225. Referring to the Canon and placement of the shroud on the holy table, the monks instruct 'at the conclusion of the troparion, the lights are extinguished except for the eternal lamp, and all retire."

60. The monastery's retention of Paschal Orthros of the received tradition stands out amidst other adaptations of cathedral elements.

adjectives: surgical, bold, innovative, and sensitive, to name a few. When one projects the magnitude of the revision itself, one word aptly summarizes the entire enterprise: creative. This implementation of renewal was not a matter of fine-tuning a few areas of the liturgy or ignoring a handful of petitions in a litany, but consisted of a wholescale, carefully considered plan underpinned by a rationale of pastoral theology. The monks reinvigorated certain cathedral traditions, such as tersext, and performed significant pruning, but the final result is not a reincarnation of some past model, but an entirely new order that claims fidelity to tradition and necessary innovation for contemporary times.

In addition to the wholescale quality of creativity, one finds creativity in specific areas as well. New Skete's sensitivity to praying in contemporary idioms with respect for the relationship between music and text resulted in an acclaimed Psalter.[61] In my view, the monastery fulfills the spirit of liturgical renewal by engaging an ongoing process of composing prayers and hymns for the liturgical year. As noted earlier in this study, the composition of new offices and hymns is not new: whenever the Church recognizes God's glorification of a saint, a new office may be composed. In the received tradition, composers of such offices consult the patterns of offices composed in honor of saints belonging to the same category. In other words, there is a certain degree of dependence on the existing repository of hymnography in the received tradition: one's contributions are gifts inspired by the Holy Spirit, not new pieces.[62]

New Skete follows this pattern in a different way. While they retain much of the hymnology of the received tradition, and reserve the right to modify it, they are also adding to the existing repository. A good example of such an addition occurs at the Vespers of Holy

---

61. Monks of New Skete, *The Psalter* (Cambridge, NY: New Skete Monastery, 1987).
62. As said by Brother Stavros, per e-mail January 2, 2014.

Thursday. New Skete composed entirely new stichera for the incense psalms, and moved some of the extant hymns to tersext in their effort to follow a sensible sequence of liturgical remembrance. The Vespers of Holy Thursday meditates on Jesus' last supper shared with his disciples in the passion sequence. Several stichera are normally sung at the incense psalms, and the first sticheron establishes the theme for the day; here is New Skete's original rendition for this first sticheron:[63]

> Brothers and sisters, let us marvel at that upper room! For there the Lord taught his friends humility by washing their feet, Judas broke with his brothers and went off to his own affair, while the Lord gave his body and blood for us and for many.

This sticheron follows tradition in many ways. First, it is hortatory, calling upon the community in the present to marvel. Second, it is didactic, referring to the events of salvation history remembered at that liturgical office, including the washing of the disciples' feet and the sharing of the supper. It also mentions Judas, who as a secondary character throughout much of Holy Week is the primary antagonist in the Church's hymnography of Holy Week. A traditional Orthodox participant would find the opening line jarring because it is deliberately gender inclusive by exhorting brothers and sisters. The non-Orthodox reader might find this point unremarkable, but for the Eastern Church, the principle of lexical equivalence tends to prevail in translation with no concern for gender neutral or inclusive devices. Here, the monastery recognizes the reality of its own mixed community consisting of male and female monastics, and addresses them appropriately in the texts.

Another sample of originality in the hymnography occurs in a sticheron from the same group, which remembers Judas's betrayal of Jesus. The originality occurs in the first verse of the hymn: "In

63. Monks of New Skete, *Passion and Resurrection*, 156.

the meantime, the unfortunate Judas arranges his deed, coming to terms with those who await him."[64] In this verse, the monks used the adjective "unfortunate." Again, this may sound unremarkable, but the Byzantine hymnography of Holy Week uses quite pejorative language to describe Judas, the antagonist: he is wicked, a traitor, impious, and treacherous.[65] New Skete was sensitive to the obsession with Judas in the hymnography of the received tradition and desired to shift some of the emphasis and focus to other themes.[66]

In this sticheron, New Skete readjusted Judas's role: he remains the one who betrayed Jesus, but he is not superimposed on the story as a character of equal interest to Jesus. Rather, Judas's deed is positioned within the larger scheme of Jesus' salvific meal: each sticheron of the series on the incense psalms ends with a reference to Jesus' body and blood given for us (sometimes "for you") and for many. Judas is mentioned only twice in all the incense hymns, while the Church praises Jesus in each one, so Judas becomes what he was in the actual New Testament narrative: the disciple who betrayed Jesus, not the antagonist who deserves a richer share in the Church's remembrance of the saving event. These two samples from the stichera New Skete composed for Vespers on Holy Thursday demonstrate their originality in creative fidelity to tradition: they composed hymns focused on the glory of God which referred to the saving events remembered at that particular liturgical office while

64. Ibid., 157.
65. See, for example, the hymnography appointed for Orthros on Holy Thursday, where Judas is "Iniquitous Iscariot" (Second Troparion on Ode 8), "the transgressor" (second sticheron at lauds), "the deceitful traitor" (third sticheron at lauds), "servant and deceiver, disciple and traitor, friend and false accuser" (fourth sticheron at lauds), in *The Lenten Triodion*, trans. Kallistos Ware and Mother Mary (South Canaan, PA: St. Tikhon's Seminary, 2002), 553–54.
66. "There seems to be an overwhelming, over-abundant, and excessive emphasis on and preoccupation with the treachery of Judas in the received usage; though retaining some of these hymns, we have preferred to underline other aspects of the season," Monks of New Skete, *Passion and Resurrection*, l.

exhorting the present community—men and women—to be thankful for Jesus' supper.

Our next example of New Skete's originality comes from their revision of the liturgy of the Hours in their Book of Prayers.[67] This edition, like the Divine Liturgy and Holy Week offices, represents the principles employed by the monastery in its enterprise of liturgical renewal. For example, the monks corrected an accident of liturgical history by restoring the biblical canticles at Orthros in place of the canon, a series of nine odes fusing the themes of the original canticles with those proclaimed by the liturgical theme of the day. Furthermore, New Skete translated the ancient sung offices from the cathedral liturgy of Constantinople, namely the vigil (pannychis) as a preferred alternative to Great Compline, based on the sung nature of the cathedral vigil. Finally, the monastery redistributed the prayers of the offices. In the received tradition, most of the prayers of the daily hours are recited quietly by the presider during the chanting of the initial psalms. This practice is a consequence of the fusion of monastic and cathedral traditions: the prayers are of cathedral provenance and many of them were clustered in the beginning of the office in favor of the order and pulse of the monastic ones. New Skete revised the offices so that the prayers would be recited aloud in their proper places.

In some instances, New Skete composed new prayers for the offices. An illustrative example is from Orthros: the first canticle sung at Orthros is the one of the Three Youths (Daniel), and New Skete composed a prayer that completes this first canticle and transitions the assembly to the next and final one, of the Theotokos (Magnificat):[68]

> O holy Father! Unfailing source and treasury of all that is good! All-powerful ruler of all things and author of all marvels We all fall down in

---

67. Monks of New Skete, *Book of Prayers* (Cambridge, NY: New Skete, 1988).
68. Ibid., 321–22.

adoration before you to assist and support us in our lowliness through your mercies and compassion. Remember us, o Lord, and accept these prayers we make to you this morning as the fragrance of incense in your sight. Do not reject any of us, but encircle our lives with your abundant loving kindness. For you are our God and we give you glory, Father, Son, and Holy Spirit: now and forever, and unto ages of ages. Amen.

This prayer is notable for its simple features. First, the prayer draws upon the language of antiquity by addressing the Father. Second, the prayer is very short, also an attribute of antiquity and in fulfillment of New Skete's objectives of liturgical renewal. The prayer makes proper reference to the morning, an element coherent with New Skete's devotion to praying offices at their appointed times. The prayer also presents an implicit acknowledgement of the realities of one's daily life; in petitioning God for assistance and support, the prayer reminds those who offer it that they need God's presence as they go about their daily business in the world.

But perhaps the best example of New Skete's creativity is the Hymn of Light appointed for Vespers of Holy Pasch (the Paschal Vigil). In the received tradition of the Byzantine Rite, the hymn of light sung at vespers is Phos Ilaron, or "Gladsome Light."[69] The antiquity of this hymn is attributed to St. Basil of Caesarea of the fourth century, who describes the hymn as ancient.[70] In the contemporary churches of the Byzantine Rite, this hymn is ubiquitous. It is common for entire assemblies to sing the hymn in its entirety to an appointed melody. Given that Gladsome Light is a fixture in the office, replacing it with a special hymn for the Holy Pasch was an audacious and creative decision on the part of New

---

69. For the history of this ancient hymn, see Robert F. Taft, *The Liturgy of the Hours in East and West: The Origins of the Divine Office and its Meaning for Today*, 2d rev ed. (Collegeville, MN: Liturgical, 1993), 36–41, 285–87.

70. Ibid., 38.

Skete. Here is the text of the hymn they sing at the Vespers of Holy Pasch:[71]

> On this sacred day of your rest, O Saviour, as you lie asleep in the tomb, make your light shine forth on our darkness as it did on those in the world beneath. On this eve of the third day, O Christ, as you await your resurrection, awaken your love in our hearts, engage all our being in your presence, and enable us to greet your rising, filled with praise for you together with your Father and Holy Spirit.

The hymn addresses Christ and petitions him to illuminate the faithful who have maintained a watchful vigil during the course of Holy Week, so that they may worship the Triune God on the solemnity of Pascha. The hymn emphasizes the ecclesiological and eschatological features of Pascha, but its originality lies primarily in its replacement of a fixed hymn for the office of Vespers. In performing this revision, the Monks of New Skete have observed a little-known pattern in Byzantine liturgy that permits the appointment of special hymns for solemnities, particularly at the Paschal Vigil. One such example is the replacement of "Alleluia" with the chanting of Psalm 81 as the responsorial psalm announcing the Resurrection Gospel, a practice which has existed in the Byzantine Rite since about the ninth century.[72] In their audacious and creative revision of the liturgy, the Monks of New Skete remain faithful to historical patterns of liturgical creativity in the Byzantine Rite.

This brief presentation on New Skete's liturgical creativity illuminates the scope of their liturgical renewal enterprise. The monastery's consultation of liturgical history led them to revise the order of offices and restore new ones. In some instances, they moved or excised existing hymns and composed new offerings in their place.

---

71. Monks of New Skete, *Passion and Resurrection*, 208-9. Brother Stavros states that the musical arrangement for this piece has become quite popular, per e-mail on December 2, 2014.
72. Nicholas Denysenko, "Psalm 81: Announcing the Resurrection on Holy Saturday," *Logos: A Journal of Eastern Christian Studies* 50 (2009): 55-88.

This liturgical creativity is both original and faithful to tradition, as I have discussed in the examples above. Here, it is worthwhile to emphasize the novelty of composing new prayers and hymns in the Byzantine liturgical tradition. Scholars devote years to studying the evolution of prayers to discover varying levels of editorship as orations make their way through the manuscript tradition and living practice of liturgical prayer. New Skete has rehabilitated the practice of composing new and fresh material that consults traditional styles. These new prayers and hymns offer a final layer to the enterprise of liturgical renewal; renewal requires not only the rearranging of furniture and the leveling and rebuilding of walls, but, in some cases, the addition of brand new elements.

New Skete and Vatican II

In the models of liturgical reform we have studied in Orthodoxy, Vatican II has had an indirect impact. In general, the scale and surgical style of Vatican II's liturgical reform has proven undesirable for Orthodox churches, which have preferred to emphasize catechesis and fine-tuning of the received tradition. Many Orthodox have embraced the same principles underpinning Vatican II's reform because those principles were developed in ecumenical conversation of pastors and scholars. Our examination of New Skete's liturgical reform suggests that Vatican II might have had more impact on New Skete than on the other Orthodox models examined here.

The reform of Vatican II employed the contributions of liturgical scholarship and drew richly from Eastern traditions to underscore the catholicity of the Church. Vatican II is also viewed as a surgical reform: offices are rearranged, elements are excised, new liturgical books are produced and distributed, the architecture was adjusted, and many new liturgical elements are created. New Skete follows the same paradigm by consulting liturgical scholarship, revising the offices, excising material for the purpose of simplifying liturgy, encouraging the active participation of the faithful, and creating new elements drawn from tradition that cohere with the contemporary environment of the church.

The monastery was formed in 1966, in the immediate memory of Vatican II, and several monks acknowledge the freedom for renewal encouraged by the Roman council. The most convincing evidence of Vatican II's influence on New Skete is in the architecture of the Holy Wisdom temple constructed in 1983. The temple facilitates a sense of one priesthood, headed by Christ and shared by laity and clergy, manifested in the large ambo, where the clergy and laity hear the word of God together. The templon surrounding the sanctuary enhances visual access into the sanctuary and mitigates the barriers between clergy and laity often promoted by ecclesial architecture. But the most telling evidence is in the iconography, particularly the murals on the four walls of the interior.

The walls above connecting the ceiling to the nave contain icons of dozens of figures central to New Skete's identity. The walls depict holy figures in groups of two to five, a procession of saints painted by Deacon Iakov Ferencz. The walls contain dozens of saints of East and West, men and women, and also pay homage to New Skete's initiative of ecumenical hope and homage to its liturgical heritage. The inclusion of numerous Western saints honors New Skete's origins in the Franciscan order of the Western church. This depiction of the past points to the future in the collection of figures who are not yet canonized in the Orthodox Church but venerated locally by New Skete, with the absence of halos denoting their interim status.[73] The depiction of Patriarch Athenagoras and Pope

73. Note that Maria Skobtsova was canonized by the Ecumenical Patriarchate in 2004, whereas Mother Theresa of Calcutta was beatified in 2003 and Dorothy Day is currently being considered for canonization.

Paul VI together on the northern wall honors the kiss of peace exchanged by the two bishops in 1964 in Jerusalem.

Likewise, the depiction of people such as Maria Skobtsova and Lev Gillet honors the labors of twentieth century figures who literally bridged east and west and contributed to ecumenical rapprochement through their actions. The inclusion of Alexander Schmemann indicates the monastery's homage to a figure who contributed to the community's formation. Partaking of worship in the nave exposes on to New Skete's powerful ecumenical ethos. The nave's iconographic program highlights the period of Christian history when East and West were united and anticipates that the assembly worshiping in the nave will share these values and promote the same ecumenical ethos. The eclectic collection of saints offers a hopeful picture for the contemporary worshipper: the communion of saints includes men and women, along with monks and married saints, emphasizing the universality of the call to holiness in the Church.

New Skete's program of liturgical renewal depended on its examination of liturgical history, but is also an exercise in discerning the signs of the times in self-honesty. The men and women of the community are a people of Western provenance who have found a home in the Eastern Church. Their reflections on identity have resulted in a veneration from their native Western home, which ultimately brought them to the Eastern Church. New Skete is an example of a monastic community that discovered the East on account of the study of the East engaged by Western scholars during the courses of the liturgical and ecumenical movements, which resulted in the groundbreaking liturgical reform of Vatican II and the recognition of the Eastern communities as real churches. Vatican II marked a new era in Western appreciation for the East. In some instances, this appreciation resulted in episodes of liturgical byzantinization of Roman sacraments and adaptation of other Eastern liturgical elements. When the community of New Skete embarked on the path of living in the Eastern Church, Vatican II had given it an encouraging push into this new world. Included with this push was a dose of the program for liturgical renewal the people of New Skete had experienced at Vatican II. New Skete has essentially implemented a variant of the liturgical reform that some of the fathers of the pre-revolutionary Russian Church had hoped for, a sentiment echoed in the modern era by some representatives of the Greek Church. This renewal is largely attributable to Vatican II.

Conclusion

New Skete's liturgical renewal program shares much in common with the other models of this study. The monks sought to draw from tradition and create a liturgy suitable for the life of the contemporary Church. Like the other models, they venerated received tradition even as they modified it. They also emphasized the significance of ritual engagement where one can encounter symbols without being overwhelmed by an enormous amount of text and venerated the important roles of liturgical presidency and musical performance. In short, New Skete sought to purify liturgy by resolving the accidents of liturgical history by a rich consultation of extant scholarship. In this way, their reform is somewhat similar to that of Schmemann and the Church of Greece, whereas their devotion to excellence in liturgical aesthetics and the *ars celebrandi* echoes that of ROCOR.

New Skete's reform are much more bold than those of the other models because their reform is more surgical and results in the removal of elements of the received tradition that others have not succeeded in treating. My assessment of New Skete's reform is that it conforms to the spirit of the proposals considered by the prerevolutionary Russian bishops and the Greek Church because it seeks to reshape liturgy itself so that it is no longer an inert object of the past venerated on the basis of charming memories, but a truly living tradition for the present generation of Orthodox Christians.

In theory, New Skete's liturgical renewal is modular, and I believe that Orthodox churches willing to adopt it would find it to be an outpouring gift of the Spirit for the building up of Christ's body. However, New Skete's reforms have had very little impact in the life of the Orthodox Church, outside of the admiration of select scholars and devoted friends of the monastery. Their remote location and history are two of the reasons for their limited impact: one has to travel a long distance to reach New Skete, and they are a small monastic community by design. Also, their openly ecumenical disposition is jarring to many Orthodox who do not trust Catholics and Protestants.

However, I believe that New Skete's reform has not had an impact on Orthodoxy for another reason: Orthodox perceive liturgy as uniform and unchangeable, an attitude communicated by Orthodox clergy who are canonically bound to remain faithful to the received tradition. The study of liturgical history demonstrates that liturgy evolves in history, just as languages, customs, and people do. Liturgy has an ossified status among Orthodox people, but this perspective on liturgy is deceiving: if people were more attentive and visited other communities, they would discover liturgical diversity even on the surface of seemingly homogenous regions.

Despite the limited impact to date, I believe that New Skete's liturgical renewal has the potential to shape Orthodox practice significantly, even in the near future, for two reasons. First, of all the models we have studied here, the theological principles underpinning liturgical reform are most manifest in New Skete's ordo. Second, rapidly changing societal conditions and globalization are demanding a response from the Church at a more rapid pace. Because New Skete's primary objective was to create a liturgical ordo that was traditional, comprehensible, engaging, edifying, inspiring, and conforming to the conditions of contemporary life, eventually it will be discovered and become a referential model by communities that desire to worship God in the idioms and circumstances of their present lives.

6

Lessons from History

Assessments and an Agenda for Liturgical Reform

This study has presented the development of liturgical reform in the Orthodox Church by examining the theological foundation of *SC*, considering the contribution of Vatican II, and by exploring four models of liturgical reform in the Orthodox Church. This chapter will synthesize the observations gleaned from this study and will propose an agenda for contemporary liturgical reform in the Orthodox and Catholic Churches, in the spirit of an ecumenical gift exchange. My proposals for contemporary liturgical reform will be based upon an analysis of the lessons we have learned from history.

The Rationale for Liturgical Reform

Throughout this study, I have prioritized the need to establish a rationale for liturgical reform. Understanding the rationale for reform is an exercise in carefully listening to the testimony of the historical witnesses that speak to us from the five models we have considered here. Our first observation is that the rationale for reform was inspired and ignited by a careful pastoral assessment of the state of the Church in all five models. The liturgy was examined by all churches through an ecclesiological lens: the visible manifestation of the Church occurs when she gathers to pray, so every aspect of the Church's prayer, namely rite, space, art, word, order, and music contributed, in some way, to pastoral reflections on the state of the Church. The processes of self-examination and assessment acknowledge that liturgy is the primary event and location where the people of the Church experience "church." Several references to examples cited in the previous chapters illustrate this point. For example, in the deliberations at Vatican II, the matter of the people's engagement of the liturgy had relevant reference points in the manner of the Church's praying.[1] The manner of distributing Holy Communion limited the people's experience of the Eucharistic covenant, along with the reservation of this sacrament to one occasion in the entire liturgical year. The Church's privileging of Latin as the sole liturgical language limited the people's comprehension of the liturgy, along with the one-year lectionary and arrangement of sacred space.

Orthodox reflections on the people's experience of the liturgy yielded similar observations. Schmemann focused on the nature of the liturgy as a corporate act involving the entire body of Christ. ROCOR identifies the selection of music as a central element in engaging the faithful in participation, as opposed to entertaining them. The Church of Greece viewed the prevailing practices of Holy

---

1. Marcel Metzger offers a brief overview of these matters in *History of the Liturgy: The Major Stages*, trans. Madeleine Beaumont (Collegeville, MN: Liturgical Press, 1997), 122-38. For a summary of the way Vatican II addressed these particular issues, see Paul Bradshaw and Maxwell Johnson, *The Eucharistic Liturgies: Their Evolution and Interpretation* (Collegeville, MN: Liturgical Press, 2012), 300-318, and Massimo Faggioli, *True Reform: Liturgy and Ecclesiology in Sacrosanctum Concilium* (Collegeville, MN: Liturgical Press, 2012), 65-71. For a complete assessment, see Kevin W. Irwin, *What We Have Done, What We Have Failed to Do: Assessing the Liturgical Reforms of Vatican II* (New York: Paulist Press, 2014), 43-64, 114-61.

Communion among the laity as an obvious symptom of the lack of engagement in the liturgy. New Skete's consultation of liturgical history resulted in their observation that the Church had not effectively taken care of the liturgy and needed to update her structures and content so that the laity would engage rituals in an environment of comprehension.

Schmemann, ROCOR, and the Church of Greece believed that the received Byzantine liturgical tradition remains suitable for the contemporary Church and emphasized catechesis and the restoration of liturgical elements that had decayed as the chief means of promoting the people's engagement of the liturgy. Vatican II and New Skete presented a different diagnosis, depicting the liturgy as having decayed to such a degree that a more surgical approach to structures and content was required. One can summarize the five models by concluding that they share a passionate pastoral concern for the Church that identifies the liturgy as the people's primary event of communion with God and one another, and differ in their approaches to revising the liturgy.

A prominent and consistent result of the pastoral assessment was the identification of the people's indifference to or boredom with the liturgy. Zizioulas's essay on the reduction and decay of symbolism identified the gradual detachment of the symbol from its theological foundation, which results in an appeal for simpler symbols that communicate meaning clearly.[2] Many theologians in the Church of Greece recognized that the liturgy retained medieval symbols that gradually lost their cultural points of reference through the socio-cultural phenomena of Turkocratia, nationalism, and modernism.[3]

2. John Zizioulas, "Symbolism and Realism in Orthodox Worship," trans. Elizabeth Theokritoff, in *Synaxis: An Anthology of the Most Significant Orthodox Theology in Greece Appearing in the Journal Synaxe*, vol. 1: *Anthropology, Environment, Creation*, trans. Peter Chamberas, ed. Liaidan Sherrard (Montreal: Alexander Press, 2006), 251-64.
3. Dimitrios Tzerpos, "ΠΡΟΣ ΜΙΑ ΑΝΑΝΕΩΣΗ ΤΗΣ ΕΚΚΛΗΣΙΑΣΤΙΚΗΣ ΜΑΣ

Metropolitan Antony (Khrapovitsky) of ROCOR recognized the permeation of Western styles of liturgical music into the Russian Church and the disengaging effect this musical style had on the people's liturgical participation.[4] New Skete Monastery similarly noted the people's struggle to engage liturgical symbols that do not communicate in contemporary idioms on account of their medieval vesture.[5] Schmemann dismissed mystagogy, the most prevalent Byzantine attempt to describe the liturgy through symbols, as illustrative symbolism that reduces liturgical meaning and impoverishes the eschatological reality of liturgy.[6] Each model offers varying proposals to restore a healthy sense of symbolism while holding the need to restore the liturgical function of symbolism as urgent.

The Academy and the Church

If pastoral assessment of the liturgy was the primary impetus for beginning the process of reform, academic scholarship on the history and theology of the liturgy likewise contributed to the rationale for reform. In this area, most of the models examined liturgical history to ascertain how it might shape reform. *SC* functioned as the apogee for a process of history manifesting potential models of reform by referring to historical models as primary sources for reforming the liturgy. In the case of Vatican II, the Church order known as

ΛΑΤΡΕΙΑΣ" ("Towards a Renewal of Our Ecclesiastical Worship") Church of Greece website, http:// www.ecclesia.gr / greek / holysynod / commitees / liturgical / liturgical-0001.htm (accessed September 15, 2014).

4. Metropolitan Antony, *О Пастырѣ?, Пастырствѣ?, и объ испов?ди*, ed. Archbishop Nikon (New York: East American and Canadian Eparchy, 1966), 290.

5. Monks of New Skete, *The Divine Liturgy* (Cambridge, NY: New Skete Monastery, 1987), xxiv-xxvi.

6. Alexander Schmemann, "Symbols and Symbolism in the Byzantine Liturgy: Liturgical Symbols and Their Theological Interpretation," in *Liturgy and Tradition: Theological Reflections of Alexander Schmemann*, ed. Thomas Fisch (Crestwood, NY: St. Vladimir's Seminary Press, 1990), 120-25.

the Apostolic Tradition attributed to St. Hippolytus was one of the privileged sources for reform, especially since it was widely accepted as authentically Roman at the time.[7] Vatican II also consulted Roman and hybrid sources illuminating liturgical structures and components in earlier stages of their historical evolution in preparation for the reform, along with Eastern liturgical sources that would honor the Church's identity as increasingly Catholic.[8]

Three of the Orthodox models examined here exhibit veneration for liturgical scholarship, especially New Skete, which constructed a liturgical ordo for the monastery that drew richly from historical studies on Constantinopolitan and hagiopolite cathedral liturgy. Schmemann's famous letter to his bishop and his course syllabi demonstrate his awareness of scholarship on liturgical history and how it might inform contemporary practice, whereas the symposia held by the Church of Greece deliberately gathered scholars and pastors to consider the historical witness. While ROCOR viewed the liturgy itself as an organism that had developed into maturity, the leaders of the Church illustrated a profound awareness of scholarly studies on Russian chant tradition and its capacity to engage the people in the liturgy, which was perhaps the chief component of ROCOR's program of liturgical enrichment. The ecumenical school of *Liturgiewissenschaft* has made remarkable progress in Oriental liturgy, and many of the Churches continue to consult the works of scholars engaged in this science to consider how their research might inform contemporary liturgy.

---

7. For an excellent assessment of the potential problems caused by this assumption, see Matthieu Smyth, "The Anaphora of the So-called 'Apostolic Tradition' and the Roman Eucharistic Prayer," in *Issues in Eucharistic Praying in East and West: Essays in Liturgical and Theological Analysis*, ed. Maxwell Johnson (Collegeville, MN: Liturgical, 2012), 71-98.
8. See Robert F. Taft, "Between Progress and Nostalgia: Liturgical Reform and the Western Romance with the Christian East; Strategies and Realities," in *A Living Tradition: On the Intersection of Liturgical History and Pastoral Practice*, ed. David Pitt, Stefanos Alexopoulos, and Christian McConnell (Collegeville, MN: Liturgical Press, 2012), 29-39; Faggioli, 34-42.

Historical efforts are not limited to structures and components, but also their interpretation and theological underpinnings. The theology of priesthood is a central theological foundation underpinning each model of reform, and this theology was retrieved and articulated through liturgical scholarship. In chapter 2, I noted the centrality of priesthood as a foundation for *SC* that functions as the catalyst for the people's engagement of the liturgy. These elements of priesthood are also present in the liturgical theology of Schmemann, ROCOR, the Church of Greece, and New Skete, though in different ways.

Schmemann's Eucharistic ecclesiology, as we have seen, emphasizes the common celebration of the liturgy by the entire body of Christ with limited physical separation between the clergy and the laity. He devoted his life to promoting this ecclesiology by building up a generation of clergy who would engage pastoral ministry in such a way that the people's priesthood would be manifest in their daily lives. The Church of Greece emphasized catechesis of the people, a program depending on clergy who have the capacity to effectively teach people, primarily through their liturgical presidency. ROCOR likewise promotes the *ars celebrandi* by placing the onus of responsibility for proper and faithful liturgical order on the clergy. ROCOR's emphasis on developing clergy capable of excellent liturgical presidency finds its primary source in the pastoral teaching of Metropolitan Antony, who demanded much from the clergy in terms of their liturgical presidency. Metropolitan Antony's teachings emphasized that the clergy should not be distracted by petty demands of entertainment coming from the laity, because only clergy who intensely focused their prayer towards God could effectively teach people how to love God and their neighbor. New Skete adopts a similar approach here by demanding that the clergy celebrate the liturgy in such a way that leads the people into the kingdom. The standard for clergy is consistently high in each model, even if the specific tasks demanded of clergy vary. One could assert that parish clergy are the most important gatekeepers of liturgical reform and restoration; if clergy are unable to fulfill their objectives for liturgical reform, the enterprise will likely fail.[9]

Having identified some of the similarities in the consultation of academic scholarship for liturgical reform, particularly the emphasis on the role of parish clergy in offering quality liturgical catechesis to the people, we should also note the stark differences between the approaches adopted in each model. I have argued here that the key figures in each model of reform performed a type of pastoral diagnosis of the liturgy through an ecclesiological lens. The most prevalent theme that runs like a thread through all of the models is the observation that the people are disengaged from the liturgy. The people tend to arrive late, they appear to be bored, and their engagement of the liturgical components that invite their participation seems to be tepid. All of our models appear to identify a restoration of the people's engagement of the liturgy as the chief catalyst that would awaken organic Christian spirituality, capacitating the people to engage the life of the world. However, the proponents of reform and restoration are not uniform in their approach to reforming the liturgy so the people can engage it.

The challenge encountered by the leaders of each model was to reform liturgy in such a way that the liturgical structures would convey the deep theology underpinning them. The analysis of the received liturgical structures and their interpretation, and the prognoses for restoration differed among the five models. The Church of Greece concluded that the problem of the laity's disengagement from the liturgy was multifaceted. The received

9. See Robert Taft's comments on the need for educated clergy in "Interviewing Liturgical Leaders: Robert Taft, SJ.," Pray, Tell Blog website, http://www.praytellblog.com/index.php/2014/06/11/interviewing-liturgical-leaders-robert-taft-s-j (accessed January 15, 2015).

tradition of the liturgy had remained largely unchanged whereas the daily lives of ordinary people had changed radically since the Byzantine liturgical synthesis was essentially fixed by the sixteenth century.

In general, Greek liturgists asserted that the gap between the evolution of Greek society and liturgical development resulted in the decreasing capacity of faithful people to apprehend and comprehend the symbols that communicate the meaning of liturgical rites. The symbols themselves were not the problem, a notion supported by Zizioulas's disappointment in the appeals for simplifying the liturgy, including clerical vestments.[10] A strong, multifaceted program of liturgical catechesis exercised primarily by parish clergy removes the barriers preventing the people's comprehension of the liturgy. The symbols themselves required minimal adjustment; the clergy needed to learn how to preside in such as way that the people would be invited and encouraged to engage the rites, which would open the doors to understanding.

ROCOR offered a different diagnosis of the liturgy by asserting that the people needed to adjust their lives to the liturgy, as opposed to the Church adjusting the liturgy to conform to people's lives. ROCOR's interpretation of the liturgy as a gift received from God that demands the faithful's attention and observation does not permit much fine-tuning of liturgical structures. That said, ROCOR's leaders acknowledged the people's disengagement from the liturgy and identified the clergy as the key ministers who could restore the people's participation. ROCOR envisioned clergy whose devotion to the liturgy would become modular for the laity. The clergy's frequent celebration of the divine offices would inaugurate the people into a regular rhythm of prayer, through which they would rehearse loving God, and from which would follow love of one's neighbor. ROCOR

10. Zizioulas, 252.

has promoted a kind of liturgical restoration through its cultivation of liturgical music following the principles and spirit of the Moscow Synodal School. This restoration seeks to develop choir directors who are competent in the received liturgical tradition and whose musical leadership will lead the faithful into a deeper comprehension of and engagement with the liturgy. ROCOR's privileging of chant-based music is designed to engage people, and not entertain them. Notably, clergy and laity both have central roles to fulfill in this restoration, which is still in progress.

ROCOR, the Church of Greece, and Schmemann cultivated restorations within the parameters of the received tradition. Our other two models, *SC* and New Skete, adopted a different approach. It is clear that *SC* and New Skete shared a similar perception on the state of the people's engagement of the liturgy as those expressed by Schmemann, the Church of Greece, and ROCOR. *SC* and New Skete also took up the challenge of reforming liturgy so that its structures could convey the theology upon which liturgy is founded. For *SC* and New Skete, the urgency of the situation required a more aggressive approach to liturgical restoration. Liturgical catechesis is necessary, but the liturgy itself is the primary catechetical event. Relying primarily on catechesis would entail a process of explaining how a rite or symbol acquired multiple layers of thematic complexity through the course of history. While the people might understand how historical circumstances inscribed certain theological notions onto symbols, these would still be present when engaged by people at liturgy, in all of their complexity. For *SC* and New Skete, this complexity would continue to function as an obstacle to the people's comprehension of the liturgy. The people's comprehension would be enabled by encountering symbols and rites that did not require them to distinguish between so many layers of meaning. Symbols and rites that communicate in contemporary idioms would permit people to enter into the process of encountering the living God without encumbering them with the task of translating symbols while simultaneously participating in the rite.

Thus, *SC* and New Skete reformed the liturgical structures themselves into forms that are suitable for contemporary Christians. The rationale for the surgical approach to liturgical reform comes from the nature of the diagnosis. For New Skete in particular, the liturgical forms themselves had not developed in conjunction with cultural, socioeconomic, and anthropological evolution. New Skete frames liturgical development in terms of time. The received liturgical tradition was fossilized and was a relic of the past, which limited the participant's engagement of ritual. Participation entailed an encounter with the ecclesial past. Encounter with the past is a reality for all Christian liturgy, but New Skete viewed the Byzantine liturgy as a collection of rituals that remained exclusively in the past, with no engagement of the present or future.[11] The only way to grant the contemporary Church complete access to the theology grounding liturgy was to reconstruct rituals and symbols so that they conform to contemporary symbolic and communicative systems of Christians.

The magnitude of such an enterprise is enormous: for New Skete, the work included the translation of the Psalter, the revision of extant hymnography, the composition of new hymns, and the reconstruction of divine services. The result was somewhat ironic: a contemporary monastic community drew primarily from ancestral cathedral traditions to create a monastic ordo of divine services that was suitable for twenty-first-century North American monastic life. In this way, New Skete's reform differs significantly from Vatican II in its scope: the magnitude of the work is similar, but its application

---

11. See Monks of New Skete, *Sighs of the Spirit* (Cambridge, NY: New Skete Monastery, 1997), xxix-xxx.

was limited to a community of monastics in Cambridge, New York; the liturgical ordo was constructed for New Skete, but the liturgical reform of *SC* was devised for the entire Roman Catholic Church. Despite the obvious variance of magnitude, *SC* and New Skete adopted a more aggressive approach to liturgical reform by performing surgery, reconfiguring liturgical structures and components, and adding an abundance of new material.

In summary, we can conclude that the five models of liturgical reform share some similarities in their consultation of academic research. Leaders in each model performed a rigorous assessment of the liturgy through an ecclesiological lens, identifying the liturgy as the Church's primary manifestation and critiquing aspects of liturgy that contributed to the people's lack of engagement. Each model also selected academic specialists in preparing programs for liturgical reform. For example, Schmemann's liturgical theology relies on the historical contributions of Catholic theologians such as Cullman, Casel, and Bouyer, and expands the pioneering work inaugurated by Russian liturgical archaeologists and their successors who developed Eucharistic ecclesiology, especially Kyprian Kern and Nicholas Afanasiev.[12] The Church of Greece honors the eighteenth-century hesychast monastic revival on Mount Athos, elaborates the work performed by premier theologians such as Panagiotis Trempelas and Ioannis Fountoulis, and consults the work by contemporary historians and theologians such as Demetrios Tzerpos, Stefanos Alexopoulos, and Petros Vassiliadis. ROCOR continues its consultation of the Moscow Synodal School of liturgical music and encourages its expansion in emigration and adaptation to new circumstances.

Our five models of liturgical reform disclose three new patterns

12. Alexander Schmemann, *Introduction to Liturgical Theology*, trans. Asheleigh E. Moorhouse (Crestwood, NY: St. Vladimir's Seminary Press, 1986), 9-32.

of liturgical scholarship informing pastoral liturgy that should be monitored by pastors, theologians, liturgists, and historians. The first pattern is the tendency to permit cross-pollination of liturgical traditions in drawing from historical models to shape contemporary practices. The reforms unleashed by Vatican II provide a good example, as the Roman church selected Eastern liturgical practices when revising and adding liturgical content.[13] Two of the three new Eucharistic prayers were based on Eastern models and the formula for anointing with Chrism was taken from the Byzantine tradition. Vatican II's purpose was unique: to enrich Roman practice by adding Eastern material in order to express veneration for the Church's catholic nature. Orthodox liturgists tend to refer to *SC* as a model to be avoided on account of the common perception that its implementation disrupted liturgical order and decorum.

However, Orthodox liturgy has also experienced cross-pollination with contributions from the West. For example, Schmemann's liturgical theology draws abundantly from his Western interlocutors, manifest in his explanation of Chrismation, which is almost identical to that of Congar. New Skete's reforms depend on Western scholarship, and while the reforms are based primarily on Eastern historical antecedents, the reformed structures are designed to flourish in a Western environment.

The most notable aspect of cross-pollination is the common articulation of the theological foundations for liturgical reform shared by Western and Eastern Churches. In this study, I have demonstrated that the scholarly and pastoral work that produced the theological rationale was not frequently performed in common. The movement for ecclesial renewal in Orthodoxy gained serious momentum with

---

13. See Taft, "Between Progress and Nostalgia," in *A Living Tradition*, ed. Pitt, Alexopoulos, McConnell, 29-39, and Anne McGowan, "Eastern Christian Insights and Western Liturgical Reforms: Travelers, Texts, and Liturgical Luggage," in *Liturgy in Migration: From the Upper Room to Cyberspace*, ed. Teresa Berger (Collegeville, MN: Liturgical Press, 2012), 179-208.

the pre-revolutionary preparations for the Russian council of 1917-1918, and liturgy was one of many topics discussed by the bishops and theologians.

Concern for the active participation of the people in the liturgy was voiced by Russian theologians independent of Western scholarship, yet both the Western and Eastern churches arrived at the same conclusion on the priority for liturgical renewal. Liturgy held the key to ecclesial renewal through the direct relationship between the primary theological foundation for liturgy and its ritualization in the liturgical assembly: the reconfiguration of priesthood where Christ is the high priest who eternally offers God the liturgy and presides over an assembly of ministerial and royal priests, whose exercise of the priesthood is manifested by active and conscious participation in the liturgy. The theological foundation and liturgical ritualization are reciprocal: engaged participation in the liturgical and sacramental life of the Church capacitates faithful to interiorize and exteriorize their priesthood in Christ. Informing the assembly of their religious identity as priests in Christ through catechesis encourages them to participate in the Church's liturgy actively and consciously.

The second pattern of liturgical scholarship informing pastoral practice is the phenomenon of implementing liturgical reform in new contexts. This pattern appears most prominently in the models of Schmemann, ROCOR, and New Skete, though elements of the pattern are also discernable in the Church of Greece and *SC*. Schmemann and ROCOR continued aspects of liturgical *ressourcement* that originated in pre-revolutionary Russia. The proponents of liturgical renewal in Russia had envisioned its implementation as the primary contribution for ecclesial renewal for the Church in Russia. Schmemann's variant of this implementation was carried out outside of Russia, primarily in North America, though his teachings have been received elsewhere. ROCOR's implementation of restoration was largely through music. ROCOR has adjusted to its context by offering summer school instruction in English and adapting the principles of the Moscow school for musicians who worship in English and also for the niceties of Church life outside of Russia. New Skete's reform was created for the particular socio-cultural environment of North America.

These three instances of reform required adaptation in progress, because the scope of reform changed in the context of immigration and of forming monastic communities that follow the Eastern tradition in the West. The phenomenon of implementing liturgical reform outside of its original scope and context raises two serious questions of assessment. First, these three models become examples of liturgical development outside of their native habitats. As of this writing, we simply do not know how the reforms of Schmemann and ROCOR would have been received in Russia. Second, given the necessity of adjusting liturgical reform so that it was possible in the new environment of the Church, we do not know if it is conceivable to apply reforms designed for specific communities to sister Churches of the world.

Schmemann acknowledged the occurrence of a Eucharistic revival in the Church, and it is clear that he established a program for forming clergy who could implement liturgical renewal in Orthodox America. Many Orthodox Churches besides the OCA have received elements of Schmemann's program, as the Antiochian and Serbian archdioceses in North America frequently send their students to St. Vladimir's. Furthermore, Alkiviadis Calivas, the most prestigious Greek Orthodox liturgical theologian in North America, acknowledges Schmemann as the figure who exercised the greatest influence on his own work, and he is a consistent and active proponent of liturgical renewal.[14]

So despite the differences in liturgical celebration and aesthetics among Orthodox in North America, many Orthodox in North America accepted the basic principles of liturgical renewal, beginning with a Eucharistic revival and an emphasis on the active participation of the laity in the liturgy. The intra-Orthodox reception of liturgical renewal suggests that the core principles of liturgical renewal resonated with most Orthodox bodies. However, this assessment of the growth of liturgical renewal requires a reminder about the historical path of Orthodox liturgical renewal in modernity. The Orthodox Churches tend to trace liturgical renewal to episodes of liturgical creativity in Byzantine history, such as the development of liturgy in the Great Church and the Studite reforms.[15] Monasteries tend to become the hosts of liturgical creativity, so even modern liturgical renewal finds its roots in phenomena such as the *Kollyvades* movement.

There is no doubt that the primary catalyst of liturgical renewal in modern Orthodoxy originated with the groundbreaking contributions of liturgical archaeology in pre-revolutionary Russia. The Revolution and emergence of the Soviet Union shifted the location of liturgical research from the prominent Russian academies to new learning centers established in the West.[16] The engagement with the West engendered the employment of scientific methods in liturgical study, a phenomenon that also occurred with Greek liturgical theologians. The most significant aspect of this historical review is that the schools of liturgical research changed locations as intellectuals who had studied liturgy in Russia were now conducting research and forming academic disciples in the west. The encounter

14. Alkiviadis Calivas, *Essays in Theology and Liturgy*, vol. 3: *Aspects of Orthodox Worship* (Brookline, MA: Holy Cross Orthodox Press, 2003), xvi-xvii.
15. Robert F. Taft, *The Byzantine Rite: A Short History* (Collegeville, MN: Liturgical Press, 1996), 56-60.
16. For an insightful presentation on the challenges posed to the émigré theologians, see Paul Gavrilyuk, *Georges Florovsky and the Russian Religious Renaissance* (Oxford: Oxford University Press, 2014), 53-59.

with the West was not only academic, but also ecclesial and domestic, and it was natural for Orthodox theologians to engage in a variety of exchanges with their new Western neighbors.[17]

If Russia was one of the original centers for the study of liturgy, the research was continued outside of Russia, and included many Catholic scholars who were devoted to studying the East.[18] The profile of the researcher of Eastern liturgy evolved to include Catholic scholars as well. The initial implementation of renewal occurred in communities of Orthodox who lived in the West, and this study is among one of the few assessments of such programs. Liturgical renewal is neither global nor uniform within Orthodoxy. The barriers to normal relations among Orthodox Churches during the Soviet period made it impossible to create a strong flow of enthusiasm for liturgical renewal to permeate the largest Orthodox Churches buffered by Soviet borders. Furthermore, the restrictions on religious freedom severely limited spontaneous and non-spontaneous initiatives for liturgical renewal in these countries.[19] Greece is an obvious exception, and we noted their careful consideration of initiatives for liturgical renewal in other Orthodox countries. Yet even Greece did not adopt a model for renewal developed elsewhere without revision and adjustment, because the primary rule for developing a rationale for revision was pastoral, to create a liturgical ordo suitable for a particular people.[20]

---

17. Ibid., 57–59. Gavrilyuk's assessment of Orthodox response to their new conditions in an actual encounter with the West is illuminating.
18. See Taft, "Between Progress and Nostalgia," in *A Living Tradition*, ed. Pitt, Alexopoulos, McConnell, 23–30.
19. For an example of an exception to this rule, see Michael Plekon's profile of Father Alexander Men in, *Living Icons: Persons of Faith in the Eastern Church*, foreword Lawrence S. Cunningham (Notre Dame, IN: University of Notre Dame Press, 2002), 236–37, 242.
20. The second symposium on Liturgical Rebirth included a paper by Father Nicolaos Ioannidis titled "Attempts at Liturgical Renewal in the Orthodox Church of Russia and the Other Slavic-Speaking Churches," at http://www.ecclesia.gr/English/holysynod/committees/liturgical/symposium_2010_1.html (accessed January 15, 2015).

We can glean two conclusions from this second pattern of scholarship forming pastoral practice. First, liturgical renewal is in motion, and in Orthodoxy, the principles born in Russia migrated to the West and were implemented there, and are now under consideration in some contexts in Russia and other countries that are no longer persecuted by Soviet rule.[21] The trajectory of the path of liturgical renewal is somewhat unclear, since the Orthodox communities that settled permanently in the West developed liturgical traditions that depend on models from the communities' original habitats.

Similarly, the results of the implementation are manifold. On the one hand, a genuine Eucharistic revival occurred, and it is now customary for most Orthodox communities of the West that received liturgical renewal to practice frequent participation in communion and employ other liturgical traditions that encourage the active and conscious participation of the people in the liturgy. In this sense, the implementation has achieved these objectives. On the other hand, Orthodox Churches in the West that adhere to liturgical renewal also face the challenge of liturgical syncretism. Because these communities are permanently established in the West, they incorporate local customs into their liturgies. It is quite common to visit Orthodox parishes that have pews, adopt Western architectural paradigms for interior and exterior design, use organs for musical accompaniment or employ Western styles of music, and adopt Western models for youth ministry and adult education. Many Orthodox leaders, educators, and communities fiercely resist the ongoing Westernization of Orthodoxy as the recurrence of the phenomenon of Western captivity.[22] I propose that the

21. See, for example, Mark Morozowich, "Liturgical Changes in Russia and the Christian East? A Case Study: The Mysteries (Sacraments) of Initiation with the Eucharistic Liturgy," *Worship* 83 (2009): 30–47.
22. For a discussion of the origins of this appellation and its occurrence in Orthodox circles,

Westernization of Orthodox communities that have settled in the West is inevitable, despite the most determined efforts to resist the influx of Western thinking and expression in the Church. In terms of the enterprise of liturgical renewal, I term this "liturgical syncretism." It is simply impossible for a community to retain and sustain the received liturgical tradition without the introduction of additions and changes because the community that offers the liturgy and receives it is always in a state of change.

In North America, for example, the profile of Orthodoxy has changed dramatically since the early-twentieth century. The people are no longer immigrants primarily, but are a complex mix of first- to fourth-generation Orthodox, converts to Orthodoxy, new immigrants, and non-Orthodox who attend an Orthodox parish with their families through marriage.[23] The urgent appeals to resist change and observe the received tradition that we see in some of the literature we have examined from leaders of ROCOR manifests the adjustments to life that occur organically as religious micro-communities develop. As people adapt to the rhythms of life in the West, it can be challenging to sustain the requirements of the inherited tradition in the new environment, which creates conflict within communities.

One of the implications of this reality is that the result of implementing liturgical renewal was always going to differ from the stated objective because renewal is always in motion on account

see Gavrilyuk, 57-59, 172-91, and Vera Shevzov, "The Burdens of Tradition: Orthodox Constructions of the West in Russia (late 19th-early 20th cc.)," in *Orthodox Constructions of the West*, ed. George Demacopoulos and Aristotle Papanikolaou (New York: Fordham University, 2013), 83-101; and Pantelis Kalaitzidis, "The Image of the West in Contemporary Greek Theology," in *Orthodox Constructions of the West*, ed. George Demacopoulos and Aristotle Papanikolaou (New York: Fordham University, 2013), 142-60.

23. Alexei Krindatch, *The Orthodox Church Today: A National Study of Parishioners and the Realities of Orthodox Parish Life in the USA* (Berkeley, CA: Patriarch Athenagoras Orthodox Institute, 2006), p. 6, available online at http:// www.hartfordinstitute.org / research / OrthChurchFullReport.pdf (accessed January 27, 2014).

of the constantly evolving constituency of the local churches. In the realm of possibility, one can imagine that Orthodoxy might integrate new Westernisms in the future, especially in aesthetics and communication idioms.

The second conclusion is that these four models of liturgical renewal might become more suitable for adoption within global Orthodoxy on account of globalization and the removal of the iron curtain. The information age and its instant dissemination has increased access to models of liturgical renewal exponentially. Clergy and musicians already have access to demonstrations of liturgy recorded by video or made available on audio, which enables the possibility of copying and importing a tradition quickly. The use of technology and social media to research, assess, and import liturgical traditions is a cautionary tale, filled with potential hazards. That said, this formidable technological reality contributes to globalization and makes the possibility of adopting a foreign liturgical model possible. Furthermore, the role of digital media in globalization suggests the possibility that cyberspace might become the preferred host for the liturgical centers of the future. Despite these trends, Orthodoxy's longstanding preference for regional autonomy and the internal culture that resists global uniformity suggest that multiple models of liturgical renewal will continue to appear alongside the currently existing ones.

The third pattern is the ongoing tension between the monastic and cathedral traditions in the process of liturgical reform, with three of the four Orthodox models privileging the cathedral and depicting it as the primary source for liturgical and ecclesial renewal suitable to contemporary circumstances. The relationship between the monastic and cathedral models is one of the most studied topics of the liturgical movement. In Byzantine liturgical history, the perception of the monastic liturgy overtaking the cathedral continues to prevail, largely as a result of the Sabaitic-Studite synthesis canonized on Mount Athos.[24] Liturgical scholars often refer to the structure of the liturgy of the hours as a primary example of the monastic hegemony in the fused office.[25] The prayers of the Euchologion were redistributed throughout the office to fit the new structure, and many of them came to be recited quietly by the presider at the beginning of the office, during the recitation of psalmody. The displacement of the prayers caused a reconfiguration in the order of the office, which in turn affected the people's experience of the liturgy. A similar development occurred in Church architecture, as the elements promoting active participation among the people in cathedral liturgy (such as open spaces, a bema or ambo, pastophoria permitting people to donate the bread and wine for the liturgy, and frequent public processions) gave way to a smaller, more confined space conducive to the less demanding requirements of a monastic liturgy, which did not require baptisteries or large, open spaces to accommodate crowds.[26]

From a historical perspective, the rearrangement of the office occurred as a result of environmental circumstances. The monks' strong leadership in the iconoclastic controversy resulted in their taking the mantle of church leadership, so that monasteries became the new liturgical centers of the Church. The invention of the printing press essentially finalized the process of making the fused liturgy, shaped mostly by its monastic quality, a uniform experience for the people. The printing press and creation of liturgical books provided a written document that stipulated the liturgical requirements and held clergy accountable to a standard established in

24. Taft, *The Byzantine Rite*, 78–83.
25. Ibid., 52–56.
26. Hans-Joachim Schulz, *The Byzantine Liturgy: Symbolic Structure and Faith Expression*, trans. Matthew J. O'Connell (New York: Pueblo, 1986), 50–59; Vasileios Marinis, *Architecture and Ritual in the Churches of Constantinople: Ninth to Fifteenth Centuries* (Cambridge: Cambridge University Press, 2014), 30–41; Cyril Mango, *Byzantine Architecture* (New York: Harry N. Abrams, Inc., 1976), 196–97.

ink. Liturgical creativity declined as the Church faced new challenges with Turkocratia, the encounter with the West and appearance of the Unia, and the Petrine reforms. In this period, the liturgy became increasingly detached from developments in the way.people lived, especially since there were no consistently predominant centers of liturgical creativity. The people's experience of the liturgy was largely colored by monasticism.

It is neither necessary nor helpful to condemn a historical development that proceeded in accordance with cultural and societal evolution. New Skete criticized the Byzantine monastic orders as a while for failing to cultivate the liturgy through these historical periods since they were the primary caretakers of the liturgy.[27] When Orthodox teachers embraced *ressourcement*, especially the scientific methods of researching texts coming from biblical studies, they permitted the possibility of revisiting the historical evolution of the liturgy. Their discovery of the cathedral tradition that had been muted in the Byzantine synthesis allowed pastors to imagine the possibility of reviving cathedral liturgy in a new way. Cathedral liturgical elements seem to promote the active participation of the people, and cathedral liturgy thus became a primary source for liturgical renewal, especially since several cathedral elements continued to exist in the received liturgical tradition.[28] The rediscovery of cathedral liturgy permitted the proponents of renewal

27. See Monks of New Skete, *Sighs of the Spirit* (Cambridge, NY: New Skete Monastery, 1997), xxix-xxx.
28. On the relationship between cathedral and monastery in liturgy, see the early essay by Anton Baumstark, "Cathedral and Monastery," in *On the Historical Development of the Liturgy*, Intro., trans., annot. by Fritz West, foreword by Robert F. Taft (Collegeville, MN: Liturgical Press, 2011), 140-49. Also see Thomas Pott, *Byzantine Liturgical Reform: A Study of Liturgical Change in the Byzantine Tradition*, trans. Paul Meyendorff, Orthodox Liturgy Series, book two (Crestwood, NY: St. Vladimir's Seminary Press, 2010), 115-51; Stelyios Muksuris, "E duobus unum in America: Rethinking the Mutual Influence between Monastic and Cathedral Liturgy," forthcoming in *St. Vladimir's Theological Quarterly*; Robert F. Taft, "'Cathedral vs. Monastic Liturgy in the Christian East: Vindicating a Distinction," *Bolletina della Badia Greca di Grottaferrata* (2005): 173-219; Idem, *The Byzantine Rite*, 52-66; Calivas, 81-101.

to devise ways to reinvigorate cathedral liturgical elements within the received tradition, which would not require a complete reconfiguration of liturgical order.

Examples of such efforts at renewal include the restoration of singing the koinonikon during communion with responsorial psalmody instead of singing a concert song, reciting certain prayers aloud so the people can hear them, and arranging sacred space that grants the people more visual access into the sanctuary while having the clergy and laity share the space of the church. Schmemann and the Church of Greece adopted this approach. New Skete's approach stands out for its originality, as the small monastic community developed liturgical offices and structures that drew primarily from the cathedral tradition.

For New Skete, reviving aspects of cathedral tradition that continued to exist within the received liturgy was insufficient. To restore the liturgy to the people, they decided that the cathedral tradition needed to become the principal guide for their liturgy. Besides the irony of a monastery constructing a cathedral liturgy for worship in monastic life, New Skete's example suggests that the nature of the structures themselves needed to become cathedral for the purpose of encouraging active participation in the liturgy.

In contrast to the example above, ROCOR did not privilege cathedral elements of the liturgy in its restoration. ROCOR was concerned with encouraging people to participate in the Church's liturgical life, but they professed confidence in the received liturgical tradition to such a degree that they attempted to mitigate obvious differences between cathedral and monastic liturgical qualities.[29] For ROCOR, the received liturgy was equally edifying for both clergy

29. The publication of Ivan Karabinov's lecture on the Typikon where the author asserts that the Church's offices are not wholly monasticized typifies this response (see the discussion in chapter 4).

and laity, and there was no need to revivify cathedral elements when the laity could fully participate in the received liturgical tradition. The example cited above from Metropolitan Antony's tenure in Volyn', when he established the liturgy of the Pochaiv Lavra as the ideal for cathedrals and parishes, presents a pattern of viewing the liturgy as granting the same blessings to all while demanding that everyone, regardless of order, toil to participate in the liturgy. While ROCOR encouraged the historical study of the liturgy, the Church leaders did not accept the idea that the liturgy needed to change. They expressed the view that a lackadaisical attitude towards the liturgy and the clergy and people's tepid observance of its requirements resulted in the ecclesial decay.

Theological Rationale for Reform

The most coveted result of the liturgical enterprise was to lead the people into a real encounter with the living God through more robust engagement with the liturgy. The varying emphases placed on the priesthood by our models illustrate a general pattern one can discern on the layers of priesthood and its manifestation in the liturgy. First, the Orthodox models emphasize the presence and activity of God in the liturgy. Schmemann accentuated the eschatological dimension of the liturgy and the community's experience of it as an epiphany of the kingdom, an encounter of all the people with the Triune God where the people gradually become transformed through their participation in God's divine life, which we might describe as a type as sacramental theosis.[30] He educated clergy of the Church to integrate this eschatological dimension into their liturgical ministry.

By contrast, Antony's liturgical theology refers to an urgent need

---

30. See, for example, Alexander Schmemann, *Of Water and the Spirit: A Liturgical Study of Baptism* (Crestwood, NY: St. Vladimir's Seminary Press, 1974), 80.

for the clergy to develop a sense of attentiveness in their exercise of liturgical ministry, as the objective of this ministry is to model love for God through faithfulness to the inherited liturgical order. Antony expected that the people would pattern their own dispositions after the clergy's, and thus love not only God, but also their neighbors. Priesthood is a staple of the liturgical renewal program of the Church of Greece, as almost every quality of the *ars celebrandi* is addressed by the symposia. The symposia suggest that the clergy avoid imposing their own affective interpretations on texts by chanting them in an individualistic style, and recite them for comprehension instead.[31] The symposia also called for the creation of post-seminary programs that would specialize in clerical formation in liturgical ministry that would ultimately strengthen catechesis, a ministry which the clergy would exercise primarily.[32] New Skete appeals to the clergy to prepare diligently for liturgy and to strive for excellence in its celebration, especially in performing their portions with clarity, comprehension, and without affectation.[33]

The Priesthood of the Laity

One of the fruits of *ressourcement* theology was the rediscovery of Christianity's notion of priesthood from late antiquity. Many of the liturgical texts and their patristic interpretations depicted the laity as a body of priests who were ordained by the imposition of hands at Baptism and anointing with oil. Early Christianity distinguished Christ the high priest from the priesthood belonging to all the

---

31. In Special Synodal Committee for Liturgical Rebirth, "The Mystery of the Holy Eucharist," Church of Greece Official Web Site, http://www.ecclesia.gr/English/holysynod/committees/liturgical/symposium_2010_1_1.html. (accessed July 10, 2013).

32. In "The First Pan-Hellenic Liturgical Symposium," Church of Greece website (English version), http:// www.ecclesia.gr / English / holysynod / committees / liturgical / symposium_1999_1.html (accessed September 15, 2014).

33. Monks of New Skete, *The Divine Liturgy* (Cambridge, NY: New Skete Monastery, 1987), xxviii.

Church, as Christ was the source of priesthood for the Church. However, as sacramental theology began to privilege the notion of administering the sacraments and the Church's growth required bishops to delegate their responsibilities to presbyters, the presbyters became known as priests, sharpening the distinctions between the orders of the Church.[34] The notion of the priesthood of the laity diminished in this scheme of priesthood, as they were the recipients of blessings invoked by the local priests, their leaders.

Ressourcement theology restored the dignity of the priesthood of the laity, which viewed their participation in the liturgical life of the Church as essential. When Nicholas Afanasiev argued that the laity is the bishop's concelebrant at the Eucharist, he contributed to the restoration of a muted theological notion that could lead to a redefinition of the priesthood of the Church.[35] Orthodox and Catholic theologians turned to liturgical and patristic sources to complete this redefinition, establishing a definition of priesthood that would conform to the liturgical structures themselves and have the capacity to renew ecclesial life.

The Orthodox paradigm of priesthood views Christ as the high priest who celebrates the liturgy, with the ordained clergy as the presiders of an ordered assembly whose primary liturgical ministry is to build up the laity into a community of priests. The laity, as liturgical concelebrants, transfer their rehearsal of liturgical ministry into their daily lives in the world, thus mitigating the barrier between sacred and profane. In other words, the entire ordered assembly

---

34. Susan Wood, *Sacramental Orders*, Lex Orandi Series, ed. John D. Laurance (Collegeville, MN: Liturgical Press, 2000), 117-26.

35. Nicholas Afanasiev, "The Ministry of Laity in the Church," in William C. Mills, ed., *Called to Serve: Readings on Ministry from the Orthodox Church* (Rollinsford, NH: Orthodox Research Institute, 2010), 8–9. Also see Nicholas Afanasiev, Трапеза Господня (*The Lord's Supper*) (Kyiv: Khram Prepodobnogo Agapita Pecherskogo, 2003), 69-90.

becomes a body of ministers of God whose task is to witness to the kingdom and transfigure the life of the world.

The historical study of the sacraments of initiation led to this ecclesiological model, and it is this notion of priesthood that serves as the primary theological rationale for liturgical reform, including that of Vatican II. In order to attempt to actualize this ecclesiological ideal, the proponents of liturgical renewal delegated the task to the clergy. The process would be twofold: the clergy themselves needed to embrace a renewed definition of priesthood in the Church, one that depicted the clergy as pastors who preside over a liturgy offered by communities of priests, as opposed to masters who are the agents of divine activity that is imparted to the people through the clergy. In the renewed scheme, the body of people invokes God through Christ's mediation, and God responds directly to the body of the people. The clergy's role is to preside as an order among the assembly, not above or outside of it.

When the clergy were formed in such a way to impart this renewed definition of priesthood, they would conduct the entirety of their pastoral and liturgical ministries so that the people would be formed in their renewed identity.[36] Over time, the people would come to understand and accept their religious identity as priests. Their primary means of learning their identity would be liturgical participation, as this is their central activity within the Church. Their repeated participation in liturgical life would reinforce and deepen their identity as priests, which would in turn shape the way they conduct ordinary life. At Church and in ordinary daily life, the laity is a body of priests that offers its life to God for the sake of the world.

---

36. On the power of liturgy to transform people, see two seminal works on liturgy as ritual participation: Mark Searle, *Called to Participate: Theological, Ritual, and Social Perspectives*, ed. Barbara Searle and Anne Y. Koester (Collegeville, MN: Liturgical Press, 2006), and Stephen Wilbricht, *Rehearsing God's Just Kingdom: The Eucharistic Vision of Mark Searle*, foreword Kevin W. Irwin (Collegeville, MN: Liturgical Press, 2013).

A vibrant liturgical life has two primary pillars. First, it depends on this renewed notion of priesthood. A body of people who encounter God through Christ the high priest can be transformed by God into people made worthy of representing him in and to the world. Ordained priests who celebrate liturgy in such a way that it informs people of their priestly identity perform the ministry of building up the body of Christ by enabling the people to exercise their priesthood. As faithful become aware of their own holy vocation, they are drawn to the liturgy as the source of divine grace that gives them the gift of the Spirit needed to exercise priesthood. Second, active participation in the liturgy is a natural consequence of exercising the lay priesthood. The reverse order of this relationship is equally powerful: as people actively engage the liturgy, they are informed of their priestly identity *a fortiori*. In other words, the two pillars of priesthood and active participation in the liturgy are inseparable; one cannot thrive without the other, and a diminishment of either pillar results in the impoverishment of the liturgy.

Catechesis

The reciprocity between priesthood and active participation in the liturgy as the primary theological foundations of the liturgy necessitated quality catechesis of both the clergy and the people. The source for the catechesis was the *ressourcement* sacramental theology and the reformed liturgy itself, and the clergy were designated as the primary catechists in this scheme. The ecumenical retrieval of this liturgical theology from late antiquity and patristic sources required translation for the people in the pew. The people might gradually recognize their holy vocation as God's priests, but only if their participation in the liturgy occurred with comprehension.

Furthermore, the catechetical process would be empowered by clergy capable of translating this theology to the people.

In the models we have explored above, catechesis appears repeatedly as one of the chief instruments of liturgical renewal. In varying ways, clergy are expected to catechize the faithful, to deepen their comprehension of the liturgy and develop love for God and one's neighbor in celebrating it. Catechesis was envisioned as both liturgical and extraliturgical. The people would receive catechesis simply by attending liturgy, whereas the Church would develop programs for further study through which the faithful would better understand the liturgy itself.

The models for reform designate several examples of liturgical catechesis. Concerning liturgical catechesis, examples include proposals for reading the Bible in the vernacular, expanding the Scriptures read in the liturgy of the Word, and exposing the faithful to prayers that were previously said quietly.[37] Such modifications represent liturgical restorations and updates that conform to the people's contemporary cultural modes of communication. The Greek Church's recommendation that clergy wear a bright vestment for the proclamation of the Gospel is a good example: the bright vestments would provide a visual complement to the message of the resurrection proclaimed in the eothina gospels at Orthros.[38] New Skete's attempt to simplify liturgical structures included acts of excising elements, revising hymns and composing new ones, decisions that sought to mitigate the problem of communicating too

---

37. Paul Bradshaw and Maxwell Johnson, *The Eucharistic Liturgies: Their Evolution and Interpretation* (Collegeville, MN: Liturgical Press, 2012), 310-11.
38. Synod of Bishops of the Church of Greece, "Ἐπαναφορά τῆς Τάξεως τοῦ Ἑωθινοῦ Εὐαγγελίου εἰς τήν κανονικήν αὐτοῦ θέσιν" ("Resetting the Order of the Eothinon Gospel according to the Canonical Order" Church of Greece website, http://www.ecclesia.gr/greek/holysynod/egyklioi/egkyklios2794.html (accessed September 15, 2014).

much information in the liturgy and replacing confusing messages with clear ones, in the language of the people.

The models also envisioned more sophisticated programs. The symposia of the Church of Greece suggested celebrating group baptisms and offering education to parents of children and couples preparing for marriage. ROCOR invested in a multifaceted school of liturgical music that would inform both clergy and musicians, in order to engage the people in the liturgy. Of course, the most salient catechetical product of the liturgical movement is the restoration of the Rites of Christian Initiation (RCIA) programs in the Roman Church, which prepare the unchurched for reception via Baptism and Confirmation.[39] The introduction to the Roman Catholic sacramentary includes several suggestions for greetings and homilies that establish the thematic tone for the occasion.[40] Catechesis includes unofficial and unsanctioned efforts carried out by local clergy. It is common for clergy to explain the meaning of the liturgy during the course of its celebration. Parishes produce their own customized explanations of the divine offices, often published online as well.

Ars Celebrandi

The models studied here seem to emphasize the liturgy itself as the primary source for catechesis. While the models are plurivocal on the means of restoration, they are united in emphasizing the development of clergy who celebrate the liturgy well. Metropolitan Antony's depiction of clergy with two types of delusion comes to mind here, especially his disapproval of clergy who engage

---

39. Maxwell Johnson, *The Rites of Christian Initiation: Their Evolution and Interpretation*, 2d ed. (Collegeville, MN: Liturgical Press, 2007), 381–405.

40. The introduction is the General Instruction of the Roman Missal, which functions as an explanation of the rite, including suggestions for the presider on celebration and catechesis. See *The Roman Missal*, English Translation according to the Third Typical Edition (Collegeville, MN: Liturgical, 2011), 17–120.

individualism during the course of the liturgy.[41] Antony's recommendation that clergy work closely with the choir to master the appointed chants and propers of the services assumes that the clergy are themselves familiar with the chants. The monks of New Skete emphasize the necessity of clergy learning how to chant and to artfully preside at the liturgy, in a manner that honors the occasion of worshiping God without distracting the people. The Church of Greece recommends that clergy recite prayers, since chanting them leads to individualistic interpretations of the texts that do not communicate their theological content. The Church of Greece also presents a vision for preparing and delivering a homily that is simultaneously theological and relevant, able to inspire and edify the faithful.[42]

One can identify a beautiful synthesis in consulting the models for liturgical reform: the clergy's aesthetic celebration of the liturgy must be guided by the liturgy itself. Since the clergy is the model for the people, they must focus on God, pray with clarity and proper reverence, and cultivate music that engages but does not entertain. The *ars celebrandi* is this the most important element of liturgical catechesis because the chief opportunity to catechize the people occurs when they are gathered for liturgy. Many people will be unable to devote time to gather for catechesis outside of Sunday, so the liturgy and its celebration will be their only teacher.

The chief lesson one can glean from catechesis as the primary means of implementing liturgical renewal is its inherent risk. The clergy have a limited window of opportunity to catechize the people, and it becomes tempting to affix as much catechetical content as possible to the liturgy. In other words, many clergy approach

41. Metropolitan Antony, *О Пастрыре, Пастырстве, и объ исповеди*, 289.

42. Synodal Encyclical, "The Hagiographical reading and Teaching at the Divine Liturgy," http://www.ecclesia.gr/greek/holysynod/egyklioi/egkyklios2791.html (accessed September 15, 2014).

catechesis with too much zeal and use so many words in their homilies and explanations that they oversaturate the people with ideas and diminish the capacity of the liturgy itself to shape and form the people.[43]

Implementing Reform: Approaches and Mechanisms

This study has shown that our five models have adopted three divergent approaches to liturgical reform and a variety of mechanisms for its implementation. The three approaches are renewal within the received liturgical tradition, surgery, and liturgical maximalism. We have discussed many of the details of these approaches in the deliberations on reform earlier in this chapter, so I will briefly remark on the ecclesiologies underpinning these approaches here. The most common approach to reform is to modify the liturgy within the received tradition, the approach adopted by Schmemann and the Church of Greece. This approach views tradition as developing in fidelity to its core principles. Ecclesiologically, liturgical structures do not need to be overhauled, but adjusted so the Church will remain faithful to tradition. The Church is her best self by retaining her liturgical core and using the language and cultural idioms of her time and place. Many of the revisions that were implemented in our models were inspired by discoveries of elements of tradition that had become impoverished: their restoration would enable the Church to be her best self and grow for witness to the world.

Proponents of surgery hold the same attitude towards tradition, but believe that the Church's liturgical structures have become so distorted that they have abandoned the interior meaning of tradition. The performance of surgery realigns liturgical structures with the core. A good example of this kind of surgery is the revision of

43. See Nicholas Denysenko, "A Proposal for Renewing Liturgy in the Twenty-First Century," *Studia Liturgica* 40 (2010): 242–44.

Holy Week performed by the monks of Holy Skete, especially their treatment of Holy Saturday. The excising of the Eucharistic liturgy not only removed the schizophrenic celebration of two Paschas separated by an interim Lenten period, but also honored the silence of demanded by Jesus' Sabbath rest. This liturgical surgery is jarring to faithful who only know the received tradition, but the reconfiguration of services restores the traditional core. Like the approach that privileges the received tradition, surgery to the core is the only possible alternative for the Church to be her best self in the present.

Proponents of liturgical maximalism dismiss the other two approaches as antiquarian, attempts to revive practices from the past that had expired for good reasons. Ecclesiologically, liturgical maximalists view the embrace of change as a betrayal of the present church. Maximalists view the Church as demanding perfection of the people, who can receive the gift of transformation and communion in the Spirit only through bona fide asceticism, practiced both liturgically and in ordinary daily life. This perspective holds that it is essential for the Church to retain the liturgical tradition she inherited from the previous generation. When the Church takes on new qualities foreign to her identity, she becomes someone other than her best self.

The three approaches to liturgical reform described above are irreconcilable because of their disparate notions of ecclesiology. In the first two approaches, some change is necessary for the people to interiorize their priestly identity and witness to the world. Without change, the status quo of tepid participation and the separation of the sacred and profane will endure. Liturgical maximalists refuse change because they believe it will dilute Orthodox liturgical ecclesiology.

Put differently, ecclesiology is inseparable from identity.[44] Making

---

44. On the interrelationships of liturgy, ecclesiology, and belonging, see Graham Ward,

a liturgical change suggests a consequential change in identity, especially since the Church will need to adjust to the new form. Change is threatening, especially when people perceive changes as having a foreign or external influence, which suggests that they are being asked to adopt a foreign identity. From this perspective, resistance to change is understandable and reasonable. The proponents of reform proposed changes to the structures and content of the liturgy to make the laity's priesthood manifest and accessible. Because many Orthodox laity and clergy received the changes introduced by modern Orthodox reform as relinquishing Orthodox identity communicated by the liturgy, they resisted, often fiercely. This raises the question on the purpose and legitimacy of reforms designed to manifest the theological rationale of the liturgy. The inseparability of liturgy and ecclesiology creates a situation where liturgical changes result in the perception of ecclesiological shifts. The desired ecclesiological shift on the part of the reformers was a potent priesthood empowered by divine grace that could transfigure the world. Some maximalists viewed the liturgical changes as attempts to adopt Catholic or Protestant ecclesiologies.

Two lessons emerge from this collection of disparate ecclesiological approaches to the liturgy. First, proponents of liturgical change need to continue to construct proposals that clearly demonstrate how the revision will enable the building up of the Church. Second, pastors and academics should attend to the relationship between liturgy and religious identity with more vigor. The second lesson on the relationship between liturgy and religious

"Belonging to the Church," in in *Liturgy in Migration: From the Upper Room to Cyberspace*, ed. Teresa Berger (Collegeville, MN: Liturgical Press, 2012), 1-18; the solid collection of essays in Dennis Doyle et al., ed., *Ecclesiology and Exclusion: Boundaries of Being and Belonging in Postmodern Times*, foreword by Richard Gaillardetz (Maryknoll, NY: Orbis, 2012); and Nicholas Denysenko, "Retrieving a Theology of Belonging: Eucharist and Church in Post-Modernity, Part 1," *Worship* 88 (2014): 543-61, and "Retrieving a Theology of Belonging: Eucharist and Church in Post-Modernity, Part 2," *Worship* 89 (2015): 21-43.

identity is the key to equipping pastors with the necessary background for constructing a potent liturgical ecclesiology with care.

In the models of reform treated by this study, there has been resistance to liturgical change within the Church. Late in his career at St. Vladimir's, Schmemann devoted time to exploring the problem of liturgical change in his courses on liturgical theology.[45] Alexopoulos emphasized the need to prepare the implementation of elements of reform in the Church of Greece, given the surprising bitterness expressed by some faithful in Athens when the practice of reading the liturgy of the word in modern Greek was introduced.[46] The monks of New Skete discuss the reluctance of people to accept new liturgical practices in many of the introductory sections of their liturgy books.

The so-called liturgy wars occur everywhere now and are not only limited to Roman Catholic orbits. Catholics are both familiar with and tired of the arguments within the Church concerning the appropriate approach to selecting liturgical music and designing sacred space. Aesthetics appear to be "ground zero" for liturgy wars, pitting proponents of traditional music and art against a contemporary camp.[47] For Catholics, Vatican II and *SC* are frequently depicted as the chief catalysts of modernist movements resulting in alternative aesthetic styles and leading to intra-church conflict.[48] Some Orthodox have likewise referred to Vatican II as the

45. Alexander Schmemann, "Liturgical Changes," course lecture Fr. Alexander Schmemann Papers at the Father Georges Florovsky Library, St. Vladimir's Theological Seminary, Box 18.

46. Stefanos Alexopoulos, "The State of Modern Greek Liturgical Studies and Research: A Preliminary Survey," in *Inquiries into Eastern Christian Worship*, Selected Papers of the Second International Congress of the Society of Oriental Liturgy, Rome, 17-21 September 2008, ed. Bert Groen, Steven Hawkes-Teeples, and Stefanos Alexopoulos, Eastern Christian Studies 12 (Leuven: Peeters, 2012), 390.

47. See, for example, the recent exchange on the renovation of Christ Cathedral in the Diocese of Orange, "Megachurches and Christ Cathedral: Continuing Dialog between Bishop Vann and Francis Mannion," Pray, Tell Blog website, http://www.praytellblog.com/index.php/2014/12/09/christ-cathedral-and-megachurches-continuing-dialog-between-bishop-vann-and-francis-mannion (accessed January 16, 2015).

scapegoat for unleashing an unprecedented freedom that permitted any number of artistic styles to permeate interior design and music.

Earlier, I concluded that Vatican II did have a tremendous impact on Orthodox liturgical reform, but not directly. Vatican II established an initiative to encourage the active and conscious participation of the people in the liturgy, but the Council did not invent this idea. The attribution of the idea to Vatican II is a result of Vatican II's stature and magnitude, which manifests a pattern of assuming that the Council created and communicated ideas for the first time in ecclesial history when this is not the case. Many Orthodox appear to have joined the public in canonizing Vatican II as the only catalyst of modern ecclesial reform. But our historical review of ROCOR's devoted enterprise of restoring chant-based liturgical music shows that liturgy wars exist in Orthodoxy. Despite the attempt to encourage styles of liturgical singing cultivated by the Moscow Synodal School and its successors, many ROCOR communities prefer the Petersburg school of music. The co-existence of two styles within the Church does not always lead to conflict and certainly not schism, but it raises the question on how much liturgical diversity is ideal and permissible. More importantly, the continuation of liturgy wars within both Orthodoxy and Catholicism manifests the tendency for liturgical style to form religious identity among the people.

Scholars and pastors have noted the people's reluctance to embrace change, which is one of the primary reasons they have recommended a strong program of pastoral catechesis to accompany liturgical change.[49] Twenty-first-century pastors and academics are tasked

---

48. On this topic, see John Baldovin's assessment of Joseph Ratzinger's (Pope Benedict XVI) theological critique of the liturgy, especially with reference to liturgical aesthetics, in *Reforming the Liturgy*, 65–86; also see Faggioli, 145–59.

49. For examples, see Schmemann, "Liturgical Changes," and Nina Glibetic, "Liturgical Renewal Movement in Contemporary Serbia," in Bert Groen, Steven Hawkes-Teeples, Stefanos Alexopoulos, eds., *Inquiries into Eastern Christian Worship*, Selected Papers of the Second

with the challenge of creating and disseminating engaging catechetical materials on the liturgy which inform the faithful. The liturgy wars waged within the Churches suggest a new direction in pastoral catechesis. The people's primary experience of Christianity and the Church occurs at liturgy. Music, word, and art are primary communicators of liturgical theology. In an imaginary poll, most people would not be able to retain the words of prayers that were not part of their daily, domestic routines. Only skilled preachers who create short refrains and integrate them into their homilies could communicate ideas people could retain and interiorize at home.

Music, however, engages the senses in such a way that people can remember passages from texts because they can remember the melody accompanying the words. Similarly, people who gaze upon a picture remember it; in this way, the arts have a greater capacity to shape and form faithful through a stronger engagement of their senses. The magnification of sensory engagement through aesthetics is a primary source for constructing religious identity: when the Arians paraded through the streets of Constantinople singing their refrains, the Orthodox beheld them with disdain on account of the effectiveness of their strategy.[50]

For contemporary Orthodox and Catholics, the unfolding of the liturgy they hear with their ears and behold with their eyes communicates the liturgy God has given them. The people learn and remember the music and become cozy with the decoration of sacred space. The processions, prayers, movements, acclamations, and refrains that occur within this space complete the picture of religious identity, which is why lay faithful who are otherwise uneducated on the theology underpinning a particular liturgical component are

International Congress of the Society of Oriental Liturgy, Rome, 17-21 September 2008, Eastern Christian Studies 12 (Leuven-Paris-Walpole, MA: Peeters, 2012), 394, 397.

50. See Robert Taft's insightful presentation on this matter in *The Byzantine Rite*, 30-33.

quite capable of correcting clergy and other liturgical ministers who err in their performance of a prescribed action. Innocuous errors are correctable; deliberate changes to liturgical order constitute minor threats to religious identity, whereas the introduction of new music or visual art is a revolutionary threat because the faithful's senses quickly register disruption to the aesthetical liturgical dimensions. The larger problem lies in the threat to religious identity, and liturgy war is the result.

To describe this phenomenon colloquially, the core people of a given parish tend to have strong preferences on music, aesthetics, and the liturgy they accompany because these form their religious identity. Introducing change to the practices of established parishes runs the risk of challenging local religious identity which tends to result in the unfortunate consequence of a liturgy war, even if the change had good intentions constructed on a solid theological foundation. People tend to misinterpret the introduction of liturgical change as an attempt to reshape religious identity because they were not consulted in the process of introducing change.

The power of liturgical aesthetics to inscribe religious identity on the people is the primary factor pastors and academics must engage in the process of developing local liturgical reform. The first element pastors must consider in considering a liturgical reform is the existing religious identity of the people, especially the core group of the parish. In today's globalized, culturally and theologically pluralistic churches, this challenge is formidable, especially since a given congregation can have dozens of disparate religious identities. Pastors must create catechetical materials that do not immediately challenge the prevailing religious identity, but clearly manifest the theological rationale of the liturgy, especially the two pillars of an ordered priesthood rooted in Christ the high priest and the obligation of the priesthood to actively and consciously participate in the liturgy. If it is possible to show how the parish's received liturgical tradition manifests the theological foundations of the liturgy, it is prudent to emphasize those areas early and often. Ideally, employing this approach will enable the pastor to gain the people's trust since he will have established himself as a person who honors their religious identity.

When pastors begin to introduce changes that are more prone to upsetting the prevailing religious identity of the liturgy, they must do so gently and gradually, by introducing new practices so that they co-exist alongside existing ones, and by consulting the people so that they know change is coming.[51] Pastors who are reluctant to consult the people should be reminded that excluding the people from participating in the process violates the dignity of the priesthood God has bestowed on them and compromises the larger goals of liturgical reform. The most important part of the catechetical process of liturgical reform is to develop a new religious identity in the people, which is exactly the kind of change many of us dread.

The key to implementing this reform is to gently and steadily encourage people to grow in their Christian life, to inform them that they are priests whose service God demands in the world. A liturgy which clearly communicates priestly identity to the people, along with their obligation to serve God, is an important objective of this enterprise. If people are consulted during the process of implementation, they will know that the leader is honoring them and will be more willing to accept something new in the liturgy, or to endure it, at minimum.

---

51. See Alexopoulos, "The State of Modern Greek Liturgical Studies and Research," 390. Also relevant is Michael Ryan's suggestion that the implementation of the third revision of the Roman Missal be postponed in "What if We said, 'Wait?'," *America*, 14 December 2009, 17-19.

The Mechanism for Implementation

Above, I treated approaches to liturgical reform and lingered at some length on the relationship between liturgy and religious identity. I also claimed that Vatican II received too much credit for proclaiming a liturgical theology while receiving too much blame for creating chaos within the Church. At the end of the section, I gave away my recommendation for adopting an approach to implementing liturgical reform in an attempt to resolve the problems caused by the inseparability of liturgy and religious identity. In this final section, I am going to backtrack by discussing the varying mechanisms for implementing liturgical reform because these processes have grave implications for understanding the contemporary phenomenon of reform while hinting towards possibilities for improvement that would strengthen the enterprise of liturgical reform without necessarily imposing it universally and simultaneously. The mechanisms for liturgical reform are shaped directly by ecclesiology: in this section, I will briefly review and analyze churchwide, autocephalous, synodal, diocesan, academic, and monastic models of renewal, concluded by a proposal for revising such processes that would enhance the permeation of liturgical renewal in the lives of the Churches.

Vatican II: Churchwide Renewal

Vatican II has become a central reference point for many aspects of liturgical reform, and in this study, I have noted the similarities between the theological rationale for reform expressed by *SC*, Schmemann, the Church of Greece, and New Skete. *SC*'s greatest contribution to liturgical theology is this theological rationale, but it is also the most underdeveloped and least appreciated aspect of the reform. Vatican II's status as a reference point for liturgical reform is attributable to the stature of the Council, but its legacy rests with its impact: the reverberations of Vatican II were experienced not only throughout the Roman Catholic Church, but also ecumenically because of the massive scope of *SC*'s implementation.[52]

Massimo Faggioli notes the irony in the bishops developing *SC* on the basis of their vision of the Church's catholicity, particularly the experience of celebrating the liturgy in a variety of traditions, with some privileging of the East.[53] *SC* aimed to achieve the central objective of the reform, for the people to actively and consciously participate in the liturgy. The reform's implementation entailed the experience of many changes: new prayers were composed, a revision of the Missal was written, translated, and disseminated, the RCIA was restored and reinvigorated, people prayed in their vernacular languages, and inculturation was encouraged.[54] This sea of change affected the entire Latin Church, and while one of the Council's priorities was to purify the liturgy and restore its Roman elements, the fascination with the East and the spirit of honoring local culture resulted in an explosion of diversity held together by a united order in the Latin rite.[55]

The newfound freedom of the Church to adopt new prayers and idioms of communication was an attempt to honor the religious identity that already existed among the people. Inculturation

52. See Bradshaw and Johnson, *The Eucharistic Liturgies*, 295-357; also see the brief but persuasive testimony of Gordon Lathrop, "Strong Center, Open Door: A Vision of Continuing Liturgical Renewal," *Worship* 75, no. 1 (2001): 35-36.
53. Faggioli, 34.
54. On the RCIA, see Johnson, *The Rites of Christian Initiation*, 381-405, and Bugnini, 584-625; on the new prayers, see Bugnini, 448-87, and Bradshaw and Johnson, 313-18; On translation, see Bugnini, 99-113, and Irwin, 114-38; and inculturation, see Anscar Chupungco, *Liturgical Inculturation: Sacramentals, Religiosity, and Catechesis* (Collegeville, MN: Liturgical Press, 1992), and *What, Then, is Liturgy? Musings and Memoir*, foreword by Mark Francis (Collegeville, MN: Liturgical Press, 2010); and Mark Francis, "Another Look at the Constitution on the Sacred Liturgy and the Substantial Unity of the Roman Rite," *Worship* 88, no. 3 (2014): 239-55.
55. Faggioli, 139-44.

envisioned an implementation of the process that differs from the one I described above: the existing religious identity of the people manifest in their cultural expressions of language, ritual, art, and music, would be honored in the liturgy, which would presumably facilitate the active and conscious participation in the liturgy. The spirit of freedom communicated by the Council contrasted the juridical tradition of the Roman Church. The Council practiced the Roman tradition of subsidiarity and delegated many of the liturgical particulars to national conferences of bishops, granting authority to new bodies of bishops organized by nation to make the ultimate pastoral determinations on reform. This delegation of responsibility to the local bishops was a result of the ecclesiology of *SC*, although tensions between bishops and Rome continue to endure at the diocesan and national levels.[56]

Other scholars have treated the legacy of Vatican II from within the Roman tradition, and I encourage readers to consider their contributions for more engaged analysis.[57] What interests me here is

---

56. Faggioli, 87-92. He notes that *Lumen Gentium* reverses course somewhat by taking a turn towards more episcopal power, disclosing some tension between the ecclesiologies of Vatican II documents (89).

57. The literary corpus is enormous. The following list summarizes the salient literature, but is not meant to be exhaustive: John Baldovin, "An Active Presence: the Liturgical Vision of Vatican II 50 Years Later," *America* 208, no. 18 (May 27, 2013): 11-14; idem, *Reforming the Liturgy*; Fernando Berrios, "The Liturgy in the Vatican Council II: Bases, Implications and Challenges of Reform," *TEOLOGIA Y VIDA* 55, no. 3 (2014): 517-47; Paul De Clerck and André Haquin, "La constitution Sacrosanctum Concilium et sa mise en œuvre: une réception toujours en cours," *Revue Théologique De Louvain* 44, no. 2 (April 2013): 171-96; Paul De Clerck, "The Liturgical Reform of Vatican II: Why Has It Only Been Partially Received?" *Worship* 88, no. 2 (2014): 170-77; André Haquin, "La réforme liturgique de Vatican II a-t-elle fait preuve de créativité et en quel sens?" *Recherches De Science Religieuse* 101, no. 1 (January 1, 2013): 53-67; Irwin, *What We Have Done*; Peter Jeffrey, "Can Catholic Social Teaching Bring Peace to the 'Liturgy Wars'?" *Theological Studies* 75, no. 2 (2014): 350-75; William H. Johnston, "Pope Benedict XVI on the Postconciliar Liturgical Reform: An Essay in Interpretation." *Antiphon* 17, no. 2 (2013): 118-38; Richter Klemens, "The Relationship Between Church and Liturgy: On the Reception of the Second Vatican Council (Vztah církve a liturgie. K recepci Druhého vatikánského koncilu)," *Studia theologica* 12, no. 3 (2010): 30-42; Patrick Prétot, "La place de la constitution sur la liturgie dans l'herméneutique de Vatican II," *Recherches De Science Religieuse* 101, no. 1 (January 1, 2013): 13-36.

the mechanism for reform when it occurs at a churchwide level. The reform implemented by Vatican II was nothing short of massive in its scope, and this leads to a seemingly irreconcilable problem in terms of ongoing pastoral implementation and assessment of the reform.

On the one hand, Vatican II's liturgical reform has been challenged from within. The decision to adopt a platform for reform was not unanimous, and restorationists have protested the unfolding of reform, along with its rationale.[58] The internal structures of the Church complicate the Church's ability to resolve liturgical conflicts. Catholics view Vatican II as an ecumenical council, possessing the highest authority within the Church, and a logical implication of this authority is that liturgical reform should continue to unfold in accordance with the principles iterated at the Council.

However, no council can implement a reform; only bishops have the power to see it through, and in the Roman Church, this task is delegated to the bishop of Rome.

Restorationists enjoyed a victory when Pope Benedict XVI issued the *motu proprio* (by his own accord), *Summorum Pontificum*, which permitted parishes to celebrate Tridentine Mass according to the Missal of Pius V.[59] Further internal conflicts ensued with the Third Revision of the Roman Missal and its translation into English, a process resulting in the humiliating isolation of many English-speaking bishops from the complex process of negotiating and vetting texts that enter the sacramentary.[60] For better or worse, the

---

58. On this topic, see Faggioli, 158.

59. On *Summorum Pontificum*, see Baldovin, *Reforming the Liturgy*, 130-33; Faggioli, 143-44; Chad J. Glendenning, "Significance of the Liturgical Reforms prior to the Second Vatican Council in Light of 'Summorum pontificium,'" *Studia Canonica* 44, no. 2 (2010), 293-342; idem, "Was the 1962 'Missale Romanum' abrogated?: a canonical analysis in light of 'Summorum Pontificum.'" *Worship* 85, no. 1 (2011), 15-37; Steven A. Kiczek, "Pope Benedict XVI's Summorum Pontificum: Reconciling Conflicting Values," *Journal of Religious & Theological Information* 8, nos. 1-2 (2009), 37-64.

60. See Kevin Seasoltz, "The Genius of the Roman Rite: On Reception and Implementation of the

publication and distribution of the third revision of the Roman Missal was a liturgical reform, and for our purposes here, this reform discloses the problem of continuing the liturgical work authorized by an ecumenical council. The texts surrounding the third revision of the Missal pledge their adherence to continuing the work of Vatican II, yet in some places, a perception that the Council's principles were violated emerged.

The massive scope of Vatican II's liturgical reform promoted instantaneous and diffuse impact, but it also compromised the ongoing work of the Council on account of the stature associated with the reform. The stature of *SC* and the Council that promoted it demands that its work be continued, but the internal mechanisms do not appear to permit the creative appearance of liturgical practices that emerge in parishes, dioceses, and religious communities. Furthermore, the reform of Vatican II is largely legislated through texts, following the longstanding pattern of implementing some semblance of liturgical uniformity by legislating the use of one book for all. The looming challenge for the Roman Church is to find a way to demonstrate the relevance of the reform of Vatican II in an increasingly globalized and pluralistic Church. The assertion that an assessment of Vatican II is somewhat premature since the Church still needs to adjust to the implementation might need to be revisited. The pastoral landscape of the Catholic Church has shifted since 1963, and it may be that the reform itself needs to be revised. The scope and authority invested in the reform by the convocation of a holy council, along with the shifting and uncertain internal dynamics of reform in intrachurch structures, makes the challenge of revising the agenda to address new needs formidable.

New Missal," *Worship* 83, no. 6 (2009): 541–49, and Nicholas Denysenko, "The Revision of the Roman Missal: An Orthodox Reflection," *Worship* 85 (2011): 306–29.

Orthodox Mechanisms for Implementing Reform

The Orthodox mechanisms for implementing liturgical reform and restoration are diverse. The Church of Greece presents the most interesting mechanisms among those encountered in this study. The symposia devoted to academic and pastoral deliberation were designed to be consultative for the bishops of the Synod, who would implement initiatives representing the principles discussed at the symposia. This model attempts to honor the potential contributions of modern scholarship while preserving the right to implement reform to the proper ecclesiological order, namely, the bishop. Notable in the model of the Church of Greece is the deliberative process, which occurs at the level of an autocephalous church. Following such deliberations, the decision to implement initiatives that would permit the principles to impact Church life belongs to bishops, at both the synodal and diocesan levels.

The Church of Greece stands out for its commitment to studying liturgical renewal in other Orthodox Churches, but this acknowledgment of instances of renewal occurring within global Orthodoxy falls short of forming a group representing all Orthodox churches devoted to the study of liturgical history and renewal. In this vein, the church of Greece is a flagship for a renewal mechanism. Other Orthodox Churches in the global community have commissions devoted to studying the liturgy and recommending actions—the Moscow Patriarchate is notable in this regard, with its publication of the celebration of the Sunday Divine Liturgy with Baptism a fruit of the process.[61] But the Church of Greece alone has created an integrative process of deliberation and implementation that has the capacity to foment positive change by deepening the faithful's engagement of Christian life.

61. Morozowich, "Liturgical Changes in Russia and the Christian East."

Critics such as Vassiliadis and Koumarianos have asserted that the mechanism needs revision, since the Synod has limited its reception of the liturgical commission and symposia. Many potentially powerful initiatives remain ideas because of the Church's conservative approach to implementing renewal. The relative inactivity of the Synod and individual bishops explain Alexopoulos's call for the establishment of several centers of liturgical study in educational institutions of Greece, an initiative which would presumably enrich the overall liturgical culture among clergy and scholars in Greece. We should also note that the commentators on liturgical renewal involved with the enterprise invested hope in the publication of a new Euchologion which would enforce the implementation of renewal. The hope invested in the publication of a liturgical book shows that Orthodox share the same pattern observed by Roman Catholics in perceiving liturgical books as authoritative documents with the teeth to enforce some semblance of uniformity.

Two traditional mechanisms of reform have been covered in this study, the first attributable to a particular figure who revises the received liturgical tradition, and the second more surgical and rooted in creativity and independence. Schmemann's liturgical renewal enterprise became a fixture at St. Vladimir's Seminary and was carried out, in part, by his students who integrated his vision of revival into their parish ministries. The cultivation of a school devoted to liturgical music also occurred in ROCOR, largely through the work of Boris Ledkovsky. The challenge with such mechanisms for reform is the opposite of what we see in Vatican II: their longevity is questionable because the initiatives largely belong to the thought of a particular figure. When the figure dies, his or her disciples are charged with continuing the project. Schmemann passed on his project to worthy successors such as Paul Meyendorff and Alkiviadis Calivas, who continued to form disciples in their respective schools.

However, Schmemann himself was similar to Vatican II in his stature: it was simply impossible for his successors to maintain continuity in impact. Ledkovsky passed on his legacy to a collegium of successors who have continued and enhanced his work.

New Skete's mechanism for reform, by contrast, follows the Eastern tradition of monastic independence where religious communities have the freedom to create their own order independent of episcopal supervision. New Skete's mechanism differs from the other Orthodox models studied here as they were inspired by the spirit of freedom engendered by Vatican II and expect Orthodox bishops to respect their relative liturgical independence. New Skete states that they endeavor to revive the monastic tradition of stewardship for the liturgy and creativity in sustaining her life, and in this vein, they follow the patterns established by their Sabaitic and Studite antecedents of late antiquity and the medieval era. The mechanism for reform is to establish an ordo and observe it, which depends on the publication and revision of books, but at New Skete, this is not a major issue since they are a small community. However, New Skete's impact on liturgical renewal within Orthodox has been limited.

The small impact of New Skete on Orthodox liturgy in North America yields three observations. First, the role of monasteries has changed, especially in North American Orthodox culture, where parishes have a modified Typikon to follow and do not rely on the practice of a given monastery. Second, New Skete is both isolated and small; one has to travel quite a distance to make a visit, and their relative isolation from a larger Orthodox population in North America represents a geographic barrier to impact. Third, the Byzantine liturgy is connected to a larger religious identity, and New Skete's liturgical order challenges this identity because of the scope of the revision performed on the liturgy. In fact, I assert that Byzantine liturgy is connected even more tightly with religious identity in North American culture because of the circumstances introduced by immigration; for immigrants, the Byzantine liturgy was the primary event of gathering for immigrants who were struggling to adjust to the demands of North American life. The liturgy provided a safe space for prayer, but also for social and political interaction and fellowship. In this vein, the liturgy delivered much more than an opportunity to worship to immigrants, which magnified their perception of the liturgy as unchanged throughout history and unchangeable in contemporary circumstances.

The Orthodox mechanisms for reform have not depended on a council, even if representatives of the Church of Greece reserved the most urgent liturgical matters for a holy council. Instead, the mechanisms for reform have relied largely on central figures: bishops and scholars entrusted with important teaching positions in theological schools. Despite the Orthodox advantage of having interdependent regional structures as opposed to an overarching central authority, the implementation of reform has been diluted by several problems. First, most reform efforts occurred either in North America or Western Europe, which have very small Orthodox populations adjusting to their statuses as minorities. Many of the largest churches in global Orthodoxy are entertaining renewal now, not even twenty-five years since the collapse of the Soviet Union.

As these Churches cultivate indigenous intellectual theological life, they will contribute thinkers and pioneers who represent the perspectives of their people at the larger table of discourse on liturgical renewal. Their absence for much of the history we have discussed here limits the potential scope of the reforms we have discussed. Second, we have discovered that the laity carries much authority on account of its reception of liturgical renewal. The laity has inspired pastors and scholars to consider liturgical renewal based on its tepid participation in liturgical life. In the deliberations on reform, the laity does not have a place at the table of discourse, which is dominated heavily by scholars, bishops, and clergy. It is insufficient to state that parish clergy represents the laity. Inclusion of a larger body of people in deliberations on the liturgy—especially women—and in identifying communities that might be strong candidates for renewal initiatives is paramount to ensuring the ecclesiological soundness of any reform effort.

Conclusion: What's New? Contemporary Challenges for Liturgical Renewal and a Proposal

In our review of the mechanisms for liturgical reform, we mentioned that the stature of Vatican II prohibited a swifter liturgical response to cultural developments in the last fifty years. In this concluding section, I will reflect on how local clergy attempt to respond to unanticipated pastoral challenges in the absence of official mechanisms permitting the updating of renewal efforts and will make one modest recommendation that might fill this lacuna.

Socioeconomic and Cultural (R)evolution

The five models covered in this study originated in the nineteenth century, with a platform for renewal deliberated in the twentieth century and implemented then as well. In a sense, all of the initiatives for renewal responded to particular diagnoses of Church life, primarily the problem of the fissure between ritualizing Christian life and rehearsing it on a daily basis. This study demonstrates that the pastoral examination of Church life illuminated issues transcending ecclesial boundaries. Liturgical structures and symbols had decayed and people used devotionals for prayer and spiritual fulfillment. Liturgical celebration was a matter of administering the sacraments with prayers read in secret and the people merely observing. The absence of the people's interiorization of liturgical life was manifest in the problems of the world, particularly war. The separation of clergy from the laity perpetuated a sense that the people did not need to do anything in the liturgy. Clergy sensitive to the people's disinterest and boredom often resorted to entertainment through brilliant aesthetics, or utilized the time of prayer for their own personal devotions.

It is outside the scope of this study to present a detailed analysis of the social, economic, and global conditions impacting Christian life during the deliberations and implementation of liturgical reform, so I will offer only a brief synthesis. The process of liturgical reform has witnessed to epic social and political upheavals on a global scale: monarchies rose and fell; two world wars claimed the lives of millions; women and minorities fought for equality and made significant advancements; the world endured a terrifying Cold War with the threat of nuclear Armageddon lingering; human trafficking and slavery has rebounded in numerous underdeveloped countries and regions; the global economy has been impacted by major financial collapses, corruption, and the hoarding and poor stewardship of natural resources and fossil fuels; terrorism, totalitarianism, and social revolutions have occurred in many regions and countries; technology has permanently changed the landscape of work and education, with women and minorities advancing higher in the workforce. Religious changes are also prominent: Christianity has weakened in traditional strongholds such as Western Europe and North America, but has strengthened in the so-called global south.[62]

---

62. See Diana Butler Bass, *Christianity for the Rest of Us: How the Neighborhood Church is Transforming the Faith* (New York: HarperOne, 2006), 6–10; "Report Examines the State of Mainline Protestant Churches," The Barna Group website, https://www.barna.org/barna-update/leadership/323-report-examines-the-state-of-mainline-protestant-churches#.UubH8xDTnIU (accessed January 27, 2014); 2007 "Religious Landscape Survey"

Women have engaged ministerial leadership in Reformed Churches since the early 1970s, and the sexual revolution permeated many churches, resulting in the acceptance of homosexuality, the revision of moral teachings on sexual relationships, marriage, and divorce, and the creations of rites for gay marriage. Globalization has mitigated social distances between countries and technology enables previously impossible encounters. In North America, people can work 24 hours a day and seven days a week with wifi and a laptop computer or tablet, and jobs tend to cluster in more populated areas resulting in selective urban growth, and the abandonment of rural or urban areas that depended on industries which are no longer thriving and thus unable to employ people. Furthermore, the American spiritual marketplace results in church shopping, and people can select a parish they find suitable to family needs that is twenty-five miles away as an alternative to attending the family parish five miles away.[63]

One can make an argument that the work of liturgical renewal is ongoing, but it would be difficult to conclude that the agenda for liturgical renewal does not need to be updated. The problem is that the current agendas for reform are attempting to address a pastoral situation that is dated: the Cold War ended and may begin again, and the spiritual marketplace poses unprecedented pastoral challenges. Simply put, a gifted pastor may do everything the "right way" and find him or herself unable to build up a local parish because people pick and choose parishes and congregations based on criteria selected by families or individuals. In the current ecclesial environment,

performed by the Pew Research Religion and Public Life Project, Pew Research website, http://religions.pewforum.org/reports (accessed January 27, 2014); Archbishop Speaks on Intentional Evangelism," Archbishop of York website, http://www.archbishopofyork.org/articles.php/3001/archbishop-speaks-on-intentional-evangelism (accessed December 11, 2013); and Kevin Seasoltz, *A Virtuous Church: Catholic Theology, Ethics, and Liturgy for the 21st Century* (Maryknoll, NY: Orbis Books, 2012), 56-63.

63. On the spiritual marketplace, with reference to Orthodoxy, see Amy Slagle, *The Eastern Church in the Spiritual Marketplace: American Conversions to Orthodox Christianity* (DeKalb, IL: Northern Illinois University Press, 2011).

Church leaders have limited authority to sternly urge people to adhere to denominational affiliation outside of creating arrangements with civil authorities that privilege a particular Church. The contemporary situation differs vastly from the one encountered by pastors at the beginning of the deliberative process of liturgical renewal in the late-nineteenth century: most people drive to Church (not walk), and attend when they can. Most people are literate and can use the Internet to browse church options on their own. Finally, clerical authority is in decline: many people simply ignore the possibility of ecclesiastical interdict and select the teachings and directives that cohere with the lifestyle they have selected. Some clergy still have significant spiritual authority, but in general, this authority must be earned very carefully over a period of time through trust.

A summary like the one offered here deserves a rigorous examination, and mine is simple: society is evolving rapidly at the macro and micro-levels, and liturgy is not keeping up in the Roman Catholic and Orthodox traditions. Orthodox scholars and pastors are acutely aware of societal upheaval and struggle to maintain peace and unity in the Church as people take sides in cultural polarization. In this sense, one might view the liturgy as the ultimate neutralizer: it unifies people who are otherwise quite different by forcing them to acquiesce to the language of prayer belonging to the catholic (according to the whole) Church.

I find this argument compelling and a potentially powerful and God-given tool to unite disparate peoples in Christ. However, a view of the liturgy as objective does not mean that liturgy should not communicate in contemporary idioms the people can engage with comprehension. Referring the people to a liturgy steeped in the past does not make the past objective; this option can actually do more harm than good by inviting people, even involuntarily, to idolize the past and attempt to restore it. An updated liturgy that conforms to the daily life of the people must be rooted in both the past and future: salvation history is the narrative of the past communicated in the liturgy, with a vision of the future life with God also shaping the present.

The Catholic and Orthodox Churches need a devoted discussion strategizing ways to update the liturgy without compromising the elements of tradition that make it holy. I offer one suggestion here that is based on the presentation of mechanisms that I have offered above. My proposal attempts to reign in tradition while learning from the lessons presented to us by our five models of reform. The current mechanisms are impoverished by the absence of viable liturgical centers. Liturgical centers emerge for a variety of reasons but they are marked by creativity.

My proposal is rooted in the hope that Catholic and Orthodox might revitalize collaborations of ecumenical *ressourcement* by allowing influential liturgical centers to emerge. I admire the ecumenical character of *SC* and its attempt to decentralize liturgical practices by restoring the authority to implement liturgical reform to diocesan bishops and national bishops' conferences. The recent past of the Catholic liturgy wars and select episodes of episcopal directives on the liturgy in the Orthodox Church expose the weaknesses of a top-heavy authority in liturgical matters. *Ressourcement* was fueled in part by the brilliant creativity of monastic centers, such as the Benedictine Abbey of Maria Laach. Likewise, the Orthodox Church has a rich history of monastic centers shaping the liturgy, epitomized by the monasteries of St. Sabas in Palestine, the Studite monasteries of Constantinople, and of course, the hesychastic tradition of Mount Athos. These monasteries tended to flourish in the aftermath of ecclesial and societal crises, nourishing the Church's liturgy by attempting to retrieve the best aspects of her identity in recovering the Christic and pneumatic DNA of liturgy preserved in "the sources." Unfortunately, it is all too apparent that a preference for centralization and a reliance on episcopal authority has stifled the creativity and potential contribution of liturgical centers. Such centers employ a divinely-mandated prophetic ministry: they vivify liturgical life and offer alternatives to a centralized liturgy that is stifled by controversy or inertia. Such models flourished historically because they were formed and shaped by *ressourcement*. Liturgical centers should not have undue authority, but they must be given the freedom to experiment and pray in accordance with their own inner rhythms so that the Church is truly a body with all of its members participating and contributing.

Three points are crucial for the emergence of bona fide liturgical centers that have the capacity to breathe life into the Church's liturgy: first, such centers must be permitted to emerge on their own and cannot merely be centers that perform the sanctioned liturgy; second, liturgical centers will ideally have vibrant lay participation; and third, it is essential that liturgical centers are viewed as communities illustrating patterns of what is possible in liturgy, and not as blueprints that one must copy. Centers which demand uniformity violate the principle of liturgical diversity that has prevailed since the first century. Liturgical centers promote creative diversity as an alternative to a church that relies on a centralized episcopal authority solely; such a church is one that will limp and stutter through the twenty-first century.

SC and the Orthodox liturgical movement had limited cross-pollination and much work remains to clarify their mutual interdependencies. One thing, however, is clear: the Holy Spirit graced both Churches with the space and freedom to explore the entirety of their heritage and recover a vision of Church that encouraged the people to exercise the priesthood given to them by Christ and seek the reconciliation of the world with God. The task of exploring the sources and seeking ways to employ them for contemporary liturgy has been handed to the present generation. Those who accept the invitation to take this task on might contribute to a formidable but promising ecumenical endeavor: to reconcile the world to God by encouraging the people to practice the priesthood God gives them at each Eucharist.

7

———

Conclusion

This study has examined contemporary liturgical reform in the Orthodox Church through four models: Alexander Schmemann, ROCOR, the Church of Greece, and New Skete Monastery. In assessing the four models, I have also explored the impact of Vatican II on liturgical reform in the Orthodox Church. The previous chapter provides a detailed analysis of this study's contributions. The conclusion has two primary objectives: first, for the reader's convenience, to summarize the study's conclusions. Second, I will conclude the study by revising the agenda for liturgical reform in the Orthodox and Catholic Churches.

The Theological Rationale for Liturgical Reform

In response to a query on the urgent need for liturgical reform, Alexander Schmemann stated that liturgical reform requires a rationale.[1] Throughout this study, I have identified a pattern

1. Alexander Schmemann, "Liturgical Theology, Theology of Liturgy, and Liturgical Reform," *St. Vladimir's Theological Quarterly* 13 (1969): 222.

appearing in the deliberative and implementation phases of liturgical reform. Reform begins as a pastoral assessment of Church life. The examination of ecclesial life is essentially a diagnosis, followed by a prognosis for building up the life of the Church.

The process of studying Church life commenced with the *ressourcement* movement in the late-eighteenth century, when theologians began to adopt a scientific approach to studying theology. Focused study of the liturgy was included in *ressourcement* and was aided not only by the adoption of scientific methods of study, but also in the discovery, collection, and categorization of liturgical texts that significantly contribute to the narrative of liturgical history. The pioneering work of the school of comparative liturgy, attributed to Anton Baumstark, illuminated patterns of liturgical development which contributed to the Church's understanding of her own tradition of praying. The work of studying the sources in the liturgical movement was ecumenical, involving representatives of West and East, and the publication of sources and composition of a liturgical history opened the doors for the Church to understand how and why liturgy has changed throughout history in dialogue with societal development. The study of liturgical history delivered a sense of understanding how liturgies grow, change, and evolve, and also provided Church leaders with a reliable blueprint of tradition which shows what is possible in the realm of liturgy.

Vatican II was an epic event in twentieth-century liturgical history which began the process of implementing liturgical reform, important because the council acted on many of the contributions of liturgical history. The fiftieth anniversary of *Sacrosanctum Concilium* in 2013 occasioned a process of reflecting on the council's impact, for two reasons: *SC* was the council's first official teaching, a symbolic gesture which attempted to restore the primacy of liturgy in Church life, and the fierce debates on the liturgy in the Catholic world referred to Vatican II as a watershed moment. The flurry of scholarship and popular literature that emerged in connection with the fiftieth anniversary of Vatican II testifies to the stature of the Council: pastors and scholars view Vatican II as a significant event that impacted the Church beyond Catholic borders, for better or worse.

I have noted the tendency of Orthodox theologians to refer to Vatican II's influence on the Orthodox Church. SC's appeals for noble simplicity, changes in the decoration of sacred space, and participation of the laity in the liturgy are examples of principles that have been committed to memory and easily misunderstood as having been invented by Vatican II. The actual impact of Vatican II on contemporary Orthodox liturgical reform is much more complex and based on both truths and misperceptions.

The first misperception is that Vatican II inaugurated the process of radical liturgical reform by performing surgery on the liturgy, one that Orthodox reformers tend to copy. When Vatican II started the process of implementing reform, a significant adjustment to the reform occurred from within the church, and this process was complicated by the sheer size of the Church and the magnitude of the reform. Celebrating the new orders of liturgy entailed a devoted learning process for clergy and laity. In many instances, they began to pray in their native languages; they adjusted to the rehabilitation of ministries (such as the diaconate); they inaugurated RCIA programs vigorously; they experimented with new styles of liturgical music, interior sacred space design, the position of the presider, and the language of newly composed Eucharistic prayers; they trained lectors and readers who assisted with the larger three-year lectionary, and they adjusted to changes in many other sacraments, including Confirmation, marriage, and reconciliation, in addition to the rite of the burial of the dead. The changes I have listed here do not exhaust all of the reforms in the Roman liturgy, and yet, they all unfolded within a period of a few years throughout the Latin-rite church.

Many Orthodox observed these changes as chaotic, but this was not a mere matter of learning how to recite the Creed together when a new translation was issued: the entire language and ritual performance of the liturgy was revised which resulted in a steep learning curve for both clergy and laity. The misperception on the part of Orthodox observers was the false idea that the relationship between implementing reform and the messiness that results from learning how to pray in a new way was caused by Vatican II which was consequently responsible for apparently similar instances of confusion that occurred in Orthodox parishes introducing renewed liturgical practices.

In this vein, Vatican II exercised enormous influence on the Orthodox approach to liturgical renewal. The stature of Vatican II and the magnitude of its liturgical reform led to its depiction among Orthodox as an inappropriate model for liturgical renewal. Most Orthodox have adopted a slow and conservative approach to renewal based on the fear that immediate implementation would yield the same result as Orthodox had observed in the Roman Church. Vatican II became a negative reference point in the eyes of the Orthodox, a model that could not be followed because the liturgical changes appeared to be dilutions of sacred symbols and ritual structures, an abandonment of tradition unacceptable to Orthodox theology. The model of reform adopted by New Skete is the exception to this norm, clearly on account of the community's experience as Franciscan friars who embraced the spirit of freedom permeating the approach to liturgy at Vatican II.

Had Orthodox theologians followed the development of Roman liturgical reform more carefully, they might have noticed that the surgical reforms performed in the Roman reform were inspired by a theological rationale to which the Orthodox subscribed. Both Catholics and Orthodox were committed to restoring the ecclesiological layers of priesthood in liturgical celebration, promoting the active and conscious participation of the laity in the liturgy, demonstrating the presence of the Paschal mystery in the liturgical offices, and redefining the liturgy as an eschatological encounter between God and the Church, an encounter which results in the Church's continued transformation and transfiguration.

When the Roman reformers drew abundantly from liturgical history to reconstruct an order of liturgy appropriate for the contemporary Church, these principles guided each decision. It was and remains difficult for Orthodox observers to behold Roman liturgical reform with more patience because on the surface, liturgy appeared to change radically, a perception which presented the illusion of an abandonment of liturgical tradition, whereas the intent was to *restore* it in its fullness.

A Shared Theological Rationale

Despite Orthodoxy's generally tepid appraisal of the contributions of Vatican II to liturgical reform, I have consistently argued in this study that the Catholic and Orthodox churches have elaborated the same theological rationale for liturgical reform rooted in priesthood and the active participation of the laity in the liturgy. All five models examined here support this assertion. In each model of reform, the priority is to restore and vitalize elements of liturgy that manifest priestly identity to the people and encourage them to actively participate in the liturgy.

In the previous chapter, I suggested that these two principles are the most deeply rooted of the theological foundations of the liturgy: they are both inseparable and reciprocal. Several prominent Catholic theologians studied the liturgical sources to articulate a theology of the priesthood of the laity where the laity is an order of the Church. Yves Congar and Nicholas Afanasiev identified the laity as the concelebrant of the liturgy, presided over by Christ, the high priest. Afanasiev and Congar argued that concelebration requires active engagement of the liturgy: it is nonsensical for the concelebrant to passively observe a ritual performed by an ordained minister.[2]

Catholic and Orthodox theologians developed the theology of priesthood and the consequential active participation of the laity in the liturgy in an environment of ecumenical dialogue. While scholars and pastors conducted their research independently, it is impossible to ignore the many areas of theological cross-pollination, evidenced by the active presence of and contribution to Vatican II by theologians such as Afanasiev and Schmemann, accompanied by Schmemann's frequent references to Western scholars in his own theological writings and course syllabi. Clearly, the liturgical movement consisted of a broad and diverse colloquy of theologians representing numerous Churches who worked through theological ideas in exchanges of ideas and positions. For liturgical reform, the restoration of the priesthood and the appeal to active and conscious participation in the liturgy were the two most salient and impactful contributions.

The models of liturgical reform elucidate the pattern of pastoral adoption of academic contributions in both the Catholic and Orthodox orbits. The problem of disinterest and boredom among the laity at the liturgy appears in the late-nineteenth-century writings of Metropolitan Antony Khrapovitsky and the contemporaneous

---

2. Nicholas Afanasiev, "The Ministry of Laity in the Church," in William C. Mills, ed., *Called to Serve: Readings on Ministry from the Orthodox Church* (Rollinsford, NH: Orthodox Research Institute, 2010), 8–9; idem, *Трапеза Господня* (Kyiv: Khram Prepodobnogo Agapita Pecherskogo, 2003), 69–90; Yves Congar, *At the Heart of Christian Worship: Liturgical Essays of Yves Congar*, ed. and trans. Paul Philibert (Collegeville, MN: Liturgical Press, 2010), 15–69.

deliberations on liturgical renewal in preparation for the All-Russian Council. Schmemann, the Church of Greece, ROCOR, and New Skete all express concern about the same problem. Each model designates the ordained clergy as having the primary responsibility for presiding at liturgy in a manner that engages the people.

In other words, the key to reinvigorating active and conscious participation of the people in the liturgy lies with the ordained clergy, whose liturgical celebration must communicate the priestly identity given to the laity at Baptism and Chrismation, and whose catechesis will help the laity understand and interiorize their identity. The ordained clergy are responsible for developing an orderly and comprehensible liturgy free of individualism and vanity and comprehensible to the laity, which facilitates their engagement.

This pastoral priority explains why theologians have directed clergy to enhance their own competence in the *ars celebrandi*. Clearly, the models do not adopt a uniform strategy for implementing the process: ROCOR emphasizes music, while New Skete and the Church of Greece address several areas in liturgical aesthetics to maximize the people's comprehension of the liturgy. In comparing the models of liturgical reform, it is tempting to dwell on the disparate strategies adopted by the Churches to emphasize reform at the risk of understating their common adherence to a theological rationale for a vibrant liturgical ecclesiology. The models have their varying points of emphases, but I have argued here that the most important ingredient of liturgical reform is its theological rationale, and it is precisely this foundation that needs to be rehabilitated in contemporary liturgical renewal.

The divergences between the five models introduce two problematic matters that undermine the potency of a common theological rationale for reform. The first problem is social, namely the tendency for liturgical reform to be implemented outside of its original liturgical habitat. Only the renewal program of the Church of Greece is unfolding in its native habitat, because the scheme for developing a program of renewal corresponds to the particular pastoral conditions in Greece. Schmemann was sensitive to the environmental conditions of reform in the North American context, which explains, in part, his attention to questions of translation and culture, his critique of secularism, and his concern that other Orthodox in North America participate in the discourse on the emergence of an Orthodox Church in America.

The reforms attributed to Schmemann were conceived outside of the North American context and implemented there and in other areas of the world. In this vein, Schmemann's Eucharistic revival is quite similar to the one energized by Vatican II. The Eucharistic revival, epitomized by frequent reception of Holy Communion, the proclamation of the anaphora loud for all to hear, and the participation of the people in the offering of the liturgy is essentially a universal reform that is not shaped by local habitat. New Skete used the received liturgical tradition, and after concluding that the liturgy cohered poorly with the local habitat, the community constructed a new order corresponding with the demands of local life.

The best examples of restorations and the preservation of a particular liturgical theology occurring outside of the original habitat occur in ROCOR's liturgical model. The first example is ROCOR's cultivation of the liturgical school of singing in the Moscow tradition. ROCOR paid careful attention to developing clergy and choir directors who mastered chants which highlighted texts and led the people in prayer; this training largely achieved the objective of the Moscow School by gradually excising the hegemony of Imperial Court chant from parish singing and replacing it with chant-based music. Obviously, some constituencies within ROCOR preferred other styles of liturgical music whose principles do not conform to those of the Moscow school. The clergy and musicians who preferred the Moscow style identified qualities in its principles that would contribute to the fulfillment of the restoration many bishops and theologians sought in the pre-revolutionary deliberations on the liturgy, summarized by Metropolitan Antony as learning how to love God by observing the fullness of the liturgy, and learning how to love one's neighbor by loving God.

In the previous chapter, I mentioned that this particular liturgical restoration went on a pilgrimage, from pre-revolutionary Russia to the West. In this sense, ROCOR's cultivation of the Moscow school of liturgical music differs from the enterprise of the Church of Greece, which seeks to cultivate traditions for the Church in its native habitat. The Russian immigrants who settled in the West assiduously preserved the traditions of their homeland, in part because their fellow Orthodox who remained in Russia were severely limited in their ability to sustain traditions. When Metropolitan Anastasy (Gribanovsky) appointed Boris Ledkovsky to serve as the choir director at the Manhattan Cathedral and train church musicians, he was motivated by the desire to create a liturgical center cultivating the Muscovite traditions of the Kremlin's Dormition Cathedral. Michael Konstantinov cultivated the Kyivan musical tradition at Holy Virgin Cathedral of San Francisco for similar reasons, especially since the Pecherskaja Lavra Monastery of Kyiv was closed for the duration of the Soviet period.

The intentional sustenance of beloved traditions that accompanied immigrants to their new homes in the West is informative in many ways. First, commitment to sustaining a migrant tradition manifests at least three potential qualities about the migrant community. Immigrants sustain traditions in new contexts because they hope and expect to return to their native homelands. They believe that their new homes will be conducive to sustaining native traditions, and often use their native music and liturgies because it is what they know. In the case of ROCOR or any migrant community, all these dynamics could be occurring simultaneously.

In ROCOR's case, I believe that their fidelity to continuing the work of the Moscow Synodal School of music was inspired by a sense of obligation for protecting a severely persecuted Church. Abandoning the project would have amounted to a betrayal of the blood shed by the new martyrs, and the opportunity to continue the project and return it to its natural habitat—Russia—would serve as another symbol of the Church's victory in Christ over the gates of hell and would be a gift from the Russians of the diaspora to their brothers and sisters who remained in Russia.

ROCOR's second example of liturgical preservation helps us understand their fidelity to continuing the school of liturgical music. ROCOR maintained a view of the liturgy as a God-given gift to the Church, one received by the previous generation of holy fathers and thus just as venerable and sacred as any other dogmatic teaching handed down to the current generation from the holy fathers. The most faithful way to honor this tradition was to observe the requirements of the liturgy even if new circumstances made fulfilling such requirements challenging. In Jordanville, the printing press bearing the name of St. Job of Pochaev continued to publish the liturgical books representing the pre-revolutionary Russian traditions, and the books bear a venerable and sacred authority.

ROCOR's fidelity to strict liturgical observance is an instance of Thomas Pott's model of "converting the faithful to the liturgy," but more important is the collective ecclesial mindset illuminated by this faithfulness.[3] The liturgy is perceived as an organism that

---

3. See Thomas Pott, *Byzantine Liturgical Reform: A Study of Liturgical Change in the Byzantine Tradition*, trans. Paul Meyendorff, Orthodox Liturgy Series, Book Two (Crestwood, NY: St. Vladimir's Seminary Press, 2010), 95–96.

grows and matures and cannot be changed. In this sense, change is akin to destruction, and the mere idea of changing the liturgy for the sake of the people represents a lack of love for the liturgy and the abandonment of holy tradition. Furthermore, this notion of the liturgy elevates the received tradition to such a stature that it attains a universal quality. The sacred liturgy inherited by the current generation is not merely a Russian variant, but is the liturgy received and beloved by global Orthodoxy.

ROCOR serves as our example here, but it is hardly the only Orthodox body that views the liturgy in this way. The prevailing perception of the liturgy among typical Orthodox Christians echoes the ideas exemplified by ROCOR. The liturgy bears the four marks of the Nicene-Constantinopolitan Creed because it is one (uniform), holy, catholic (universal), and apostolic, and to this we might add a fifth "mark": it is canonical, which means that the Church is required to observe it in its fullness, especially the clergy.

I have lingered on ROCOR's examples here because I believe that comparing ROCOR to our other Orthodox models enhances our comprehension of the way collective attitudes towards the liturgy impact efforts to assess and restore it for the purpose of building up the body of Christ. A complex amalgamation of circumstances has resulted in a plethora of attitudes towards the liturgy that strongly discourage the performance of any surgery in attempts to renew the liturgy and the Church. For ROCOR, the only elements that needed to be excised from the liturgy were foreign ones, especially works of sacred art and music that were of Western provenance. A recovery of the Church's ancient chant tradition would enable choirs to lead the people in engaged prayer without necessitating a reconfiguration of liturgical order or components.

Schmemann, the Church of Greece, and New Skete did not adopt the same approach to the liturgy because their reading of liturgical history led them to conclude that the liturgy developed in conjunction with the evolution of people's lives in particular historical periods, contexts, and regions. In fact, history demonstrates that there were examples of the radical reconfiguration of liturgical components and the provision for creativity where new prayers and hymns were added to the Church's existing corpus. This fundamental difference in the perception of the way liturgies develop inspired Schmemann and the Church of Greece to envision restorations which would affect the performance of the received tradition. Modest revisions to liturgical structures would facilitate the communication of the theology of the priesthood underpinning the liturgy.

The Eucharistic revival was symbolized by the faithful's frequent reception of Holy Communion, and other restorations were deemed possible, such as the celebration of Baptism with the Divine Liturgy. But Schmemann and the Church of Greece stopped short of a more surgical approach to reform, whereas New Skete embraced it. One of the chief reasons for a more conservative approach to liturgical reform is an understanding of the people's fixed perceptions of the liturgy on the part of Schmemann and those involved with renewal in the Church of Greece. The slow, careful approach to the liturgy emphasized liturgical catechesis of the laity by the clergy; once the clergy were equipped to explain the history and meaning of the liturgy to the people, they would be able to engage the central elements of liturgy within the received tradition. New Skete's approach stands in contrast to the other Orthodox models because they viewed the received tradition as having accumulated far too many superficial elements that concealed the inner meaning of liturgy; excision and the creation of new elements were the most effective ways to reconstruct the liturgy for the people's comprehension and engagement. New Skete enjoyed a privilege unavailable to the others: the monastic freedom to worship according to an order that diverged from the received tradition.

A Right Approach?

Given the multiple approaches adopted in liturgical renewal, is there one that stands out above the others? Have any of the models of liturgical renewal achieved their objectives? These questions are difficult to answer for several reasons, partially because the programs of liturgical renewal remain ongoing in several of the models we have examined. I will begin with the thorny issue of evaluating success.

Each model of reform has yielded a desired outcome. The models of Schmemann, the Church of Greece, and New Skete have contributed to a serious paradigm shift in Eucharistic participation and discipline. In North America and the West, the pattern of receiving Communion infrequently has given way to regular participation. Many clergy read prayers aloud for people to hear, and the encouragement of assembly participation in the liturgy has been enhanced by architectural innovations and the promotion of assembly singing. ROCOR has succeeded in developing a cadre of choral directors who are capable of developing parish music ministries that authentically lead worship by engaging the people as opposed to entertaining them.

An iconographic renaissance is also underway, as master iconographers who have retrieved the principles of Byzantine and medieval Russian iconography form apprentices who reshape the interior design of parish structures. The scope of renewal is somewhat limited, however, as noted by the symposia of the Church of Greece, since Orthodox liturgical reform has been largely limited to minority churches of the diaspora outside of the older autocephalous churches. The first outcome of both the conservative and assertive approaches to liturgical reform is that it is limited by region and philosophy within Orthodoxy. Unlike the prevailing perceptions of liturgy among Orthodox people, creating programs for liturgical renewal and implementing them is not universal.

For the Churches that implemented even limited renewal programs, the ultimate outcome was difficult to measure, because it could only be manifest by the fruits of ecclesial renewal, namely the building up of a royal kingdom and nation of priests that transformed and transfigured society. In other words, the only way to accurately assess liturgical renewal is through the fruits of the communities that have embraced it. The customary criteria for assessing such a program would examine areas such as parish growth, the creation and flourishing of new communities, solid financial stewardship.

In these areas, Orthodox churches tend to disappoint. Despite multiple influxes of converts into the Antiochian Archdiocese, OCA, and ROCOR, these churches have experienced attrition similar to the decline experienced by Reformed congregations in America.[4] Orthodoxy has also been no stranger to scandal, as all of these churches have experienced episodes of sexual abuse, financial corruption, and conflict between laity and episcopal leaders.[5] A superficial evaluation of liturgical reform performed through this prism might lead one to believe that renewal programs are impotent.

The aims of liturgical reform run much deeper than statistics measuring Church growth or breaking news on Church scandals could ever indicate. The aim of liturgical reform is repentance and conversion of the Christian who hears God inviting him or her to be a priest in his service. The Christian accepts this invitation and spends the rest of his or her lifetime claiming it and attempting to learn how

4. See the discussion of this matter in chapter 7.
5. See Nicholas Denysenko, "Rituals and Prayers of Forgiveness in Byzantine Lent," *Worship* 86 (2012): 140–60, and "Pastoral Principles for Orthodox Clergy in America," in William C. Mills, ed., *Church and World: Essays in Honor of Michael Plekon* (Rollinsford, NH: Orthodox Research Institute Press, 2013), 29–54.

to interiorize it. The transformation of the Christian into a Christ, an anointed one in God's service, does not occur instantaneously. It is instead a gradual process requiring the participant to hear and receive the invitation to be a priest over and over again, and to actively participate in the liturgy. As the participant attempts to embody these qualities taken from Jesus' humanity, he or she fails, only to return to the liturgy again, to begin the process of rehearsal anew.

The reality of the human participation in the liturgy is such that at any point, a participant can reject the divine invitation to be a priest in his service, or simply ignore it while focusing on other matters. Evaluating the success and impact of liturgical renewal will always be a tricky matter because the point of renewal is to create a clear path for God to communicate his invitation to serve the Church and the world in the liturgy; today, there is very little pastors can do to ensure that people will heed this divine invitation beyond joyously welcoming them. Attempts to coerce people through the threat of ecclesial interdict or personal humiliation is a gross violation of free human will to engage the liturgy, and it is this human will which requires the creation of a custom evaluative matrix for liturgical reform.

We can imagine the potential fruits of liturgical reform; here are a few examples of life situations that would indicate people who had interiorized liturgical renewal. A family that sings the core hymns of the Church together, by memory, manifests liturgical renewal. Men, women, and children who are happy to volunteer their time to help those in need express the values expressed by liturgical renewal. Men, women, and children who genuinely want to attend church because it is good to be there respond to God's invitation to assemble for worship, a sign of liturgical renewal. Men and women who work incessantly on their marital life without abandoning it when times get tough are rehearsing the commandment to love one another which is featured in liturgical renewal. Men and women who share their good fortune and yield with the less fortunate around them without asking for assistance are exercising priestly service to those in need, an important theme of liturgical renewal. Men, women, and children who work at developing their talents and share them freely with the world, especially in presenting innovative products and services that affirm life, are engaging the world as priests of the new creation as envisioned by liturgical renewal. Men, women, and children who voluntarily place themselves in unfamiliar environments as a response to discerning God's will for them are responding to the divine invitation featured in liturgical renewal. Men, women, and children who carry their crosses even through long, arid periods of divine silence are rehearsing the daily struggle to encounter God demanded by liturgical renewal. Men, women, and children who make time during the day to offer even feeble prayers on their own or in a group, despite the demands of a busy schedule, and living the liturgy in ordinary daily life. Men, women, and children who want to join a community in church even if they do not know them because they recognize that the opportunity to thank God in community is a privilege that many in the world do not enjoy, and that thanksgiving always precedes and shapes petition, are responding to God's invitation to assemble. All of these examples represent the interiorization of liturgical renewal in diverse ways.

One can recognize the fruits of liturgical renewal when one meets and greets people whose Paschal joy and immediate acceptance of others is simultaneously uplifting and infectious. The careful construction of a metric to evaluate programs of renewal is possible if an interdisciplinary study employing ethnographic methods attempts to measure the impact of liturgical participation on a variety of communities. The undertaking of such a project would be both worthy and also potentially enriching for those committed to the liturgical renewal enterprise.

I do not know if communities that have a critical mass of people who exhibit such behaviors employ any of the programs of liturgical renewal I have discussed here, but I am confident that such communities prioritized the theological rationale underpinning the models of liturgical renewal featured in this study, namely the invitation to become a priest of God and to live out one's priesthood in ordinary, daily life by receiving the divine energy emanating from active and conscious participation in the liturgy. Thus, the right approach to liturgical renewal begins with collaborative thinking about the theological rationale underpinning it.

Revising the Agenda for Liturgical Reform

In the preceding section, I stated that it is difficult to evaluate the effectiveness of a given program for liturgical reform because the Churches typically do not employ adequate assessment mechanisms. The primary problem with evaluating liturgical reform is that the mechanisms tend to have no reference whatsoever to the outcomes we have explicated above. In fact, the entire assessment enterprise is superficial because of a common ecumenical misinterpretation of the meaning of active participation in the liturgy. Christian obsession with liturgical aesthetics leads to the false conclusion that liturgy begins and ends with its sensory experience, which is essentially a betrayal of Christian anthropology.

In terms appropriate to liturgy, we feel relieved when a liturgical experience has unfolded in accordance with our expectations. I remember celebrating Pascha (Easter) in an Orthodox parish that had an elderly priest. As we processed around the Church, he expressed his joy that we were observing the proper order and that there was nothing out of place. His comment exemplifies a common pastoral reaction to liturgy. At liturgical celebrations of solemn seasons, we want everything to go well. It's important for the lectors to be prepared, for the music to be good so that people can leave the Church with a sense that it was good to be there.

In the Orthodox Church, no liturgy embodies this sense of liturgical satisfaction better than the hierarchical liturgy. The ritual performance of this service is exceedingly difficult for choir directors, singers, deacons, and subdeacons because of the elements from the Byzantine imperial court that have become affixed to the liturgy. When these liturgies have concluded, the prevailing sense among the clergy, servers, and singers is relief that we have survived. It is as if the desired outcome of the hierarchical liturgy is survival, not the deepening of the faithful's communion with one another and God.

The more liturgy is assessed from the perspective of instantaneous post-liturgical reaction, the more superficial the assessment becomes, and the theological foundations of liturgy are hopelessly obfuscated when this happens. Men and women leave church and thank the homilist for a good homily, and perhaps congratulate the musicians for an inspiring performance. There is no doubt that our models have focused on the *ars celebrandi* as a key for inaugurating the faithful into the deeper meaning of the liturgy, but the typical evaluative criterion remains at this superficial level which robs liturgy of its power to transform participants into the *christs* God has called them to become.

It is essential that proponents of liturgical reform toil towards the objective of changing the internal ecclesial culture into one that recognizes the desired outcome of liturgy: that her participants become priests who serve God in this world. Thus, the first part of the agenda is the most important point: pastors and theologians must recover the theological foundations of the liturgy, namely that Christ the high priest offers the liturgy to God with his concelebrants, the ordained and royal priests. Through their active participation in the liturgy, these priests are equipped to proclaim God's message of Paschal joy to the world. Recovering these theological foundations of liturgical reform requires asceticism on the part of pastors and theologians. We must relinquish our obsession with our favorite aspects of liturgy which we will fight tooth and nail to see favored in any given place and turn to these central theological foundation as the collective prism through which we approach the task of updating liturgical reform. For both Catholics and Orthodox, this task begins with learning the theological foundations of the liturgy anew.

The second task is to dig deeper into the nature of the liturgy and inquire about the existence of other theological foundations that have been mute, ignored, or underdeveloped for one reason or another. Beholding the enterprise of liturgical reform through a twenty-first-century lens could be a tremendous asset for this endeavor. Perhaps the greatest ecumenical contribution to the liturgical reform enterprise was the restoration of the dignity of the laity with multiple references to their royal, priestly, and prophetic dignity God bestowed on them in Baptism and Chrismation.

The reemergence of the laity as the first order of the Church reverberated throughout global Christianity and its manifestation was not limited to the Eucharistic revival and numerous instances of lay leadership exercised within the Church, but also in Church architecture, where new structures were deliberately designed to reduce the inherited tradition of physical barriers separating the clergy form the laity.[6] Despite the significant advancements made through the restoration of the laity, severe power struggles between clergy and laity continue to afflict Christian churches throughout the world. In the Orthodox world, the laity has exercised its dignity as the first order of the Church and has held the clergy accountable in

---

6. Jeanne Halgren Kilde, *Sacred Power, Sacred Space: An Introduction to Christian Architecture and Worship* (Oxford: Oxford University Press, 2008), 188–89.

select instances of scandal.[7] However, the tug of war between clergy and laity continues and the sacramental theology defining the laity as God's priests has not translated into more opportunities for the laity to participate in the governance of the Church. The vast majority of Orthodox Churches in the world privilege the synodal ecclesiological model, in which bishops make all decisions and issue all teachings on matters of faith and order.

Three steps are required to elevate the contribution of the laity to the Church's liturgical ministry. First, pastors and theologians must learn the theology of the priesthood of the laity thoroughly. Second, pastors and theologians need to identify ways in which ritual engagement faithfully fulfills the theological principle of the priesthood of the laity. Much progress has occurred in this area with the recitation of prayers aloud, the more frequent reception of communion, and the encouragement of congregational singing. Another step would be to reduce the distance between the laity and the clergy in liturgical celebration, primarily by having the whole assembly gathered in the same space without any physical barriers so that one experiences the liturgy with the clergy, and not merely by watching them.

The clergy's appointed liturgical roles should not change: the deacon should continue to lead the people in prayer, and the priest and bishop should continue to preside. Whenever possible, the clergy should stand with the people, which would require significant revision of the received tradition's rubrics, since the clergy's usual place is at the holy table in the sanctuary. It is possible to create innovative architectural designs for interior sacred space that honors the traditional tripartite structure of the Church (sanctuary, nave, and narthex), without creating too much separation between nave (occupied by the laity) and sanctuary.

7. See n. 5 above.

The third step in this process requires focused study on the orders of the church (bishop, priest, and deacon), their relationship with the laity, and their exercise of ministry with the laity. Several scholars have contributed landmark studies that inaugurated this process of reflection, especially Afanasiev, James Puglisi, Susan Wood, John Zizioulas, and John Chryssavgis.[8] New studies which define pastoral ministry in light of the priesthood of the laity can explain the distinctions between ecclesial orders while assisting the clergy in their primary task of promoting and building up the lay priesthood.

In addition to renewed studies on laity and clergy concelebration, a rejuvenated priesthood of the laity should lead to adjustments in the mechanism for implementing liturgical reform. The matter is elementary: the prominent theological stature of the laity in liturgical theology should be mirrored in the deliberative and implementation phases of reform. This is not an appeal to convert the process into a democratic deliberation where the laity has an equal vote in the process. I am urging both the Orthodox and Catholic churches to deliberately integrate laity into these processes so that their representation is consistently present throughout. Appeals to the clergy's representation of the laity are inadequate: the real presence of the laity and their contribution to the formation and implementation of every liturgical program should be threaded through the entirety of the process.

8. Nicholas Afanasiev, *The Church of the Holy Spirit*, ed. Michael Plekon, trans. Vitaly Permiakov (Notre Dame, IN: University of Notre Dame Press, 2007); James Puglisi, *The Process of Admission to Ordained Ministry: A Comparative Study*, 3 vols., trans. Michael Driscoll and Mary Misrahi, pref. by Hervé Legrand (Collegeville, MN: Liturgical Press, 1996); Susan Wood, *Sacramental Orders*, Lex Orandi Series, ed. John D. Laurance (Collegeville, MN: Liturgical Press, 2000); John Zizioulas, *Eucharist, Bishop, Church: The Unity of the Church in the Divine Eucharist and the Bishop During the First Three Centuries*, trans. Elizabeth Theokritoff (Brookline, MA: Holy Cross Orthodox Press, 2001); John Chryssavgis, *Remembering and Reclaiming Diakonia: The Diaconate Yesterday and Today* (Brookline, MA: Holy Cross Orthodox Press, 2009).

Liturgical Eschatology and Sacred Symbols

The next theological tenet requiring further study is the eschatological dimension of the liturgy. As with the priesthood of the laity, the *ressourcement* movement yielded an abundance of scholarship highlighting liturgical eschatology. For Catholics, the recovery of pneumatology and its careful integration into the liturgy made an enormous impact on the landscape of sacramental theology. Notable here are the seminal works of Odo Casel, Kevin Irwin and Louis Chauvet.[9] *SC* epitomizes the Catholic understanding of the liturgy when it says "in the earthly liturgy we take part in a foretaste of that heavenly liturgy which is celebrated in the holy city of Jerusalem toward which we journey as pilgrims, where Christ is sitting at the right hand of God, a minister of the holies and of the true tabernacle."[10] The inscription of a stronger eschatological dimension into Catholic liturgy occurred with the composition of new Eucharistic prayers, the addition of pneumatic epicleses, and other elements that communicate the notion of the Church as a body in motion, ascending toward the kingdom of God.

Orthodox theology has also recovered the eschatological dimension of the liturgy, with special deference to Schmemann, Zizioulas, Boris Bobrinskoy, and more recently, Petros Vassiliadis.[11]

---

9. Odo Casel, *The Mystery of Christian Worship, and Other Writings*, ed. Burkhard Neunheuser, preface by Charles Davis (Westminster, MD: Newman Press, 1962); Louis Chauvet, *The Sacraments: The Word of God at the Mercy of the Body*, trans. Madeleine Beaumont (Collegeville, MN: Liturgical Press, 2001); idem, *Symbol and Sacrament: A Sacramental Reinterpretation of Christian Existence*, trans. Patrick Madigan and Madeleine Beaumont (Collegeville, MN: Liturgical Press, 1995); Kevin Irwin, "A Sacramental World—Sacramentality As the Primary Language for Sacraments," *Worship* 76, no. 3 (2002): 197-211.

10. *SC* no. 8, Vatican Web Site, http://www.vatican.va/archive/hist_councils/ii_vatican_council/documents/vat-ii_const_19631204_sacrosanctum-concilium_en.html (accessed November 7, 2014).

11. For Schmemann and Vassiliadis, see chapters 3 and 5, respectively. For Bobrinskoy, see *The Mystery of the Trinity: Trinitarian Experience and Vision in the Biblical and Patristic Tradition*, trans. Anthony Gythiel (Crestwood, NY: St. Vladimir's Seminary Press, 1999).

The Orthodox mystagogical tradition had already privileged liturgical eschatology, epitomized by the reflection on the liturgy of St. Maximus Confessor.[12] Schmemann relentlessly referred to a restoration of eschatology as a theological correction of the tendency of theologians to reduce liturgy to an allegorized mimesis of the past.

These advances have reshaped the landscape of sacramental theology, but something is still amiss in liturgical eschatology. The most glaring evidence of a deficiency is the continued misinterpretation and erroneous apprehension, comprehension, and explanation of sacred symbols. In both the Catholic and Orthodox churches, discussions on symbols continue to concentrate on the distinction between symbol and reality, especially with reference to the matter of the true presence of Christ in the consecrated bread and cup of the Eucharist. Furthermore, the continued fascination with relics and their capacity to produce miracles suggests that the function of symbols in liturgy is magical.[13]

In my teaching experience, defining symbols with reference to narratives communicating salvation history (the past), contemporary life (the present), and the life to come (the future) discloses a prevailing sense of ignorance that classical Christian kerygma refers primarily to the future kingdom of God as the primary reality permeating all sacred symbols. In their respective essays, Zizioulas and Vassiliadis emphasize the tendency to ignore the future in interpreting symbols as the chief contributor to their decay in liturgical function. Following their lead, , theologians must find new and creative ways to teach symbols to varied audiences while also

12. Specifically, Maximus's mystagogy of the Church, in *Selected Writings*, trans. George C. Berthold, intro. Jaroslav Pelikan, preface by Ir'en'ee-Henri Dalmais (New York: Paulist Press, 1985).

13. For examples, see Jim Forest, "Icons and Miracles: An Intensity of Faith," *Christianity and Crisis* 45, no 9 (May 27, 1985): 201-5, and Wendy Slater, "Relics, Remains, and Revisionism: Narratives of Nicholas II in Contemporary Russia." *Rethinking History: The Journal of Theory and Practice* 9:1 (2005): 53-70.

developing innovative approaches to depicting them so that they convey Christian destiny and are not reduced to their accompanying historical period of the figures or events. The reinvigoration of this theological rationale and its integration into liturgical symbols is particularly crucial in the twenty-first-century milieu where each Christian encounters a flood of images on electronic devices daily, resulting in image oversaturation and overstimulation.

Women

No attention to the matter of continuing the restoration of the priesthood of the laity is complete without studying the role of women in the liturgy. The reforms implemented in our models have all yielded a significant increase in the role of women in liturgical ministry. In the Catholic Church, women can preside at offices of the Liturgy of the Hours and also on Sunday celebrations in the absence of a priest. Women can also assist in liturgical celebration by serving as acolytes and assisting with the distribution of Holy Communion as extraordinary ministers of the rite.

For a Church that steadfastly reserves ordination to the major orders for men only, women have advanced about as far as is possible in liturgical ministry in the Roman Church. Many voices within the Roman church continue to debate the possibility of ordaining women to the diaconate, with an assist from scholarship on women deacons in the Eastern churches.[14] Vatican II honored the catholicity of the Church by incorporating many elements from the Eastern ecclesial tradition into Roman practice. This precedent allows for the possibility of ordaining women to the diaconate in the Roman church.

The question of women and liturgy is more complicated in the

---

14. See Phyllis Zagano, *Women in Ministry: Emerging Questions About the Diaconate*, foreword by William T. Ditewig (New York: Paulist Press, 2012).

Orthodox Church because of the existence of a female diaconate in Orthodox history. An increase in women's leadership at the liturgy has not been commensurate with the restoration of the priesthood of the laity, the order to which women belong. Women are permitted to exercise two liturgical ministries that were once closed to them: choral leadership and chanting. Women's participation in chanting is somewhat misleading, as Orthodoxy has a minor order of reader which is typically reserved to men. Some women have been tonsured readers, and such instances have been criticized since the prayer for tonsuring a reader suggests that the reader might be ordained a priest.[15] In reality, one can exercise the ministries of reader without ever seeking ordination to the major orders, so an initial positive step that would manifest the fullness of the priesthood of the laity would be to admit women to this minor order so that they can exercise a ministry that is needed in parishes.[16]

But the integration of women into liturgical ministry should not end here. Women and girls should also be permitted to serve as acolytes and enter the sanctuary. Many Orthodox churches prohibit women from entering the sanctuary on account of rules of ritual impurity, a theological problem exacerbated by a limited episcopal directive in the United States that prohibited women from holding the cloth during Holy Communion.[17] The prohibition of women and girls from serving as acolytes depends on the faulty theology underpinning rules of ritual impurity and the dubious connection

15. For a discussion of this matter, see Nicholas Denysenko, "Towards an Agenda for Byzantine Pastoral Liturgy: A Response to Peter Galadza," *Bolletino della Badia Greca di Grottaferrata* 7 (2010): 60-62.
16. See "The Definition of the Sacred Council of the Orthodox Church of Russia on the Active Participation of Women in Various Areas of Church Ministry," in Hyacinthe Destivelle, *The Moscow Council (1917-1918): The Creation of the Conciliar Institutions of the Russian Orthodox Church*, ed. Michael Plekon and Vitaly Permiakov, trans. Jerry Ryan, foreword by Metropolitan Hilarion (Alfeyev) (Notre Dame, IN: University of Notre Dame Press, 2015).
17. See Nicholas Denysenko, "Liturgical Maximalism in Orthodoxy: A Case Study," *Worship* 87 (2013): 338-62.

between serving as an acolyte and seeking ordination to a major order.

In her scholarship, Vassa Larin has persuasively demythologized the taboos of ritual purity and thus liberated women from its prohibitions, which leaves no theological reason to exclude women from expanding their liturgical ministry.[18] In fact, the policies on women's participation in liturgical ministry are inconsistent within Orthodoxy, as some countries do not abide by the prohibitions. The insistence that Orthodox continue to exclude women from most liturgical ministries both violates the theology of the priesthood of the laity and results in blatant ecclesial misogyny.

To amend this theological deficiency, the Orthodox Churches should permit women to be tonsured as readers and serve as acolytes with no prohibitions. The Orthodox Church should also create a commission of pastors and theologians representing global Orthodoxy to take up the proposal of the Church of Greece to restore the female diaconate, especially since this major order has a reliable antecedent in Church history.[19] To honor the Church's tradition of engaging discourse on controversial matters, the Orthodox Church should continue to permit the scholarly study of the possibility of ordaining women to the presbytery, with Catholic theologians also invited to participate in this dialogue. Lastly, on the topic of women, the rejuvenation of the Christic offices of priest, prophet, and king was the primary impetus for the program of identity formation accompanying Baptism and Chrismation in the twentieth century. To grant women greater access to the gifts of the Spirit in the Church, Catholics and Orthodox should collaborate for the

18. See Vassa Larin, "What is Ritual Im/Purity and Why?" in *St. Vladimir's Theological Quarterly* 52, nos. 3-4 (2008), 275-92.
19. Phyllis Zagano, "Grant her Your Spirit," *America* (February 7, 2005), http://americamagazine.org / node / 147165 (accessed January 20, 2015).

expansion of liturgical vocabulary that is more gender inclusive by adding new terms to priest, prophet, and king.[20]

The Problem of Liturgiolatry

One of the most formidable and unexpected issues requiring assessment is the problem of liturgiolatry. The *ressourcement* and *Liturgiewissenschaft* movements have allowed liturgy to ascend to new heights among theologians, symbolized by SC's proclamation that the liturgy is the Church's summit and font from which her power flows. The development of liturgy as *theologia prima* is largely attributable to the school bearing the unofficial title of "Schmemann-Kavanagh-Lathrop-Fagerberg," and including many other pioneers such as Diekmann, Michel, and Irwin. This school of liturgical theology has a natural partner *in Liturgiewissenschaft*, which comprises a much larger school of scientists devoted to the craft of comparative liturgy. The work of comparative liturgists makes liturgical theology possible and enhances the notion that liturgy is the first order of theology.

The liturgical movement had a practical impact on the academy and the Church. *SC* had called for liturgical studies to take on much more prominence in seminary and graduate-level theological study so that even undergraduates in most Catholic universities take courses on liturgical history and theology. The academy fueled a new approach to educating people about the liturgy, which deviated from liturgy's former subservient position in systematic theology. In the Church, the rediscovery of the riches of liturgiology generated pastoral opportunities for catechesis. Furthermore, the capacity of liturgy to form people into God's priests who serve the world had

---

20. Nicholas Denysenko, *Chrismation: A Primer for Catholics* (Collegeville, MN: Liturgical Press, 2014), 196.

appeal, which reinforced the opportunity at every Sunday and feast. The translation of texts into the vernacular in both the Orthodox and Catholic churches expanded a comprehensive horizon. Texts which were either unheard or incomprehensible were now available to the faithful, aided (in some instances) by improvements in the performance of liturgical music.

The liturgical movement resulted in a type of convergence that placed an enormous burden of responsibility on the liturgy. Now that Vatican II had proclaimed the liturgy as source, summit, and font, the temptation to view the liturgy as the only impactful force in Christian life surfaced, despite the cautionary phrase of SC: "The sacred liturgy does not exhaust the entire activity of the Church." These are some of the factors contributing to what I am calling "liturgiolatry," which is a perception of the liturgy as the sole focus of Christian life.

It is tempting to view liturgiolatry as a sibling of liturgical maximalism, but liturgiolatry is a misinterpretation of classical liturgical theology laced with good intentions. Liturgiolatry is another candidate for an ethnographic study of pastoral practices and their impact on people. Pastors and laity know and recognize liturgiolatry because it is pervasive in ecclesial culture. For example, Orthodoxy privileges the role of hymnography in liturgy, as hymnography explains and proclaims dogma and salvation history while exhorting people to deepen their Christian commitments; it is a staple of the cycles of the liturgical year.

The discovery of the richness of liturgical sources has led some pastors to overestimate their power to convert the faithful. In Orthodoxy, it is not uncommon for a pastor to preach on the appointed hymns of the day for thirty minutes. Pastors are also prone to catechizing the people on the meaning of the liturgy during the course of its celebration, without considering the impact this has on the various levels of conscious engagement of ritual, combined with intellectual, personal, and emotional processing of messages. The recognition of the potential power of the liturgical year and the liturgy of the Hours leads some pastors to schedule as many liturgical offices as possible in a week and add as much content as they can to the Sunday service, followed by episodes of frustration when people leave early or fail to attend the services.

If the liturgical movement sought to move liturgy's position on the Christian pendulum to the most prominent position, in many cases, pastors perceived this shift as a domino effect where liturgy was the only domino standing at the end of the shift. Liturgiolatry is an attitude that views the Church's primary obligation as having to gather for liturgy, not only to honor God, but also to receive as much sanctification as possible. The negative consequence of liturgiolatry is the same as any idolatry: liturgy changed from an ideal to the utopian, and there was a significant difference between illusion and reality in the outcome.

The phrase from *SC* reminds the reader of the limits of liturgy, and pastors and theologians would be wise to heed the lessons from the phrase. *Liturgiewissenschaft* unleashed a new movement of mystagogy that informed people on the power and meaning of the liturgy. The time to update this approach has arrived, and an important part of the agenda for revision is to begin the process of creating a new mystagogy where the domestic shapes the liturgical as much as the liturgical shapes the domestic.

The new mystagogy will be founded upon two guiding principles: to initiate the faithful and seekers into the communion of the Holy Spirit, and to introduce them to the God who alone can save their souls. For this reason, I propose that the Orthodox and Catholic churches create a new program of parish mystagogy that we might view as a new branch that strengthens pastoral ministry. The task of translating *Liturgiewisscenschaft* into pastoral ministry is ongoing and must continue.[21] The liturgy is the primary event of encounter, not only of a meeting between God and his people, but also between the pastor and people, and the people with one another.

Mystagogy's native home is liturgy and liturgical renewal is the ministerial branch best equipped to form people into faithful citizens of God's kingdom. As a branch in the liturgical renewal movement, the new mystagogy is designed to reach people wherever they are: we might think of the branch as a liturgical one that performs its task even when the faithful are not gathered for liturgy. The liturgy is the primary source and inspiration for this mystagogical method, but in this scheme, liturgy is larger than sacraments or the celebration of divine offices. Liturgy is all of life, even ordinary daily life, so that the people partake of liturgy at home, work, school, and in social gatherings.

I am not attempting to blur the distinction between liturgical and domestic gatherings, but to remove circumscription from liturgy, so that liturgy is empowered to permeate each aspect of ordinary, daily life. This approach would strengthen the connection between liturgy and life and enable pastors to effectively communicate the reality that one can be truly and fully Christian in everything that one does; that being Christian is not limited to the number of prostrations one performs or the number of canons one prays before receiving Holy Communion. I am proposing an initial program for parish mystagogy which occurs in seven steps. The steps are as follows: first, demystify sacred space by extending its utility as a place of encounter and openness, where every aspect of personal, domestic, and community life can be openly addressed. Pastors should consider convoking assemblies of people into the church for non-liturgical gatherings, to show that the sacred space of the Church is not

---

21. The essays honoring Maxwell Johnson's contributions to the academy and the Churches are designed to produce such outcomes. See *A Living Tradition*, ed. Pitt, Alexopoulos, McConnell.

threatened by the profanity of the world. The sacred space of the Church can and should become a place of honest dialogue and discussion about people's daily experiences and struggles. We live in an epoch of query and questioning, and understanding is at a premium because the dissemination and circulation of information includes much misinformation. If local parish communities can become places where honest discourse about the topics of our epoch (such as sexuality, economics, gender, marriage, and so on) can occur without fear, then sacred space will be demystified and can become a place where people feel as if they belong, even if they do not fit the paradigm perfectly.[22]

Second, create a Typikon that presents liturgical structures corresponding to peoples' lives and celebrate liturgy based on the abilities and competence of available personnel. The requirements of many of our liturgical offices are arduous because the received liturgical tradition is a hybrid of monastic and cathedral, with the monastic dominating liturgical performance. I have visited many parishes where the community tries to observe the requirements of the Typikon but lacks the resources; I have also been in parishes where the community simply cannot fulfill the demands of the liturgical schedule because of work commitments or commuting distance. In the current environment, pastors should be encouraged to adjust liturgical offices so that the community can actually be present and come away with joy. Coming away from liturgy stunned by cacophony or feeling guilty because of time constraints does not amount to a joyous encounter. Pastors should consider adjusting the liturgy in accordance with the desired outcome: that people would go home adjusting to God's presence and prompted to respond,

22. Another example, even though it makes me uncomfortable as a father of a young daughter: perhaps church is the safest place for our adolescents to ask questions about sex without fear of punishment or shame?

instead of distracted by a poor or unsuitable liturgical performance.[23] The principle pastors should consider is to make liturgy memorable. When faithful remember participating in the liturgy, this memory has inaugurated the process of enfleshing and interiorizing the divine-human synergy of the liturgy itself. This study has noted the revisions of the Typikon that occurred in the Ecumenical Patriarchate in the nineteenth century. The figures who authorized the revision recognized the need for a parish practices that are possible. The revisions made to the Typikon were relatively insignificant. My recommendations for the creation of a new parish Typikon envisions the deconstruction of the current Typikon and careful reconstruction of a parish rule that is based on the core of the received tradition. The outcome of this revision would illuminate new and more obvious differences between monastic and parish liturgy. The undertaking of such a project should occur at local levels and require the collaborative study and contributions of a variety of international theologians with a background in liturgics and vast experience in pastoral liturgy. Such a team must also include men and women from the laity and practicing musicians since a revised parish Typikon would significantly impact their experience of worship. To honor the hopeful appearance and development of this project, I will not flesh out an exhaustive list of desiderata here, but will instead begin with a short list of principles and areas of the Typikon that demand our attention:

23. By adjustment, I have in mind Aidan Kavanagh's description of a liturgical act: "A liturgical act *is* a theological act of the most all-encompassing, integral, and foundational kind. It is both precipitator and result of that adjustment to the change wrought in the worshiping assembly by its regular encounter in faith with its divine Source. This adjustment to God-wrought change is no less critical and reflective an act of theology than any other of the secondary sort. Unlike these, however, it is *proletarian* in the sense that it is not done by academic elites; it is *communitarian* in the sense that it is not undertaken by the scholar alone in his study; and it is *quotidian* in the sense that it is not accomplished occasionally but regularly throughout the daily, weekly, and yearly round of the assembly's life of public liturgical worship," in Kavanagh, *On Liturgical Theology* (New York: Pueblo, 1984), 89.

1. Autocephalous churches would adopt and implement the creation of the parish Typikon since the areas demanding the most rigorous revision will be common to all Orthodox churches, in all likelihood;

2. The underlying assumption is that the parish Typikon will refer to the received liturgical tradition as the basic liturgical core, to ensure the best chance of the Church's reception of the parish Typikon; the creation of a new Typikon will inaugurate a spirit of freedom which permits the Church to respond to pastoral needs by revising the liturgy with more surgery in the future, if necessary;

3. Furthermore, a slightly more conservative approach will ease the process of learning the *ars celebrandi* necessary to celebrate the new parish Typikon;

4. Each parish Typikon will be structured so that certain liturgical elements can be customized by a parish in accordance with their ability to perform particular rites;

5. The first and foremost liturgical element to be addressed is the Church lectionary.[24] The principle to be implemented in the parish Typikon is to increase the place of the proclamation of the word of God in liturgical celebration and improve biblical literacy by broadening the lectionary and integrating more Scripture into the weekly and seasonal cycles of the Church year. Features of the revised lectionary would include one Old Testament lesson for each Divine Liturgy, the removal of lessons that are repeated and their replacement with new material, and the study of the balance of New Testament books in the annual cycle;

24. New Skete Monastery has constructed a revised lectionary for the liturgical year through a gradual process lasting more than thirty-five years. See Chapter 6, n. 35 for a brief description of their lectionary.

6. The following elements of the Divine Liturgy would be examined: study groups will consider a variety of possibilities to encourage a more tangible participation of the laity in the performance of the offering;[25] the ritual performance of the entrances should involve movement throughout the entirety of the church building; several options should be permitted for the number of hymns taken after the Little Entrance (parishes which prefer a more complete observance of the current Typikon would have the option of retaining that practice); the litanies following the homily can be adjusted; all commemorations should be restored to their proper place at concluding the anaphora, entailing the removal of commemorations at the Great Entrance; and the repetitions between the two litanies of supplication will be removed (the litany before the "Our Father" should be the one chanted in its entirety);

7. The parish Typikon would include an option for a Vesperal Liturgy to be celebrated for each feast of the liturgical year;[26]

8. Options for the number of hymns to be taken at various portions of the divine offices would be established. This revision is especially crucial for parishes lacking the musical competence to sing several hymns set to varying tones. The principle of balancing hymnography with psalmody should also be applied here.

It is essential to note that individual clergy and parishes already

---

25. A good example here is Robert Taft's suggestion to place the Prothesis chamber (the place where the ministers prepare the bread and cup for the liturgy) near the entrance of the Church to encourage greater lay participation in this action. See Taft, *A History of the Liturgy of St. John Chrysostom*, vol. 2: *The Great Entrance, A History of the Transfer of Gifts and Other Pre-anaphoral Rites,* 4th ed., Orientalia christiana analecta 200 (Rome: Pontifical Oriental Institute, 2004), 427-28.

26. The celebration of festal Vesperal liturgies has been a controversial topic in the Orthodox Church. For background, see Denysenko, "Liturgical Maximalism in Orthodoxy," 349-53.

employ many of the revisions I have suggested here. Some parishes limit the number of litanies taken after the Gospel at the liturgy; other parishes sing the first three hymns assigned to Psalm 140 at Vespers; many communities only sing the first, third, sixth, and ninth odes of the canons at Orthros. In any given parish, the priest may perform the great entrance through the entirety of the Church. These are all examples of local fine-tuning of the liturgy that occur in response to need. Some of the practices are more widespread (e.g., the omission of litanies after the Gospel). Scholars and pastors disagree on the motivation for implementing local changes: some would attribute such decisions to clerical vanity, whereas others would describe them as a normal pastoral response motivated by necessity.

The creation of a Typikon that allows for options in these areas meets the needs of diverse congregations. Small parishes lacking experienced singers can learn the core liturgical elements without the added strain of singing numerous consecutive hymns in different tones. Maximalist congregations that want to observe the fullness of the Typikon can live in accordance with the ideal. The key factor is to honor unwritten liturgical reform by permitting it in print and perfecting it by bringing such elements to teams for study and feedback.

We have already seen that theologians and pastors perceive liturgical books as bearing the authority of the whole Church. Legalizing liturgical diversity in accordance with parish need can significantly contribute to the demythologizing of liturgical uniformity as required by the canons while permitting parishes to retain a sense of their liturgical identity. The creation of such Typika would also liberate both parishes and monasteries from the permanence of liturgical fusion. History has demonstrated how and why the monastic and cathedral traditions were fused, with the monastic preferred, but moving forward, it would be preferable to liberate both traditions from coerced cross-pollination which permits that process to occur organically while facilitating more freedom within the monastic and parish environments.

Third, fine-tune liturgy so that it is done well and allow the liturgy and its structures to speak for themselves so that it is memorable. The principle pastors should consider is to make liturgy memorable. When faithful remember participating in the liturgy, this memory has inaugurated the process of enfleshing and interiorizing the divine-human synergy of the liturgy itself. If sensory overstimulation and information overload are problems, as I claim they are, pastors might consider fine-tuning the liturgy to emphasize retention of key themes and ideas so that they might shape one's consciousness and heart. For example, encourage music that everyone can sing so that they will remember the short refrains, litanies, and psalmody of our ritual.

Fourth, accentuate the domestic dimension of Christian life. My primary concern here is not the protection of marital and family life, but encouraging awareness that domestic life is essentially liturgical and a participation in the divine life of God. In fact, it is domestic activity that shapes the liturgical. We prepare a table and share food and drink at the Eucharist because these are domestic realities on which our physical and social lives depend.[27] We take a cleansing bath in Baptism because we wash domestically. There are numerous strategies pastors might employ to awaken an awareness of relational living and becoming at home (meaning that one continues the process of becoming Christian while at home). Pastors should encourage families to optimize the time they spend together at table and view sharing meals as a microcosm of the Eucharist. I am not

---

27. Irwin, "A Sacramental World," 197-211; Peter Bouteneff, "Sacraments as the Mystery of Union: Elements in an Orthodox Sacramental Theology," in *The Gestures of God: Explorations in Sacramentality*, ed, Geoffrey Rowell and Christine Hall (London, New York: Routledge, 2004), 91-108.

encouraging anyone to claim that a family meal of fish sticks and *piroshky* is the Eucharist. This is a way of breaking open the real relational dynamics that occur at table when people merely share the banal reports of their ordinary days while breaking bread.

The banal act of listening briefly to another is a relational icon of God hearing our petitions. An awareness of the power of sharing and just being with the other in a domestic setting can open into a recognition of one's identity as a Christian playing out in ordinary daily life. A pastor can apply this one example to multiple domestic activities. The point of such exercises is not to attempt to locate liturgical rituals in domestic activities, but rather to magnify domestic relationships as living out the liturgy in daily life. The central point of the exercise is to equip people to recognize that they are being Christian in every facet of daily life, and that the rituals one rehearses in church (e.g., exchanging the kiss of peace, processing in line together to receiving communion) are relevant and shape the way one lives life, so that the domestic becomes the liturgical.

Fifth, adopt St. Maria Skobtsova's challenge of the Church engaging the world. This step is based upon St. Maria Skobtsova's important essay on human communion.[28] In this essay, St. Maria caricatures the Orthodox notion of "churching" as a reduction, where one takes pride in having constructed a small chapel at home, thus churching it. St. Maria challenges the reader to follow the primary example of Christ, who completely poured himself out for the life of the world, without reserving anything for himself. She states that the notion of Eucharistic sacrifice might be adopted in such a way that Orthodox faithful enact mimesis and pour themselves out for the other.[29] St. Maria refers to the powerful imagery of the iconostasis

28. *Mother Maria Skobtsova: Essential Writings,* trans. Richard Pevear and Larissa Volokhonsky, intro. Jim Forest, Modern Spiritual Master Series (Maryknoll, NY: Orbis, 2003), 75-83.
29. Ibid., 78.

and challenges people to view the world itself as an iconostasis; the people adorning the iconostasis are actually the ones who annoy us, the different other who is not like-minded.[30] St. Maria's reference to the Eucharist as the primary source for reconciliation and developing one's veneration of the image of God seated in the other is an essential mystagogy that illuminates the Eucharist as a sacrament that builds up community for the common good, as opposed to a brief, private event between the communicant and God.

Sixth, emphasize thanksgiving in liturgical celebration. Most people approach liturgy in a spirit of petition, asking God to grant their requests. Petition is a staple of liturgical practice, along with thanksgiving. People tend to attend liturgy with fervor and enthusiasm in times of personal or community difficulty, to petition God to make things better. However, the hegemony of petition in liturgy has the unfortunate theological effect of depicting God as a divine problem solver or one who grants miraculous healings to the worthy.

Almost the entirety of Christian history has emphasized petition over thanksgiving in liturgy. Pastors and theologians should reconfigure the relationship so that thanksgiving establishes petition, which honors the anamnetic repository of Christian history. Liturgy that consistently communicates thanksgiving depicts God as the divine Philanthropist, the gift-giver who loves humankind through all joys and sorrows. Thanksgiving and petition can be practiced anywhere, but making thanksgiving primary encourages the people to assemble and makes their petitions more meaningful.

Seventh, demonstrate the power of epiclesis in ordinary life. My seventh and initially final step draws from the liturgical practice of invoking the descent of the Holy Spirit upon the assembly. The twentieth century experienced such a strong pneumatological revival

30. Ibid., 80-81.

and appreciation for its integration into the liturgy that we occasionally reduce Christianity to liturgical celebration. All of us, clergy included, must live our lives with family, friends, colleagues, and a litany of formidable challenges. Many of us are frustrated by the imperfections of our lives. We want better relations with our family and friends; we want to advance in our careers; we want deliverance from addictions and vices; we want to become the people God has called us to become. It can be disappointing when we invest solely in church attendance and find that liturgy is not magic, that the process of working out each angle of salvation continues in the many hours we spend outside of Church.

God sends the Spirit on us for this very purpose: to work out our salvation when we are not in church. The point of the descent of the Spirit is for the Spirit to be with us in those banal moments of having a tough discussion with our spouse, trying to figure out how to say "no" to an unreasonable request from the boss, conjuring up the courage to ask our children for forgiveness when we have been impatient with them, and acting charitably toward our neighbors whose branches fall on our lawns or whose parties keep us awake at night. In other words, we begin the process of rehearsing Christian identity when we participate in liturgy; that process intensifies during the week when we go about our business. The process is like a journey, but the destination is not one we can earn; it is given to us by God, in the second coming.

Graduate and Post-graduate Formation of the Clergy

Among the commonalities shared by our five models is the role of the clergy in liturgical reform. The local parish clergy are the gatekeepers of parish life and the primary Church leaders who the people come to know. Seminary education offers an introduction to liturgical history and theology with a crash course in liturgics. While such courses are foundational and necessary, they simply cannot offer the detail and texture clergy need to understand to enrich their own liturgical presidency.

There are two factors complicating the liturgical formation of the clergy. First, as Schmemann's courses indicate, clergy have to adjust their liturgical presidency upon arriving in the local parish. In such instances, implementing every principle of reform or renewal becomes difficult if pastoral emergencies take precedence or the local parish liturgical tradition cannot accommodate reform. Second, and most important, because the Church is a community of people who live in the present, clergy must find creative ways to modify liturgical elements so that they cohere with the life of the community.

As a community, the Church is growing and becoming shaped by (for better or for worse) its local and global environments. It is not sufficient to refer to a model that excelled in a different time and place. Most clergy cannot rely on their own skills to modify liturgy that retains the core of their native tradition (e.g., Roman or Byzantine) while simultaneously developing organically in concert with the local cultural environment. For this reason, Church leaders and theologians should devote resources for the ongoing education of clergy in liturgical formation and presidency. Such programs must be built upon the principles that honor the theological foundations of the liturgy and do not attempt to constrict the Church from offering her liturgy in motion, as she evolves in time.

Another essential component of the formation of clergy who are able to liturgize in the spirit of renewal is to permit creativity and innovation. If pastors and theologians offer communities freedom to discover liturgical orders that are gifts from the Spirit, liturgical centers will emerge that respond to contemporary conditions and times with divine grace. It is tempting to list concrete examples of needed innovations, but this would betray the spirit of the liturgy in motion, as my suggestions could become irrelevant in a matter of months. Kevin Irwin has recently published a reflection on the ongoing work needed for the Roman communion, and I refer readers to his book for the suggestions.[31] I will offer a few suggestions for the Orthodox Church that honor the theological principles I have privileged throughout this study:

1. The current liturgy is overrun with hymnography, which overshadows the proclamation of God's word in the liturgy. In the received tradition, the people experience a detailed poetic reflection on Scripture and sanctoral narratives with only a sampling of the word of God proclaimed. Orthodox scholars and pastors should begin the process of lectionary reform which will enhance the Church's hearing of God's word and create a real balance between the proclamation of Scripture in liturgy and hymnographical reflection on that Scripture—New Skete's revised lectionary for Holy Week and Pascha establishes a potentially modular pattern for this task.

2. The Liturgy of the Hours requires rehabilitation. This need is even more dire in the Roman communion, but also necessary for Orthodoxy. Orthodox people are generally deprived of the Liturgy of the Hours, yet seem to find it an engaging experience when they are able to participate. Most parishes will not observe the monastic rule for the Liturgy of the Hours; pastors and theologians might revise the rule so that monthly services might be celebrated in one parish with nearby communities invited, perhaps in conjunction with a lecture, concert, or liturgical remembrance of the dead. Furthermore, there is an unofficial grassroots movement among Orthodox where the laity gathers for the liturgy of the Hours without an ordained presider.

---

31. Kevin Irwin, *What We Have Done, What We Have Failed to Do: Assessing the Liturgical Reforms of Vatican II* (New York: Paulist Press, 2013).

Pastors and theologians should encourage the continuation of this practice and consider creating a variety of downloadable offices a group might use for prayer to be followed by fellowship.

3. The Orthodox Church should consider increasing its repository of new prayers used for several liturgies. The current reliance of the Church on the liturgies of Chrysostom and Basil limits the people's exposure to the broader liturgical tradition. The reintroduction of the liturgy of St. James into the life of the Orthodox Church has proven to be positive, and Orthodox leaders should consider making the liturgy of St. James a part of the regular rotation of Sunday celebrations. Furthermore, pastors and leaders should affirm the possibility of celebrating Vesperal liturgies in parishes to encourage the people to gather when they are able to. All Orthodox churches compose new offices of the sanctoral cycle which follow established patterns in the received tradition, but Orthodoxy should seize the spirit exhibited by New Skete and the Roman church by composing a variety of new prayers and hymns for the liturgy—even Eucharistic prayers.

4. Orthodoxy has employed communion via intinction and imparted with a spoon since the tenth century.[32] New Skete's modification of the communion rite which requires everyone to receive from the hand of another, to realize the Eucharist as a gift received and not given to one's self, is modular and should be considered for adoption. Orthodoxy should consider restoring the older form of the rite of communion where all the people receive the Lord's body and blood separately. The adoption of this form would honor the theological principle of

---

32. Robert F. Taft, "Byzantine Communion Spoons: A Review of the Evidence," *Dumbarton Oaks Papers* 50 (1996), 209-38.

the priesthood of the laity, which would be reinforced by the clergy's rehearsal of receiving communion.

Relativism, Minimalism, or Something Else?

The attentive reader will note that the liturgical reforms I have recommended for the Orthodox Churches favor the principles employed by New Skete in their reform. I have essentially illuminated the model Thomas Pott presents of modifying the liturgy for the sake of the people, as opposed to converting the people to the liturgy.[33] I have made this conscious selection because the liturgy is a work of God that was founded by Christ's incarnation as a human being who lived among particular people and spoke their language, and shared their culture. The same Christ speaks to every culture through their idioms of communication and ritual. The received Byzantine tradition is varied and has evolved in dialogue with local cultures. Many elements of liturgy are universal, including the basic order of each rite, but there are also many movable and adjustable parts, a process of liturgical development evidenced by the contributions of liturgical historians.[34]

My recommendations are motivated by the aspects of globalization impacting most cultures, including increasing demands of employment, congested traffic patterns, time conflicts, and the maintenance of social networks. My recommendation to reduce the number of hymns is not motivated by some deficiency in hymnography, but by my conviction that participants should not be overwhelmed with too many messages in a given liturgy, and that hymnography not supersede the proclamation of God's word. The laity's ability to receive God's invitation to be his priests and

---

33. Pott, 95-96.
34. See Maxwell Johnson, "Can We Avoid Relativism in Worship? Liturgical Norms in the Light of Contemporary Liturgical Scholarship," *Worship* 74, no. 2 (2000): 135-55.

serve him through active liturgical participation is the overarching principles guiding each recommendation.

If parishes attempted to implement these principles, their liturgies would probably be shorter and have less overall content. The actual outcome might bear the appearance of minimalism, which could lead one to interpret my proposed enterprise as relativistic. This is not my intent; I envision a liturgy that is possible, where the outcome can be accurately described as edifying and inspiring, and not burdensome or difficult to comprehend. Essentially, I am recommending retention of the received tradition with some serious trimming and reconfiguration that allow the theological foundations of the liturgy to shine forth with clarity to the participants. In this sense, this proposed revision would result in a restoration of the liturgy to its fullness because its parts would work together in a more pleasant harmony, without unnecessary dissonance.

There are many other areas of liturgy that need to be addressed, and my hope is that readers committed to liturgical renewal will seriously consider the principles I have identified as common to the Orthodox and Catholic traditions and apply them with renewed vigor to their own communions. It is possible for Christians to work together in the enterprise of liturgical renewal, because the accomplishments of Vatican II not only impacted Orthodoxy, but were also a result of earnest dialogue with the East, as I hope to have demonstrated. I hope that I have also persuaded the reader that Christianity has benefited from the liturgical reforms attributed to Vatican II, but must free herself from the inertia inadvertently created by the Council. The community of the Church offers the liturgy, and the liturgy must be adjusted because the community changes as it evolves in time, place, and space. An ecumenical commitment to reinvigorating the principles of liturgical reform yielded by this study has the capacity to begin achieving the desired outcomes of liturgical reform: the creation of a global church that receives and interiorizes its priestly identity and serves the world in the spirit of Paschal joy. This outcome is admittedly bold and perhaps utopian, but I continue to believe that it is possible because there have been episodes in contemporary history where the Church has fomented change by making God present through active liturgical participation; for this and for what is yet to come, we have reason to be thankful.

Bibliography

Afanasiev, Nicholas. *The Church of the Holy Spirit*. Edited by Michael Plekon and Vitaly Permiakov. Notre Dame, IN: University of Notre Dame Press, 2007.

―――――. *Трапеза Господня* (The Lord's Supper). Kyiv: Temple of the Venerable Agapit of the Caves, 2003.

Alexopoulos, Stefanos. "Did the Work of Fr. Alexander Schmemann Influence modern Greek Theological Thought? A Preliminary Assessment." *St. Vladimir's Theological Quarterly* 53, nos. 2-3 (2009): 273-99.

―――――. "The State of Modern Greek Liturgical Studies and Research: A Preliminary Survey." In *Inquiries into Eastern Christian Worship*, Selected Papers of the Second International Congress of the Society of Oriental Liturgy, Rome, 17-21 September 2008, edited by Bert Groen, Steven Hawkes-Teeples, and Stefanos Alexopoulos, 375-92. Eastern Christian Studies 12. Leuven: Peeters, 2012.

Anashkin, D. P., ed. *Законодательство Русской Православной Церкви Заграницей (1921-2007) (Legislation of the Russian Orthodox Church Outside of Russia, 1921-2007)*. Moscow: Foundation of Russian History, Publication of St. Tikhon's Orthodox University, 2013.

Arjakovsky, Antoine. *The Way: Religious Thinkers of the Russian Emigration in Paris and Their Journal, 1925-1940*. Edited by John Jillions and Michael

Plekon. Translated by Jerry Ryan. Foreword by Rowan Williams. Notre Dame, IN: University of Notre Dame Press, 2013.

Artemov, Nikolai. "О сотериологии митрополита Антония (Храповицкого)" ("On the Soteriology of Metropolitan Antonii (Khrapovitsky))." In *Metropolitan Antonii (Khrapovitskii): Archpastor of the Russian Diaspora*, ed. Vladimir Tsurikov, 19-68. Readings in Russian Religious Culture 5. Jordanville, NY: Foundation of Russian Culture, 2014.

Athanasopoulou-Kypriou, Spyridoula. "Emancipation through Celibacy? The Sisterhoods of the Zoe Movement and the Role in the Development of 'Christian Feminism' in Greece, 1938-1960." In *Innovation in the Orthodox Tradition? The Question of Change in Greek Orthodox Thought and Practice*, edited by Trine Stauning-Willert and Lina Molokotos-Lierman, 101-21. Aldershot, Burlington: Ashgate, 2012.

Aune, Michael. "Liturgy and Theology: Rethinking the Relationship, Part 1, Setting the Stage." *Worship* 81, no. 1 (2007): 46-68.

Balashov, Nikolai. *На пути к литургическому возрождению (On the Path of Liturgical Renewal)*. Moscow: Round Table on Religious Education and Service, 2001.

Baldovin, John. "An Active Presence: the Liturgical Vision of Vatican II 50 Years Later." *America* 208, no. 18 (May 27, 2013): 11-14.

————. *Reforming the Liturgy: A Response to the Critics*. Collegeville, MN: Liturgical Press, 2008.

Beal, Rose. "Priest, Prophet and King: Jesus Christ, the Church and the Christian Person." In *John Calvin's Ecclesiology: Ecumenical Perspectives*, edited by Gerard Mannion and Eddy van der Borght, 90-106. London, New York: T & T Clark, 2011.

Belcher, Kimberly. *Efficacious Engagement: Sacramental Participation in the Trinitarian Mystery*. Collegeville, MN: Liturgical Press, 2011.

Berrios, Fernando. "The Liturgy in the Vatican Council II: Bases, Implications and Challenges of Reform." *TEOLOGIA Y VIDA* 55, no. 3 (2014): 517-47.

Bertonière, Gabriel. *The Historical Development of the Easter Vigil and Related Services in the Greek Church*. Orientalia christiana analecta 193. Rome: Pontifical Oriental Institute, 1972.

Bobrinskoy, Boris. *The Mystery of the Trinity: Trinitarian Experience and Vision in the Biblical and Patristic Tradition*. Translated by Anthony P. Gythiel. Crestwood, NY: St. Vladimir's Seminary Press, 1999.

Bordeianu, Radu. "(In)Voluntary Ecumenism: Dumitru Staniloae's Interaction with the West as Open Sobornicity." In *Orthodox Constructions of the West*, edited by George Demacopoulos and Aristotle Papanikolaou, 240-53. New York: Fordham University Press, 2013.

Bouteneff, Peter. "Sacraments as the Mystery of Union: Elements in an Orthodox Sacramental Theology." In *The Gestures of God: Explorations in Sacramentality*, edited by Geoffrey Rowell and Christine Hall, 91-108. London, New York: Routledge, 2004.

Bradshaw, Paul and Maxwell Johnson. *The Eucharistic Liturgies: Their Evolution and Interpretation*. Collegeville, MN: Liturgical Press, 2012.

Bresciani, David. "La reception de la théologie liturgique du père Alexandre Schmemann dans l'Église catholique romaine." In *La joie du Royaume: Actes du colloque international "l'heritage du père Alexandre Schmemann," Paris, 11-14 décembre 2008*, edited by André Lossky et al., 196-202. Paris: YMCA Press, 2012.

Butler Bass, Diana. *Christianity for the Rest of Us: How the Neighborhood Church is Transforming the Faith*. New York: HarperOne, 2006.

Calabretta, Rose B. *Baptism and Confirmation: The Vocation and Mission of the Laity in the Writings of Virgil Michel*. Tesi gregoriana, Serie Teologia 47. Rome: Gregorian University Press, 1998.

Calivas, Alkiviadis. *Essays in Theology and Liturgy*, vol. 3: *Aspects of Orthodox Worship*. Brookline, MA: Holy Cross Orthodox Press, 2003.

————. *Great Week and Pascha in the Greek Orthodox Church*. Brookline, MA: Holy Cross Orthodox Press, 1992.

Chauvet, Louis. *Symbol and Sacrament: A Sacramental Reinterpretation of Christian Existence.* Translated by Patrick Madigan and Madeleine Beaumont. Collegeville, MN: Liturgical Press, 1995.

_____. *The Sacraments: The Word of God at the Mercy of the Body.* Translated by Madeleine Beaumont. Collegeville, MN: Liturgical Press, 2001.

Chryssavgis, John. *Remembering and Reclaiming Diakonia: The Diaconate Yesterday and Today.* Brookline, MA: Holy Cross Orthodox Press, 2009.

Chupungco, Anscar. *Liturgical Inculturation: Sacramentals, Religiosity, and Catechesis.* Collegeville, MN: Liturgical Press, 1992.

_____. *What, Then, is Liturgy? Musings and Memoir.* Collegeville, MN: Liturgical Press, 2010.

Clément, Olivier. "Vers un dialogue avec le catholicisme." *Contacts* 14 (1965): 16-37.

Congar, Yves. *At the Heart of Christian Worship: Liturgical Essays of Yves Congar.* Edited and translated by Paul Philibert. Collegeville, MN: Liturgical Press, 2010.

_____. *Lay People in the Church: A Study for the Theology of the Laity.* Translated by Donald Attwater. Westminster, MD: Newman Press, 1957, 1963 reprint.

_____. *My Journal of the Council.* Translated by Mary John Ronayne and Mary Cecily Boulding. Edited by Dennis Minns. Collegeville, MN: Liturgical Press, 2012.

_____. "Sur la trilogie: prophìte-roi-prêtre." *Revues des sciences philosophiques et théologiques* 67 (1983): 97-115.

Constantelos, Demetrios. "The Zoe Movement in Greece." *St. Vladimir's Theological Quarterly* 3 (1959): 11-25.

Corner, Martin. "Protection, Autonomy and Reform: the Russian Orthodox Church 1905-29." *Sobornost* 10 no 1 (1988): 6-21.

Cunningham, James. "Reform Projects of the Russian Orthodox Church at the Beginning of the Twentieth Century." In *The Legacy of St. Vladimir: Byzantium, Russia, America*, edited by John Breck, John Meyendorff, and Eleana Silk, 107-38. Crestwood, NY: St. Vladimir's Seminary Press, 1990.

_____. *A Vanquished Hope: The Movement for Church Renewal in Russia, 1905-1906.* Crestwood, NY: St. Vladimir's Seminary Press, 1981.

De Clerck, Paul. "The Liturgical Reform of Vatican II: Why Has It Only Been Partially Received?" *Worship* 88, no. 2 (2014): 170-77.

_____ and André Haquin, "La constitution Sacrosanctum Concilium et sa mise en œuvre: une réception toujours en cours." *Revue Théologique De Louvain* 44, no. 2 (April 2013): 171-96.

De Lubac, Henri. *The Splendour of the Church.* Trans. Michael Mason. New York: Sheed and Ward, 1956.

Demacopoulos, George and Aristotle Papanikolaou, eds. *Orthodox Constructions of the West.* New York: Fordham University Press, 2013.

Denysenko, Nicholas. *Chrismation: A Primer for Catholics.* Collegeville, MN: Liturgical Press, 2014.

_____. "Liturgical Maximalism in Orthodoxy: A Case Study." *Worship* 87 (2013): 338-62.

_____. "Pastoral Principles for Orthodox Clergy in America." In *Church and World: Essays in Honor of Michael Plekon,* edited by William C. Mills, 29-54. Rollinsford, NH: Orthodox Research Institute Press, 2013.

_____. "A Proposal for Renewing Liturgy in the Twenty-First Century." *Studia Liturgica* 40 (2010): 231-59.

_____. "Psalm 81: Announcing the Resurrection on Holy Saturday." *Logos: A Journal of Eastern Christian Studies* 50 (2009): 55-88.

_____. "Retrieving a Theology of Belonging: Eucharist and Church in Post-Modernity, Part 1." *Worship* 88 (2014): 543-61.

_____. "Retrieving a Theology of Belonging: Eucharist and Church in Post-Modernity, Part 2." *Worship* 89 (2015): 21-43.

————. "The Revision of the Roman Missal: An Orthodox Reflection." *Worship* 85 (2011): 306-29.

————. "The Revision of the Vigil Service." *St. Vladimir's Theological Quarterly* 51, nos. 2-3 (2007): 221-51.

————. "Rituals and Prayers of Forgiveness in Byzantine Lent." *Worship* 86 (2012): 140-60.

————. "Towards an Agenda for Byzantine Pastoral Liturgy: A Response to Peter Galadza." *Bolletino della Badia Greca di Grottaferrata* 7 (2010): 45-68.

Destivelle, Hyacinthe. *The Moscow Council (1917-1918): The Creation of the Conciliar Institutions of the Russian Orthodox Church.* Edited by Michael Plekon and Vitaly Permiakov. Translated by Jerry Ryan. Foreword by Metropolitan Hilarion (Alfeyev). Notre Dame, IN: University of Notre Dame Press, 2015.

Dmitrievsky, Aleksei. *Описаніе Литургическихъ Рукописей*, 3 vols. Kiev: Typographia G. T. Korchak-Novitskago, 1895. Reprint, Hildesheim: Georg Olms Verlagbuchhandlung, 1965.

Doyle, Dennis et al., eds. *Ecclesiology and Exclusion: Boundaries of Being and Belonging in Postmodern Times.* Foreword by Richard Gaillardetz. Maryknoll, NY: Orbis, 2012.

Drillock, David. "My Life in Liturgical Music." Lecture delivered at the Institute of Liturgical Music and Pastoral Practice at St. Vladimir's Seminary, Crestwood, NY, June 2004.

Evdokimov, Paul. *Ages of the Spiritual Life.* Translated by Michael Plekon and Alexis Vinogradov. Crestwood, NY: St. Vladimir's Seminary, 1998.

————. *L'Esprit Saint et l'Église. Catholiques, orthodoxes et protestants de divers pays confrontent leur science, leur foi et leur tradition: l'Avenir de l'Église et de l'oecuménisme,* ed. Académie internationale des sciences religieuses. Paris: Fanyard, 1969.

————. *The Sacrament of Love: The Nuptial Mystery in the Light of the*

Orthodox Tradition. Translated by Anthony P. Gythiel and Victoria Steadman. Foreword by Olivier Clément. Crestwood, NY: St. Vladimir's Seminary Press, 1995.

Fagerberg, David. "The Cost of Understanding Schmemann in the West." *St. Vladimir's Theological Quarterly* 53, nos. 2-3 (2009): 179-207.

———. *On Liturgical Asceticism.* Washington, DC: The Catholic University of America Press, 2013.

Faggioli, Massimo. *True Reform: Liturgy and Ecclesiology in* Sacrosanctum Concilium. Collegeville, MN: Liturgical Press, 2012.

Faros, Philotheos. "Ecclesial Life and Theology: From Mutual Fulfilling to Mutual Undermining." In *Synaxis: An Anthology of the Most Significant Orthodox Theology in Greece Appearing in the Journal Synaxe,* vol. 1: *Anthropology, Environment, Creation,* translated by Peter Chamberas. Edited by Liaidan Sherrard, 213-19. Montreal: Alexander Press, 2006.

Fenwick, John and Bryan Spinks. *Worship in Transition: The Liturgical Movement in the Twentieth Century.* New York: Continuum, 1995.

Ferrone, Rita. *Liturgy: Sacrosanctum Concilium.* New York: Paulist Press, 2007. *Festal Menaion.* Translated by Kallistos Ware and Mother Maria. South Canaan, PA: St. Tikhon's Seminary Press, 1969, 1990.

Filia, C. N. "Ο Ιερέας ως διδάσκαλος του Ευαγγελίου" ("The Priest as a teacher of the Gospel"). Church of Greece website, http://www.ecclesia.gr/greek/holysynod/commitees/liturgical/z_symposio_3.html.

Fisch, Thomas, ed. *Liturgy and Tradition: Theological Reflections of Alexander Schmemann.* Crestwood, NY: St. Vladimir's Seminary Press, 1990.

Fitzgerald, Thomas. "Le père Alexandre Schmemann, l'autocephalie de la Métropole de l'OCA et la réponse du Patriarche œcuménique Athénagoras." In *La joie du Royaume: Actes du colloque international "l'heritage du père Alexandre Schmemann," Paris, 11-14 décembre 2008.* Edited by André Lossky et al., 243-51. Paris: YMCA Press, 2012.

Florovsky, Georges. *Collected Works*, vol. 4: *Aspects of Church History*. Belmont, MA: Nordland Publishing Co., 1975.

Forest, Jim. "Icons and Miracles: An Intensity of Faith." *Christianity and Crisis* 45, no. 9 (May 27, 1985): 201-5.

Fountoulis, Ioannis. "Η ΛΕΙΤΟΥΡΓΙΚΗ ΑΝΑΝΕΩΣΗ ΣΤΗΝ ΟΡΘΟΔΟΞΟ ΕΚΚΛΗΣΙΑ ΔΥΝΑΤΟΤΗΤΕΣ ΚΑΙ ΕΜΠΟΔΙΑ" ("Liturgical Renewal in the Orthodox Church: Opportunities and Obstacles"). *Kleronomia* 21 (1989): 325-34.

Fox, Zeni. "Laity, Ministry, and Secular Character." In *Ordering the Baptismal Priesthood: Theologies of Lay and Ordained Ministry*, edited by Susan Wood, 121-51. Collegeville, MN: Liturgical Press, 2003.

Francis, Mark. "Another Look at the Constitution on the Sacred Liturgy and the Substantial Unity of the Roman Rite." *Worship* 88, no. 3 (2014): 239-55.

Freeze, Gregory. "Dechristianization in Holy Rus'? Religious Observance in Vladimir Diocese, 1900-1913." In *Orthodox Christianity in Imperial Russia: A Source Book on Lived Religion*, edited by Heather Coleman, 208-28. Bloomington, IN: Indiana University Press, 2014.

Galadza, Peter. "Baumstark's Kievan Contemporary, Mikhail N. Skaballanovich (1871-1931 [?]): A Sketch of his Life and Heortology." *Orientalia christiana analecta* 265 (2001): 761-75.

————. "Liturgy and Life: The Appropriation of the 'Personalization of Cult' in East-Slavic Orthodox Liturgiology, 1869-1996." *Studia Liturgica* 28 (1988): 210-31.

————. "Schmemann Between Fagerberg and Reality: Towards an Agenda for Byzantine Christian Pastoral Liturgy." *Bollettino della Badia Greca di Grottaferrata* 3, no. 4 (2007): 7-32.

————. "Seventeenth-century Liturgicons of the Kyivan Metropolia and Several Lessons for Today." *St. Vladimir's Theological Quarterly* 56, no. 1 (2012): 73-91.

Gardner, Johann von. *Russian Church Singing, Vol. 1: Orthodox Worship and*

Hymnography. Translated by Vladimir Morosan. Crestwood, NY: St. Vladimir's Seminary Press, 1980.

————. *Russian Church Singing,* vol. 2: *History from the Origins to the Mid-Seventeenth Century.* Translated and edited by Vladimir Morosan. Crestwood, NY: St. Vladimir's Seminary Press, 2000.

————. "Several Observations on Congregational Chanting During the Divine Services." In *Russian Liturgical Music Revival in the Diaspora: A Collection of Essays,* edited by Marina Ledkovsky and Vladimir von Tsuripov, Readings in Russian Religious Culture, vol. 4, 263-71. Jordanville, NY: Foundation of Russian History, 2012.

————. "Still More on Congregational Chanting of the Divine Services." In *Russian Liturgical Music Revival in the Diaspora: A Collection of Essays,* edited by Marina Ledkovsky and Vladimir von Tsuripov, Readings in Russian Religious Culture, vol. 4, 272-77. Jordanville, NY: Foundation of Russian History, 2012.

Gavrilyuk, Paul. *Georges Florovsky and the Russian Religious Renaissance.* Oxford: Oxford University Press, 2014.

Getcha, Job. "Les études liturgiques russes aux XIXe-XXe siècles et leur impact sur la pratique." In *Les mouvements liturgiques: corrélations entre pratiques et recherché, conferences Saint-Serge, Le Semaine d'études liturgiques,* Bibliotheca Ephermerides Liturgicae, Subsidia, 279-91. Rome: Edizione liturgizhe, 2004.

————. "From Master to Disciple: The Notion of 'Liturgical Theology' in Fr. Kiprian Kern and Fr. Alexander Schmemann." *St. Vladimir's Theological Quarterly* 53, nos. 2-3 (2009): 251-72.

————. *Le Typikon décrypte: manuel de liturgie byzantine.* Preface by Hieromonk Macarius. Paris: Cerf, 2009.

Glendenning, Chad J. "Significance of the Liturgical Reforms prior to the Second Vatican Council in Light of 'Summorum pontificium.'" *Studia Canonica* 44, no. 2 (2010): 293-342.

————. "Was the 1962 'Missale Romanum' abrogated?: a Canonical

Analysis in Light of 'Summorum Pontificum.'" *Worship* 85, no. 1 (2011): 15-37.

Glibetic, Nina. "Liturgical Renewal Movement in Contemporary Serbia." In *Inquiries into Eastern Christian Worship*, edited by Bert Groen, Steven Hawkes-Teeples, Stefanos Alexopoulos, Selected Papers of the Second International Congress of the Society of Oriental Liturgy, Rome, 17-21 September 2008, Eastern Christian Studies 12, 393-414. Leuven-Paris-Walpole, MA: Peeters, 2012.

Goar, Jacques. *Euchologion sive rituale graecorum.* Second Edition. Venice: Typographia Bartholomaei Javarina, 1730; Graz: Akademische Druck und Verlagsanstalt, 1960.

Goergen, Donald J. "Priest, Prophet, King: The Ministry of Jesus Christ." In *The Theology of Priesthood*, edited by Donald Goergen and Ann Garrido, 187-210. Collegeville, MN: Liturgical Press, 2000.

Gouneras, Soteris. "Notes on Urgent Issues Concerning Orthodox Christians in Greece and in the World." In *Synaxis: An Anthology of the Most Significant Orthodox Theology in Greece Appearing in the Journal Synaxe*, vol. 3: *Ecclesiology and Pastoral Care.* Translated by Peter Chamberas, edited by John Hadjinicolaou, 203-13. Montreal: Alexander Press, 2006.

Haquin, André. "La réforme liturgique de Vatican II a-t-elle fait preuve de créativité et en quell sens?" *Recherches De Science Religieuse* 101, no. 1 (January 1, 2013): 53-67.

Hovorun, Cyril. "Kollyvadic Fathers." In *The Encyclopedia of Orthodox Christianity*, vol. 2, ed. John McGuckin, 365. Chichester, West Sussex: Wiley-Blackwell Publications, 2011.

Ioniţă, Viorel, ed. *Orthodox Theology in the 20th Century and Early 21st Century: A Romanian Orthodox Perspective.* Translated by Adrian Agachi et al. Bucharest: Basilica, 2013.

Irwin, Kevin. "A Sacramental World—Sacramentality As the Primary Language for Sacraments." *Worship* 76, no. 3 (2002): 197-211.

_____. *What We have Done, What We Have Failed to Do: Assessing the Liturgical Reforms of Vatican II.* New York: Paulist Press, 2014.

Janeras, Sebastià. *Le vendredi-Saint dans la tradition liturgique byzantine: structure et histoire de ses offices.* Analecta liturgica, Studia Anselmiana 99. Rome: Abbazia S. Paolo, 1988.

Jeffrey, Peter. "Can Catholic Social Teaching Bring Peace to the 'Liturgy Wars'?" *Theological Studies* 75, no. 2 (2014): 350-75.

Jillions, John A. "Ecumenism and the Paris School of Orthodox Theology." *Theoforum* 39, no. 2 (2008): 141-74.

Johnson, Maxwell. "Can We Avoid Relativism in Worship? Liturgical Norms in the Light of Contemporary Liturgical Scholarship." *Worship* 74, no. 2 (2000): 135-55.

_____. *The Rites of Christian Initiation: Their Evolution and Interpretation.* Second Edition. Collegeville, MN: Liturgical Press, 2007.

Johnston, William H. "Pope Benedict XVI on the Postconciliar Liturgical Reform: an Essay in Interpretation." *Antiphon* 17, no. 2 (2013): 118-38.

Kalaitzis, Pantelis. "Challenges of Renewal Facing the Orthodox Church." *The Ecumenical Review* 61, no. 2 (2009): 136-64.

_____. "The Image of the West in Contemporary Greek Theology." In *Orthodox Constructions of the West*, ed. George Demacopoulos and Aristotle Papanikolaou, 142-60. New York: Fordham University, 2013.

Kartachoff, Antoine. "Orthodox Theology and the Ecumenical Movement." *The Ecumenical Review* 8, no. 1 (1955): 30-35.

Kavanagh, Aidan. *On Liturgical Theology.* New York: Pueblo, 1984.

Kern, Kyprian. *Eucharistia.* Paris: YMCA, 1947.

_____. "Reminiscences of Metropolitan Anthony (Khrapovitskii)." Translated by Alexander Lisenko. ROCOR Studies: Historical Studies of the Russian Church Abroad website, http://www.rocorstudies.org/church-people/lives-of-bishops/2012/10/03/reminiscences-of-metropolitan-anthony-khrapovitskii/.

Khrapovitsky, Metropolitan Antony. *Confession: A Series of Lectures on the Mystery of Repentance.* Translated by Father Christopher Birchall. Jordanville, NY: Holy Trinity Monastery, 1983.

_____. *О Пастырѣ, Пастырствѣ, и объ исповѣди* (On the Pastor, Ministry, and on Confession). Edited by Archbishop Nikon. New York: East American and Canadian Eparchy, 1966.

_____. "Преданіе или произволъ?" ("Tradition or arbitrariness?") *В?ра и разумъ* 14 (1914).

Kiczek, Steven A. "Pope Benedict XVI's Summorum Pontificum: Reconciling Conflicting Values." *Journal of Religious & Theological Information* 8, nos. 1-2 (2009): 37-64.

Kilde, Jeanne Halgren. *Sacred Power, Sacred Space: An Introduction to Christian Architecture and Worship.* Oxford: Oxford University Press, 2008.

Kilmartin, Edward. *The Eucharist in the West: History and Theology.* Edited by Robert Daly. Collegeville, MN: The Liturgical Press, 1998, 2004.

Kinnamon, Michael and Brian E. Cope, eds. *The Ecumenical Movement: an Anthology of Key Texts and Voices.* Grand Rapids: Eerdmans, 1996.

Kizenko, Nadieszda. "Sacramental Confession in Modern Russia and Ukraine." in *State Secularism and Lived Religion in Soviet Russia and Ukraine,* 190-217. Edited by Catherine Wanner. Oxford: Oxford University Press, 2012.

Klemens, Richter. "The Relationship Between Church and Liturgy: On the Reception of the Second Vatican Council (Vztah církve a liturgie. K recepci Druhého vatikánského koncilu)." *Studia theologica* 12, no. 3 (2010): 30-42.

Kniazeff, Alexis. *L'Institut Saint-Serge: de l'académie d'autrefois au rayonnement d'aujourd'hui.* Paris: Beauchesne, 1974.

Koumarianos, Pavlos. "Liturgical Rebirth in the Church of Greece Today: A Doubtful Effort of Liturgical Reform." *Bolletino della Badia Greca di Grottaferrata* 3 (2007): 119-44.

_____. "Liturgical Problems of Holy Week," *St. Vladimir's Theological Quarterly* 46, no. 1 (2002): 3-22.

Kourelis, Kostis and Vasileios Marinis. "An Immigrant Liturgy: Greek Orthodox Worship and Architecture in America." In *Liturgy in Migration: From the Upper Room to Cyberspace*, edited by Teresa Berger, 155-75. Collegeville, MN: Liturgical Press, 2012.

Krindatch, Alexei. *The Orthodox Church Today: A National Study of Parishioners and the Realities of Orthodox Parish Life in the USA*. Berkeley, CA: Patriarch Athenagoras Orthodox Institute, 2006.

Larin, Vassa. "The Opening Formula of the Byzantine Divine Liturgy, 'Blessed is the Kingdom,' among Other Liturgical Beginnings." *Studia Liturgica* 43:2 (2013): 229-55.

_____. "What is Ritual Im/Purity and Why?" *St. Vladimir's Theological Quarterly* 52, nos. 3-4 (2008): 275-92.

Lathrop, Gordon. "Strong Center, Open Door: A Vision of Continuing Liturgical Renewal," *Worship* 75, no. 1 (2001): 35-45.

Ledkovsky, Marina. "Dedication to the ROCM Foundation." In *Russian Liturgical Music Revival in the Diaspora: A Collection of Essays*, edited by Marina Ledkovsky and Vladimir von Tsuripov, Readings in Russian Religious Culture, vol. 4, 21-24. Jordanville, NY: Foundation of Russian History, 2012.

_____. "The Dispute Between Moscow and Petersburg about Canonical Singing in the Middle of the Nineteenth Century." In *Russian Liturgical Music Revival in the Diaspora: A Collection of Essays*, ed. Marina Ledkovsky and Vladimir von Tsuripov, Readings in Russian Religious Culture, vol. 4, 136-47. Jordanville, NY: Foundation of Russian History, 2012.

_____. "The Renaissance of Russian Orthodox Liturgical Music in the Russian Diaspora." In *Russian Liturgical Music Revival in the Diaspora: A Collection of Essays*, edited by Marina Ledkovsky and Vladimir von

Tsuripov, Readings in Russian Religious Culture, vol. 4, 64-75. Jordanville, NY: Foundation of Russian History, 2012.

Lloyd-Moffett, Stephen. *Beauty for Ashes: The Spiritual Transformation of a Modern Greek Community.* Crestwood, NY: St. Vladimir's Seminary Press, 2009.

Lukianov, Valerii. *Богослужебныя заметки: Опытъ разъясненія практической стороны богослуженія Православной Церкви* (Liturgical Notes: Expert Explanations of Practical Aspects of the Liturgy of the Orthodox Church). Third Edition. Jordanville, NY: St. Job of Pochaev, Holy Trinity Monastery, 2006.

Mango, Cyril. *Byzantine Architecture.* New York: Harry N. Abrams, Inc., 1976.

Marinis, Vasileios. *Architecture and Ritual in the Churches of Constantinople: Ninth to Fifteenth Centuries.* Cambridge: Cambridge University Press, 2014.

Mastrogiannopoulos, Elias. "Περί συμμετοχής των πιστών στην Θ. Κοινωνίαν" ("On the Participation of the Faithful in Holy Communion"). Church of Greece website, http://www.ecclesia.gr/greek/holysynod/commitees/liturgical/z_symposio_11.html.

Mateos, Juan. *La célébration de la parole dans la liturgie byzantine.* Orientalia Christiana Analecta 121. Rome: Pontifical Oriental Institute, 1971.

Maximus Confessor, Saint. *Selected Writings.* Translated by George C. Berthold. Introduction by Jaroslav Pelikan. Preface by Ir'en'ee-Henri Dalmais. New York: Paulist Press, 1985.

Mazza, Enrico. *The Celebration of the Eucharist: The Origin of the Rite and the Development of its Interpretation.* Translated by Matthew O'Connell. Collegeville, MN: Liturgical Press, 1999.

McGowan, Anne. "Eastern Christian Insights and Western Liturgical Reforms: Travelers, Texts, and Liturgical Luggage." In *Liturgy in Migration: From the Upper Room to Cyberspace*, edited by Teresa Berger, 179-208. Collegeville, MN: Liturgical Press, 2012.

McPartlan, Paul. *The Eucharist Makes the Church: Henri de Lubac and John Zizioulas in Dialogue*. Foreword by Edward Yarnold, SJ. Edinburgh: T & T Clark, 1993.

_____. *Sacrament of Salvation: An Introduction to Eucharistic Ecclesiology*. Edinburgh: T & T Clark, 1995.

Metzger, Marcel. *History of the Liturgy: The Major Stages*. Translated by Madeleine Beaumont. Collegeville, MN: Liturgical Press, 1997.

Meyendorff, Paul. "The Liturgical Path of Orthodoxy in America." *St. Vladimir's Theological Quarterly* 40, nos. 1-2 (1996): 44-49.

_____. "The Liturgical Reforms of Peter Moghila: A New Look." *St. Vladimir's Theological Quarterly* 29, no. 2 (1985): 101-14.

_____. *Russia, Ritual, and Reform: The Liturgical Reforms of Nikon in the 17th Century*. Crestwood, NY: St. Vladimir's Seminary Press, 1991.

Mills, William C, ed. *Called to Serve: Readings on Ministry from the Orthodox Church*. Rollinsford, NH: Orthodox Research Institute, 2010.

_____. *Church, World, and Kingdom: The Eucharistic Foundation of Alexander Schmemann's Pastoral Theology*. Chicago: Archdiocese of Chicago: Liturgy Training Publications, 2012.

Mojzeš, Marcel. *Il movimento liturgico nelle chiese bizantine. Analisi di alcune tendenze do riforma nel XX secolo*. Bibliotheca Ephemerides Liturgicae Subsidia 132. Rome: Edizione Liturgiche, 2005.

Monks of New Skete Monastery. *Book of Prayers*. Cambridge, NY: New Skete Monastery, 1988.

_____. *The Divine Liturgy*. Cambridge, NY: New Skete Monastery, 1987.

_____. *In the Spirit of Happiness*. Boston: Little, Brown, and Company, 1999.

_____. *Passion and Resurrection*. Cambridge, NY: New Skete Monastery, 1995.

_____. *The Psalter*. Cambridge, NY: New Skete Monastery, 1987.

_____. *Sighs of the Spirit*. Cambridge, NY: New Skete Monastery, 1997.

Morosan, Vladimir. *Choral Performance in Pre-Revolutionary Russia*. Russian Music Studies no. 17. Madison, CT: Musica Russica, 1986.

———. "Liturgical Singing or Sacred Music? Understanding the Aesthetic of the New Russian Choral Music." In *The Legacy of St. Vladimir: Byzantium, Russia, America*, edited by John Breck, John Meyendorff, and Eleana Silk, 69-78. Crestwood, NY: St. Vladimir's Seminary Press, 1990.

Morozowich, Mark. *Holy Thursday in Jerusalem and Constantinople: The Liturgical Celebrations from the Fourth to the Fourteenth Centuries*, forthcoming in Orientalia christiana analecta.

———. "East Meets West in Liturgy: Mutual Influence Throughout the Centuries." In *Liturgies in East and West: Ecumenical Relevance of Early Liturgical Development. Acts of the International Symposium Vindobonense I, Vienna, November 17-20, 2007*, 295-305. Vienne: International Specialized Book Services, 2013.

Nedelsky, Samuel. "Archbishop Antonii (Khrapovitskii), Imiaslavie, and Hesychasm." In *Metropolitan Antonii (Khrapovitskii): Archpastor of the Russian Diaspora*, ed. Vladimir Tsurikov, Readings in Russian Religious Culture 5, 69-91. Jordanville, NY: Foundation of Russian Culture, 2014.

Nichols, Aidan. *Theology in the Russian Diaspora: Church, Fathers, Eucharist in Nikolai Afanasiev, 1893-1966*. New York: Cambridge University Press, 1989.

O'Collins, Gerald. "*Ressourcement*, Vatican II, and Eucharistic Ecclesiology." In Ressourcement: *A Movement for Renewal in Twentieth-Century Catholic Theology*, edited by Gabriel Flynn and Paul D. Murray, 392-404. New York: Oxford University Press, 2012.

O'Malley, John. *What Happened at Vatican II*. Cambridge: Belknap Press of Harvard University Press, 2008.

Oulis, D., G. Makris, and S. Roussos. "The Orthodox Church of Greece: Policies and Challenges under Archbishop Christodoulos of Athens

(1998-2008)." *International Journal for the Study of the Christian Church* 10, nos. 2-3 (2010): 192-210.

Papkova, Irina. "The Freezing of Historical Memory? The Post-Soviet Russian Orthodox Church and the Council of 1917." In *Religion, Morality, and Community in Post-Soviet Societies*, edited by Mark Steinberg and Catherine Wanner, 55-84. Washington, DC: Woodrow Wilson Center Press; Bloomington, IN: Indiana University Press, 2008.

Patapios, Hieromonk and Archbishop Chrysostomos. *Manna from Athos: The Issue of Frequent Communion on the Holy Mountain in the Late Eighteenth and Early Nineteenth Centuries*. Byzantine and Neohellenic Studies, vol. 2, edited by Andrew Louth and David Ricks. New York: Peter Lang, 2006.

Paul, Archbishop. *Feast of Faith*. Crestwood, NY: St. Vladimir's Seminary Press, 1988.

Pecklers, Keith. *The Unread Vision: the Liturgical Movement in the United States of America, 1926-1955*. Collegeville, MN: Liturgical Press, 1998.

Perekrestov, Peter. *Владыка Иоанн—Святитель Русского Зарубежья* (Vladyka John—A Saint of the Russian Diaspora). Third Edition. Серия "Жития святых." Moscow: Strentensky Monastery, 2009.

_____. *Man of God: Saint John of Shanghai and San Francisco*. Richfield Springs, NY: Nikodemus Orthodox Publication Society, 1994: 2012 printing.

Pivarnik, Gabriel. *Towards a Trinitarian Theology of Liturgical Participation*. Foreword by Kevin Irwin. Collegeville, MN: Liturgical Press, 2012.

Plekon, Michael. *Living Icons: Persons of Faith in the Eastern Church*. Foreword by Lawrence Cunningham. Notre Dame, IN: University of Notre Dame, 2002.

_____. "Nicholas Afanasiev," in *Key Theological Thinkers: From Modern to Postmodern*, 371-78. Edited by Staale Kristiansen and Svian Reis. Farnham, Burlington: Ashgate, 2013.

Pomazansky, Michael. *Selected Essays.* Jordanville, NY: Holy Trinity Monastery, 1996.

Popivchak, Ronald. "The Life and Times of Peter Mohyla, Metropolitan of Kiev." *Logos: A Journal of Eastern Christian Studies* 43-45 (2004): 339-59.

Pospielovsky, Dimitry. *The Orthodox Church in the History of Russia.* Crestwood, NY: St. Vladimir's Seminary Press, 1998.

Pott, Thomas. *Byzantine Liturgical Reform: A Study of Liturgical Change in the Byzantine Tradition.* Translated by Paul Meyendorff. Orthodox Liturgy Series, Book Two. Crestwood, NY: St. Vladimir's Seminary Press, 2010.

Power, David. "Priesthood Revisited: Mission and Ministries in the Royal Priesthood." In *Ordering the Baptismal Priesthood: Theologies of Lay and Ordained Priesthood,* ed. Susan Wood, 97-120. Collegeville, MN: Liturgical Press, 2003.

Prétot, Patrick. "La place de la constitution sur la liturgie dans l'herméneutique de Vatican II." *Recherches De Science Religieuse* 101, no. 1 (January 1, 2013): 13-36.

Psarev, Andrei. "Metropolitan Kallistos Ware: 'ROCOR's Emphasis on Ascetic and Liturgical Tradition is very much Needed Today." ROCOR Studies website, http://www.rocorstudies.org/interviews/2014/03/27/metropolitan-kallistos-ware-rocor-emphasis-on-assetic-and-liturgical-tradition-is-very-much-needed-today/.

Puglisi, James. *The Process of Admission to Ordained Ministry: A Comparative Study,* 3 vols. Translated by Michael Driscoll and Mary Misrahi. Preface by Hervé Legrand. Collegeville, MN: Liturgical Press, 1996.

Radovic, Amfilohije. "Reformes liturgiques dans L'Église de Grec." In *Liturgie de l'Église particuliére, Liturgie de l'Église universelle,* Bibliotheca ephemerides liturgicae subsidia 7, 261-74. Rome: Edizione liturgiche, 1976.

Russo, Nicholas. "The Validity of the Anaphora of Addai and Mari: Critique of the Critiques." In *Issues in Eucharistic Praying in East and West: Essays in Liturgical and Theological Analysis*, edited by Maxwell Johnson, 21–62. Collegeville, MN: Liturgical Press, 2012.

Schidlovsky, Nicolas. "Sources of Russian Chant Theory." In *Russian Liturgical Music Revival in the Diaspora: A Collection of Essays*, edited by Marina Ledkovsky and Vladimir von Tsuripov, Readings in Russian Religious Culture, vol. 4, 45–57. Jordanville, NY: Foundation of Russian History, 2012.

Schmemann, Alexander. "Confession and Communion." http://www.schmemann.org / byhim / confessionandcommunion.html.

_____. *For the Life of the World: Sacraments and Orthodoxy*. Crestwood, NY: St. Vladimir's Seminary Press, 1963, fourth printing: 1988.

_____. *The Eucharist: Sacrament of the Kingdom*. Translated by Paul Kachur. Crestwood, NY: St. Vladimir's Seminary Press, 1987.

_____. *Introduction to Liturgical Theology*. Translated by Asheleigh E. Moorhouse. Crestwood, NY: St. Vladimir's Seminary Press, 1986.

_____. *The Journals of Father Alexander Schmemann, 1973–1984*. Crestwood, NY: St. Vladimir's Seminary Press, 2000.

_____. "Liturgical Theology, Theology of Liturgy, and Liturgical Reform." *St. Vladimir's Theological Quarterly* 13 (1969): 217–24.

_____. *Liturgy and Life: Christian Development through Liturgical Experience*. New York: Department of Religious Education, Orthodox Church in America, 1974.

_____. "Notes and Comments: On the Question of Liturgical Practices, A Letter to my Bishop." *St. Vladimir's Theological Quarterly* 7, no. 3 (1973): 227–38.

_____. *Of Water and the Spirit: A Liturgical Study of Baptism*. Crestwood, NY: St. Vladimir's Seminary Press, 1974.

_____. "Problems of Orthodoxy in America: The Liturgical Problem." *St. Vladimir's Seminary Quarterly* 8, no. 4 (1964): 164–85.

_____. Syllabus. "Liturgical Theology 22/31A," Spring 1982–83. Fr.

Alexander Schmemann Papers at the Father Georges Florovsky Library, St. Vladimir's Theological Seminary, Box 18, Document 8.

———. Syllabus. "Liturgical Theology 57," Winter 1978. Fr. Alexander Schmemann Papers at the Father Georges Florovsky Library, St. Vladimir's Theological Seminary, Box 18, Document 9.

———. "Transformation of the Parish." Lecture at St. Andrew's parish, 1971. Fr. Alexander Schmemann Papers at the Father Georges Florovsky Library, St. Vladimir's Theological Seminary, Box 17, Document 12.

———. *A Virtuous Church: Catholic Theology, Ethics, and Liturgy for the 21st Century.* Maryknoll, NY: Orbis Books, 2012.

Schulz, Günther. "Das Landeskonzil der Orthodoxen Kirche in Russland 1917/1918 und seine Folgen für die russische Geschichte und Kirchengeschichte." *Kirche im Osten* 42-43 (1999-2000): 11-28.

Schulz, Hans-Joachim. *The Byzantine Liturgy: Symbolic Structure and Faith Expression.* Translated by Matthew J. O'Connell. New York: Pueblo, 1986.

Searle, Mark. *Called to Participate: Theological, Ritual, and Social Perspectives.* Edited by Barbara Searle and Anne Y. Koester. Collegeville, MN: Liturgical Press, 2006.

Seasoltz, Kevin. "The Genius of the Roman Rite: On Reception and Implementation of the New Missal." *Worship* 83, no. 6 (2009): 541-49.

Senyk, Sophia. "Antonij Xrapovickij in Volyn': 1902-1914." In *Metropolitan Antonii (Khrapovitskii): Archpastor of the Russian Diaspora,* ed. Vladimir Tsurikov, Readings in Russian Religious Culture 5, 249-54. Jordanville, NY: Foundation of Russian History, 2012.

Service and Akathist to Our Father Among the Saints John, Archbishop of Shanghai and San Francisco, The Wonderworker. San Francisco: Russkiy pastyr, originally published in 2004; 2013 revision.

Ševčenko, Ihor. "The Many Worlds of Peter Mohyla." *Harvard Ukrainian Studies* 8, nos. 1-2 (1984): 9-40.

Shevzov, Vera. "The Burdens of Tradition: Orthodox Constructions of the

West in Russia (late 19th-early 20th cc.)." In *Orthodox Constructions of the West*, edited by George Demacopoulos and Aristotle Papanikolaou, 83-101. New York: Fordham University, 2013.

_____. *Russian Orthodox on the Eve of the Revolution*. Oxford: Oxford University Press, 2004.

_____. "The Russian Tradition." In *The Orthodox Christian World*, edited by Augustine Casiday, 15-40. London and New York: Routledge, 2012.

Shkurla, Metropolitan Laurus. "Наследие митрополита Антония (Храповицкого)." In *Metropolitan Antonii (Khrapovitskii): Archpastor of the Russian Diaspora*, ed. Vladimir Tsurikov. Readings in Russian Religious Culture 5, 11-18. Jordanville, NY: Foundation of Russian Culture, 2014.

_____. "The Significance of the Practical Study of Liturgics." *Orthodox Life* 45 (1995): 42-48.

Sippo, Arthur. "Liturgical Reform Did Not Start with Vatican II." *New Oxford Review* 03 (2011): 40-43.

Skobtsova, Saint Maria. *Mother Maria Skobtsova: Essential Writings*. Translated by Richard Pevear and Larissa Volokhonsky. Introduction by Jim Forest. Modern Spiritual Master Series. Maryknoll, NY: Orbis, 2003.

Slagle, Amy. *The Eastern Church in the Spiritual Marketplace: American Conversions to Orthodox Christianity*. DeKalb, IL: Northern Illinois University Press, 2011.

Slater, Wendy. "Relics, Remains, and Revisionism: Narratives of Nicholas II in Contemporary Russia." *Rethinking History: The Journal of Theory and Practice* 9:1 (2005): 53-70.

Smyth, Matthieu. "The Anaphora of the So-called 'Apostolic Tradition' and the Roman Eucharistic Prayer." In *Issues in Eucharistic Praying in East and West: Essays in Liturgical and Theological Analysis*, edited by Maxwell Johnson, 71-98. Collegeville, MN: Liturgical Press, 2012.

Святитель Іоаннъ (Максимовичъ) и Русская Зарубежная Церковь (Saint

John (Maximovich) and the Russian Church Abroad). Jordanville, NY: Holy Trinity Monastery, 1996.

Synod of Bishops, Church of Greece. "Τά Ἁγιογραφικά ἀναγνώσματα καί τό κήρυγμα εἰς τήν Θείαν Λειτουργίαν" ("The Hagiographical Reading and Teaching at the Divine Liturgy"). Church of Greece website, http://www.ecclesia.gr/greek/holysynod/egyklioi/egkyklios2791.html.

————. "Ἐκφωνητική σημειογραφία ἐν τῇ πράξει τῆς Ὀρθοδόξου Λατρείας" ("Ekphonetic Notation in Orthodox Liturgical Practice"). Church of Greece website, http://www.ecclesia.gr/greek/holysynod/egyklioi/egkyklios2793.html.

————. "Ἐπαναφορά τῆς Τάξεως τοῦ Ἑωθινοῦ Εὐαγγελίου εἰς τήν κανονικήν αὐτοῦ θέσιν" ("Resetting the Order of the Eothinon Gospel according to the Canonical Order"). Church of Greece website, http://www.ecclesia.gr/greek/holysynod/egyklioi/egkyklios2794.html.

————. "Ὁ καιρός τῆς Θείας Λειτουργίας καί ἡ δυνατότης τελέσεώς της τό Ἑσπέρας" ("The Time of the Divine Liturgy and the Possibility of Celebrating it in the Evening"). Church of Greece website, http://www.ecclesia.gr/greek/holysynod/egyklioi/egkyklios2786.html.

————. "Ἡ Μυστηριακή ζωή τῆς Ἐκκλησίας καί τά Ραδιοτηλεοπτικά Μέσα Ἐνημερώσεως" ("The Sacramental Life of the Church and Broadcast Media"). Church of Greece website, http://www.ecclesia.gr/greek/holysynod/egyklioi/egkyklios2792.html.

————. "Περί τῆς συμμετοχῆς τῶν πιστῶν εἰς τήν Θείαν Εὐχαριστίαν" ("On the Participation of the Faithful in the Divine Eucharist"). Church of Greece website, http://www.ecclesia.gr/greek/holysynod/egyklioi/egkyklios2785.html.

————. "Περί τοῦ τρόπου ἀναγνώσεως τῶν εὐχῶν τῆς Θείας Λειτουργίας" ("On the Method for Reading the Prayers of the Divine Liturgy"). Church of Greece website, http://www.ecclesia.gr/greek/holysynod/egyklioi/egkyklios2784.html.

Sysyn, Frank E. "The Formation of Modern Ukrainian Religious Culture." In

Religion and Nation in Modern Ukraine, edited by Serhii Plokhy and Frank E. Sysyn, 1-22. Edmonton and Toronto: Canadian Institute of Ukrainian Studies Press, 2003.

Taft, Robert F. "Between Progress and Nostalgia: Liturgical Reform and the Western Romance with the Christian East; Strategies and Realities." In *A Living Tradition: On the Intersection of Liturgical History and Pastoral Practice*, edited by David Pitt, Stefanos Alexopoulos, and Christian McConnell, 19-39. Collegeville, MN: Liturgical Press, 2012.

_____. "Byzantine Communion Spoons: A Review of the Evidence." *Dumbarton Oaks Papers* 50 (1996): 209-38.

_____. *The Byzantine Rite*. Collegeville, MN: Liturgical Press, 1996.

_____. "Cathedral vs. Monastic Liturgy in the Christian East: Vindicating a Distinction." *Bolletina della Badia Greca di Grottaferrata* (2005): 173-219.

_____. *A History of the Liturgy of St. John Chrysostom*, vol. 2: *The Great Entrance, A History of the Transfer of Gifts and Other Pre-anaphoral Rites*. Fourth Edition. Orientalia christiana analecta 200. Rome: Pontifical Oriental Institute, 2004.

_____. "The Liturgical Enterprise Twenty-five Years after Alexander Schmemann." *St. Vladimir's Theological Quarterly* 53, nos. 2-3 (2009): 139-77.

_____. "The Liturgy of the Great Church: An Initial Synthesis of Structure and Interpretation on the Eve of Iconoclasm." *Dumbarton Oaks Papers* 34 (1980-81): 45-75.

_____. *The Liturgy of the Hours in East and West: The Origins of the Divine Office and its Meaning for Today*. Second Revised Edition. Collegeville, MN: Liturgical Press, 1993.

_____. "Mass Without the Consecration? The Historic Agreement on the Eucharist Between the Catholic Church and the Assyrian Church of the East Promulgated 26 October 2001." *Worship* 77, no. 6 (2003): 482-509.

————. "Mount Athos: A Late Chapter in the History of the Byzantine Rite," *Dumbarton Oaks Papers* 42 (1988): 179-93.

————. "Response to the Berakah Award: Anamnesis." *Worship* 59 (1985): 305-25.

————. "A Tale of Two Cities: The Byzantine Holy Week Triduum as a Paradigm of Liturgical History." In *Time and Community: Essays In Honor of Thomas Julian Talley (NPM Studies in Church Music and Liturgy)*, edited by J. Neil Alexander, 21-41. Washington, DC: The Pastoral Press, 1990.

————. *Through Their Own Eyes: Liturgy as the Byzantines Saw It.* Berkeley, CA: InterOrthodox Press, 2005.

Taushev, Archbishop Averky. *Литургика (Liturgics)*. Jordanville, NY: St. Job of Pochaev Press, Holy Trinity Monastery, 2000.

Theophan the Recluse, Saint. *The Path to Salvation: A Manual of Spiritual Transformation.* Translated by Seraphim Rose and the St. Herman of Alaska Brotherhood. Platina, CA: St. Herman of Alaska Brotherhood, 1996.

Townsend, John. "Order of Prayer and Worship for Orthodox Faithful." *Orthodox Life* 48 (1998): 29-39.

Turner, Jack. "Journeying Onwards: An overview of the Liturgical Books in Western-rite Orthodoxy." *St. Vladimir's Orthodox Theological Quarterly* 56, no. 1 (2012): 93-112.

————. "The Journey thus Far: A Review of the Literature of Western-rite Orthodoxy." *St. Vladimir's Orthodox Theological Quarterly* 53, no. 4 (2009): 477-505.

————. "Western Rite Orthodoxy as an Ecumenical Problem." *Journal of Ecumenical Studies* 47, no. 4 (2012): 541-54.

Tzerpos, Dimitrios. "Ο Ιερεύς ως Λειτουργός" ("The Priest as Liturgist"). http://www.ecclesia.gr/greek/holysynod/commitees/liturgical/z_symposio_6.html.

————. "Η ΟΡΘΟΔΟΞΗ ΛΑΤΡΕΙΑ ΣΤΑ ΗΘΗ ΚΑΙ ΕΘΙΜΑ ΤΟΥ ΕΛΛΗΝΙΚΟΥ ΛΑΟΥ" ("Orthodox Worship in the Customs of the

Greek People"). Church of Greece website, http://www.ecclesia.gr/greek/holysynod/commitees/liturgical/latreia_ethima.html.

_____. "ΠΡΟΣ ΜΙΑ ΑΝΑΝΕΩΣΗ ΤΗΣ ΕΚΚΛΗΣΙΑΣΤΙΚΗΣ ΜΑΣ ΛΑΤΡΕΙΑΣ" ("Towards a Renewal of Our Ecclesiastical Worship"). Church of Greece website, http://www.ecclesia.gr/greek/holysynod/commitees/liturgical/liturgical-0001.htm.

Valliere, Paul. Conciliarism: A History of Decision-Making in the Church. Cambridge, U. K., and New York: Cambridge University Press, 2012.

Vassialidis, Petros. "Greek Theology in the Making: Trends and Facts in the 80's—Vision for the 90's." St. Vladimir's Theological Quarterly 35 (1991): 33-52.

_____. "Liturgical Renewal and the Orthodox Church." Unpublished essay taken from Professor Vassiliadis's academia web page, https://www.academia.edu/3581957.

_____. "The Liturgical Use of the Bible in Greek Orthodoxy: An Orthodox Critical Approach in 12 Steps." Unpublished Essay. Published by Professor Vassiliadis on his academia web page, https://www.academia.edu/3852656.

_____. "Orthodox Theology Facing the Twenty-First Century." Greek Orthodox Theological Review 35, no. 2 (1990): 139-53.

Ward, Graham. "Belonging to the Church," in in Liturgy in Migration: From the Upper Room to Cyberspace, edited by Teresa Berger, 1-18. Collegeville, MN: Liturgical Press, 2012.

Ware, Kallistos, and Mother Maria. The Lenten Triodion. South Canaan, PA: St. Tikhon's Seminary, 2002.

White, James. "Where the Reformation Was Wrong on Worship," Christian Century 99, no. 33 (1982): 1074-77.

Wilbricht, Stephen. Rehearsing God's Just Kingdom: The Eucharistic Vision of Mark Searle. Foreword Kevin W. Irwin. Collegeville, MN: Liturgical Press, 2013.

Winner, Brother Stavros. "Liturgical Renewal: Have We Missed the Boat?" Unpublished essay.

————. "Liturgy: Theory and Practice—An Example from Finland." *St. Vladimir's Theological Quarterly* 33, no. 2 (1989): 180-89.

————. "The Monastery and Applies Liturgical Renewal." In *Worship Traditions and Armenia and the Neighboring Christian East: An International Symposium in Honor of the 40th Anniversary of St. Nersess Armenian Seminary*, ed. Roberta R. Ervine, 307-23. Crestwood, NY: St. Vladimir's Seminary Press, St. Nersess Armenian Seminary, 2006.

Wood, Susan. *Sacramental Orders*, Lex Orandi series, ed. John Laurance. Collegeville, MN: Liturgical Press, 2000.

Wooden, Anastacia. "Eucharistic Ecclesiology of Nicholas Afanasiev and Catholic Ecclesiology: History of Interaction and Future Perspectives." A Paper presented at the 50th International Eucharistic Congress in 2012. http://www.iec2012.ie/media/1AnastaciaWooden1.pdf.

————. "Eucharistic Ecclesiology of Nicolas Afanasiev and its Ecumenical Significance: A New Perspective." *Journal of Ecumenical Studies* 45, no. 4 (2010): 543-60.

Woods, Michael. *Cultivating Soil and Soul: Twentieth-Century Catholic Agrarians Embrace the Liturgical Movement.* Collegeville, MN: The Liturgical Press, 2009.

Zagano, Phyllis. *Women in Ministry: Emerging Questions About the Diaconate*, foreword by William T. Ditewig. New York: Paulist Press, 2012.

Zelensky, Natalie. "Chanting the Homeland: Discourses of Authenticity and Sacrality in Competing Styles of Church Music in the Russian Orthodox Diaspora of New York." *Oxford Handbook of Music and World Christianities*. Edited Jonathan Dueck and Suzel Ana Reily. Oxford: Oxford University Press, January 2015, online version. DOI: 10.1093/oxfordhb/9780199859993.013.18.

Zernov, Nicholas. *The Russian Religious Renaissance of the Twentieth Century.* Salisbury, MA: Regina Orthodox Press, 1999.

Zizioulas, John. *Eucharist, Bishop, Church: The Unity of the Church in the Divine Eucharist and the Bishop During the First Three Centuries.* Translated by Elizabeth Theokritoff. Brookline, MA: Holy Cross Orthodox Press, 2001.

_____. "Symbolism and Realism in Orthodox Worship." Translated by Elizabeth Theokritoff. *Synaxis: An Anthology of the Most Significant Orthodox Theology in Greece Appearing in the Journal Synaxe,* vol. 1: *Anthropology, Environment, Creation,* translated by Peter Chamberas, edited by Liaidan Sherrard, 251-64. Montreal: Alexander Press, 2006.

Index

Serbia, 30, 111, 128, 337

Sergianism, 18, 144

Sergiev Posad, 148

Sergius, Metropolitan, 148

sermon. *See* homily

Shanghai, 159, 160, 161, 162

Shevzov, Vera, 14, 26, 181, 320

singing: canonical (*see* chant, canonical); congregational, 111, 126, 183, 184-88, 199-200, 231, 369, 376. *See also* music, liturgical.

Skaballanovich, Mikhail, 12-13, 83, 94, 117

Skobtsova, Maria, 298, 299, 393-94

Slagle, Amy, 352

Smolensky, Stepan, 183-84, 193

Society of Jesus, 26, 36, 180, 181-82, 261

solea, 271

spiritual marketplace, 352-53

St. Andrew's Ukrainian Orthodox College, 135-36

St. Job of Pochaev Press, 174-75, 366

St. Sabas monastery, 24, 150, 354

St. Sergius Institute, 39, 54, 94, 98, 188

St. Vladimir's Orthodox Theological Seminary, 16,

17-18, 39, 83-84, 86-87, 97, 110-11, 113-14, 119, 126, 133, 135, 140, 142, 190-93, 199, 200, 250, 316, 336, 347

Staniloae, Dumitru, 41

stichera, 150, 152, 186, 292, 293

Summorum Pontificum, 344

Swan, Alfred, 192

symbol, 74, 104, 110, 112, 117, 213, 223-25, 236, 242, 257, 265, 300, 305-6, 310-12, 360, 379-80

Synaxis (liturgy), 225, 232

Synaxis (periodical), 208

synod, Greek, 20, 58, 209, 214, 217, 218-23, 225-28, 229, 230-45, 253, 255-56, 330, 346-47; encyclicals of, 20, 220-21, 225-27, 232-35, 238, 240-44, 332; symposia of, (*see* Synodal Committee for Liturgical Rebirth)

synod, Orthodox Church in America, 133-34

synod, Pan-Orthodox, 215-16, 227, 256

synod, Russian, 13, 94

synod, Russian Orthodox Church outside of Russia, 147, 162, 174-75, 177-78

Synodal Committee for Liturgical